A Digital Europe for Citizens

Graça Enes · Inês Neves · Tiago Morais Rocha
Editors

A Digital Europe for Citizens

Data Governance, Data Markets, Data Services

Springer

Editors
Graça Enes
Faculty of Law, CIJ-FDUP; Jean Monnet Module DigEUCit "A Digital Europe for Citizens. Constitutional and Policymaking Challenges"
University of Porto
Porto, Portugal

Inês Neves
Faculty of Law, CIJ-FDUP; Jean Monnet Module DigEUCit "A Digital Europe for Citizens. Constitutional and Policymaking Challenges"
University of Porto
Porto, Portugal

Tiago Morais Rocha
Faculty of Law, CIJ-FDUP; Jean Monnet Module DigEUCit "A Digital Europe for Citizens. Constitutional and Policymaking Challenges"
University of Porto
Porto, Portugal

ISBN 978-3-032-02499-2 ISBN 978-3-032-02500-5 (eBook)
https://doi.org/10.1007/978-3-032-02500-5

This work was supported by ERASMUS-JMO-2022-HEI-TCH-RSCH (101085671) and CIJ (Centre for Interdisciplinary Research on Justice) (FCT grant UIDB/00443/2020).

This Springer imprint is published by the registered company Springer Nature Switzerland AG
The registered company address is: Gewerbestrasse 11, 6330 Cham, Switzerland

Foreword

Europe as an economic, political, cultural, scientific and social union exists first and foremost for its citizens and for the promotion of their well-being and prosperity. As enshrined in the Treaty on European Union, "the Union is founded on the values of respect for human dignity, freedom, democracy, equality, the rule of law and respect for human rights", seeking to achieve and consolidate a plural, tolerant, fair, open and equitable citizenship.

The digital reality that has imposed itself on us in recent decades, and its prevalence in the most varied areas of human activity, cannot and must not endanger those basic principles of European integration. Technology and digital infrastructures today play a critical role in our lives, in the relationships we establish, and in different environments: at work, in communication, in business, in the progress of science and knowledge, and also in the urgent fight against global social and environmental problems. Therefore, it is up to Europe and its national and transnational institutions to guarantee the mechanisms capable of ensuring effective digital citizenship, by providing all citizens of our common space with access to the tools, advantages, and potential of this reality, as well as free, fair, and safe access to digital services and markets, without excluding anyone and ensuring effective and transparent regulation.

This conference is based on The DigEUCit Project—Digital Europe for Citizens, which is a project that aims to contribute to teaching and research rooted in excellence on constitutional challenges and the formulation of public policies related to Digital Europe. In addition, it seeks to promote dialogue and the debate of ideas between stakeholders on a local, national, and international level, with a focus on citizens. The DigEuCit Project addresses the challenges, risks, and legal and policy developments related to the European Digital Strategy, the Digital Single Market, the European Data Space, and Cybersecurity, with an emphasis on fundamental rights, digital citizenship, democracy, and European values.

We can observe that today's conference schedule is very much in line with the project's objectives and therefore represents an important milestone in pursuing the DigEUCit project's mission. The dematerialised and, to some extent, totalitarian digital space is everywhere. It poses, after all, similar challenges to the common world. If institutions and companies already have the necessary tools to aggregate and process our data, using them to their advantage, citizens should also be given the possibility to protect their individuality and privacy. I would stress that the digital field exposes us to the same dangers, risks and challenges as common citizenship, so it is up to the institutions to ensure that the same principles that governed the creation of the European Union are guaranteed and that we can derive the same benefits from them.

Effective digital citizenship should therefore ensure the quality of habits, actions, activities, and consumption patterns of the entire European community. The university cannot and should not shy away from actively participating in the progress of this field, including the promotion of a much-needed ethical, political, deontological, and economic debate regarding the implementation of a digital space of communication and knowledge. It is up to us to educate our students on citizenship, on their rights and responsibilities as members of a community. The digital society also demands that we safeguard the same ethical principles on which Europe was built so that everyone can play a responsible and productive role in current digital Europe and in the future. The consolidation and competitiveness of our shared economy and the possibility to enjoy the benefits of the progress we are striving for depend on ensuring that every citizen can master digital skills and technologies.

Universities thus have a fundamental and dual role: to create and develop the necessary tools for the material progress of our common area, ensuring Europe's technological autonomy and strengthening our technical and ethical skills in this field, but also to promote knowledge so that the benefits of this progress can reach all European companies and citizens. Therefore, it is of great importance for the mission of the University of Porto to acknowledge, in particular, the DigEuCit project and the training initiatives of the Faculty of Law, which provide students and professionals with integrated knowledge about the regulatory framework, challenges, and opportunities of a Digital Europe. They offer a critical and extended reflection on the new challenges, benefits, and risks arising from the construction of a European Digital space. Also, at the level of organisations, emerging technological advances in fields such as artificial intelligence, data science, automation, or the Internet of Things, and their integration into business models, have contributed to transforming the way the economy and society are organised. The increasing pace of digital innovation and transformation has improved the efficiency and productivity of industries and services in the public and private sectors. It has also facilitated access to information, education, and lifelong learning, bringing new tools to address global societal challenges and promoting the prosperity of communities and society as a whole. Perhaps there was a time when cyberspace pretended to be beyond sovereignty or even the Law, but nowadays, the importance of the Law in the Digital Society is consensual. Markets, companies, the government, and infrastructures of this new digital era should be approached in an integrated way, under a constitutional perspective. Today's conference shows the importance of this integrated perspective on the theme of Digital Europe, and demonstrates the relevance of the debate of ideas on central themes of Digital Transformation in our society.

You can count on the University of Porto to actively participate in solving the multiple and demanding challenges we face in Europe's Digital Transformation.

Given the great relevance of the topics addressed in the programme and the quality of the speakers and guests here, I am confident that today will be a memorable and enriching day for all. I wish everyone a productive conference.

Ana Camanho
Vice-Rector of the University of Porto
Porto, Portugal

Preface

This book corresponds to the Proceedings of the First International Conference "A Digital Europe for Citizens", organised by the Jean Monnet Module Dig*EU*Cit, "A Digital Europe for Citizens. Constitutional and Policymaking Challenges" and CIJ (Centre for Interdisciplinary Research on Justice, Faculty of Law of the University of Porto). It was held at the Faculty of Law of the University of Porto, on 14 April 2023. The book focuses on three main topics: data governance, digital markets, and digital services. It is composed of chapters authored by legal experts who address EU's accomplishments and future perspectives on the ongoing Digital Revolution, and the impact of digitalisation on the European Union. A comparative approach with other legal systems is also included. This comprehensive work will interest legal scholars, academics, researchers, and practitioners of European and Constitutional Law, data protection, competition or consumer law, and a larger audience of policymakers and digital entrepreneurs. The Book follows a holistic perspective with a focus on citizens and is aimed at recalling that constitutionalism shall also be considered in its role of ensuring democracy, an open and inclusive society, and a fair economy. It presents an original, cross-sectoral, and cutting-edge approach, already recognised by the Conference's participants and audience. Besides two broader texts, from Professors Ana Camanho (on the fundamental issues raised by the digital revolution) and Professor Oreste Pollicino (on "Digital Constitutionalism"), the book structures itself around three main subjects: Data Governance, Digital Markets, and Digital Services. As regards Data Governance, Jean-Paul Triaille writes about "The approach of the European Commission. Legal openness. Do as you preach"; Graça Enes authors the chapter "European Data Space(s). A governance model 'the European way'?"; and, finally, in this section, Maria Novella Campagnoly, Luca Panico, and Luigi Prosia's explore "Rights, Freedom, Equality and Security: prevention and control strategies". The following chapters regard Digital Markets: "Which Data Governance for a Social Post-Pandemic Recovery?", by Maria Francesca De Tullio; "Digital markets, positive duties of protection and the freedom to conduct a business: how to have your cake and eat it too", authored by Inês Neves, as well as a chapter from Alba Ribera Martínez, entitled "If I Could Have, I Would Have: Multi-Level Governance and Trust in the DMAs Effectiveness". The last chapters focus on Digital

Services and count with a text by Esther Arroyo authors "Online Marketplaces in the Digital Services Act"; Fernanda Magalhães and Irene Calle co-author the chapter entitled "Consumer Protection in the Digital Age: a reflection on Regulation 2022/2065 (Digital Services Act) and Agenda 2030"; Tiago Rocha explores the "Digital Services Act: towards the digital rule of law?"; and finally, Martim Farinha and Diogo Brandão present the chapter "Who moderates the moderators?: A brief overlook into how the Digital Services Act impacts the economics of content moderation against «overblocking»". The authors discuss the fundamental values and principles. They also analyse concrete and practical questions that arise from the policy and the legal framework being adopted by the EU. The aim is to bring constitutionalism to the digital stage and to advance solutions and a proper framework, building on solid foundations.

We would like to thank Lara Carvalho (B.A. and Masters in Criminology, Research Fellow at CIJ, 2024) for her editorial support.

Porto, Portugal

Graça Enes
Inês Neves
Tiago Morais Rocha

Contents

Introduction

Graça Enes, Inês Neves, and Tiago Morais Rocha

The current digital transformation represents one of the most profound and far-reaching phenomena of our time, with ramifications that extend across a vast array of domains. The pace, scope, and impact of this phenomenon are pervasive, affecting every aspect of our lives, including the ways in which we work, communicate, consume, engage with governments, businesses, and one another. As the European Union ('EU') persists in defining and redefining its role in this rapidly evolving landscape, it is confronted with the urgent need to reconcile the promises of innovation with the protection of fundamental rights, democratic values, and constitutional principles.

This book represents the outcome of the inaugural International Conference, entitled "A Digital Europe for Citizens", which was organised by the Jean Monnet Module Dig*EU*Cit. "A Digital Europe for Citizens. Constitutional and Policymaking Challenges". The conference was held on 14 April 2023 at the Faculty of Law of the University of Porto and it brought together leading legal scholars, practitioners and policymakers to examine the interconnections between digitalisation, law and society in the context of the European Union's regulatory framework and approach to digitalisation.

The book presents the work of experts from a range of legal fields. In particular, it examines three critical areas of digital policy and governance, building on the discussions and insights derived from the event. The subject matter of the conference

G. Enes (✉) · I. Neves · T. Morais Rocha
Faculty of Law of the University of Porto, Porto, Portugal
e-mail: gef@direito.up.pt

CIJ—Centre for Interdisciplinary Research on Justice, Porto, Portugal

I. Neves
e-mail: ineves@direito.up.pt

T. Morais Rocha
e-mail: trocha@direito.up.pt

G. Enes et al. (eds.), *A Digital Europe for Citizens*,
https://doi.org/10.1007/978-3-032-02500-5_1

was data governance, digital markets and digital services. This structured approach, reflected in this book, allows readers to navigate the key implications of European Digital Constitutionalism (*lato* sensu) with ease, thereby fostering a better understanding of the evolving digital landscape in Europe.

In light of the accelerated evolution of the digital landscape in the EU, the establishment of a robust protective framework for European citizens is of heightened importance. In order for this to occur, it is essential to begin with the fundamentals and gain an understanding of the central characteristics of digital constitutionalism and its capacity to safeguard citizens in the digital domain while also guaranteeing accountability and the rule of law in the context of rapid technological developments that challenge traditional legal frameworks. Given the ongoing digital transformation of the European landscape, this book seeks to emphasise the continued relevance of upholding democratic values, ensuring the protection of citizens' rights, and fostering an open and inclusive society. It examines how the EU's regulatory frameworks can facilitate the attainment of these objectives while also acknowledging the inherent complexity and dynamic nature of the digital world.

From this point onwards, an examination of specific aspects of the digital landscape and paradigmatic shifts can be undertaken, with a particular focus on the role of data in the digital economy. Data has emerged as a vital asset for economic growth and social development, with the European Union acknowledging the necessity for effective data governance, fair access and uses. The discussion held on 14 April 2023, and now reflected in this book of proceedings, presents the approach of the European Commission and elucidates the concept of European data spaces and the EU's objective of ensuring equitable data sharing among various stakeholders, while adhering to EU values and principles.

Moreover, it addresses the regulatory challenges of digital markets, which present distinctive challenges that traditional competition law and regulations seem inadequate to address. In view of the pivotal role played by the Digital Markets Act in addressing the fairness and contestability issues prevalent in contemporary digital markets, this book emphasises the necessity for an interpretation of the Act in conjunction with the freedom to conduct business for both gatekeepers and business users.

Although they originate from the same legislative package and are typically regarded as two aspects of a single entity, the Digital Services Act has a distinct focus. The objective is to establish a more secure online environment for users (citizens) and to ensure that digital platforms are held to account, irrespective of their scale. It is therefore related to the field of consumer protection in the context of the digital age, a relationship which is also addressed in this book.

As the digital realm continues to expand, it is of the utmost importance that the European Union demonstrates its commitment to upholding fundamental rights while fostering innovation, in order to ensure the creation of a fair and inclusive digital economy. The discussions held at the conference, together with the conclusions set out in this book, provide a valuable guide for policymakers, legal experts and citizens alike.

This collection of texts provides readers with a unique opportunity to examine the ongoing digital transformation from a distinctly European perspective. By drawing on the expertise of legal scholars and practitioners, readers will be able to gain insights into the EU's successes, its challenges, and the road ahead in managing the complexities of data, digital markets, and digital services, which are all the more important in the current geopolitical context. In contrast to numerous other texts that concentrate narrowly on a single aspect of digital law, this work integrates a diverse array of issues within a unified framework, thereby establishing a foundation for discussion on the broader constitutional principles of digital constitutionalism. The contributions presented here are unified in their commitment to ensuring that the digital revolution does not bypass the fundamental values of justice, equality, and fairness.

In conclusion, as indicated by the motto of the Jean Monnet Module, this book is not merely about the digitalisation of Europe; it is about the construction of a digital Europe that serves the interests of its citizens following a holistic constitutional perspective. The contributions presented here encourage engagement with the intricate and evolving domain of digital law, and prompt reflection on the future that is being shaped through our legal frameworks and policies.

A New Geometry for Digital Constitutionalism?

Oreste Pollicino

1 Introduction

In the last twenty years, the development of digital technologies has not only challenged the protection of individuals' fundamental rights such as freedom of expression and data protection. Even more importantly, this new technological framework has also empowered transnational corporations operating in the digital environment as platforms to perform quasi-public functions in the transnational context. These two drivers have created a new phase of modern constitutionalism: the digital constitutionalism.

Given this new context, it is necessary to raise some important questions: what are the signs and constituent elements of the constitutional categories in the actual digital context? Which are the rights and duties in this digital context? What tools are available to constitutionalism to counter the transfiguration of economic actors in private powers, taking into account of the relevant constellation of the rights in play, from freedom of expression through the protection of freedom of enterprise to the right to privacy?

These are the questions that the following pages will attempt to answer.

On this matter, there is a growing literature related to the relationship between constitutional law and the evolution of the digital context, as well as to the emerging notion of digital constitutionalism (De Gregorio 2021). However, until now, there have been little analyses of the constitutive elements of the geometry of digital power (Balkin 2018), of new actors' roles in the digital context, as well as on the reaction that new changes and challenges have triggered on modern constitutionalism.

This contribution is based on the author's article "The quadrangular shape of the geometry of digital power(s) and the move towards a procedural digital constitutionalism", European Law Journal 2023, 1–21, John Wiley & Sons Ltd.

O. Pollicino (✉)
Department of Law, Boconni University, Milan, Italy
e-mail: oreste.pollicino@unibocconi.it

G. Enes et al. (eds.), *A Digital Europe for Citizens*,
https://doi.org/10.1007/978-3-032-02500-5_2

Specifically, using a comparative approach, this work aims to shift the focus from a classical vertical approach juxtaposing authority and freedom towards a horizontal approach. The objective will be to highlight the importance of redress mechanism as the instruments for limiting and containing the emerging digital powers (Pollicino 2023).

Within the context illustrated here, the geometry of the season of digital constitutionalism will be conceptualized as having a triangular shape corresponding to the following three constitutive dimensions: (1) values; (2) actors; and (3) redress mechanisms.

Therefore, three dimensions will be analyzed.

First, a focus will be done on the European values that should be—and are—the foundation of the EU constitutional legal order and on which, for example, the Digital Service Act, the Digital Market Act, as well as the Data Governance Acts are based (paragraph 3.1).

Then, the analysis will move to the actors that play a role in the digital context. Particularly, it is necessary to assess whether these actors need to be regulated and how. In this context, it is interesting to notice that while the European legislator has enacted different pieces of legislation, the United States are adopting a different approach that it is directed to a lower degree of regulation (paragraph 3.2).

Lastly, the reaction of the European constitutionalism to these new challenges will be pointed out, specifically referring to the redress mechanism that are put in place (paragraph 3.3).

From a methodological point of view, the investigation will cover, from a transatlantic perspective, the European Union and US experiences. This choice does not wish to deny the emergence and consolidation of other regional areas with a significative impact on a geopolitical digital landscape, such as the Chinese model. Nevertheless, the privileged focus of this analysis aims, on the one hand, to be confined to liberal democracy experiences and, on the other, to critically point out the need to take more seriously the transatlantic bridge related to the biunivocal migration of constitutional ideas, from one side of the Ocean to the other one.

2 Newless of the Digital Context

Before illustrating the three dimensions of the new geometry of digital constitutionalism mentioned aboce, it is necessary make an important premises. Indeed, particularly in this field, the trap of the 'newless of the digital context' should be avoided, as applying the law in new technological context could rise the question on whether a new branch of the law must be brought to life.

One important aspect of this evaluation is descriptive. Particularly, it should be considered how does the disruptive potential of an emerging digital technology fits within existing law and policy regimes. A second step is more normative. Specifically, it should be understood whether new technologies change the paradigm of current law or regulation that the underlying rules should change. And together, these questions raise a series of normative issues: How do we know if a change is in action? Are there any calls for a different legal process or rule limited to a particular technical context, or do they also extend more generally to other areas of law and life?

On this matter, the 'law of the horse' example is emblematic to understand the chosen approach to the digital context.[1]

Specifically, in the mid-1990s, Judge Frank Easterbrook warned that the topic of 'property in cyberspace' was tantamount to a 'law of the horse'. He cautioned that adopting a 'new law' for cyberspace risked not only isolating technology from broader systems of law, but also undermining the hard work necessary to 'put the law of the [tech] horse in the context of broader rules' (Easterbrook 1996). An emphasis on a discrete body of tech law for the burgeoning internet age, in other words, risked skipping right past the extant 'unifying principles' that law already provided (Lawrence 1999). Broadly speaking, the debate concerned the question whether cyberlaw constitutes an independent academic field, and the ancillary question of whether it should be taught in law schools. Aside from this, this debate has become a point of reference to illustrate the competing understandings of cyberspace in the late 1990s and their corresponding ideas on how the Internet could and should be regulated.

Following these ideas in the context of new digital powers the focus should not be on special new rules just because new technological challenges are raising. Although it is not possible to affirm that the classical categories of sovereignty, of protection of fundamental rights, of territory plainly apply in a digital context, the use of traditional legal categories in all fields of the law is of uttermost importance to approach and regulate new digital powers.

Therefore, offline European constitutional values should be taken into account, trying to see how those values are changing, are challenged, as they maybe need to be updated, but not betrayed in the digital context.

3 Three Dimensions of Digital Constitutionalism

The reason for the division in three dimensions may be summarized as follows. Within the new algorithmic society, private transnational corporations (operators) are de facto increasingly performing public functions through the 'governance' of digital spaces (space). Within this context, the value framework that characterizes the European legal order on the one hand and the US system on the other hand, especially as regards the balancing of the rights at play (axiological dimension), is fundamental in understanding why different constitutional reactions by different legal orders are heavily influenced by the value-based approach which characterizes the respective bills of rights and the constitutional case-law of the legal orders at stake. The last relevant corner is the one corresponding to the constitutional remedies dimension. It bears the question of what instruments are available to public law to counter and

[1] Please note that this is the author's chosen approach.

limit private digital powers, which appear, however, to be following an increasing growth trajectory.

Therefore, the following paragraphs will be structured according to this tripartite understanding corresponding to the geometry of digital power(s). Section 3.1 will focus, looking at the first constitutive element, on trans-Atlantic diversity in terms of the values and judicial frames endorsed, respectively, by European courts and by the US Supreme Court as regards their approach to technology. Section 3.2 will then focus on the second constituent element, involving the major platforms and their metamorphosis into private powers. Finally, section 3.3 will examine the potential responses from US and European constitutionalism to limit the amplification of private digital power (Pollicino 2023).

3.1 Values

Starting with the 'value' dimension, the debate should concern the protection of the rights at stake as well as the value framework used as a backdrop for balancing operations by courts and lawmakers, which has, as such, an effect on the reinforcement, weaking or containment of new digital powers. This is not an irrelevant debate as it vividly exemplifies the existence of different regulatory models underpinning the predominance of equally different values. It is no coincidence that such values represent the keystones of respectively US and European constitutionalism (Rosenfeld and Sajó 2005), which are not always readily reconciled with each other.

Considered from this perspective, it may be interesting to point out the difference between the major values between the EU and the US in order to understand how they are balanced with other rights in both legal orders.

In this context, it should be noted that the main value in the European digital context is dignity, as its violations during the Second World War gave rise to reaction of constitutional law, as well as the creation of rigid constitutions all over Europe. Whereas, if we try to point out which is the most important value in the US digital context the answer is freedom, and specifically freedom of expression. Particularly, it is considered as an 'holy freedom', as it has basically no borders, no limits.

Therefore, although these values are not irreconcilable, their adoption has led to a different approach in the balancing those values with other fundamental rights. Indeed, whereas in Europe the right to freedom of expression is guaranteed by article 10 of the European Convention of Human Rights, it is not considered as an 'holy freedom', since the article codifies some limits to it, stating that 'the exercise of these freedoms, since it carries with it duties and responsibilities, may be subject to such formalities, conditions, restrictions or penalties as are prescribed by law and are necessary in a democratic society, in the interests of national security, territorial integrity or public safety, for the prevention of disorder or crime, for the protection of health or morals, for the protection of the reputation or rights of others, for preventing the disclosure of information received in confidence, or for maintaining the authority and impartiality of the judiciary'.[2]

As such, considering the different significance that it is given to the freedom of expression in both legal orders, we shall focus in particular on how the different framework values adopted respectively by the ECtHR in Strasbourg and the US Supreme Court in relation to the protection of this right can be decisive in identifying the level of protection that should be granted to that freedom when it comes into conflict with other fundamental rights. This is obviously crucially important in assessing those balancing operations that are necessary in order to deal with new digital powers.

There is a profound underlying fissure between the US approach focused on the First Amendment and a strictly European approach based on the axiological predominance of data protection rights (Pollicino 2023).

Particularly, freedom of expression has historically been interpreted as the North Star of US constitutional law, as the right characterizing the entire legal order. This approach is apparent within the value framework embraced by the Supreme Court, which, since its very first judgments in this area, has been inclined to exalt the unprecedented libertarian dimension to the Internet. In the eyes of the US Supreme Court, the new free marketplace of ideas immediately offered a framework and a new space for the exercise of this freedom, which must be considered through lenses and according to categories that differ from those applied to traditional media. This resulted in the choice in *Reno v. ACLU* to adapt the metaphor of the free marketplace of ideas from Justice Holmes' famous dissenting opinion, the enduring relevance of which could be called into question in the light of the changes that affected the Internet over the first few years of its life. This ruling is indicative of a clear inclination of the US Supreme Court to safeguard the exercise of free speech rights, and consequently to guarantee a kind of 'carte blanche' for Internet service providers through an instrument that was considered to be capable of ensuring an extraordinary expansion in their margin for manoeuvre. This value framework evidently resulted in the expansion of private digital power, especially during the period immediately following the creation of cyberspace.

Moving now to the judicial frame that has characterized the relevant case-law of the European courts, the European legal order has a different value framework in axiological terms as regards protection for freedom of expression. In simple terms, we can state that in Europe this right competes on an equal footing with other fundamental rights and does not enjoy the axiological priority that is afforded to the status and interpretation of the First Amendment under US law.

This configuration is confirmed by at least two elements, both of which can be identified within the text of the ECHR. First and foremost, as previously stated, Article 10(2) ECHR codifies limits and hence restrictions on that freedom, and also on all other rights and freedoms provided for in the Convention, where justified based on the principle of proportionality, representing a paramount element of European constitutionalism. Second, the ECHR (and also the EU Charter of Fundamental

[2] Article 10, paragraph 2, of the European Convention on Human Rights.

Rights) expressly provides for the possibility of the abuse of rights,[3] confirming the approach based on non-absolutism, balancing and equal status among rights that is characteristic of the constitutional traditions common to the Member States.

It is therefore no surprise that, starting from value contexts with such different facets (as well as even more fundamental differences), an analysis of the relevant case-law appears to point towards a judicial frame that is generally opposed to that prevailing within US courts. Rather than exalting the Internet as a driving force for freedom of expression, that value frame conceptualizes and gives weight above all to those aspects of it that are critical in the face of competing rights.

Turning now to the cases in which the ECtHR has been called upon to rule on applications resulting from supposed violations of freedom of expression online, a clear trend is apparent to rein in the expansive scope which had distinguished the previous case-law concerning the application of Article 10 in the world of atoms (Pollicino and Bassini 2014). This new nuanced view of the scope of freedom of expression online appears to be rooted in the conviction that the use of digital technologies entails a greater potential to cause harm to the other interests with which the exercise of free speech must engage (Pollicino and Bassini 2014). Naturally, this "relative" and "fall-back" status within operations concerning the balancing of the fundamental rights protected by the ECHR is certainly nothing new. However, this status appears to have been accentuated within Internet case-law, which has had immediate repercussions on attempts to rein in the expansive reach of digital technology, as well as the algorithmic power behind that technology.

To summarize and inevitably simplify the respective scope of the US and European judicial frames with regard to online regulation, and hence the containment of digital power, they appear to be inspired by diametrically opposite approaches. The US approach, which is inspired by a firm conviction that digital technology is inherently capable of amplifying freedoms (digital trust), assumes that any content regulation will not provide any increased benefits for freedom; the European approach, on the other hand, views new technologies with greater skepticism (digital distrust), considering it likely that technology will jeopardize other rights, and as such asserts the need for, and indeed the legitimacy of, corrective measures that may limit the exercise of free speech rights.

Based on this analysis, the key distinction appears to be between a (judicial) frame of resistance to technology (rooted in Europe) and an alternative frame that is more open to technology (which prevails within the relevant US case-law) (Pollicino 2023).

3.2 Actors

Having pointed out which are the main values underlying the digital context, the analysis should focus on which actors play a role in the aforementioned context.

[3] European Convention on Human Rights, Nov. 4, 1950, 213 UNTS 221, art. 17.

As such, the problem concerning the relationship between public law and private powers arises (Lombardi 1970). Specifically, in the digital context, gatekeepers, platforms and internet providers have gained a central role in letting users exercise their values.

In this context, how should such platforms be regulated?

It is well known that the large companies that now control the technology market (and beyond) have been able to develop in a very favorable regulatory regime, characterized by few constraints and many incentives (Kosseff 2019). This poor regulatory environment was a decisive condition for the creation of innovative services, the transformation of startups into platforms of enormous global scale, as well as for the still ongoing growth of investment and market. Indeed, the belief that regulation would have hindered and, perhaps, made innovation impossible spread, as well as the idea that a more interventionist approach would have entailed more disadvantages than advantages. Consequently, excluding platforms and new services from the relevant regulations has allowed their transformation into vertically integrated players, gradually operating as oligopolists or even monopolists. Particularly, we have witnessed a 'season of digital liberalism', during which, no rules or few rules were established. Indeed, both in Europe and in the United States a minimalist approach spread aimed at promoting the wide circulation of content. Specifically, the dominant concern within the lawmakers was to establish rules that could guide the actions of service providers in order not to impede the circulation of content online.

The structure underpinning these legislative acts reflects above all the openness to freedom of expression that is inherent to US constitutionalism. As was also confirmed by the US Supreme Court's interpretation of freedom of expression in *Reno v. ACLU*, the US lawmakers chose a paradigm, set out in Section 230 of the Communications Decency Act, which is still an object of debate. This Act, which is still in force, gives effect to that libertarian fervor embodied in the First Amendment, which was celebrated at the dawn of the Internet (Kosseff 2019). The legislation exempts service providers from any responsibility for any moderation of defamatory content: irrespective of whether the service provider has chosen to remove content or to leave it online, that choice cannot result in any liability for it, save under exceptional circumstances. The reason for this choice, which massively favored service providers, was to avoid any room for doubt regarding the legal classification of service providers. This hence solved the dilemma that had arisen within US case-law over whether to classify them as 'distributors' or 'publishers'. It has been noted that the choice made, which, moreover, resulted in an enhancement of the protection provided for under the First Amendment (Goldman 2019), resulted from the need to avoid virtuous forms of content moderation and policing by websites based on appropriate implementation mechanisms. As scholars have stressed, Section 230 CDA resulted from a bipartisan initiative aimed at avoiding the paradox, as is clearly apparent in the *Stratton Oakmont v. Prodigy* judgment[4] of the Supreme Court of New York, that the efforts made by a platform to carry out content policing in good faith could subject

[4] Stratton Oakmont v. Prodigy, 23 Media L. Rep. 1794 (N.Y. Sup. Ct. 1995).

the operator of such a site to a more severe liability standard, such as that applicable to publishers and content providers.[5] The need to maintain separate liability standards flowed from the need to favor as far as possible the spread of new 'virtual *agorà*' that could host and retransmit third party content, including content created by individual users themselves. Within this perspective, considering platforms as equivalent to content creators would have severely penalized the aim of favoring the exercise of freedom of speech in cyberspace. It was considered that this aim could be most readily achieved by providing that service providers should not incur any liability. Besides, the imposition of "direct" liability for content published by third parties would have significantly undermined the business models of content-sharing platforms.

This idea of digital liberalism readily migrated from one side of the Atlantic to the other. Indeed, albeit several years later, Europe also adopted a regulatory framework inspired by concerns not to inconvenience the business models of 'information society service providers': in other words, to favor e-commerce as much as possible. The (few) provisions dedicated to the liability regime were set out within Directive 2000/31/EC, known as the 'E-Commerce Directive' (Edwards 2005), which laid down two fundamental rules: first of all, the lack of any general requirement of preventive supervision for service providers; second, the provision of a 'notice and take down' mechanism, which was imported from the special rules contained in the US Digital Millennium Copyright Act (DMCA). This framework is based on the absence of any direct liability on the part of the service provider for any unlawful content; it provides, by contrast, that the service provider incurs liability where it fails to ensure the removal of any manifestly unlawful content, despite effectively being aware of it.

This approach has, then, lead to a transformation of such actors in kind of digital forum often exercising para-constitutional functions. As such, it is necessary to consider why, at a particular moment in time, operators doing business in cyberspace transformed into full-blown private powers in competition with public authorities, thereby inevitably increasing the relevance of constitutional law arguments.

In order to provide an adequate response, we must look back a few decades and consider who, at the end of the last century (Lessig 1999), was the first to point out the initial transformation, which ultimately ended up representing a significant step.

The key aspects of the debate into cyberspace regulation is, starting from the centrality of the role of technology for effective regulation, the fact that a shift was underway within fundamental decision-making over that regulation from the lawmaker to the IT technician, in other words to the expert capable of deciphering the code. As has been pointed out (Bassini 2019), it is no coincidence that the first provisions laid down by lawmakers in this area concerned the role of intermediaries, in awareness of the central importance of their technical role (which at the time still

[5] Just a few years earlier, the US District Court for the Southern District of New York, in Cubby, Inc. v. CompuServe Inc., 776 F. Supp. 135 (S.D.N.Y. 1991) had seemingly seconded the assimilation of online platforms to distributors, suggesting a similarity with news-stands, libraries and book-shops as far as control over content is concerned.

did not have any oligopolistic features and was thus unaffected by competition law) in relation to operations impinging on user activity and behavior.

Today we are witnessing a kind of 'code reloaded', in light of the metamorphosis referred to above, whereby digital intermediaries have transformed from economic operators into full-blown private powers, in competition with public authorities. Indeed, these operators are distant relatives of the operators that were (not) regulated under European law during the era of digital liberalism. They are much less neutral, much less passive, and yet much more sophisticated and much more capable of altering the content hosted within their virtual spaces.

On the other hand, from the start of the 2010s, algorithmic power and the resulting machine-learning capability shifted decision-making from humans—whether politicians or IT experts—to machines. These algorithms formed part of the automation architecture of the new ecosystem rooted in AI which, along with the exponential growth of the data available, completed the new intermediaries' transformation from economic operators into political forces. It should be added that in many cases the algorithm is opaque and non-transparent, thereby further enhancing the power of platforms (Pollicino 2023).

In light of these preliminary reflections, as anti-trust law was not anymore enough to meet the new challenge constitutional law had to be taken into account. This is exactly where and when constitutional law enters into the scene, as constitutional law has the force to limit powers. Indeed, two different reactions can be observed in Europe. The first one is related to the 'judicial activism' according, as, because of the inertia of the European legislator, judges, basically, played the role of lawmakers. Indeed, for example in the field of personal data protection, before the entry into force of the GDPR, the European Court of Justice decided to play the role of legislator, particularly in three very important decisions as Digital Rights Ireland, Google v. Spain and Schrems. The positive implication was an increase of the protection of the rights, especially an increase of the protection of individuals. However, the drawback was, for example, in Google v. Spain, to delegate to a private operator a public exercise: the exercise to be an arbiter between two fundamental rights in contrast—the right to be forgotten, on one hand, and the right to be informed, on the other hand. Then, the second season is related to the legislative reaction. Thus, in Europe (more than in the United States), proposals are now multiplying for the adoption of new rules and constraints aimed at regulating and containing such a concentration of power that have few precedents.

In this sense, it is possible to affirm that, at certain point, the judicial fragmentation was replaced by legislative fragmentation, but, unfortunately, the final problem remained the same: harming legal certainty.

3.3 Redress Mechanisms

Having highlighted all the concerns related to the role of private actors in the digital context, we must consider what appropriate instruments are available to modern constitutionalism in order to counter or limit the expansion of this private digital power.

How can liberal democracies exercise their own "digital" sovereignty over private powers that are competing on an increasingly equal footing with public authorities?

In this context, the major differences between the respective value frameworks that characterize US and European law also explain the issues at stake within the debate on digital sovereignty under which different legal systems, which may make specific claims in relation to the governance of cyberspace, apply different 'visions' of the same rights and different standards of protection.

Remaining true to the trans-Atlantic focus sketched out at the start, these reactions must be illustrated—also in the light of the extremely different value framework, which this study has sought to present—by focusing on the US system as well as on the EU.

Particularly, if we start by considering the US context, American constitutional law does not provide for the horizontal application of the rights contained in the Bill of Rights, in contrast to the position in Europe. The reason underlying the resistance towards acceptance of a general horizontal effect for the rights contained in the federal Constitution can be found in the fertile ground in which US constitutionalism took root, based on the values of liberty and individual freedom, which constitute the bedrock for private autonomy.

In other words, as Mark Tushnet has observed, 'the judicialisation of relations between private persons [is] an intolerable intrusion of the state into the sphere of private autonomy'. This leads naturally into the question, with specific reference to our field of enquiry, as to whether such an intrusion could be considered to be intolerable even in cases involving private powers that often de facto exercise public or para-constitutional functions, which can hence be considered to be state actors latu senso? The Supreme Court's answer has been sufficiently clear and confirms that such an intrusion would be intolerable. In the only substantial decision to be considered newsworthy,[6] the Court held that a private person could not be regarded as a state actor, despite the massive size of the platform YouTube.

Moreover, as has rightly been pointed out, 'according to the interpretation embraced by the Court of Appeal, there is absolutely no potential similarity between a service provider such as YouTube and the notion of state actor within US constitutional law: there is no involvement in that specific range of functions that have been traditionally reserved on an exclusive basis to the state' (Bassini 2019); on the contrary, they are nothing other than private operators that make decisions relating to the governance of their own respective spaces.

Given the insuperable nature of the obstacles presented by the state action doctrine, the reference to governance of the space managed by the platforms represented a second attempt by US constitutional law to more effectively (de)limit the emerging digital power. This involved, in particular, the interpretative option that sought to establish equivalence between the spaces offered by digital platforms providing social network services, on the one hand, and a public forum, on the other. The aim of this

[6] Prager University v. Google LLC, n. 18–15,712 (9th Cir. 2020).

was to apply the 'public forum doctrine', which allows extremely limited scope for interference with the exercise of free speech rights in locations, such as parks, roads, and squares, that are considered to be naturally designed to host exchanges of ideas and opinions between different people.

It has been pointed out in the literature (Bassini 2019) that this assertion is often made metaphorically with the aim of describing social networks as the new public forum; however, to vest it with a normative effect would be something entirely different. The US case-law has endorsed this account to date solely in relation to social network accounts used by state officials, i.e., persons acting in a public capacity, holding that measures such as the blocking or removal of comments effectively violate freedom of expression.[7] It is important to note that the case-law does not consider private ownership to preclude classification as a public place, noting that there may indeed be 'designated public forums'; these are spaces that, whilst being private, 'become' essentially public in nature, being subjected to the same process of metamorphosis that we have seen to apply in relation to private cyberspace operators.

The attempts referred to above to reclassify the role of platforms, and in particular social networks, have a variety of implications with regard to the values at stake within digital space, with which the new 'powers' must inevitably engage. To state that a social network is equivalent to a public service, or a state is not a neutral act as it entails subjection to a range of guarantees that are normally associated with the actions of public operators. Although on paper such a development might mark progress in the sense of providing greater guarantees, on the other hand it may entail some pitfalls. In particular, to subject private operators to the same standard of protection as that imposed on public bodies could have difficult consequences in terms of some of the strategies that have been developed at the European level. This is relevant above all in relation to content that is not unlawful but may need to be removed or to be subject to technical action according to strategies to combat certain content developed within the ambit of self-regulation or co-regulation. Disinformation is a particularly striking example of this. This is a warning which, as has been acknowledged in the literature (Bassini 2019), was previously given by Justice Alito in his concurring opinion in *Packingham v. North Carolina*,[8] in which he criticized the excessively relaxed way in which the Supreme Court's opinion had suggested that the Internet—and social networks in particular—constituted new 'public forums' within the digital reality, without considering the normative implications of this dictum. This is not all: any requirement that content moderation by social networks must comply with the 'public' standard would risk entirely frustrating the promise of freedom inherent within these platforms, jeopardizing their possible use as instruments of protest or for combatting propaganda or public censorship. This would result in social networks being steered by state authorities. Although the authorities may in some cases operate

---

[7] Knight First Amendment Inst. at Columbia Univ. v. Trump, n. 1:17-cv-5205 (SDNY); Knight First Amendment Inst. at Columbia Univ. v. Trump, n. 18–1691 (2d Cir.); Biden v. Knight First Amendment Institute at Columbia University 593 U.S. (2021); Davison v. Randall, n. 17–2002 (4th Cir.).

[8] Packingham v. North Carolina, in 582 U.S. (2017).

for virtuous purposes, in some cases they may be inspired by less commendable goals, especially within immature democracies or during armed conflict, as we are already sadly aware of.

We turn now to the ways in which sovereignty has been expressed in Europe in response to, and in order to 'contain', the new digital power, with emphasis placed on how these actions contrast with the approach in the United States. It is posited that actions taken in Europe, in contrast to what has occurred in the United States, are feasible on the grounds of being consistent with the constitutional traditions common to the Member States. The option involves the possibility of recognizing European charters of rights as having horizontal effect against private operators.

For its part, the ECJ has demonstrated the potential for horizontal application of provisions of the Treaties, even when they were directed exclusively at the Member States.

A number of cases have subsequently resulted in the horizontal application of general principles of EU law[9] and, albeit in a line of case-law that is not always entirely transparent, also of some provisions of the Charter of Fundamental Rights (Frantziou 2020; Piccone and Pollicino 2018).[10]

However, within this context there is a singular aspect of the ECJ's reaction to the emergence of digital power, which during those years was not, moreover, being resisted by a neo-liberal legislature, which took the view that digital operators should not be regulated, or simply remained inactive, as is apparent from the extremely long gestational period necessary in order to adopt the General Data Protection Regulation (GDPR) in 2016. This aspect was the surreptitious, and by all means not expressed, horizontal application of Articles 7 and 8 of the Charter of Fundamental Rights (concerning, respectively, the respect for private life and data protection) within the case-law adopted in 2014 and 2015 (Google Spain and Schrems in particular) concerning the enforcement of digital privacy rights against the emerging power of algorithms.

This period of judicial activism by the ECJ, which can in some sense be accounted for both with reference to the threat of global surveillance originating from the United States and the inertia of European lawmakers (De Gregorio 2022), having repeatedly kicked the long-awaited GDPR into the long grass, evidently amounted to a clear rejection by the ECJ of the previous approach characterized by digital liberalism. This approach prevailed on both sides of the Atlantic and favored the transformation of private entities from economic operators into full-blown powers.

Although the period of creative reaction from the ECJ is certainly understandable and even consistent (at least as regards the specific level of protection afforded to

---

[9] See, among others, Case 26/62, Van Gend en Loos v. Administratie der Belastingen, ECLI:EU:C:1963:1; Case 2/74, Reyners v. Belgian State, ECLI:EU:C:1974:68; Case 33/74, Van Binsbergen v. Bestuur van de Bedrijfsvereniging voor de Metaalnijverheid, ECLI:EU:C:1974:131; Case 41/74, Van Duyn v. Home Office, ECLI:EU:C:1974:133.

[10] Case 414/16, Egenberger, ECLI:EU:C:2018:257; Case 569/16, Bauer, ECLI:EU:C:2018:871; Case 684/16 Max-Planck-Gesellschaft zur Förderung der Wissenschaften, ECLI:EU:C:2018:874; Case 68/17, IR v. JQ, ECLI:EU:C:2018:696; Case 193/17, Cresco Investigation, ECLI:EU:C:2019:43; Case 55/18, CCOO, ECLI:EU:C:2019:402.

data protection) with the values embraced by the constitutional traditions common to the Member States, there were nonetheless some downsides which forced a rethink of the way in which European digital sovereignty was expressed in the face of the digital "threat". The first evident downside was the amplification of an imbalance, in terms of the separation of powers, between the judicial branch and the political/legislative branch.

In light of these considerations, it is clear within the European context that it was necessary, if not to rebalance, then at least to mitigate the imbalance referred to above in terms of the separation of powers, ensuring that decision-making mechanisms involved also and in particular the democratic-representative input from the legislative process.

This imbalance is not the only drawback to the expression of digital sovereignty through case-law. It is also compounded by a process of fragmentation, also at the national level, of the rules developed through case-law for specific individual scenarios, thereby significantly undermining the principle of legal certainty. More specifically, given the lack of legislative action, having failed to regulate, amongst other things, the liability exemptions (or rather limitations) provided for under Directive 2000/31, both European and national courts have established new roles and definitions for Internet service providers. These have been both active and passive roles,[11] although also 'sophisticated' roles,[12] thereby resulting in the creation of a variety of new figures (despite the legislation remaining unchanged) corresponding to the different levels of responsibility for the private gatekeepers of the digital ecosystem, which have not only become much larger but have also changed fundamentally in terms of their essence. All of this has obviously played out against a backdrop characterized by a significant level of fragmentation within the case-law, and consequently the weakening of the principle of legitimate expectations.

A third downside to this period of judicial activism has been the—certainly unintended but extremely risky—consequences of the decisions discussed, including in particular Google Spain. In fact, one of the effects of the creation within the case-law of the right to be forgotten has been for the ECJ to vest a search engine (i.e., a private operator/power) with the task of striking the delicate balance between a user's right to be forgotten and the right to be informed of the majority of Internet users. Where an operation that should fall within the exclusive purview of a judicial or para-judicial authority is delegated to a private operator vested with almost complete discretion and without adequate procedural guarantees, this inevitably ends up enhancing that operator's power.

These issues have resulted in the emergence of a new approach, which has been defined as 'digital constitutionalism' (De Gregorio 2021), in which political actors have reasserted control over the expression of digital sovereignty with a view to containing the new private powers. Leaving aside specific labels and the potential

[11] See, among others, Joined Cases 236/08, C-237/08 and 238/08, L'Oréal and others, ECLI:EU:C:2010:159; Case 18/18, Glawischnig-Piesczek, ECLI:EU:C:2019:821. With respect to Italian case-law, see, most notably, Cass. Pen. 19 marzo 2019, n. 7708.

[12] See Tribunale di Roma, sez. IX, 27 aprile 2016, n. 8437.

conceptual confusion that has been associated with them (not always rightly) due to the alleged (although in fact unfounded) resemblance between theories of global constitutionalism (Betzu 2021) and the different manifestations of digital constitutionalism, one thing is certain. This new approach has been characterized by the re-appropriation of European legislators' role as lawmakers.

The first somewhat concentrated dose of this 'injection' came with the entry into force of the GDPR in 2016, which, moreover, codified many of the rules that had previously been developed within the case law of the ECJ. It elevated the right to data protection from an economically informed interest under Directive No 95/46 into a right to privacy inherent to the constitutional framework, which had in the meantime been codified in the Charter of Fundamental Rights, in both its static (Article 7) and dynamic (Article 8) manifestations (Martinico 2017).

The GDPR has acted as a model for various jurisdictions, giving rise to a form of legal 'colonisation', or, as it has also been defined, a 'Brussels effect' (Bradford 2020) that is almost global in reach, extending from California to China.

This enhancement of fortress Europe has been a common feature of the various legislative changes introduced in recent years: from the reform of copyright law[13] through the changes to the law governing the provision of audio-visual media services[14] to European legislation on the prevention of terrorism.[15] This could be regarded as the initial phase of digital constitutionalism, which has de facto emerged as a response by European political representatives to the considerably high judicial power of the previous era, the processes, and pitfalls of which have been described above.

A defining feature of this first phase has been a strong axiological-substantive configuration, which in turn, however, suffers from two underlying drawbacks, despite being fundamentally consistent with European constitutional roots. Due to the variety of sectoral legislation, the first drawback concerns the risk (as seen during the phase of judicial activism) of triggering a process of internal fragmentation. This would result in the application of different rules, also in relation to the different liability models for the major digital platforms, depending upon the specific relevant legislation, subject, moreover, to a not insignificant margin for the Member States, considering the extremely large number of open clauses contained in the relevant regulations, which are often tantamount to masked directives (De Gregorio 2020).

---

[13] Directive (EU) 2019/790 of the European Parliament and of the Council of 17 April 2019 on copyright and related rights in the Digital Single Market and amending Directives 96/9/EC and 2001/29/EC [2019] OJ L130/92.

[14] Directive (EU) 2018/1808 of the European Parliament and of the Council of 14 November 2018 amending Directive 2010/13/EU on the coordination of certain provisions laid down by law, regulation or administrative action in Member States concerning the provision of audiovisual media services (Audiovisual Media Services Directive) in view of changing market realities [2018] OJ L303/69.

[15] Regulation (EU) 2021/784 of the European Parliament and of the Council of 29 April 2021 on addressing the dissemination of terrorist content online [2021] OJ L172/79.

It is clear that, although this obviously buttresses fortress Europe against possible external attacks, it also risks causing an implosion, or in any case an internal weakening, due to the excessive sectoral specialization within the relevant provisions. This has evident repercussions, once again, on the principle of legal certainty.

The second drawback results from the risk that, in focusing exclusively on a regional value framework—the characteristic features of which are extremely specific—in order to regulate the digital ecosystem, which is by definition transnational, fortress Europe may end up becoming seriously isolated due to a lack of bridges connecting it with other significant regional hubs.

This clearly raises the possible risk that European rules may not be enforced, and more generally that Europe and the United States may drift further apart, thereby undermining the solidity of the trans-Atlantic bridge. However, maintaining that bridge is crucially important in order to ensure the effective containment by modern constitutionalism of the now consolidated private digital power.

The drawbacks illustrated in the previous section have resulted in a second phase (which is currently ongoing and is set to continue into the near future) within digital constitutionalism in Europe. This phase is characterized not only by an axiological-substantive approach but also by a procedural dimension as well as its 'horizontal' scope, as it is not focused on individual sectors, precisely in order to avoid the fragmentation mentioned above.

4 Conclusion

As a last point, what will happen in the future?

As mentioned, after a first phase of reaction to the emerging digital powers by the European constitutional powers (firstly, the European Court of Justice with its 'wild' judicial activism and, secondly, starting with the adoption of the GDPR, the EU lawmaker with its hypertrophic approach) there is the need to focus on the substantive values at the heart of European constitutional law. The focus has been not (only) on the mentioned values, in the light, it should be added, of a sectorial vertical approach, but rather, as has been described by commenting on the new EU legislation's added value, on a horizontal and procedural application thereof, which might be seen as the main features of the second season of European digital constitutionalism.

In particular, the mentioned legislation does so by providing procedural guarantees to remedy the absence of substantive guarantees comparable to those applicable to relations with public bodies. However, it is important to note that, whilst focusing much more on the procedural dimension than the previous exclusively axiological-substantive approach did, this new manifestation of digital constitutionalism must not be confused with a radicalization of that approach that would risk transforming the state into what Forsthoff would have called 'a macro-administration shorn of political capacity' (Betzu 2021). Moreover, one must not be so naive as to overlook the possibility that any attempt at proceduralist that is detached from a reference value foundation is destined to degenerate into a sterile exercise of "procedural fetishism".

The great benefit of stressing the procedural dimension, which may be defined as a European application of due (data) process (Crawford and Schultz 2014) on a horizontal level between private parties, is that it is potentially able to consolidate that trans-Atlantic bridge. This is because it is a dimension (and a principle, i.e., due process applied in the digital realm) that is absolutely not alien to US constitutionalism (Redish and Marshall 1985). Moreover, the particular focus on the valorizations of the principle of transparency points towards another benefit that is often not visible: that of ensuring that the actions of 'private powers' are open to control where they implement strategies or measures that have been adopted by public authorities, which may have threatened major financial sanctions in the event of non-compliance.

As is clear from the investigation carried out, the classic categories of constitutional law—sovereignty, territory, people and power—far from being outdated in the new digital context, are very much contemporary and indeed crucial in order to understand and contextualise the new threats to constitutionalism which must be, at the same time, able to show the needed flexibility to address such threats and remain faithful to its genetical code: limiting power(s) (Pollicino 2023).

References

Balkin JM (2018) Free speech is a triangle. Colum l Rev 118:2011

Bassini M (2019) Internet e libertà di espressione: prospettive costituzionali e sovranazionali. Aracne Editrice

Betzu M (2021) I poteri privati nella società digitale: oligopoli e antitrust. Diritto Pubblico 27(3):739–760

Bradford A (2020) The Brussels Effect: How the European Union Rules the World. Oxford University Press, New York

Crawford K, Schultz J (2014) Big data and due process: Toward a framework to redress predictive privacy harms. BCL Rev 55:93

De Gregorio G (2020) Democratising online content moderation: A constitutional framework. Comput Law Secur Rev 36:105374

De Gregorio G (2021) The rise of digital constitutionalism in the European Union. Int J Const Law 19(1):41–70

De Gregorio, G. (2022). Digital constitutionalism in Europe: Reframing rights and powers in the algorithmic society. Cambridge University Press

Easterbrook FH (1996) Cyberspace and the Law of the Horse. U Chi Legal F 207

Edwards L (ed) (2005) The new legal framework for e-commerce in Europe. Bloomsbury Publishing

Frantziou E (2020) The Horizontal Effect of the Charter: Towards an Understanding of Horizontality as a Structural Constitutional Principle. Camb Yearb Eur Legal Stud 22:208–232. https://doi.org/10.1017/cel.2020.7

Goldman E (2019) Why Section 230 is better than the First Amendment. Notre Dame l Rev Reflection 95:33

Kosseff J (2019) The twenty-six words that created the Internet. Cornell University Press

Lawrence L (1999) Commentaries the Law of the Horse: What Cyberlaw Might Teach. Harv Law Rev 113:501–549

Lessig L (1999) Code: And other laws of cyberspace. ReadHowYouWant.com

Lombardi G (1970) Potere privato e diritti fondamentali

Martinico G (2021) Rispetto della vita privata e della vita familiare. In Codice della privacy e data protection, vol 1, Giuffrè, pp. 17–35
Piccone V, Pollicino O (eds) (2018) La carta dei diritti fondamentali dell'Unione europea: efficacia ed effettività. Editoriale scientifica
Pollicino O, Bassini M (2014) Free speech, defamation and the limits to freedom of expression in the EU: a comparative analysis. In Research Handbook on EU Internet Law (pp. 508–542). Edward Elgar Publishing
Pollicino O (2023) The quadrangular shape of the geometry of digital power(s) and the move towards a procedural digital constitutionalism. Eur Law J 29(1–2):10–30. https://doi.org/10.1111/eulj.12472
Rosenfeld M, Sajó A (2005) Spreading liberal constitutionalism: an inquiry into the fate of free speech rights in new democracies. Cardozo Legal Studies Research Paper (144).
Redish MH, Marshall LC (1985) Adjudicatory independence and the values of procedural due process. Yale LJ 95:455

The Approach by the European Commission "Legal Openness—*Do as You Preach!*"

Jean-Paul Triaille

1 Introduction

In this contribution, we will describe how the concepts of legal openness and transparency apply respectively to Commission's documents, data (including scientific data), software and scientific publications.

Amongst the EU institutions, the European Commission is the biggest "producer" of documents, data, software and probably the most advanced in terms of legal openness.

2 Copyright and EU Documents

It is generally accepted that there is no copyright or other intellectual property right on official documents such as legislative texts (or drafts thereof), for instance EU directives or regulations, decisions by the European Court of Justice or speeches in

The views expressed by the author do not necessarily reflect the official views of the European Commission.

The European Commission's Central Intellectual Property Service (CIPS) is the Commission's competence centre for intellectual property management and legal support to Commission's services. The Service operates in accordance with the guiding principles established by the Commission Communication of 3 March 2022, C(2022) 1225 final ("*Consolidating the corporate intellectual property management framework at the European Commission*"). The activities of the Central IP Service can be grouped under three main pillars: legal support, management of the IP portfolio of the Commission and awareness raising.

J.-P. Triaille (✉)
Central Intellectual Property Service (CIPS), European Commission, Brussels, Belgium
e-mail: Jean-Paul.TRIAILLE@ec.europa.eu

G. Enes et al. (eds.), *A Digital Europe for Citizens*,
https://doi.org/10.1007/978-3-032-02500-5_3

the European Parliament[1] or alternatively that the copyright protection, if it exists at all, should not be exercised in a manner which prevents access by citizens to these official acts.[2] As a consequence thereof, all these texts may be freely reproduced and reused (translated, published) by everybody, including for commercial purposes and regardless of whether the person or legal entity concerned is established in the EU or not.

Regarding other documents which may not qualify as such as "official" documents, such as preparatory materials, datasets, reports, computer programs, they may be subject to copyright protection (provided they are "original" in the copyright sense of the word); the copyright will belong to the European Union and not to the Commission itself (which has no separate legal entity – as opposed to some EU agencies, which may be the owners of copyright on their own publications). Such documents would however usually qualify as "public sector information" in line with the PSI and Open Data Directive.

Directives are addressed to Member States and do not strictly speaking apply to EU institutions and bodies, but they will usually serve as principles determining the Commission's own policy. As a consequence thereof, in line with the Public Sector Information and Open Data Directive, the Commission, as is recommended to Member States, "*should [...] exercise [its] copyright in a way that facilitates re-use*" (see paragraph 54 of the preamble). As regards data and the intellectual property rights on data (in particular the so-called *sui generis* right on databases), the Commission, as is recommended to Member States, "*should not exercise that right in order to prevent reuse or to restrict the re-use of existing documents beyond the limits provided for in this Directive*" (see paragraph 61 of the preamble).

3 Commission Documents: Reusable

The reuse by third parties of Commission documents is governed by the Commission Decision on the reuse of Commission documents (2011/833/EU) (the "Reuse Decision"). As per its article 2, the Decision applies to "*public documents produced by the Commission or by public and private entities on its behalf: (a) which have been published by the Commission or by the Publications Office on its behalf through publications, websites or dissemination tools; or (b) which have not been published for economic or other practical reasons, such as studies, reports and other data*". The

[1] See article 2.4. of the Berne Convention for the Protection of Literary and Artistic Works: "*It shall be a matter for legislation in the countries of the Union to determine the protection to be granted to official texts of a legislative, administrative and legal nature, and to official translations of such texts*".

[2] See on this issue the recent opinion of the Advocate General in Case C-588/21P (Public.Resource.Org. Inc., Right to Know CLG v. European Commission), in particular par. 66 et s.; the Advocate General suggests that if a harmonised standard is to be considered as part of EU law, it "*should, in principle, not benefit from copyright protection*".

Reuse Decision is in many ways an application to the Commission of the principles and mechanisms of the PSI and Open Data Directive.

The Decision must be distinguished from Regulation 1049/2001 regarding public access to European Parliament, Council and Commission documents, which applies by definition to documents which have not been published – and which therefore is also a legal instrument aiming at ensuring transparency of the administration towards citizens and third parties.

According to article 3.2., "reuse" covers the use by persons or legal entities (EU or non-EU), for non-commercial but also for commercial purposes "*other than the initial purpose for which the documents were produced*" (in line with the terminology of article 2.4. of the PSI and Open Data Directive; the "initial purpose" for which the document was produced has normally and by definition already been fulfilled, the "reuse" thus covers all other uses of it.

Examples of reuse include republication on another media, distribution (or selling) of exemplars, translation, adaptations,[3] etc.

In line with article 3.1., "document" means: "*a) any content whatever its medium (written on paper or stored in electronic form or as a sound, visual or audio-visual recording); (b) any part of such content*".

The following items are outside the scope of the Decision[4]:

(a) software or documents covered by industrial property rights such as patents, trademarks, registered designs, logos and names;
(b) documents for which the Commission is not in a position to allow their reuse in view of intellectual property rights of third parties;
(c) documents which pursuant to the rules established in Regulation (EC) No 1049/2001 (on access to documents) are excluded from access or only made accessible to a party under specific rules governing privileged access[5];
(d) confidential data, as defined in Regulation (EC) No 223/2009 of the European Parliament and of the Council (1);
(e) documents resulting from ongoing research projects conducted by the staff of the Commission, when their reuse could interfere with the validation of provisional research results or constitute a reason to refuse registration of a patent (for lack of novelty, as a result of the prior reuse).

As a consequence of the Reuse Decision therefore, *once* a document has been published by the Commission, it becomes freely reusable by everyone. It is worth noting that the decision *to publish or not to publish* the document is not governed by the Reuse Decision and remains at the discretion of the services concerned.

[3] See however, concerning the possibilities to adapt the document, article 3.4. of the Reuse Decision, which provides as follows: "*Nothing in this Decision authorises reuse of documents in a manner calculated to deceive or to defraud. The Commission shall take the appropriate measures to protect the interests and the public image of the EU in accordance to applicable rules*".

[4] For more details, see article 2.1.

[5] The reasoning here is that if some unpublished documents should not be allowed to be made available upon the individual request of an applicant, *a fortiori* they should not fall in the scope of the Reuse Decision.

4 Commission Data: Reusable as Open Data

As indicated above, the notion of document in the Reuse Decision covers any content whatever its medium (written on paper or stored in electronic form or as a sound, visual or audio-visual recording) as well as any part of such content. This clearly covers data (as also confirmed explicitly in article 2.1.b. and in various paragraphs of the preamble of the Decision).

As for other documents, internal and administrative data are out of the scope of the Decision which only applies to "public" documents and data. But any data collected in preparation of a policy initiative or in the context of the evaluation of an existing policy falls in scope of the Reuse Decision.

5 Research Data: Reusable and Open Data

Data resulting from research conducted by Commission services (in particular by researchers from the Commission's Joint Research Centre) is also included. Research data differs from scientific articles.[6] Whereas the initial PSI Directive did not apply to "research data", the Commission had decided to include research data from its own research centre when the initial version of the Reuse Decision was reviewed in 2011 (see indeed paragraph 10 of the preamble).

The PSI and Open Data Directive did later include research data in its recast version, in its article 10 which also clarifies that "*concerns relating to intellectual property rights, personal data protection and confidentiality, security and legitimate commercial interests, shall be taken into account in accordance with the principle of 'as open as possible, as closed as necessary'*".

The PSI Directive in its initial version had introduced *minimum* rules for the reuse of public sector information throughout the European Union. In its recitals, it was encouraging Member States "*to go beyond these minimum rules and to adopt open data policies, allowing a broad use of documents held by public sector bodies*"[7]: on research data, the Commission took advantage of this invitation and was somehow in advance of what the PSI and Open Data Directive imposed only later on for Member States.

And to further ensure the implementation of open data principles, the Joint Research Centre (JRC) of the Commission has adopted an elaborate data policy,[8] aiming at a "*free, full, open and timely*" access to its data, in line with the so-called

---

[6] See article 2.9. of the PSI and Open Data Directive: "*'research data' means documents in a digital form, other than scientific publications, which are collected or produced in the course of scientific research activities and are used as evidence in the research process, or are commonly accepted in the research community as necessary to validate research findings and results*".

[7] As recalled in paragraph 6 of the Reuse Decision.

[8] https://joint-research-centre.ec.europa.eu/system/files/2019-05/jrc115832_2019_jrc_data_policy_2.pdf.

FAIR principle (findability, accessibility, interoperability, and reusability). The data flowing from the JRC's research feed into the EU Open Data Portal; and to further encourage the effective implementation of this open data policy, the JRC also developed an online "data policy implementation tool" to assist its own researchers in the publication process and it ensures that all researchers also receive appropriate trainings on this.

6 For Documents and Data: Which Open Licence?

Until 2019, documents and data published on behalf of the European Commission by the Publications Office as well as the Commission's website were carrying a copyright notice which was labelled as follows:

> © *European Union, [year of publication]*
>
> *Reuse is authorised, provided the source is acknowledged. The Commission's reuse policy is implemented by the Decision of 12 December 2011 - reuse of Commission documents.*

It was for candidate reusers and for readers in general to look and find out what the Reuse Decision was stating, which was suboptimal in terms of user-friendliness and accessibility. Also, this notice was not machine-readable and could not be identified as such by robots and search engines; finally, it was a Commission bespoke solution, rather than a standard solution as the Commission itself had advocated in its own guidelines addressed to Member States on how to implement the PSI Directive.[9]

In 2019, on the recommendation of the Commission's Central IP Service,[10] the Commission adopted Creative Commons as "the" instrument to implement the Reuse Decision, more precisely the licence CC BY 4.0 as the default solution, and CC 0 (public domain dedication) for special cases (such as machine-generated data, to which no copyright applies).[11] This development was notably welcomed by the Creative Commons organisation itself.[12]

As a result, documents (be it on-line or in print formats) and datasets published by the European Commission now carry the following copyright notice (with small variations where needed):

> © *European Union, 20XX [year of first publication]*

---

[9] See Commission Notice, Guidelines on recommended standard licences, datasets and charging for the reuse of documents, 24 July 2014, Official Journal, 2014/C 240/01.

[10] EC Reuse policy: a study on available reuse implementing instruments and licensing considerations (europa.eu), European Commission's Central IP Service, EUR 29,685 EN, Publications Office of the European Union, Luxembourg, 2019, https://doi.org/10.2760/95373, JRC115947, available here: https://publications.jrc.ec.europa.eu/repository/handle/JRC115947.

[11] Commission Decision adopting Creative Commons as an open licence under the European Commission's reuse policy, Brussels, 22 February 2019 C(2019) 1655 final.

[12] https://creativecommons.org/2019/04/02/european-commission-adopts-cc-by-and-cc0-for-sharing-information/.

> *The Commission's reuse policy is implemented by Commission Decision 2011/833/EU of 12 December 2011 on the reuse of Commission documents (OJ L 330, 14.12.2011, p. 39 –*https://eur-lex.europa.eu/eli/dec/2011/833/oj*).*
>
> *Unless otherwise noted, the reuse of this document is authorised under the Creative Commons Attribution 4.0 International (CC BY 4.0) licence (*https://creativecommons.org/licenses/by/4.0/*).*
>
> *This means that reuse is allowed, provided that appropriate credit is given and any changes are indicated.*

Internally, guidelines and practical documents have been prepared by the Commission's Central Intellectual Property Service and the Office of Publications to ensure a proper implementation of the Commission's decision to opt for Creative Commons, and trainings are regularly organised for interested staff members.

As is well known, the use of Creative Commons has various advantages: CC BY 4.0 offers technology-ready features (in particular, machine-readability) out of the box, can be adopted with minimum effort and resources, is widely known and used (including by online platforms and publishing services) and is a user-friendly solution that can incentivise reuse. The language of the CC licences has been scrutinised by copyright experts in most if not all EU jurisdictions and has already been enforced by courts in various jurisdictions.

Amongst the various CC licences, CC BY was identified as the one which best implemented the principles of the Reuse Decision. Differentiating between commercial and non-commercial uses, preventing modifications or imposing a share-alike condition (as this is made possible via the other CC licences) would unnecessarily restrict possibilities for reuse. This would not be in line with the Commission's Reuse Decision.

CC BY 4.0 is a worldwide, royalty-free, non-sublicensable, non-exclusive, irrevocable licence. When applied to a document (which can be done simply by mentioning that the document is licensed under it), the licence allows third parties to reuse that document, provided that they comply with a few conditions (in essence, mentioning the source and mentioning if changes have been made by the person re-distributing the work).

Third parties are entitled to copy and redistribute the material in any medium or format, remix, transform, and build upon the material for any purpose, even commercially, as long as the reuser identifies the source of the document in a reasonable manner. This is in line with Article 6(2)(a) of the Reuse Decision, which mentions '*the obligation for the reuser to acknowledge the source of the documents*' as one of only few the conditions that can be imposed on the reuse of Commission documents.

In addition, if the reuser modifies the work, it must state what changes have been made. Although the reuser is obliged to acknowledge the source, it cannot in any way assert or imply that the copyright owner is connected with the reuse or that it is thereby sponsored, endorsed, or granted official status. This is in line with Articles 2(4) and 6(2)(b) of the Reuse Decision, preventing the reuse of Commission documents in a manner calculated to deceive or to defraud and making sure that any changes to a document are clearly pointed out, to prevent its original meaning or message from being compromised.

The licence applies only to copyright and related rights; it does not affect any other rights. Publicity, privacy and other similar personality rights are not licensed. Similarly, patent and trade mark rights are excluded from the scope of the licence (as they are from the Reuse Decision).

Finally, the licence is granted together with a disclaimer of warranties and limitation of liability. Thus, in using this licence, the licensor does not guarantee that it gives the reuser all the authorisations necessary for its intended use. This is also in line with Article 6(2)(c) of the Reuse Decision (which allows such waiver of liability by the Commission).

The full text of CC BY 4.0 is available at https://creativecommons.org/licenses/by/4.0/legalcode. A 'human-readable' summary of the licence is available at https://creativecommons.org/2009/02/18/the-value-of-human-readable-licenses/.

7 Commission Software: Open Source

The Reuse Decision does not apply to software, as explained above (see article 2.2.a.). The preamble to the PSI Directive introduced a minimal harmonisation system regarding open data and the reuse of public sector information. Recital 30 of that Directive had clarified however that, while it is not intended to cover computer programs, Member States could decide to extend the Directive's application to computer programs. Here again, the Commission decided to opt for this reuse and sharing option.

On 21 October 2020, the Commission had adopted a new strategy on open source software[13] encouraging the use of open source software by the Commission, the Commission's contribution to third-party open source projects and the sharing of Commission software as open source. In that Communication, it was stated that, wherever possible and appropriate, the Commission would share the source code for any computer programs where it holds the intellectual property rights on behalf of the Union. The Open Source Strategy contributes to the goals of the overarching Digital Strategy of the Commission and the Digital Europe programme.

Open source licensing has become an integral part of business models in the software industry and is largely used by public institutions in the EU and elsewhere; the Commission had already taken a number of initiatives in this area, such as adopting

[13] Communication to the Commission, Open Source Software Strategy 2020–2023, Think Open, 21 October 2020, C(2020) 7149 final.

its own open source licence, i.e. the European Union Public Licence (EUPL) in 2007, the current version of which was published in May 2017.[14]

On 8 December 2021, the Commission adopted new rules on open source software that enable its software solutions to be made publicly accessible whenever there are potential benefits for citizens, companies or other public services.[15] Commission services are now able to publish the software source code they own in much shorter time and with less paperwork and are encouraged (though not obliged) to do so. This should then enable other public services, companies, start-ups as well as citizens to use and further develop Commission software, facilitating also the sharing of knowledge and expertise.

The Decision of 8 December 2021 on the open source licensing and reuse of Commission software includes similar exceptions as the Reuse Decision for Commission documents (i.e. for software to which third-party rights apply in a manner which does not allow its distribution under an open licence, where distribution would entail security risks to the Commission's IT systems, etc.).

In line with article 5 of the Decision, the choice of the open source licence should be made as follows:

- by default, the open source licence shall be the EUPL;
- however, where the use of another open source licence is made obligatory due to reciprocal clauses ('copyleft') that apply to parts of the software originating from a third party, or where an alternative open source licence is deemed preferable to the EUPL for a particular software, notably if it is deemed more adequate in order to facilitate its adoption by the community of users, an alternative open source licence may be used, provided it is a standard open source licence;
- where, as a result of the licences applicable to pre-existing parts of the software a choice exists between several standard open licences, preference shall be given to the open source licence granting the broadest rights of use to the users (i.e. to the most "permissive" licence).

It is worth noting that while the Decision encourages the open source licensing of Commission software, it does not make it obligatory: as per article 10,[16] the Commission may still decide that a Commission software, rather than as open source software, will be made available under the terms of a proprietary licence, possibly to one or several selected licensees only, for instance for the provision of a service in the public interest or in cases which are objectively justified, for public policy interests, policy reasons or technology transfer considerations.

The Commission will progressively make its software available as open source in one single repository to facilitate access and reuse (code.europa.eu). Before its

---

[14] Commission Implementing Decision (EU) 2017/863 of 18 May 2017 updating the open source software licence EUPL to further facilitate the sharing and reuse of software developed by public administrations (OJ L 128, 19 May 2017, p. 59).

[15] Commission Decision of 8 December 2021 on the open source licensing and reuse of Commission software (2021/C 495 I/01), OJ C 495I, 9 December 2021, p. 1.

[16] See also paragraph 5 of its preamble.

release, each software is checked to avoid security or confidentiality-related risks, data protection issues or infringement to intellectual property rights of third parties (for instance due to an incompatible copyleft licence applying upstream).

The Commission also encourages its software developers to contribute to open source projects with improvements that they developed as part of their work.

The Commission already shares hundreds of software projects as open source, including software developed for the Connecting Europe Facility, Eurostat, the Interoperable Europe Programme (the former ISA programme) or by its Joint Research Centre.

Where models or artificial intelligence components developed by Commission services include software elements, the Decision should apply to those elements, without prejudice to the possible application of the Reuse Decision to the other elements such as the accompanying data. The choice of the appropriate open licence in such cases should be made according to the nature and function of the relevant elements (software or data?).

Building on the minimal character of the PSI Directive, the Commission has thus decided to go further in terms of transparency and reuse and to apply a similar logic to its own computer programs.

And again, in order to ensure the effective implementation of this policy, guidelines have been drafted for EC developers by the Central Intellectual Property Service (as provided for by article 8 of the Decision), and trainings are regularly organised.

8 Scientific Articles: Under Open Access

Most scientific articles authored by Commission staff originate from the researchers of the Joint Research Centre. The Centre has a strong open access policy, providing for the publication of these articles under gold open access (i.e. with no embargo period, except in more and more rare cases), and under the Creative Commons CC BY licence (or equivalent for the accompanying data sets). Similar rules are thus followed (even though on another legal basis) than those applying to scientific publications stemming from Horizon Europe research grants.

The Reuse Decision allows for a limited exception to its reuse logic, when it comes to scientific articles, in its article 11.4., whereby *"[E]xclusive rights may be granted to publishers of scientific and scholarly journals for articles based on the work of Commission officials for a limited period*". In practice however, this exception is only very rarely used, only where it is unavoidable to accept it, i.e. mostly where the publication is part of a print monography and the publisher requires a limited exclusivity period.

In order to ensure the effective open access availability of these scientific publications, guidelines have been drafted by the Central Intellectual Property Service, which also regularly organizes information trainings on these issues.

9 A Prerequisite to All This: IP Ownership for the Commission

For all the assets mentioned above (writings, data, software, scientific articles), in order for the Commission to allow its reuse, it is obviously required that it owns the intellectual property rights on it (essentially, the copyright and, where applicable, the *sui generis* right on databases).[17] This is rightly confirmed by both the Reuse Decision and the Decision on the open source licensing and reuse of Commission software which both exclude assets where third-party pre-existing rights do not allow the reuse of the asset.[18]

For all documents and works created by Commission staff, article 18.1. of the Staff Regulations (applying to both permanent and temporary staff) caters for this concern and provides as follows: "*All rights in any writings or other work done by any official in the performance of his duties shall be the property of the Community to whose activities such writings or work relate. The Communities shall have the right to acquire compulsorily the copyright in such works*".

As to works commissioned from third parties under a service contract or study contract, the standard clauses in the templates generally used by Commission services do provide that all intellectual property rights in the results (i.e. the elements that are produced specifically for the Commission as a result of the contract) will belong to the European Union. And in order to be fully transparent vis-à-vis the contractors, the standard agreement explicitly provides that, when the intellectual property rights are transferred to the Commission (the Union) and the results are in the form of documents (or data), the Commission obtains notably "*the right to authorise the reuse of the documents in conformity with the Commission Decision of 12 December 2011 on the reuse of Commission documents (2011/833/EU), to the extent it is applicable and the documents fall within its scope and are not excluded by any of its provisions*": in this way, the circle is complete.

More recently, an internal service has also been set up (the "Better Regulation Evidence Transparency Service") to further help services ensuring that documents, data and evidence used in policy initiatives are, as much as possible, made available to the public for consultation and reuse.

[17] Strictly speaking, it is more correct to say that the European Union, and not the European Commission, is the owner—as the Commission as no legal personality of its own.

[18] See respectively article 2.2.b. of the Reuse Decision and article 4.a. of the Decision on the open source licensing and reuse of Commission software.

10 Conclusion

As it has hopefully been demonstrated in this contribution, when it comes to authorising the reuse of its assets, the Commission "walks the talk": documents are reusable, data (including scientific data) is available as open data and reusable, software is distributed as open source and scientific articles are published under open access. Creative Commons CC BY has become the norm for publications and data, while for software the specific EUPL open source licence is used but may, when it facilitates distribution, be replaced by another standard open source licence.

Efforts are also made to ensure that the rules and the policies are effectively being followed and implemented: detailed guidelines (and some online tools) are available for the Commission staff, trainings are regularly organised and the Commission's Central IP Service provides a dedicated intellectual property-related legal support service.

Finally, as it was also explained, on some issues (scientific data and software), the Commission has even been ahead of what it suggested for Member States. It is therefore no wonder that the other EU institutions and the EU agencies are looking at the Commission for inspiration and guidance.

The Common European Data Space(s). A Governance Model "the European Way"

Graça Enes

1 Introduction

We live in a world of data. Digitalisation and especially the development of IoT made data ubiquitous. In 2018, the volume of data in the world was of 33 zettabytes. In 2025, it is expected to reach 175 zettabites (European Commission 2020a, p. 2). This explosion of data feeds a flourishing data economy even if it is complex and there are different methods for the assessment of its value (OECD 2022). The numbers are impressive. In 2019, the value of data was estimated over € 400 billion. The economic impact of sharing was estimated in between 1% and 2,5% of GDP (OECD 2019, p. 11). In the EU27, in 2020 that value has been estimated in €388 billion (European Data Portal 2020, p. 24), in 2023 it exceeded the threshold of €544 billion (European Commission 2024b, p. 8), and in 2027 it is expected to reach €829 billion.[1]

Maximizing the usefulness and value of data depends on its reuse for purposes other than those for which it was initially collected. Data is a non-rivalrous asset, which means it can be used multiple times, by multiple agents without losing value.[2]

In addition to the economic benefits for the creation of new goods and services and improving efficiency, including the training of AI models (European Commission 2024a, p. 3), opening data has important societal benefits (Scerri et al. 2022, pp. 347–353). Reusing data in R&D or in policymaking are good examples of the

G. Enes (✉)
Faculty of Law, University of Porto, Porto, Portugal
e-mail: gef@direito.up.pt

CIJ—Centre for Interdisciplinary Research on Justice, Porto, Portugal

[1] https://commission.europa.eu/strategy-and-policy/priorities-2019-2024/europe-fit-digital-age/european-data-strategy_en#a-single-market-for-data.

[2] It can be affected by obsolescence (OECD 2022, p. 14).

G. Enes et al. (eds.), *A Digital Europe for Citizens*,
https://doi.org/10.1007/978-3-032-02500-5_4

potential benefits for society (LIU 2022).[3] Combating diseases and climate change are the ultimate arguments for data sharing (Ruhaak and Algorithm Watch 2020, p. 5). The United Nations Organisation speaks of a «data revolution» and signals its importance for Sustainable Development Goals (SDGs) (Maaroof N.D.; United Nations Organisation N.D.). The European Commission, too, underlines the social and environmental benefits of data (greater accountability, more transparency, better planning (European Commission 2020b; c). Besides that, data reuse can correct asymmetries and "challenge the dominance of Big Tech" (Meadway 2020).

Data access has been receiving an increasing attention at international level and "open data" has been in the agenda of policymakers around the world for a decade (European Commission/European Data Portal 2015, pp. 24–25): the OECD Recommendations (OECD 2020, 2021), the G8's Open Data Charter (G8, 2013), the UN's "Cape Town Global Action Plan for Sustainable Development Data" (UN Statistical Commission 2017), the United Nations Development Group's "Data Privacy, Ethics and Protection. Guidance note on big data for achievement of the 2030 Agenda" (United Nations Development Group N.D.), just to mention a few.

When lawyers focus on data, the risks and problems of sharing are usually highlighted. The General Data Protection Regulation (GDPR) pays great attention to these issues imposing the express consent or one of the other reasons of Article 6 to the (re)use of personal data. This has not prevented the concentration of the benefits of data mining in the hands of a few companies. Yet, there is a "bright side of the moon" of data sharing and its "light" should benefit not only tech and marketing companies but the broad economy and society according to the European values. To foster the benefits of data three conditions have to be met: it is necessary to empower the individuals and data subjects with control on their data; moreover, it is necessary to establish a level playing field for all stakeholders in the data economy with a fair redistribution of value along the chain, instead of the factual oligopoly now in place; finally, a new model of data governance should be discussed where collective agency is considered (Ruhaak and Algorithm Watch 2020, p. 4).

In its European Data Strategy, the European Commission mentions a governance "the European way" with a focus on economic growth but also on other societal benefits. What are the features of this "European way" of "Data4Social Good" (D4SG)? Its regulatory framework deals with the following issues: who should benefit from data and how? What is the appropriate governance model for enabling a "vision" that makes the EU "a society empowered by data to make better decisions—in business and the public sector" (European Commission 2024a, p. 3)?

The EU regulatory approach has been incremental. Since 2015, with the Digital Single Market strategy,[4] the regulatory progress evolved significantly. In 2017, the European Commission adopted the Communication "Building a European

[3] Destination Earth project (https://destination-earth.eu/), a digital twin of the Earth being built in the common European green deal data space, is an example presented by the European Commission (European Commission 2024a, p. 5).

[4] https://ec.europa.eu/digital-single-market/en/news/public-consultation-building-european-data-economy.

Data Economy" (European Commission 2017) and, in 2018, the Communication "Towards a common European data space" (European Commission 2018a). The open data policy that started with the Directive 2003/98/EC ("PSI Directive"), in 2003, became a general policy objective aimed at overcoming the EU's lag in this area. The starting point recognises intervention is necessary but must be cautious not to stifle innovation. The regulatory approach is based on a common "ground" with different legal frameworks according to the type of data. Common data spaces were considered an important part of the European strategy. In 2024, there are initiatives in 14 sectors. Yet, their implementation is not uniform, and fragmentation still reigns.

This chapter provides a "macro" overview of the EU policy on data and data spaces, focusing especially on the common European data spaces. The brief description of common data spaces (section 2) is followed by an analysis of the European data policy (section 3) and of the common European data space(s) that are in place or being implemented (section 4), including their governance (section 5).

2 What and What for are Data Spaces? Between Principles and a Taxonomy

Data value is dependent on data use(s). In that view, the extraction of value aimed at guaranteeing social good must meet several principles. Data spaces are an important way to implement data sharing according to these principles.

Data access/use should follow one general principle: "as open as possible, as closed as necessary", according to the type of data and the purpose of its (re)use. Access and reuse of public data ought to be free for any purpose, subject to some conditions and with the limits imposed by public interest or other legitimate reasons. Personal data (re)use ought to be submitted to the sovereign will of its subject. On the other hand, private non personal data ought to be shared in a fair and non-discriminatory way.

To foster the value of data that general principle should be implemented respecting other relevant principles: in general, the "FAIR" principles, meaning that data is "Findable, Accessible, Interoperable, Reusable"; as an economic asset data should follow the "STREAM" principles, meaning "sovereign" (controlled by its subject/owner), "trusted", "reusable", exchangeable", "actionable", and "measurable"; from another view point, in a data economy subject to the dominance of big players data access and reuse should be "fair", "reasonable", and "non-discriminatory" ("FRAND" principles). Those requirements aim to promote the maximization of the usefulness of data in a non-discriminatory way that respects the subject/owners' will. At the same time, it aims to guarantee the quality of data available on different systems.

In a digital world of permanent data creation by millions of people and millions of things, with an infinity of possible reuses, data spaces can be most useful for creating and exploiting data value. The objectives of establishing data spaces are, among others, fostering competitive growth and innovation, technical efficiency, informational/political sovereignty, promoting education, etc. (Gaia-X, Hub Germany 2022). Data spaces may be the key "to overcome legal and technical barriers to data sharing across organisations, by combining the necessary tools and infrastructures and addressing issues of trust" (European Commission 2020a, p. 16). The motivations for sharing are diverse: reciprocity; profit; innovation; reputation; responsibility, legal obligation.

The concept of "data space" was first introduced in 2005 (Franklin et al. 2005).[5] A data space is not a data platform; the latter is one of its components, the former has institutional and contractual dimensions. A data space should also be distinguished from a neighboring concept such as a data marketplace.[6] This one refers instead to the commercial exchange of data and consists of a channel for the transfer of data. In our view, this last one is not properly a common data space but instead a data intermediary service provider (DISP)[7] that facilitates the exchange between the supplier and the user of data in atomized markets (Micheli et al. 2023, p. 59), although it can be similar to a data space if the data marketplace also provides other services, such as processing or payment clearance. The Data Governance Act (DGA) regulates some of the DISP and at the same time sets a policy to support the creation of common data spaces, as an instrument of the European data strategy. In fact, a data space can be one of the intermediaries foreseen on the DGA. Nevertheless, these two concepts should be distinguished. Data intermediation can take place in a data space, but a data space is more than intermediation and intermediation can take place outside data spaces. One of the complex issues is the prohibition imposed on data intermediaries of using the data "for purposes other than to put them at the disposal of data users" (Article 12, a) of the DGA), limiting legitimate reuses data spaces could intend to make (metadata aggregations or reports) and a way to fund its functioning (Duisberg 2022, pp. 72–73). "Personal Information Management Systems (PIMS)",[8] or other similar entities, such as personal data wallets or clouds, too, are not common data spaces even if they share a common infrastructure. They are intermediaries aimed solely at leveraging control on data (Micheli 2023, p. 44).[9]

Data spaces are complex and encompass a governance framework that is implemented by one or more interlinked data space infrastructures that enable one or more use cases. The Data Spaces Support Centre (DSSC) defines a data space as "a distributed system defined by a governance framework that enables secure and trustworthy data transactions between participants while supporting trust and data

---

[5] Several definitions can be found in Curry et al. (2022, p. 4).

[6] Some authors consider "Data marketplaces" as data spaces (Micheli et al. 2023, p. 8), as well as "data unions".

[7] And these are two different concepts.

[8] Some use cases are not for individuals but can also be for business, especially SMEs (Micheli et al. 2023, pp. 45–46).

[9] The EUDI wallet is an example. MyData has promoted several initiatives but with a relative success (https://mydata.org/).

sovereignty" (DSSC 2024a). In data spaces data stays at the source and its integration and reuse can rely on sharing vocabularies on a semantic level (Otto 2022, p. 7). The data space governance framework consists of "the structured set of principles, processes, and practices that guide and regulate the governance, management and operations within a data space to ensure effective and responsible leadership, control, and oversight. It defines the functionalities the data space provides and the associated data space roles, including the data space governance authority and participants" (DSSC 2024a). The data space infrastructure is made of a technical, legal, procedural and organisational set of components (data models, datasets, ontologies, data sharing contracts), services, and soft competencies that together enable data transactions to be performed in the context of one or more data spaces (DSSC 2024a). The sharing of data within a data space does not have to entail a transfer of data but simply the access to information (Gaia-X, German Hub 2022, p. 9).

A common data space involves a large group of stakeholders, data owners, data users and data intermediaries, though it may or may not have an open/limited number of participants, public and/or private. It is an ecosystem (Nagel and Lycklama 2021), composed of a federated information technology infrastructure to pooling and sharing data, including technical and semantic standards,[10] and legislative, administrative, and contractual governance rules and standards, as well as common governing bodies. Together, they constitute a secure environment for processing and sharing a category of data that foster innovation and more equitable prosperity (Otto 2022, p. 4). The framework of rules can be set by the participants, or based on international, European, and national laws. The federated infrastructure allows for continuous openness and growing of data spaces but requires interoperability of the participating systems. Common data spaces include:

i) Tools and services for processing and sharing data in a certain domain by a number of organisations/individuals, as well as the federation of reliable and energy-efficient cloud capacities and related services;
ii) Data governance structures, compatible with applicable legislation, which determine, in a transparent and fair manner, data access and processing rights;
iii) The promotion of data availability, quality, and interoperability—both in domain-specific configurations and across sectors.

The diversity of sectors and the multiplicity or even divergence of interests and potential uses (e.g. selfish and/or altruistic) make any single solution insufficient and inadequate. Several classifications are possible. Yet, even if the governance features are diverse, it is important to have a common framework that encourages cross-fertilization between sectors or domains, including the overlapping of data spaces (Otto 2022, p. 7).

Besides differentiation resulting from different use values and objectives, a taxonomy of data spaces distinguishes several categories of spaces, according to different criteria. The main criteria of a possible taxonomy are the following: the stakeholders; the objectives; value redistribution; governance; and interactions.

[10] On semantic integration see Auer (2022).

Among the possible categories of common data spaces, "Data Sharing Pools", "Data Trusts", and "Data Cooperatives" are the most relevant.[11]

In "Data sharing pools" data is an asset, and the objective of sharing is leveraging the economic benefit for the participants (Michelli et al. 2023, pp. 43, 59–60). Members share a purpose, especially focused on innovation, and there are cooperation and coordination efforts—at technical, legal and organisational levels—among the different actors. It is expected that data sharing pools reduce the information asymmetries between participants and enhance a fair distribution of value (Michelli et al. 2023, p. 60), upon the condition of neutrality of the intermediary governance structure of the space. The concrete economic benefit for participants can take the form of a price charged for granting access or allowing the reuse of data and the potential benefits from accessing the data available in the pool. The value resulting from sharing is mainly distributed among the participants, but it can indirectly promote social benefits resulting from the innovation it promotes or resulting from increased competition on a level playing field. Regarding marketing failures, the effects are not so clear (Martens et al. 2020). Although "Data sharing pools" can be private (with profit or not-profit purpose) or public, the key stakeholders are business organisations and their purpose is business oriented. Some of he most successful data pools combine complementary business and complementary data. Economies of scale and/or scope are the most important factors for building this type of common data space (Michelli et al. 2023, p. 61).

"Public data trusts" are inspired on "trusts", providing an independent stewardship of data in which the public and social interest prevail. A data trust (with a public or private legal status) may involve public and private participants. The key stakeholders are mainly individuals but there is an independent entity (public or private, including for profit) with the capacity to manage the data in the interest of the data subjects/holders or in the public interest (World Economic Forum 2022, p. 14). A public entity is usually the promotor and is responsible for coordinating the data trust. Data trusts are based on a fiduciary duty of the intermediary who is entrusted with the control of the data (Ada Lovelace Institute, UK AI Council 2021, p. 35; Delacroix and Lawrence 2019, p. 240). Independence is its main feature and it may be necessary to set measures for scientific and democratic scrutiny (Ada Lovelace Institute, UK AI Council 2021, p. 45). The covid-19 pandemic favored the creation of public data trusts in health, but it also revealed their difficulties. The respect for sovereignty and self-determination of data subjects and owners is mandatory and trust and raising awareness are the greatest challenges data trusts face. The potential benefits seem self-evident although there are also shortcomings because the benefits are not exclusive. Health is a good example: sharing may help improve the quality of health services or research, but an individual may not have any advantage to share such sensitive personal data. That is why sometimes sharing becomes mandatory, like in Finland (Ministry of Social Affairs and Health N.D.). In the UK, the "General Practice Data

[11] Another category is the one of "Data Unions". This one, like workers' unions, have a common bargaining purpose. It's not clear the difference with data cooperatives, except that the key stakeholders can be only individuals.

Trust pilot" within the "Data Trusts Initiative" focuses on how overcome the bias that resulted of the opt out by over a million people of NHS Digital's General Practice Data for Planning and Research (GPDPR).[12]

"Data cooperatives", in turn, are especially fit for the sharing of existing or future data between individuals, civil society organisations, NGOs, research institutions, and SMEs (Micheli et al. 2023, p. 47), and they can allow sharing with a profit or not. Their objectives are to benefit the members of the community (for instance, the common space is limited to a specific agriculture sector), or its purpose is some collective/societal benefit, for instance health, environment or mobility (Meijer and Potjer 2018; Ponti and Craglia 2020).[13] Experience reveals growth and sustainability difficulties (Micheli et al. 2023, p. 51), and their greatest challenge is raising capital, since the venture capital model used by capitalist platforms is not suitable (Borkin 2019, pp. 26–37). The governance model is participatory with a horizontal direct data stewardship (Delacroix and Lawrence 2019, p. 240) and a democratic approach to governance (Borkin 2019, p. 20), with elective management and members directly or indirectly responsible for the stewardship of data. "Services of data cooperatives" are included in the category of data intermediation services.[14] In agriculture they could be an interesting initiative for existing producer cooperatives, so common in Portugal.[15] Some may fit the category of data altruism organisations, according to the DGA,[16] with a social benefit as their purpose, especially regarding fundamental research aimed at innovation. This model, however, may not be the best suited for that purpose. The data trust model may be more suited instead.[17]

There is no ideal model nor a "one size fits all purposes". The sector and the aims of the concrete data space will determine the specific form. The diversity of stakeholders (data subjects, data owners, data purchasers, data intermediaries, public, private, profit or non-profit) will shape the different categories of data spaces and will pose specific challenges to setting the specific governance framework aimed at ensuring autonomy and freedom, but also equity. What is fundamental is to ensure the control of data subjects/owners and the accountability of the governing entities.

Real common data spaces may be a hybrid of different types. Any of these categories can simultaneously correspond to the category of "data intermediaries" enshrined in the DGA if they abide by the conditions set in the regulation (Otto

[12] https://datatrusts.uk/pilot-projects-gpdata. For case studies see Delacroix and Lawrence (2019, pp. 248–252).

[13] Salus.Coop, in Barcelona is one example in health (https://www.salus.coop/). On mobility, one example is Posmo (https://posmo.coop/).

[14] Article 10 (c).

[15] One American example is Grower's Information Service Cooperative (GISC) – https://www.gisc.coop/. In Scotland, one example is SAOS - https://saos.coop/what-we-do/data/.

[16] Article 17.

[17] Data unions, built on the idea of "data dignity", have the purpose of leveraging the negotiation capabilities of a community of data subjects towards the platforms they interact with (Micheli et al. 2023, p. 55).

2022, p. 8). Public data trusts and data cooperatives can be data altruism organisations if they are non-profit and fulfill the other conditions.[18] Data intermediaries can be important participants in common data spaces as enablers and facilitators matching the demand and supply of data; on the other hand, common European data spaces can be "controlled environments" favoring data intermediaries' activities. (Micheli et al. 2023, p. 64). Notwithstanding, data intermediaries are not a necessary feature of common data spaces, since these can be governed in a participatory and horizontal manner (Farrell et al. 2023). The participants can be classified into four categories: Core participants (data owner, data provider, data consumer, data user, app provider); Intermediary participants (metadata broker service provider, clearing house, identity provider, app store, vocabulary provider); Software and services (software provider, service provider); Governance bodies, including certification and auditing (Pettenpohl et al. 2022, pp. 34–37).

Common data spaces face several challenges. The first one is the lack of a robust regulatory governance framework, as well as capable intermediaries that guarantee trust. The security of access and the conditions of reuse of data (personal and non-personal) raise problems of confidentiality and respect for rights, and, on the other side, there are concerns about data quality. That demands the setting of an appropriate technical infrastructure and an adequate regulatory framework. The reinforcement of standardization, the establishment of sharing protocols, and the new category of data intermediaries will be fundamental throughout the network of spaces. The DGA and the Data Act intend to tackle some of these challenges.

Another challenge, especially for individuals and SMEs, is to assess the value they are owed for sharing their data. What is the best model? contractual negotiation; mediation/fixation by an intermediary? This challenge is especially significant for personal data since the information may be inferred from the interaction with others, making the problem of inverse privacy practically impossible to solve.[19] Digital sovereignty, meaning control and agency by individuals or organisations that produce data over who can use it, for what purpose and under what conditions, still requires a better definition of the regulatory and management framework to ensure the intended "human-centric approach (…) anchored in European values and fundamental rights" (Micheli et al. 2023, p. 20). Standards are being defined, and it is not certain that the data intermediaries foreseen in the DGA will be trustworthy entities capable of this task. Storage at the source is a central feature to guarantee sovereignty (Pettenpohl et al. 2022, p. 29).

---

[18] Until August 2025 only Spain and Belgium had notified the registration of data altruism organisations. https://digital-strategy.ec.europa.eu/en/policies/data-altruism-organisations. Six EU Member States had notified the registration of 25 data intermediation services https://digital-strategy.ec.europa.eu/en/policies/data-intermediary-services. The Commission Implementing Regulation (EU) 2023/1622 of 9 August 2023 already approved the official logo for altruism data organisations and data intermediation services recognised in the UE. https://digital-strategy.ec.europa.eu/en/library/logos-data-intermediaries-and-data-altruism-organisations-recognised-union.

[19] It is also imperative to combat the widespread lack of knowledge and misunderstanding of the GDPR.

The rules governing common data spaces are fundamental in defining the general conditions for participation and data sharing, data use and control, including aspects such as confidentiality, transparency, fair competition, non-discrimination, commercialization, and monetization of data, as well as the conditions for exercising rights over data, consent and its withdrawal. These conditions can be administrative, regulatory, technical, or organizational, and include procedural rules and protocols for participation and on operation, including contractual ones. Certain categories of data, e.g. sensitive personal data, demand for special conditions. Codes of conduct, such as the "EU Code of Conduct on agricultural data sharing" or the "SITRA rulebook" in the healthcare sector,[20] have also an important role as recognized by the Data Act (Recital 27). Moreover, these conditions must ensure the compliance with applicable legislation and the prevention of illicit access and use of data, be it the protection of personal data, intellectual property and trade secrets, the respect for criminal law or competition law. Finally, governance, operating and contractual rules must be accompanied by technical solutions that ensure control throughout the data lifecycle.

3 Data Policy in the European Union. "From Strategy to Regulation"

Data governance is a spectrum that goes from the macro-global to the micro-corporate and individual. At a fundamental level, data governance comprises the goals, principles, policies, and legal mechanisms, from legal rules to standards and contracts, the stakeholders' relations and practices, decision-making and processes established to collect, share and reuse data. The DSSC glossary refers to the "data space governance framework" as the "structured set of principles, processes, and practices that guide and regulate the governance, management and operations within a data space to ensure effective and responsible leadership, control, and oversight. It defines the functionalities the data space provides and the associated data space roles, including the data space governance authority and participants" (DSSC 2024a). Micheli et al. (2020, p. 3) define data governance as "the power relations between all the actors affected by, or having an effect on, the way data is accessed, controlled, shared and used, the various socio-technical arrangements established to generate value from data, and the way this value is redistributed between actors." According to Janssen et al. (2020, pp. 3–5), different approaches are possible between complete control and lack of control. Data governance mechanisms set "the ways data is controlled, what value is created, who benefits from it, and it ranges from a system of thoughts, policies, regulations, committees, contracts, terms of service, standards, algorithms, interfaces and other socio-technical systems that form the governance mechanisms of today's data infrastructure" (Micheli et al. 2020, p. 5). In fact, data governance

[20] https://www.sitra.fi/app/uploads/2020/10/towards-trustworthy-health-data-ecosystems-2.pdf. This code of conduct was applied by the Portuguese national health service (SNS).

"determines the value produced from data and how it is distributed between actors and across society." (Micheli et al. 2023, p. 17).

Today, in the EU, there is a growing awareness that the data governance model, which exists de facto, is unbalanced and asymmetrical (Zygmuntowski et al. 2021), and does not provide security. In contrast, an inclusive model "for the benefit of all, not the few" must put forward "initiatives for data sharing, control and use that promote alternatives to dominant monopolistic and exploitative data practices", supporting "more horizontal relations between actors involved in data collection and use", diversifying the use of data by multiple stakeholders for "different purposes", offering "means to access and share data assets for smaller economic players in the data market", fostering "data sharing for public interest purposes", allowing "data subjects to decide about how to use their data", reinforcing transparency and accountability and promoting the redistribution of benefits of data through "different kinds of economic and social value" (Micheli et al. 2023, pp. 18–20). Common European data spaces are one way to enable those data governance objectives.

3.1 The Overall Objective: Maximizing the Value through the Free Access and the Free Flow of Data

A European single market for data exchange has been in place for long. Regardless of whether it is characterised as a good or a service, whether personal or non-personal, data is an asset, and as such it is part of the internal market. Nevertheless, the aim of building an area of freedom and data circulation faces several barriers: interoperability and communication barriers between the systems and platforms on which the data is stored; barriers resulting from the uncertainty of the legal framework applicable to data; restrictions imposed by Member States for security and public policy reasons; the costs of compliance with rules and the costs of licensing; organisational challenges to ensure the effectiveness of law and the respect for fundamental values, such as the control over reuse, misappropriation, shortage of competent human resources.

The main objective of European data policy is also a principle: freedom of movement within European (and potentially global) territory, provided the respect for consent and legitimate interest for access and reuse, in the case of personal data, and contractual autonomy, in the case of the reuse of non-personal data. The freedom of movement implies the prohibition of any territoriality requirements related to the storage of data imposed by Member States (except for reasons of public security, with respect to proportionality) and the right to portability of personal data. There is no right to portability of non-personal data. The strategy has been to foster portability through promoting the industry initiatives with that purpose (European Commission 2019). The working group, promoted by the European Commission following Article 6 of the Free-Flow Regulation, SWIPO (Switching Cloud Service Providers and Porting Data) adopted the "High Level Principles" (SWIPO 2020a), the "Code of Conduct and transparency statement for Infrastructure as a Service" (SWIPO 2020b) and the "Code of Conduct for Software as a Service" (SWIPO 2020c), defining good practices and information for cloud service providers, as well as complaints and appeals forms and procedures (SWIPO 2020d). These results were criticised (CICREF 2019) and its preliminary assessment (European Commission 2020d) finds severe insufficiencies concerning the prevention of lock-in or fairness and concludes they cannot meet Article 6 objectives, focusing mainly on transparency. Few stakeholders adopted the SWIPO codes of conduct. The Data Act recognizes the shortcomings of that voluntary approach and declares the need to "to adopt a set of minimum regulatory obligations for providers of data processing services to eliminate pre-commercial, commercial, technical, contractual and organisational obstacles (…) which hamper effective switching between data processing services" (Recital 79).

Starting with the PSI directive (Directive 2003/98/EC on the re-use of public sector information) to the Open Data Directive (Directive (EU) 2019/1024), Member States were increasingly encouraged to open and facilitate the re-use of the data they own, forbidding any charges that exceed the cost of making public sector information available. The European Union created the European Data Portal, an infrastructure that now gathers 1 754 943 datasets.[21] In 2015, the European Commission started publishing the "Open Data Maturity" studies to benchmark and gain insights into the development achieved in the field of open data in Europe.[22] In 2016, Article 1 (3) of the GDPR expressly stated the free movement of personal data within the EU.

In 2017, the Communication "Building a European Data Economy" launched an extensive stakeholder consultation (European Commission 2017). In 2018, the Communication of the European Commission "Towards a Common European data space" set the goal of building a "common data space for Europe" (European Commission 2018a, p. 1) in which it will be "easier for businesses and the public sector to access and re-use data coming from different sources, sectors and disciplines in the EU" (European Commission 2018a, p. 14). Private sector data was labelled as a "key driver of innovation and competitiveness in Europe" (European Commission 2018a, p. 8) but the consultation held before was not in favor of a horizontal legal act, showing preference for an autonomous contractual approach on "Business2Business" data sharing. On the other hand, there was support for non-regulatory measures such as the use of APIs or standard contract terms (European Commission 2018a, p. 9). Finally, with the intent to provide guidance, the Communication outlines "key principles" that should be respected in contracts related to non-personal machine-generated data (European Commission 2018a, p. 10), and in "Business to Government" (B2G) data sharing for public interest purposes (European Commission 2018a, pp. 13–14). The key principles related to IoT presented are the following: transparency; shared value creation; respect for each other's commercial interests; undistorted competition; minimising lock-in (although portability is not a "right" as it is in personal data). The second set of key principles aims to clarify the

[21] https://data.europa.eu/en.

[22] https://data.europa.eu/en/publications/open-data-maturity.

preferential conditions for re-use by public bodies of private sector data: proportionality in the use of private sector data; purpose limitation; 'do no harm' (protection of trade secrets and other commercially sensitive information); preferential and non-discriminatory conditions for data re-use; mitigate limitations of private sector data; transparency and societal participation. These principles guide the DGA and the Data Act.

In 2018, the Regulation on the Free flow of non-personal data was adopted (Regulation (EU) 2018/1807). This act aimed at enhancing digital transformation and contributing to the objectives of the digital decade, promoting innovation and the creation of new data-driven products and services, while at the same time respecting the rights of data subject/owner/holder, individuals and companies. This regulation promotes an internal market for data, in which data can be used regardless of the place of its physical storage location. A special attention to the most vulnerable was required following the principle "design for all".

3.2 *Besides the Free Flow of Data. Common European Data Spaces as the Strategic and Structural Dimension of the European Data Policy*

Although the free flow of data across borders is a paramount goal (European Commission 2024a, p. 3), freedom of movement and a data single market is not enough to build a European data space. The situation at present corresponds to a liberal data governance model that has failed to prevent the data extractivism on marketplaces (Zuboff 2022, p. 8). These are not fair, transparent, or accountable, and are asymmetric and monopolistic (Micheli et al. 2023, p. 18). Data owners cannot truly control the reuse of their data, and the lock-in effect persists. Furthermore, there is "nudging manipulation" with unethical incentives, bias and discrimination, and a general lack of respect for fundamental rights and the rule of law. Scandals follow one another with huge leaks of personal data or the scrapping of face images.

The European Commission proposed several acts putting forward an incremental approach: the most important one was the Open Data directive, with a view of enhancing further the access and reuse of public sector data; the other two were "soft law" acts: an update of the Recommendation on access to and preservation of scientific information (Bjornsson et al. 2020), and a Guidance on sharing private sector data in the European data economy (European Commission 2018b). In 2020, the Commission takes a step further setting an encompassing approach and proposes a "European Strategy for Data" (European Commission 2020a). The Data Governance Act was adopted in May 2022 [Regulation (EU) 2022/868] and is in force since 4 June 2022. In December 2022, the Commission approved the Implementing Regulation (EU) 2023/138, specifying the high-value datasets. The legislative cycle on data was completed with the Data Act adopted in 2023, mostly concerned with unlocking machine generated data and vendor lock-in [Regulation (EU) 2023/2854], in force since 11 January 2024.[23]

The intended European model of data governance involves the different stakeholders as the best way to overcome the asymmetries of the current undeliberated model. Instead of the unilateral and private model (Nagel and Lycklama 2022, p. 19), which was designed by the "big tech", it aims to build one that is more participatory, with reciprocity and fairness, involving public support and supervision at European and national level, following a constitutional approach (Pollicino and De Gregorio 2021). As highlighted by Bodó et al. (2021), the European way of data governance tries to combine these objectives with innovation and economic growth. That may look paradoxical. On the one hand, the goal is to foster the creation of value (individual and collective) with trust and sovereignty (individual sovereignty giving data subjects and owners the power to decide the conditions of use and access to their data throughout the chain, and collective sovereignty, aka strategic autonomy of the EU[24]). On the other hand, there is a concern with accessibility for the most vulnerable following the principle of "design for all" and the moto "human being at the centre" (European Commission 2020a, p. 41). Data spaces can be seen as "2.0 data sharing" benefiting all the stakeholders, the economy and the society (Lycklama 2022, p. 522).

The common European data spaces in priority sectors and areas of public interest are strategic and a structural dimension of the EU data policy. This "European way of data governance" has at its core a federation of data ecosystems (Otto 2022, p. 11), with infrastructures, rules, and mechanisms for access, sharing and (re)use, which are secure and in line with the European values, at the same time maximising the social and economic benefits of data and preventing risks.[25] A parallel goal is to create a gold standard which, like the GDPR, can become a global standard through the "Brussels Effect" (Bradford 2019). The extraterritorial effects of the rules and the "territorialization" of third states' operators, imposing on them the appointment of a representative in the Union, will enhance that goal.

The "European Strategy for Data" makes a commitment to support the creation of common data spaces in ten areas: one horizontal research data space—the Open Science Cloud; Industry; Green Deal Data; Mobility; Health; Financial Sector; Energy; Agriculture; Public Administration (through the OOTS - Once-Only Technical System[26]—and the PPDS—Public Procurement Data Space); and Skills. A media (2020) and a cultural heritage data space (2021) soon followed as well as two

[23] There are several sector specific acts with effects on data: automotive (Regulation (EU) 2018/858), payment service providers (Directive (EU) 2015/2366), smart metering information, electricity network data (Directive (EU) 2019/944), etc.

[24] The concept of "strategic autonomy" means setting the competitive and regulatory conditions to ensure that the EU is not dependent on others to fulfill its technological needs and compete according to its values and interests (Micheli et al. 2023, p. 15).

[25] On 25.03.2021, the Council recognized the importance of European Data Spaces and invited the Commission to present the progress achieved. The European Commission provided that first assessment in 2022 (European Commission 2022a).

[26] The OOTS will form an EU-wide government-to-government data space, which will be seamlessly integrated into the common European data space for public administrations, and link

other, one related to tourism (EU Code of Conduct for data sharing in tourism,[27] developed by the industry and supported by the Commission) and another related to construction. Other data spaces were put in place, especially related to public services (e.g. a European data space for smart communities, a procurement data space). The fast development of AI LLMs led to the creation of a language data space.[28] Meanwhile, common European data spaces for law enforcement are under study (European Commission & Flynn 2021). The proposal for a European Health Data Space (European Commission 2022b), has already been agreed upon by the Parliament and the Council. The OPEN DEI Project highlighted core domains: manufacturing, health, energy, and agri-food.[29]

These data spaces are intended to facilitate the access to data, including across sectors, enhancing the creation of value while giving users control over their data. Reusing data across sectors is a paramount goal and the interconnection of the different common data spaces "will form a pillar of the single market for data" and contribute to foster innovation and the competitiveness of the EU in AI, especially regarding start-ups and SMEs (European Commission 2024a, pp. 3, 51). Achieving this goal needs the adequate technology, especially regarding interoperability,[30] process knowledge to leverage it and continuous maintenance, all based on sound macro and micro governance. Since the first assessment, in 2022, there was substantial progress. Yet not only the progress is differentiated between the data spaces but there is a lot to be done regarding the interconnection between data spaces and towards enhancing participation and use (European Commission 2024a, p. 52).

The EU data policy is a cross-sectoral and multi-level governance framework built on different dimensions. One dimension is empowering people, investing in skills and SMEs through the Digital Education Action Plan,[31] through the promotion personal data spaces and eIDAS.[32] There is also a regulatory dimension mainly set by the DGA and the Data Act. This dimension differentiates between a data intermediation regime with a low/medium regulatory intensity based on principles such as neutrality, fairness, non-discrimination, transparency, and mandatory notification, and a low regulatory intensity, in which good practices defined by the actors prevail; finally, there is a higher regulatory intensity, with greater intervention, regarding data

public authorities that act as trusted authentic sources of information (base registries) (European Commission 2024a), p. 42.

[27] The tourism sector is made mostly of SMEs and the non-binding EU Code of Conduct aims, through general guidance, to promote trust for data sharing through contractual (European Commission 2024a, p. 49).

[28] Until January 2024, 14 common European data spaces had been created (European Commission 2024a, p. 3).

[29] https://www.enlit.world/projects/open-dei/.

[30] Interoperability standards are an important feature for an inclusive data governance with cross-sector data re-use and for fostering competition, preventing lock-in effects (Borgogno and Colangelo 2019; Micheli et al. 2023, p. 21, Recital 90 of the Data Act).

[31] https://education.ec.europa.eu/focus-topics/digital-education/action-plan.

[32] Regulation (EU) No 910/2014 of the European Parliament and of the Council of 23 July 2014 on electronic identification and trust services for electronic transactions in the internal market.

altruism. The DGA also strengthened the sharing and reusing data held by the public sector with a framework of low/medium regulatory intensity. The regulatory dynamic is of the co-regulatory type with a top–bottom incentive and a flexible horizontal regulatory development based on good practices with limited binding rules.

To achieve its' aims the EU data policy has at its disposal facilitating elements promoted by the Union, such as investment funding in order to reinforce Europe's capacities and infrastructures for hosting, processing, and using data, interoperability, especially for developing common European data spaces and interconnecting cloud computing infrastructures. In 2024, there are 74 EU-funded common European data space initiatives (European Commission 2024a, Annex I), using mainly the Digital Europe and Horizon programs. Their progress is differentiated, with some still at its preparatory stage whereas others are already functioning, as can be seen in Figs. 1, 2, 3, and 4 (European Commission 2024a, Annex II).

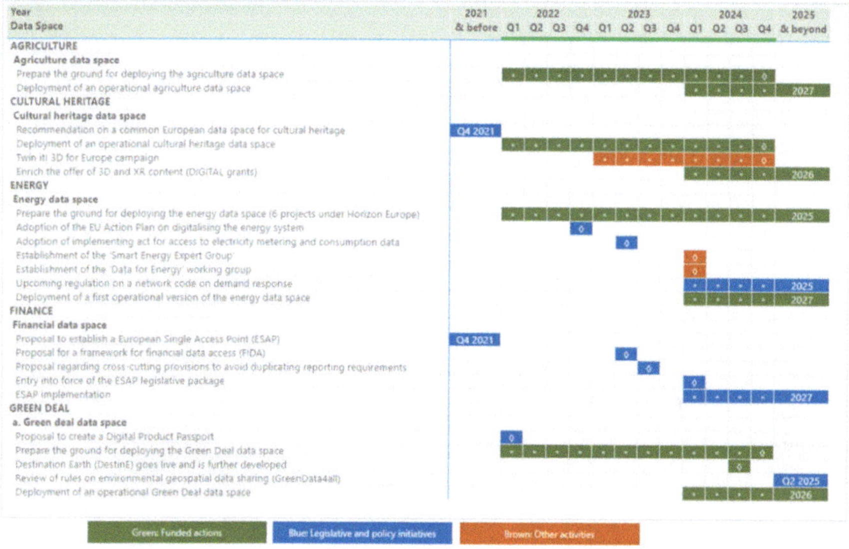

Fig. 1 Timeline for common European data spaces Part I. (Source: European Commission 2024a, Annex II)

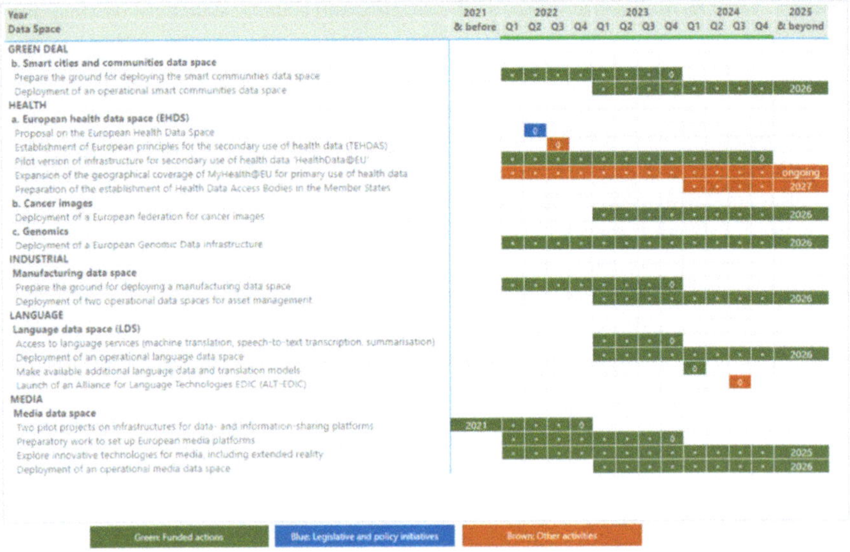

Fig. 2 Timeline for common European data spaces Part II. (Source: European Commission 2024a, Annex II)

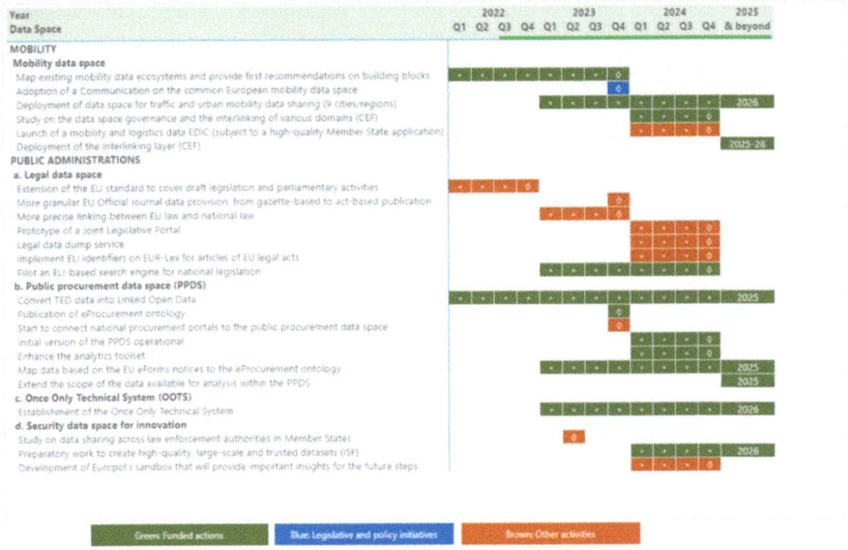

Fig. 3 Timeline for common European data spaces Part III. (Source: European Commission 2024a, Annex II)

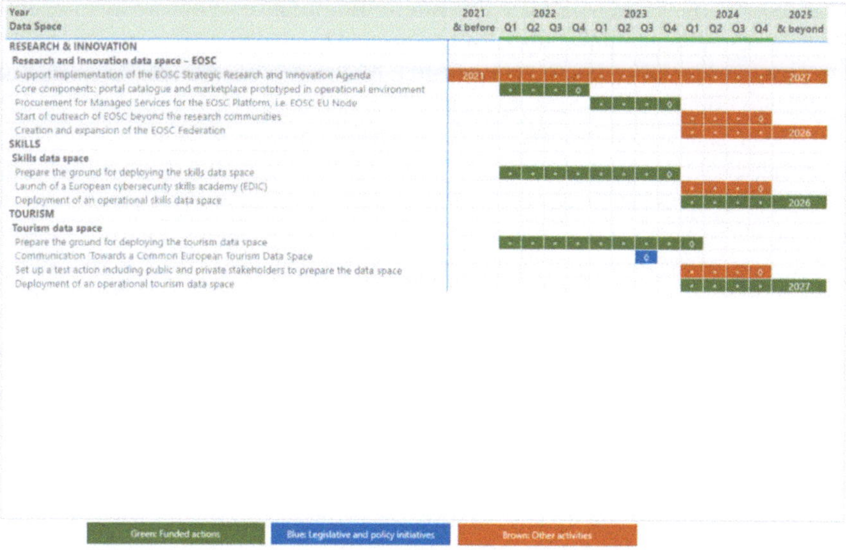

Fig. 4 Timeline for common European data spaces Part IV. (Source: European Commission 2024a, Annex II)

4 The European Data Space(s). General Principles and Implementation towards an Ecosystem of Data Spaces

4.1 General Principles and the (Non-accomplished) Promise of Personal Data Spaces

The EU model aims to achieve innovation and guarantee trust in data respecting sovereignty, both individual and collective. Individual sovereignty means that data subjects can determine the conditions of use and access to their data throughout the entire chain, following the *moto* "the human being at the center". This goes hand in hand with the freedom of movement within the EU territory. The freedom of movement implies the prohibition of any territoriality requirements related to the storage of data imposed by Member States (except for reasons of public security, respecting proportionality) and the right to portability of personal data. From that follows the need for consent under the GDPR (or equivalent) for the reuse of personal data and the respect for the principle of contractual freedom for the reuse of non-personal data. No right to portability of non-personal data is recognized, but the Data Act imposes fairness and non-discrimination requirements.

The common European data spaces are meant to be the answer to guarantee trust, autonomy, sovereignty, and equity, ensuring innovation and competitiveness with protection of rights and values and a fair distribution of value between the stakeholders. The main goal of the common European data spaces is to enable researchers, public administrators, companies, and individuals to share and make better use of data. Through the participation of an open number of organizations/ individuals, common European data spaces can play a pivotal role in cross-border, cross-sector, and cross-domain collaborations regarding the challenges we are facing as a society.

Those objectives can be complementary but also contradictory. It is necessary to integrate the different stakeholders and to ensure that the model can overcome the asymmetries of the current, de facto, model. Regarding data spaces, the Commission highlights several fundamental principles: control of the data subject, appropriate governance, respect for EU values. Other principles, less mentioned by jurists, are technical robustness, interconnection and interoperability, and openness to all relevant actors. Relating to governance, one principle emerges, the principle of subsidiarity, meaning that each common European data space is autonomously organised by participants "taking into account the unique characteristics of the specific sector/domain" (European Commission 2024a, pp. 3–4).

In today's world of digital gadgets and of general digitalisation one major difficulty is the lack of awareness of data subjects/owners that their own data are being registered in millions of devices and the value that it generates, a phenomenon labelled as "inverse privacy" (Gurevitch et al. 2015). In addition to privacy concerns, there is enormous value that is appropriated without any compensation to the data subject or data owner. The Commission envisages personal data spaces and sector common data spaces as a possible solution to allow data subjects/owners to get back control of their data and benefit from its value in an equitable manner.

Personal data spaces are secure, privacy-preserving infrastructures for grouping, accessing, sharing, processing, and using data (Lähteenoja 2023).[33] They may contain static personal data, such as name, address, or date of birth, as well as dynamic data generated by a person, for example through using an online service or an internet connected object. They can be used to store verified identification information, such as passport numbers or social security information, as well as credentials, such as driver's licenses, diplomas, or bank account information. These personal data spaces may facilitate the provision or acquisition of public and private goods and services without transmitting personal data to third parties, maximizing the protection of personal data and privacy. At the same time, they enable the reuse of data, personal and non-personal (metadata), according to the will and the conditions determined by the data subject/owner, including the respective price or other compensation for sharing. There are some examples of personal data spaces in place. KRAKEN[34] is an example of a personal data space in healthcare and education, offering discounts on insurances and access to innovative services (Gabrielli 2022). Notwithstanding, personal data spaces have not been successful until now (Curry et al. 2022, pp. 6–7). There are several reasons explaining that lack of success: most of the information with commercial value can be inferred from the interaction of the data subjects with each

[33] «PIMS» ("Personal Information Management Systems") were precursors of personal data spaces.

[34] https://www.krakenh2020.eu/.

other and there is a true loophole in the GDPR regarding the absence of this consent (for instance forwarding files or posting "likes"); another reason is the atomization of data subjects and owners and the asymmetry in power between them and tech actors; finally, there is widespread ignorance among individuals and the widespread "nudging" in the digital environment does not favor containment. Diversely, the reuse of personal data is often seen as remuneration for providing a service, especially a digital service such as communicating through an online platform. Directive (EU) 2019/770 admits this business model (recital 24),[35] but it raises several issues, and one of them is its fairness. In fact, the situation is similar with the data produced by SMEs.

The first problem is the difficulty in overcoming the atomization, ensuring autonomy, and respecting contractual freedom at the same time given the difference in power between actors. Regarding individuals, the solutions seem more difficult, although the new "data intermediaries" provided in the DGA (allowing for data stewardship), namely data cooperatives, and the implementation of technical solutions, such as dynamic consent, seem promising. Data intermediaries can act as "orchestrators of data-sharing ecosystems" (European Commission 2024a, p. 6) that open the market in the context of common European data spaces. There are examples that can serve as inspiration, namely the well-known cooperatives or associations of authors in the field of intellectual property. The implementation of the DGA will demonstrate whether these possibilities will be viable or not. Several public and industry-led initiatives have been under development for some time, many with European support, and it is hoped, even if they are different, that the know-how and even the software building blocks will be a basis for common European data spaces (Farrell et al. 2023, p. 20).

4.2 The Common European Data Space(s). General Principles and Implementation of an Ecosystem of Data Spaces

The European Strategy for Data envisages a "single European data space" which is an ecosystem that combines secure sectoral data spaces with personal and non-personal data from across the world, in strategic and public interest sectors offering access within each space and across spaces to high-quality data that are now fragmented (European Commission 2020a; Farrell et al. 2023, pp. 12–13), according to European values and rules. Although there have been various initiatives, public and private, the common European data spaces are a policy endeavor of the European Commission aiming "to overcome legal, organisational, semantic and technical barriers to data sharing between diverse actors by combining the necessary tools and infrastructures,

[35] This model of "payment of services with personal data" needs critical assessment (Parrillo and Carvalho 2024).

and by way of common rules and standards, always in compliance with the applicable laws." (Farrell et al. 2023, p. 13). Despite being a political initiative of the EU, the European data space is not a top-down building but instead it is the result of decentralised and voluntary initiatives (Nagel and Lycklama 2022 19–20). Common European data spaces are defined as "[d]ecentralised, governed and standard-based structure[s] to enable trustworthy data sharing between the participants on a voluntary basis" (European Commission, JRC Dataspaces Knowledge Base N.D.a). Certainly, there will be differences between sectoral data spaces, but they should be interconnected to "enable cross-exploitation and collaboration for innovation" (Farrell et al. 2023, p. 16[36]).

The common European data spaces are seen as a powerful tool for fostering a single data market in which data could be used irrespective of its physical storage location in full respect of the EU values and principles. Sectoral common data spaces are seen as the solution that will enable the sharing of data in an equitable manner, thus ensuring the maximization of economic benefit and the respect for the sovereignty of the data subject and owner, especially SMEs. Data is currently in "silos", and their subjects/producers and other stakeholders cannot grasp the full potential of their value to create new products and services or for research, especially the development of AI technologies. The Commission introduced the concept of "common European data space" in the European Data Strategy. It can be defined as a mix of data infrastructure, data governance rules and community building whose aim is to enhance data sharing within economic sectors in the EU. A common data space has a technical dimension, and a regulatory and contractual governance infrastructure aimed at ensuring a secure processing and sharing space, with the widest possible scale of participation to ensure optimization of utility. It involves legal sharing obligations, but above all they will be based on voluntary sharing with or without compensation. Its key elements are the following (European Commission 2024a, p. 4): (1) a secure, privacy-preserving infrastructure to pool, access, share, process and use data; (2) a clear and practical structure for accessing and using of data in a fair, transparent, proportionate and/or non-discriminatory manner and clear and trustworthy data governance mechanisms; (3) European rules and values, in particular the protection of personal data, consumer protection legislation and competition law, are fully respected; (4) Data holders will have the possibility, in the data space, to grant access to or to share certain personal or non-personal data under their control; (5) Data that is made available can be reused against compensation, including remuneration, or for free; (6) Participation of an open number of organisations/individuals.

A European data space has three features: a large pool of data; a technical infrastructure; a governance framework regarding the rules for sharing, access and reuse. Some of the principles of common European data spaces relate to organizational requirements (e.g., rules and practices of data governance, data protection, open participation, transparency, sustainability, scalability, security), and technical requirements (e.g., data transfer and exchange, identification, data findability and

[36] The author believes this is especially important with the Green Deal Data Space.

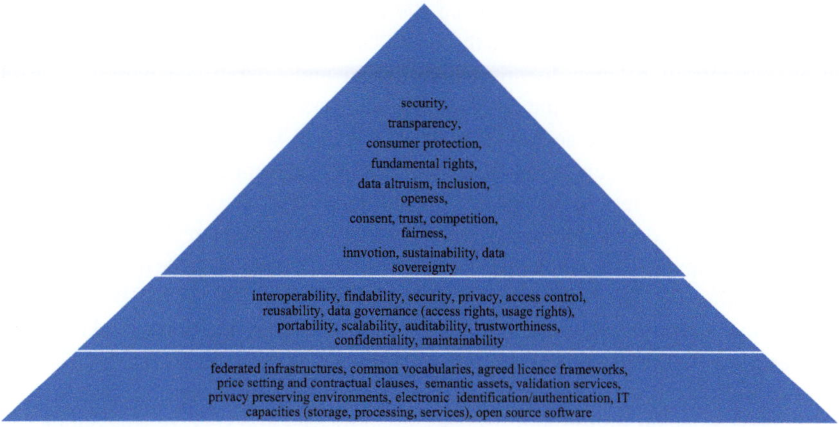

Fig 5 requirements of a common European data space

reusability, privacy preservation, authentication and access control, and interoperability) (Farrell et al. 2023, p. 13). Some relate to the participants; others relate to the common infrastructure. Moreover, these requirements must be embedded into the software for access, governance and processing, and must allow the exchange and transfer between the participants (e.g. portability) and between the different common data spaces (e.g. interoperability). That embedment further demands the definition of other more granular functional and non-functional requirements throughout the design cycle of components and the architecture of the data space. Standards will be fundamental regarding software and middleware (Farrell et al. 2023, p. 21, Article 33, (3) and (4) of the Data Act).[37]

The requirements of a common European data space may be presented as a pyramid with overarching principles at the top, the requirements in the middle and the technical, management and the regulatory and contractual features at the bottom (see Fig. 5).[38]

There are functional and non-functional requirements for common data spaces as well as horizontal principles, and a community-based inclusive approach is necessary but not a single technical or organisational solution because of the specific context of each data space (Farrell et al. 2023, p. 7). To ensure the objective of cross-sectoral flow of data, some neutral technical common protocols and specifications that can be used in a federated, decentralised manner are needed (Farrell et al. 2023, p. 7). The right balance between the common features and the sector-specific rules has not been achieved with some initiatives, probably because they have been developing in isolation (Farrell et al. 2023, p. 16).

---

[37] The author presents a table with functional and non-functional requirements (Farrell et al. 2023, pp. 22–23).

[38] Farrell et al. present a similar pyramid (2023, p. 14).

In every common European data space, there are key actors involved in the creation and the governance of the data space through a "soft infrastructure consisting of rules and agreements of a legal, functional, technical and operational nature" (Farrell et al. 2023, p. 17). They are the relevant stakeholders of the data value chain, from the public and the private sector, academia, and civil society (Farrell et al. 2023, p. 17). They play different roles in the ecosystem. Some may be data producers, others may be data receivers, data rights holders, data users or consumers, data service providers, data intermediaries, and they can include technology services providers and standardisation bodies. The same actors can participate in different data spaces. Another key actor is the European Data Innovation Board (EDIB). EDIB is a Commission expert group, and it is supposed to bring together different stakeholders, Member States' authorities on data intermediaries and data altruism organisations, EU personal data protection bodies, ENISA (cybersecurity), representatives from SMEs, and "relevant public and private bodies in specific sectors and public and private bodies with specific expertise".[39]

Another dimension of the European strategy is the support to initiatives that may develop the building blocks for common European data spaces. Some initiatives are sector and domain-specific initiatives, others are led by the DSSC, and a third one is "Simpl": smart open-source middleware, in order to ensure that the data spaces will be deployed based on a common technical infrastructure (European Commission 2024a, pp. 10, 12). Standards harmonisation initiatives promoted by the Commision are also foreseen in the Data Act to overcome interoperability barriers (Recital 103 and Article 33, (3) and (11)).

There may be common data spaces that are not supported or recognized by the Commission and resulting of the autonomous initiative of the industry. Several sectoral associations, such as the Big Data Value Association (BDVA), the Data Spaces Business Alliance (DSBA), the International Data Spaces Association (IDSA), GAIA-X, or the Digital Transport and Logistics Forum (DTLF) are developing complementary initiatives in data infrastructure. Aiming to guarantee a functioning ecosystem the DSSC works in close partnership with the sectoral initiatives in relation to the definition of: (1) the data space reference architecture, building blocks and common toolboxes; (2) common standards, including semantic standards and interoperability protocols,[40] both domain-specific and cross-cutting; and (3) data governance models, business models and strategies for running data spaces." (European Commission 2024a, p. 10). The Multi-Country Project on European Common Data Infrastructure and Services (European Commission 2023, p. 12) will deliver a technical infrastructure for the deployment of data spaces. There are two instruments: the Important Projects of Common European Interest (IPCEI) to develop the Next-Generation Cloud Infrastructure and Services; and the European Digital

[39] Commission Decision of 20 February 2023 setting up the European Data Innovation Board, C(2023) 1074 final, Brussels, 20 February 2023 (Article 3).

[40] These deserve a special attention by the Data Act (Recital 103), imposing special requirements (Article 33 (1)).

Infrastructure Consortium (EDIC). SIMPL[41] is a middleware platform funded by the European Commission that is developing the open source free components, namely the "Minimum Viable Product" (MVP), meeting the general needs of most data spaces secure data sharing across European data initiatives. The network of European Digital Innovation Hubs (EDIHs) will also work closely with the data spaces, together with European AI Testing and Experimentation Facilities (TEFs),[42] especially with the aim of promoting the use of these infrastructures by SMEs (Farrell et al. 2023, pp. 22–23).

Initial public funding is necessary, especially where the main stakeholders are public bodies, citizens/consumers and SMEs (Nagel and Lycklama 2021, p. 94). European financial support comes first through the Digital Europe Program (DIGITAL). In 2021–2022, €410 million has been earmarked to support the development of common European data spaces, for the DSSC and for core cloud-to-edge infrastructure and services. The Commission's "Coordination and Support Actions" have supported sectoral data spaces. The Recovery and Resilience Facility also contributes to this support. Eight data spaces have been developed with the support of the DIGITAL program[43]—cultural heritage, health (genome, cancer images), language, manufacturing, media, mobility, public administrations (public procurement) and smart communities. The Horizon Europe financed the creation of an energy and a research and innovation data space. The EU's Recovery and Resilience Facility (RRF) and the recovery and resilience plans of several Member States also support actions related to common European data spaces (European Commission 2024a, p. 11). At present, 74 initiatives within 14 sectors/domains are being supported (European Commission 2024a, Annex 1).[44] It is expected between six to eight years will be enough to reach financial break-even. Their societal impact can be compared to critical infrastructures such as sewages or the electricity grid (Nagel and Lycklama 2021, p. 94) and in the same way that happened with these infrastructures only "common agreements from large and small industry, policymakers, educators, researchers, and society at large" will foster the development of common European data spaces (Curry et al. 2022, p. 16).

Some of the common European data spaces that are being implemented correspond to "Data Sharing Pools" (e.g. industry; agriculture). Others are "Public Data Trusts" (e.g. Health, Open Science Cloud). The first ones are promoted and supported by the European Union because, although the central interests are the stakeholders' ones, there is an indirect benefit for innovation and economic growth.

The potential benefits of common European data spaces are broad and cross-sectoral. The gradual interconnection of the sectoral data spaces will profit from synergies enabled by common practices, communication concepts, services and/or components, which in turn will increase data space interoperability (DSSC 2024b) and is expected to create a wide data ecosystem and market. This will consist of a

[41] https://simpl-programme.ec.europa.eu/book-page/simpl-mission-and-vision.

[42] https://digital-strategy.ec.europa.eu/en/activities/testing-and-experimentation-facilities.

[43] Specific grants were available for SMEs regarding cultural heritage, manufacturing and media.

[44] https://digital-strategy.ec.europa.eu/pt/policies/data-spaces.

Industrial ecosystems \ EU data spaces	Manufacturing	Green Deal	Mobility	Health	Financial	Energy	Agricultural	Legal	Procurement	Security	Skills	Open Science	Media	Cultural heritage	Tourism	Construction	Smart communities
Construction	✓	✓			✓	✓		✓	✓		✓	✓		✓		✓	✓
Tourism		✓	✓	✓		✓	✓	✓		✓	✓	✓	✓	✓	✓		✓
Textile	✓	✓						✓	✓		✓	✓					
Proximity and social economy	✓	✓	✓	✓	✓	✓	✓	✓	✓		✓	✓		✓	✓	✓	✓
Mobility-Transport-Automotive	✓	✓	✓			✓		✓			✓	✓					✓
Health	✓	✓		✓				✓			✓	✓					
Energy intensive industry	✓	✓	✓	✓	✓	✓	✓	✓	✓		✓	✓				✓	✓
Energy renewables	✓	✓	✓		✓	✓	✓	✓	✓		✓	✓				✓	✓
Retail	✓	✓	✓		✓		✓	✓			✓	✓			✓		
Electronics	✓	✓				✓		✓			✓	✓					
Digital industries	✓	✓	✓	✓	✓	✓	✓	✓	✓	✓	✓	✓				✓	✓
Cultural and creative industry	✓	✓						✓			✓	✓	✓	✓	✓	✓	
Agri-food	✓	✓					✓	✓			✓	✓			✓		
Aerospace & Defence	✓	✓	✓	✓	✓	✓	✓	✓	✓	✓	✓	✓	✓	✓	✓	✓	✓

Fig. 6 Mappings between industrial ecosystems and common European data spaces based on types of data it would need to have access to. (Source: European Commission 2022a, Annex 2)

set of interoperable API-based IT platforms, where users control the data flow by means of advanced dynamic identity and consent management mechanisms.

The measurement of the impact of these European data spaces presented in the following table demonstrates that the "Skills common data space", the "Open science data space" and the "Legal data space" are the ones with the most impact on every field. Figure 6 shows that even the health data space is expected to induce benefits beyond the health sector, on tourism, the digital sector, and other fields (European Commission 2022a, Annex 2).

It is expected that AI start-ups and SMEs will be among the beneficiaries of the common European data spaces (European Commission 2024a, p. 3).

5 Governance of the Common European Data Space(s)

Several approaches to data governance are possible (Janssen et al. 2020). Data governance guarantees the legal and adequate leadership, strategy, management of resources, and maintenance of data assets and related aspects such as stewardship, data rights, data privacy, and data security or sustainability (Farrell et al. 2023, p. 26) with the aim of maximizing the benefits of data. Some are common to every data space, others are specific to each data space (Farrell et al. 2023, pp. 24, 26). The DSSC's Data Spaces Start-up Kit (2023a) refers to several legal issues that must be considered when a data space is created relating to data substantive rights and obligations, contracts, competition, organization, interoperability, and regulatory aspects. Besides a regulatory dimension, both public and private (Fritzenkötter et al. 2022), legal and contractual (DSSC 2024c), data governance has also functional dimensions (e.g. technical and organisational). Social, economic, political, and cultural factors should be considered as well (Liu 2022).

The governance of the common European data spaces faces some challenges and it can be a complex endeavour (Farrell et al. 2023, p. 26). First and foremost, it is necessary to promote adherence to ensure scalability, otherwise there will be no optimization of results (Otto 2022, p. 12). As any ecosystem there is a need for a soft common infrastructure, based on an interoperable legal, functional, and technical framework—a "SoS" (System of Systems), capable of integrating data from different sources and relating at different levels (Curry et al. 2022, p. 3). Moreover, it is necessary to guarantee that the multiple data spaces interact and can cooperate. Only considering a broad concept of interoperability[45] that includes the four levels of interoperability (legal, organizational, semantic and technical) can the objectives set in the European policy be achieved. On the other hand, the biggest governance challenge is not of a technical nature but of organization and coordination (Nagel and Lycklama 2022, p. 25; Ahle and Hierro 2022, p. 416).[46]

The most important challenges to European data spaces governance are: (1) the diversity of main stakeholders (interests, capabilities, power): data subjects/data holders; data acquirers/users; others (e.g. intermediaries); (2) the different nature of stakeholders: private/public, individuals/corporations, profit/non-profit, etc.; (3) the existence of conflicting and/or converging objectives: openness/privacy/control; social value/private value; (4) the criteria for distributing value along the stakeholders' chain: autonomy/freedom; equity/progress. Some implementing principles can respond to these challenges: decentralization, scalability, collaboration, support, federation, interoperability, compatibility, trust management, and auditability (Nagel and Lycklama 2022, p. 23).

The DSSC has developed governance building blocks, both organizational and data sharing governance (DSSC 2023b), as well as legal, concerning the regulatory compliance and contractual framework (DSSC 2023c). The International Data Spaces Association (IDSA) also provides a framework with guidance rules (IDSA 2023).

5.1 A Multilevel Continuous Governance on the Path to Harmonisation

Data space governance is a multilayered framework (IDSA 2022; Torre-Bastida et al. 2022; Bodó et al. 2021). The layers range from the intra-organisational within a data space, with business, functional, contractual, operational layers, to the macro layer of the legislative framework and institutional coordination and supervision (Nagel and Lycklama 2022, p. 20). Governance encompasses the strategic vision and values,

[45] https://joinup.ec.europa.eu/interoperable-europe.

[46] Scerri et al. (2022) exhaustively list the challenges of the spaces.

European, national and infranational policies and legal norms, general and contractual rules, and standardization.[47] It also includes interoperability features and coordination between stakeholders, cross-border, cross-sector, and cross-data spaces issues (European Commission, JRC Knowledge Base N.D.b). Farrell et al. (2023, p. 8) also include political and sociological aspects in the governance framework political and sociological features, and define it as "the set of rules, policies, relations, decision-making structures and processes established among different kinds of actors to collect, share and use data."

The fundamental and overarching regulatory framework of common European data spaces is composed of some norms and principles enshrined at international level (e.e. G7, Council of Europe, OECD), in the Charter of Fundamental Rights and the Treaties, the GDPR,[48] the ePrivacy Directive, eIDAS, the Data Governance Act, the Data Act. These acts enshrine horizontal rules, some of which leave room for private autonomy. (e.g. personal data protection, portability and freedom of movement, freedom of enterprise and contract, non-discrimination, transparency, fairness). Policy documents such as the European Strategy for Data are also important. Other relevant acts are the Open Data Directive, the Free Flow Regulation and acts relating to cybersecurity. This layer also encompasses policies and rules at the different levels from European to local and sectoral, as well as horizontal ones such as intellectual property, competition or consumer law rules.

The middle layer encompasses organization features defined by the stakeholders and governing bodies of the data space, as well arrangements, practices, and technical features that determine how data spaces are managed, be they private, public or public–private partnerships (PPP). It concerns the roles (e.g. data producers, data rights holders, data providers, data user, data intermediaries, data brokers, data consumers, data altruism organisations, public authorities, regulatory agencies, standardization and certification bodies, technology providers, etc.), the duties, rights, and responsibilities of every data space participant and stakeholder (Torre-Bastida et al. 2022), which must be clearly defined (Farrell et al. 2023, p. 26). It also includes contracts regarding access and reuse of data (e.g. licensing contracts, compliance rules), management rules, decision procedures or data processing rules, accountability, control, and appeal procedures (Farrell et al. 2023, p. 27). There may be different business models, contracts and use cases coding for the specific data space sharing context (Farrell et al. 2023, p. 30) and for the flows of data between different stakeholders. "Cultural practices" and "mentality" (Torre-Bastida et al. 2022, p. 67) are also relevant and may differ between sectors. The governance building blocks include organizational governance protocols, from business agreements to organizational agreements.

Technical and operational requirements constitute another middle layer and include the technical building blocks (e.g. network protocols, middleware components, standardized APIs) and tools necessary to ensure that the legal requirements

[47] Farrell et al. (2023, p. 28) present an illustrative scheme.

[48] In common data spaces it is possible that there is joint controllership of personal data and because of that it is necessary to take that into consideration when defining the rules and governance.

(e.g. privacy and consent), the policy options (e.g. fostering the reuse of data across sectors), and management decisions are accomplished, facilitating the sharing of data between different parties in a secure and trustworthy way. The operational aspects of interoperability and sovereignty are part of this common infrastructure and include issues such as identity, legal terms, and security, as well as the categories of participants and responsible parties.

Regarding the conditions for interoperability the Regulation (EU) 2024/903 ("Interoperable Europe Act") laying down measures for a high level of public sector interoperability across the Union, according to the "OOTS", can provide a model to follow (Farrell et al. 2023, p. 31), although some fundamental differences are expected since private sector data cannot be subjected to the exact same principles and contractual autonomy is an imperative. On the other hand, it is necessary to ensure trust and prevent a lock-in of the less powerful stakeholders and of the regulators. Cross-space and cross-domain interoperability, including legal interoperability, must be guaranteed to prevent silos and the aforementioned risks (Farrell et al. 2023, p. 32). Standardisation, namely international standards such as INSPIRE standards, and the coding of best practices are "key enablers"[49] (European Commission 2024, p. 15). The European Blockchain Services Infrastructure (EBSI)[50] may be useful. The participation of stakeholders from industry is indispensable in defining the building blocks to implement interoperability. In turn, transparency is fundamental to ensure that this multilevel governance does not end up in a lock-in of regulators.

The DSSC has developed 17 building blocks covering business, organizational and technical features (DSSC 2024d).[51]

Finally, there is a layer relating to oversight and control. Its features range from internal conflict resolution mechanisms to external auditing and control by regulatory agencies and coordinating bodies at the European and national level. At the European level the most important are the European Data Innovation Board (EDIB), the Data Spaces Support Centre (DSSC), the Interoperable Europe Board (IEB), and the European Data Protection Board. Other national and sectoral authorities have also an important role. Especially, National competent bodies and authorities (NCAs) will be competent for supervision and the authorization of data intermediaries and data altruism authorities (Articles 13 and 23 of the DGA).

Those different layers of governance are in fact a *continuum* (Fritzenkötter 2022) going from broad strategic and values setting to narrower structures of technical and organizational kind, such as standards setting and process rules, as well as reference code lists to manage interoperability.

It is expected that, respecting similar principles, objectives and rules, and using similar governance, business and technical building blocks, not only interoperability

---

[49] Such as the "EU Code of Conduct on Agricultural Data Sharing" (COPA & COGECA 2020), or the "SITRA Rulebook" (Luoma-Kyyny and Pitkänen 2022).

[50] https://ec.europa.eu/digital-building-blocks/sites/display/DIGITAL/European+Blockchain+Services+Infrastructure+%28EBSI%29+dashboard?preview=/187107372/703791819/EBSI%20(dashboard).pdf.

[51] These blocks are built based on others already developed by entities such as IDSA or FIWARE.

will be achieved but also "a more uniform, de-facto 'soft infrastructure'" may emerge (Nagel and Lycklama 2021, p. 84). That soft infrastructure is a framework of "design decisions, rules, agreements and processes concerning how to share, manage and use data, that would include common aspects for all data spaces, including (but not limited) to identity, metadata, consent, legal terms, and security", guaranteeing citizens, business and governments control of their data across different data spaces (Farrell et al. 2023, p. 27).

A final layer of governance concerns governance between data spaces and the relation of data spaces with the different sectoral and general policies. This layer is fundamental to achieve the societal policy objectives and grasp the full benefits of data. This layer mostly consists of a multi-level institutional structure of variable geometry, involving both public and private stakeholders, with one common and several specific frameworks of different normative intensity. Co-regulation and horizontal regulation with soft vertical coordination are examples of this variable governance.

5.2 The European Institutional Framework for Data Governance

The European Data Space is not intended to be the juxtaposition of sectoral common data spaces. The planned European institutional framework aims to ensure that these multiple spaces are part of a global ecosystem. In that view, the Data Governance Act is "the key building block for the common European data spaces" (European Commission 2024a, p. 6).

The DGA entails a "two-tier governance" (Nagel and Lycklama 2021), in which each data space has its own governance structure that is integrated into a European soft institutional structure led by the Commission.

The European institutional framework is multilevel. Article 29 (1) of the DGA stipulates the creation of an expert group chaired by the Commission, the 'European Data Innovation Board' (EDIB), which is at the centre of this governance framework. The EDIB was established by Commission Decision of 20 February 2023 [C(2023) 1074 final] with the aim of promoting the development of common European data spaces. This expert group is an advisory body of the Commission and is made up of MS representatives from the competent authorities for data intermediation services and for the registration of data altruism organisations, and from the European Data Protection Board (EDPB), the European Data Protection Supervisor (EDPS), the EU Agency for Network and Information Security (ENISA), the European Environment Agency, European Union Agency for the cooperation of energy regulators, Statistics Estonia, the SME envoys network, and other representatives of relevant bodies in specific sectors selected by the Commission, including promoters of common data spaces.[52] The DSSC has an observer status.

According to Article 30 (h) of the DGA and Article 42 of the Data Act, the EDIB will advise the Commission regarding establishing consistent practices of data sharing and exchange, developing guidelines, maintaining the general authorisation framework, ensuring cross-sectoral interoperability of data spaces, and facilitating collaboration with National Competent Authorities (NCAs). A special concern is the clarification and distinction of standards and practices that are cross-sectoral and those that are sectoral, security requirements, the respect for fundamental principles and rules, such as non-discrimination and competition, with a special attention to international data transfers.

The DSSC is the operational arm of this European governance structure and was established in 13 October 2022.[53] The DSSC supports the work of the EDIB, especially relating to the definition of guidelines, building blocks and tools for common European data spaces enhancing the interoperability promoting data-sharing services between different sectors and domains, in compliance with existing EU legislation on data protection (European Commission 2024a, pp. 11–12).[54] It is expected that it will contribute to a coherent development of common data spaces. A starter kit and a blueprint were adopted. The blueprint contains a glossary, a data space conceptual model and building blocks, as well as a collection of standards and specifications from the data space technology landscape.

The multistakeholder approach is present and the DSSC has a stakeholder network encompassing diverse organisations and initiatives relevant to the development of data spaces, comprising three subsets: (1) the Community of Practice (currently consists of the EU-funded common European data space initiatives), (2) the Strategic Stakeholder Forum (The Strategic Stakeholder Forum (SSF) is a think-and-do-tank that supports the DSSC objectives and offers recommendations on governance and sustainability), and (3) Liaisons and Collaborations (other relevant initiatives and stakeholders for the development of data spaces).[55]

The NCAs will be responsible for the oversight of many data spaces and its participants of common European data spaces, namely because they can be data intermediaries and data altruism organisations regulated by the DGA. There have been proposals for a Data Exchange Board (DEB) focusing on "the tactical and operational level" (MyData 2020).

---

[52] https://ec.europa.eu/transparency/expert-groups-register/screen/expert-groups/consult?lang=en&groupID=3903.

[53] https://dssc.eu/.

[54] https://dssc.eu/space/DDP/117211137/DSSC+Delivery+Plan+-+Summary+of+assets+publication.

[55] https://dssc.eu/space/DC/28016695/Communities.

5.3 *Fundamental Governance Principles of Common European Data Spaces*

These principles are outlined in relevant EU policy and legislative Acts. Besides the Treaties and the Charter of Fundamental Rights, the "European declaration on digital rights and principles" that was published in 2022 sets the basic principles framework. The other core acts are the DGA and the Data Act.

The basic principles presiding the governance of common European data spaces correspond to the already mentioned STREAM, FAIR and FRAND principles and must apply throughout the data value chain from production and collection to usage and sharing (European Commission, JRC Knowledge Base N.D.c). They should integrate the "design principles" of data spaces. Nagel & Lycklama present four "design principles": Data sovereignty, Level playing field for data sharing and exchange, Decentralised soft infrastructure, Public–private governance (2021, pp. 27–28). The DSSC has developed building blocks to implement these principles (DSSC 2024d). Finally, general principles such as innovation, sustainability, competition or consumer protection too are to be considered within the governance and technical infrastructure of data spaces.

Sovereignty means control and self-determination. Free and informed consent is paramount in guaranteeing that principle. Technical tools, model contracts and organizational arrangements must be in place (Nagel and Lycklama 2021, p. 23; Gaia-X, Hub Germany 2022, p. 9) to facilitate the upload of data into data spaces, give or revoke their authorization, decide on and change access rights for how the data can be accessed and reused, including remuneration. The technical infrastructure must be built according to the principle of cybersecurity by design and respect the personal data protection by design. Although the DGA and the Data Act safeguard the prevalence of GDPR and the protection of personal data there are complex issues regarding data ownership, control, and use, namely related to data resulting from the use of connected devices and inferred data. The Data Act recognises that in the "context[s] of multiple users, each user may contribute in a different manner to the data generation and have an interest in several forms of use" (Recital 18). These issues are ignored by the DGA and the soft "approach" of the Data Act of "assigning rights regarding access to and the use of data is preferable to awarding exclusive rights of access and use" raises doubts (Recital 6 of the Data Act). This approach seems to follow the perspective that believes the "ownership" concept is not appropriate in a data economy striving for innovation and favors private contractual solutions (Duisberg 2022, pp. 62, 75–76, Recitals 25, 43, and 60 of the Data Act). It excludes "information inferred or derived from such data, which is the outcome of additional investments into assigning values or insights from the data, in particular by means of proprietary, complex algorithms, including those that are a part of proprietary software (…) unless otherwise agreed between the user and the data holder" (Recital 15 of the Data Act). On the other hand, the Data Act regulates B2G data sharing justified by exceptional need of public interest (Recitals 64 to 77, and Articles 14 to 21 of the Data Act).

A level playing field for data sharing and exchange must implement the principles of security, trust, transparency, openness, fairness, and non-discriminatory inclusion. That demands for a participatory governance structure with proper organizational, technical and contractual arrangements complying with existing provisions of horizontal legislation, EU sectoral legislation, and WTO rules. According to the fairness, openness and non-discrimination principles all actors (organisations/individuals), European or non-European, who comply with the rules of the data space can participate, their rights and interests must be taken into due consideration and must be treated fairly, with a special attention to SMEs (Recitals 49, 51, 57, and 58, and Article 7 of the Data Act). Notwithstanding, there is awareness of difficult issues relating to transparency, fairness and access by users of connected devices to the data produced (Recitals 20, 21, 24, 44 and 45 of the Data Act).

The Data Act aims to facilitate data sharing in business-to-business (B2B) and business-to-consumer (B2C) along the data value chain ensuring fairness and data protection, including provisions regarding portability and interoperability for providers of data processing services (Recitals 26 to 28, Article 13 and Articles 23 to 31 and 33 to 35 of the Data Act). A decentralized infrastructure relies on interoperability. The Data Act provides that data space participants that offer data or data services to other participants are obliged to comply with a few essential requirements to facilitate the interoperability of data, data sharing mechanisms and services (Article 33 (1)[56]).

The governance framework of common European data spaces corresponds to a multilevel and multistakeholder public–private model (see Sect. 4.2).

6 Concluding Remarks

The reuse of data is an important factor in innovation and wealth creation and its free circulation within the Union is necessary. Common data spaces have been a tool for data sharing in various economic sectors, but their development faces several challenges and difficulties. The European data strategy proposed the implementation of the European data space having as cornerstones several common European data spaces in priority sectors, setting several principles of a "European way of data governance", decentralized and built bottom-up but with a European coordination.

[56] (a) the dataset content, use restrictions, licenses, data collection methodology, data quality and uncertainty shall be sufficiently described, where applicable, in a machine-readable format, to allow the recipient to find, access and use the data; (b) the data structures, data formats, vocabularies, classification schemes, taxonomies and code lists, where available, shall be described in a publicly available and consistent manner; (c) the technical means to access the data, such as application programming interfaces, and their terms of use and quality of service shall be sufficiently described to enable automatic access and transmission of data between parties, including continuously, in bulk download or in real-time in a machine-readable format where that is technically feasible and does not hamper the good functioning of the connected product; (d) where applicable, the means to enable the interoperability of tools for automating the execution of data sharing agreements, such as smart contracts shall be provided.

The development of these common data spaces has been differentiated, with some still in an embryonic phase. Several acts adopted in the meantime, in particular the DGA and the Data Act, enshrined relevant principles and rules to ensure respect for these principles and enhance the implementation of common European data spaces, in particular the conditions of interoperability so that a true ecosystem of data is possible. However, some inadequacies and uncertainties emerge, and some doubts arise whether the regulatory approach, partly through soft law, and the multi-level and multi-stakeholder institutional framework will be suitable to meet the objectives of a European data space.

References

Ada Lovelace Institute, UK AI Council (2021). Exploring legal mechanisms for data stewardship, https://www.adalovelaceinstitute.org/wp-content/uploads/2021/03/Legal-mechanisms-for-data-stewardship_report_Ada_AI-Council-2.pdf

Ahle U, Hierro JJ (2022) FIWARE for Data Spaces. In: Otto B et al. (eds) Designing Data Spaces. The ¬Ecosystem Approach to Competitive Advantage. Springer, pp. 395–417. https://doi.org/10.1007/978-3-030-93975-5

Auer S (2022) Semantic Integration and Interoperability. In: Otto B et al. (eds) Designing Data Spaces. The Ecosystem Approach to Competitive Advantage. Springer, pp. 195–210. https://doi.org/10.1007/978-3-030-93975-5

Bjornsson A et al. (2020) Access to and preservation of scientific information in Europe. Report on the implementation of Commission Recommendation C(2018)2375 FINAL, European Commission, https://op.europa.eu/pt/publication-detail/-/publication/6e5718ef-f179-11ea-991b-01aa75ed71a1

Bodó B et al. (September 30 2021) Personal Data Ordering in Context: The Interaction of Meso-Level Data Governance Regimes with Macro Frameworks, Internet Policy Rev 10(3). https://doi.org/10.14763/2021.3.1581

Borgogno O, Colangelo G (2019) Data Sharing and Interoperability Through APIs: Insights from European Regulatory Strategy, Stanford—Vienna Transatlantic Technology Law Forum, https://papers.ssrn.com/sol3/papers.cfm?abstract_id=3288460

Borkin S (2019) Platform co-operatives—solving the capital conundrum, https://media.nesta.org.uk/documents/Nesta_Platform_Report_FINAL-WEB_b1qZGj7.pdf

Bradford A (2019) The Brussels Effect: How the European Union Rules the World, Oxford Academic Books

CICREF (2019) SWIPO: Failure to regulate the European cloud market, https://www.cigref.fr/swipo-failure-regulate-european-cloud-market

COPA & COGECA (2020) EU Code of Conduct on Agricultural Data Sharing", https://fefac.eu/wp-content/uploads/2020/07/eu_code_of_conduct_on_agricultural_data_sharing-1.pdf

Curry E et al. (2022) Data Spaces: Design, Deployment, and Future Directions. In: Curry E et al. (eds) Data Spaces Design, Deployment and Future Directions. Springer, pp. 1–17. https://doi.org/10.1007/978-3-030-98636-0_4

Delacroix S, Lawrence ND (2019) Bottom-up Data Trusts: Disturbing the 'One Size Fits All' Approach to Data Governance, International Data Privacy Law, October 1, 2019, https://doi.org/10.1093/idpl/ipz014

DSSC (2023a) Starter Kit for Data Space Designers, https://dssc.eu/space/SK/29523973/Starter+Kit+for+Data+Space+Designers+%257C+Version+1.0+%257C+March+2023?attachment=%2Fdownload%2Fattachments%2F29523973%2FDSSC-Starterkit-Version-1.0.pdf&type=application%2Fpdf&filename=DSSC-Starterkit-Version-1.0.pdf

DSSC (2023b) Building Blocks, Governance, https://dssc.eu/space/BBE/178422080/Governance
DSSC (2023c) Building Blocks, Legal, https://dssc.eu/space/BBE/178422156/Legal
DSSC (2024a) Blueprint V1.0, 2 Core concepts, https://dssc.eu/space/BVE/357073747/2+Core+Concepts
DSSC (2024b) Blueprint v1.0, 3 Data space use cases and business mode, https://dssc.eu/space/BVE/357073771/3+Data+space+use+cases+and+business+model
DSSC (2024c Blueprint v1.0, Legal Building Blocks, https://dssc.eu/space/BVE/357074679/Legal+Building+Blocks
DSSC (2024d) Blueprint v1.0, Building blocks, https://dssc.eu/space/BVE/357073899/Building+Block+Overview
Duisberg A (2022) Legal Aspects of IDS: Data Sovereignty—What Does It Imply? In: Otto B et al. (eds) Designing Data Spaces. The Ecosystem Approach to Competitive Advantage. Springer, pp. 61–90. https://doi.org/10.1007/978-3-030-93975-5
European Commission/European Data Portal (2015) Creating Value through Open Data, https://data.europa.eu/sites/default/files/edp_creating_value_through_open_data_0.pdf
European Commission (2017) Communication from the Commission to the European Parliament, the Council, the European Economic and Social Committee and the Committee of the Regions "Building a European Data Economy", COM(2017) 9 final, Brussels, 10.1.2017, https://eur-lex.europa.eu/legal-content/EN/TXT/?uri=COM:2017:9:FIN
European Commission (2018a) Communication from the Commission to the European Parliament, the Council, the European Economic and Social Committee and the Committee of the Regions "Towards a common European data space", COM(2018) 232 final, Brussels, 25.4.2018, https://eur-lex.europa.eu/legal-content/EN/ALL/?uri=COM:2018:0232:FIN
European Commission (2018b) Commission Staff Working Document Guidance on sharing private sector data in the European data economy Accompanying the document Communication from the Commission to the European Parliament, the Council, the European economic and social Committee and the Committee of the Regions "Towards a common European data space", SWD/2018/125 final, https://eur-lex.europa.eu/legal-content/EN/TXT/?uri=CELEX%3A52018SC0125
European Commission (2019) Communication from the Commission to the European Parliament, the Council, the European Economic and Social Committee and the Committee of the Regions "Guidance on the regulation on a framework for the free flow of non-personal data in the European Union", COM(2019) 250 final, Brussels, 29.5.2019, https://eur-lex.europa.eu/legal-content/EN/TXT/?uri=COM:2019:250:FIN
European Commission (2020a) Communication from the Commission to the European Parliament, the Council, the European Economic and Social Committee and the Committee of the Regions. A European strategy for data, Brussels, 19.2.2020, COM(2020) 66 final, https://eur-lex.europa.eu/legal-content/EN/TXT/?uri=CELEX%3A52020DC0066
European Commission (2020b) Inception Impact Assessment on Legislative framework for the governance of common European data spaces—Ares(2020)3480073, https://eur-lex.europa.eu/legal-content/EN/ALL/?uri=pi_com:Ares(2020)3480073
European Commission (2020c) Commission Staff Working Document. Impact Assessment Report Accompanying the document Proposal for a Regulation of the European Parliament and of the Council on European Data Governance (Data Governance Act), SWD(2020)295, Brussels, 25.11.2020, https://eur-lex.europa.eu/legal-content/EN/TXT/PDF/?uri=CELEX:52020SC0295
European Commission (2020d) Preliminary Assessment Reports on SWIPO IaaS AND SaaS Codes of Conduct, https://digital-strategy.ec.europa.eu/pt/library/study-presenting-assessments-codes-conduct-data-porting-and-cloud-switching
European Commission (2022a) Commission Staff Working Document on Common European Data Spaces, SWD(2022) 45 final, Brussels, 23.2.2022, https://data.consilium.europa.eu/doc/document/ST-6532-2022-INIT/en/pdf

European Commission (2022b) Proposal for a Regulation of the European Parliament and of the Council on the European Health Data Space, COM(2022) 197 final, Brussels, 3.5.2022, https://eur-lex.europa.eu/legal-content/EN/TXT/?uri=CELEX:52022PC0197

European Commission (2023) Commission Staff Working Document Implementation of multi-country projects. Accompanying the document Communication from the Commission to the European Parliament, the Council, the European Economic and Social Committee and the Committee of the Regions. Report on the state of the Digital Decade 2023, SWD(2023) 573 final, Brussels, 27.9.2023, https://digital-strategy.ec.europa.eu/en/library/implementation-multi-country-projects-digital-decade-report-2023

European Commission (2024a) Commission Staff Working Document on Common European Data Spaces, SWD (2024) 21 final, Brussells, 24.1.2024, https://digital-strategy.ec.europa.eu/en/library/second-staff-working-document-data-spaces

European Commission (2024b) The European data market monitoring tool key. facts & figures, first policy conclusions, data landscape and quantified stories. D2.9 Final Study Report. Executive summary, https://digital-strategy.ec.europa.eu/en/library/results-european-data-market-study-2021-2023

European Commission, Flynn MJ (2021) Study on technical requirements for data spaces in Law enforcement. Executive Summary, https://op.europa.eu/en/publication-detail/-/publication/2cf9cd6e-6c1a-11eb-aeb5-01aa75ed71a1/language-en

European Commission, JRC Knowledge Base (N.D.a) https://wikis.ec.europa.eu/display/jrcdataspaceswiki/1.3++Definitions

European Commission, JRC Knowledge Base (N.D.b) https://wikis.ec.europa.eu/display/jrcdataspaceswiki/3.+Governance

European Commission, JRC Knowledge Base (N.D.c) https://wikis.ec.europa.eu/display/jrcdataspaceswiki/1.4++Principles

European Data Portal (2020) The Economic Impact of Open Data Opportunities for value creation in Europe", https://data.europa.eu/sites/default/files/the-economic-impact-of-open-data.pdf

Farrell E et al. (2023) European Data Spaces—Scientific Insights into Data Sharing and Utilisation at Scale, EUR 31499 EN, Publications Office of the European Union, Luxembourg, 2023, ISBN 978-92-68-03166-7, https://doi.org/10.2760/400188, JRC129900, https://publications.jrc.ec.europa.eu/repository/handle/JRC129900

Franklin M, Halvey A, Maier D (2005) From databases to dataspaces: a new abstraction for information management. ACM SIGMOD Rec 34(4):27–33. https://doi.org/10.1145/1107499.1107502

Fritzenkötter J et al. (2022) Governing the Environment-Related Data Space, Govlab, https://files.thegovlab.org/erdgovernance.pdf

G8 (2013) Open Data Charter, https://g7g20-documents.org/fileadmin/G7G20_documents/2013/G7/United%20Kingdom/Leaders/1%20Leaders%27%20Language/G8%20Open%20Data%20Charter_18062013.pdf

Gabrielli S (2022) Kraken: A Secure, Trusted, Regulatory-Compliant, and Privacy-Preserving Data Sharing Platform. In: Curry E et al. (eds) Data Spaces Design, Deployment and Future Directions. Springer, pp. 107–129. https://doi.org/10.1007/978-3-030-98636-0_4

Gaia X, Hub Germany (2022) "What is a Data Space. Definition of the data space concept", White Paper 1/2022, https://gaia-x-hub.de/wp-content/uploads/2023/11/GX-White-Paper-Data-Space.pdf

Gurevitch Y et al. (2015) Inverse Privacy, https://arxiv.org/pdf/1510.03311

IDSA (2022) IDS Reference Architecture Model, Version 4.0, https://docs.internationaldataspaces.org/ids-knowledgebase/v/ids-ram-4

IDSA (2023) IDSA Rule Book, White Paper, https://docs.internationaldataspaces.org/ids-knowledgebase/v/idsa-rulebook

Janssen et. al. (2020) Data governance: Organizing data for trustworthy Artificial Intelligence. Gov Inf Q 37(3):101493. https://doi.org/10.1016/j.giq.2020.101493

Lähteenoja V (2023) What Are "Personal Data Spaces"?, Companion Proceedings of the ACM Web Conference 2023, ACM, Austin TX USA, 2023, pp. 1458–1461. https://doi.org/10.1145/3543873.3587656

Lycklama D (2022) Data Space Functionality. In: Otto B et al. (eds) Designing Data Spaces. The - Ecosystem Approach to Competitive Advantage. Springer, pp. 521–534 https://doi.org/10.1007/978-3-030-93975-5

Liu J (July 2022) 'Social Data Governance: Towards a Definition and Model'. Big Data & Society 9(2). https://doi.org/10.1177/20539517221111352

Luoma-kyyny J, Pitkänen O (2022) Rulebook for a fair data economy, SITRA, https://www.sitra.fi/en/publications/rulebook-for-a-fair-data-economy/

Maaroof A (N.D.) Big Data and the 2030 agenda for sustainable development. Final draft report-open for comment, https://www.unescap.org/sites/default/files/Final%20Draft_%20stock-taking%20report_For%20Comment_301115.pdf

Martens B et al. (2020) Business to business data sharing: an economic and legal analysis, Digital Economy Working Paper 2020–05, European Commission, Seville, 2020, JRC121336 https://joint-research-centre.ec.europa.eu/document/download/c48fbb97-7e53-4082-a5a1-9a4ad1b6577c_en?filename=jrc121336.pdf

Meadway J (2020) Creating a digital commons, IPPR, https://www.ippr.org/research/publications/creating-a-digital-commons

Meijer A, Potjer S (2018) Citizen-generated open data: An explorative analysis of 25 cases. Gov Inf Q 35(4):613–621. https://doi.org/10.1016/j.giq.2018.10.004, https://dspace.library.uu.nl/bitstream/handle/1874/410120/1_s2.0_S0740624X17303015_main.pdf?sequence=1&isAllowed=y

Micheli M et al. (July–December 2020) Emerging models of data governance in the age of datafication. Big Data & Society 1–15. https://doi.org/10.1007/s12525-019-00362-x

Micheli M et al. (2023) Mapping the landscape of data intermediaries. Emerging models for more inclusive data governance, Publications Office of the European Union, Luxembourg, https://doi.org/10.2760/261724, JRC133988, https://publications.jrc.ec.europa.eu/repository/handle/JRC133988

Ministry of Social Affairs and Health (N.D.) Secondary use of health and social data, https://stm.fi/en/secondary-use-of-health-and-social-data

MyData (2020) Why We Need a Data Exchange Board to Improve the EU Data Governance Act?, https://mydata.org/2020/12/09/why-we-need-a-data-exchange-board-to-improve-the-eu-data-governance-act/

Nagel L, Lycklama D (2021) Design Principles for Data Spaces. Position Paper, Version 1.0, April 2021, https://www.researchgate.net/publication/351307125_Design_Principles_for_Data_Spaces_-_Position_Paper

Nagel L, Lycklama D (2022) In: Otto B et al. (eds) Designing Data Spaces. The Ecosystem Approach to Competitive Advantage. Springer, pp. 17–28. https://doi.org/10.1007/978-3-030-93975-5

OECD (2019) Enhancing Access to and Sharing of Data: Reconciling risks and benefits for data re-use across societies. OECD Publishing, Paris,. https://doi.org/10.1787/276aaca8-en

OECD (2020) Enhanced Access to Publicly Funded Data for Science, Technology and Innovation, https://www.oecd-ilibrary.org/science-and-technology/enhanced-access-to-publicly-funded-data-for-science-technology-and-innovation_947717bc-en

OECD (2021) Recommendation of the Council on Enhancing Access to and Sharing of Data, https://legalinstruments.oecd.org/en/instruments/OECD-LEGAL-0463

OECD (2022) Going Digital Toolkit Note: Measuring the economic value of data, 2022, https://one.oecd.org/document/DSTI/CDEP/GD(2021)2/FINAL/en/pdf

Otto B (2022) The Evolution of Data Spaces. In: Otto B et al. (eds) Designing Data Spaces. The Ecosystem Approach to Competitive Advantage. Springer, pp. 3–15. https://doi.org/10.1007/978-3-030-93975-5

Parrilla C, Carvalho M (2024) "Pay or ok". Pagar con datos personales tras la Directiva 2019/770: Una visión comparada entre España y Portugal, RED ANO 2024 No.

2 Vol. 34, https://cij.up.pt/pt/red/ultima-edicao/ldquopay-or-okrdquo-pagar-con-datos-personales-tras-la-directiva-2019770-una-vision-comparada-entre-espana-y-portugal/

Pettenpohl H et al. (2022) International Data Spaces in a Nutshell. In: Otto B et al. (eds) Designing Data Spaces. The Ecosystem Approach to Competitive Advantage. Springer, pp. 29–40. https://doi.org/10.1007/978-3-030-93975-5

Pollicino O, De Gregorio G (2021) Constitutional Law in the Algorithmic Society. In: Micklitz HW et al. (ed) Constitutional Challenges in the Algorithmic Society. Cambridge University Press, pp. 3–24, 4

Ponti M, Craglia M (2020) Citizen-generated data for public policy. A brief review of European citizen-generated data projects, European Commission, Ispra, 2020 JRC120231, https://marisaponti.org/wp-content/uploads/2020/03/ponti_jrc-report-final.pdf

Ruhaak A, Algorithm Watch (2020) Data Trusts in Germany and under the GDPR, Algorithm Watch, https://algorithmwatch.org/en/wp-content/uploads/2020/12/Data-trusts-in-Germany-and-under-the-GDPR-Anouk-Ruhaak-AlgorithmWatch-2020.pdf

Scerri S et al. (2022) Common European Data Spaces: Challenges and Opportunities. In: Curry E et al. (eds) Data Spaces Design, Deployment and Future Directions. Springer, pp. 337–357. https://doi.org/10.1007/978-3-030-98636-0

SWIPO (2020a) Common Scope and Approach to Article 6 of the Free Flow of Non-personal Data Regulation and use of Codes of Conduct for Cloud Services, https://swipo.eu/wp-content/uploads/2020/07/SWIPO-Codes-of-Conduct-Common-high-level-principles.pdf

SWIPO (2020b) Code of Conduct for Data Portability and Cloud Service Switching for Infrastructure as a Service (IaaS) Cloud services, https://swipo.eu/wp-content/uploads/2020/07/SWIPO-IaaS-Code-of-Conduct.pdf

SWIPO (2020c) SWIPO AISBL Code of Conduct Switching and Portability of data related to Software as a Service (SaaS), https://swipo.eu/wp-content/uploads/2020/07/SWIPO-SaaS-Code-of-Conduct.pdf

SWIPO (2020d) Appeals and Complaints Procedures (Version November 23, 2020), https://swipo.eu/wp-content/uploads/2021/01/SWIPO_AISBL_Complaints-and-Appeals_V2.pdf

Torre-Bastida et al. (2022) Technological Perspective of Data Governance in Data Space Ecosystems. In: Curry E et al. (eds) Data Spaces Design, Deployment and Future Directions. Springer, pp. 65–87. https://doi.org/10.1007/978-3-030-98636-0_4

United Nations Development Group (N.D.) Data privacy, ethics and protection. Guidance note on big data for achievement of the 2030 agenda, https://unsdg.un.org/sites/default/files/UNDG_BigData_final_web.pdf

United Nations Organisation (N.D.) https://www.un.org/en/global-issues/big-data-for-sustainable-development; https://www.un.org/en/UN-system/big-data

UN Statistical Commission (2017) Cape Town Global Action Plan for Sustainable Development Data, https://unstats.un.org/sdgs/hlg/Cape_Town_Global_Action_Plan_for_Sustainable_Development_Data.pdf

World Economic Forum (2022) Advancing Digital Agency: The Power of Data Intermediaries, https://www3.weforum.org/docs/WEF_Advancing_towards_Digital_Agency_2022.pdf

Zuboff S (2022) Surveillance Capitalism or Democracy? The Death Match of Institutional Orders and the Politics of Knowledge in Our Information Civilization. Organization Theory 3:1–79. https://journals.sagepub.com/doi/epub/10.1177/26317877221129290

Zygmuntowski JJ et al. (September 30 2021) Embedding European Values in Data Governance: A Case for Public Data Commons. Internet Policy Rev 10(3). https://doi.org/10.14763/2021.3.1572

Rights, Freedom, Equality, Security: Open Questions. For an Appeal to European Legal Science

Maria Novella Campagnoli, Luca Panico, and Luigi Prosia

1 Introduction

The effective protection of the fundamental rights and freedoms of European citizens within the digital habitat—acephalous and dominated by the emergence of new powers—certainly represents one of the most difficult challenges facing the EU and its member States. It is enough to think about the multiple dysfunctional situations that can threaten the right to freedom of thought and speech, privacy, information, as well as the right to image and reputation. Situations detrimental to the fundamental rights of European citizens that have also been highlighted by the recent pandemic, which—consistently implementing the use of ICT and access to platforms—has, on the one hand, demonstrated their usefulness, but, on the other hand, emphasized their opacity and dangers.

Among the various profiles that deserve attention, there is certainly the fact that collecting, processing, and analyzing personal data in real time—now on the agenda in the private sector dominated by big digital players—can also play a fundamental role in the public sphere, to plan, monitor and make responsible decisions, in view of a truly inclusive, democratic, and participatory development. The use of sophisticated data mining techniques can enable governments to obtain increasingly detailed and timely information on which to build better intervention strategies in every field

Text of the Report presented at the DigUECit International Conference "A digital Europe for citizens. Data Governance. Digital market. Digital Service", held in Porto on 14 April 2023.
Section 3 of the chapter, attributed to Luigi Prosia, contains material partly previously published in the author's article "Big Data and Digital Nudging. Insights, Into Freedom of Choice, Sustainability, and Cybersecurity", Humanities and Rights, Vol. 5, No. 2 (2023).

Section 1 is written by Maria Novella Campagnoli and Luigi Prosia. Section 2 is written by Luca Panico. Section 3 is written by Luigi Prosia. Sections 4 and 5 are written by Maria Novella Campagnoli.

M. N. Campagnoli (✉) · L. Panico · L. Prosia
University of Rome "Tor Vergata", Rome, Italy
e-mail: marianovellacampagnoli@gmail.com

G. Enes et al. (eds.), *A Digital Europe for Citizens*,
https://doi.org/10.1007/978-3-032-02500-5_5

(social, environmental, and economic), the effectiveness of which can then be verified. However, to safeguard personal freedoms and rights, which can be harmed by unlawful or arbitrary data processing, it is necessary that the great opportunities offered by big data analytics must be embedded into a framework where technological sustainability is the key factor. This is even truer since behavioral economics has definitively removed the paradigm of rationality of *homo œconomicus*, highlighting the cognitive errors inherent in its very nature. Bias of the mind that facilitate mechanisms of libertarian paternalism (or neuromarketing), able to silently alter the formation of wills, although they are often legitimized with the supposed purpose of improving individual and collective well-being.

European citizens and individuals in general cannot—and must not—be reduced to mere informational entities to evaluate, profile, exploit and "monetize" for the most disparate purposes, as the logics that move certain powers would often like. Today more than ever, it is therefore necessary to return to reflect—with the spectacles of the philosopher of law and the legal informatics—on the structural elements of law and justice: equality (of subjects), symmetry (of positions), and proportionality (of interventions and law enforcement measures). The intent must obviously be to avert inequality, discrimination, and prevarication.

On this horizon, in addition to the "IA Act",[1] the "Digital Services Act",[2] the "Digital Markets Act"[3] and the "Data Governance Act"[4]—to which the various speakers who took part in the "DigUECit International Conference" devoted extensive coverage and to whose texts we refer for a more in-depth normative discussion—important is the "European data strategy",[5] whose echo in Italy has been widely felt not only by the National Recovery and Resilience Plan (NRRP),[6] but also by the National Cybersecurity Agency (NCA) with the National Cybersecurity Strategy 2022–2026.[7]

In the light of the state of the art quickly recalled and these very brief prodromal considerations, the essay will deal with: firstly, (1) the birth of new spaces and new powers, which go beyond state sovereignty; then, (2) on the impact of open data in social regulation and on the possible use of nudging strategies also and especially in the public sphere; and finally, (3) on the imperative need to prevent and effectively combat abuses and violations carried out in cyberspace.

---

[1] https://www.europarl.europa.eu/RegData/etudes/BRIE/2021/698792/EPRS_BRI(2021)698792_EN.pdf.

[2] https://eur-lex.europa.eu/legal-content/EN/TXT/?uri=celex%3A32022R2065.

[3] https://eur-lex.europa.eu/legal-content/EN/TXT/PDF/?uri=CELEX:32022R1925.

[4] https://eur-lex.europa.eu/legal-content/EN/TXT/?uri=celex%3A52020PC0767.

[5] https://commission.europa.eu/strategy-and-policy/priorities-2019-2024/europe-fit-digital-age/european-data-strategy_en.

[6] https://www.governo.it/sites/governo.it/files/PNRR.pdf.

[7] https://www.acn.gov.it/documents/ACN%20Manuale%20Operativo%20implementazione%20misura-82.pdf.

2 Looking for a New *Nomos*. Reflections about the Relatisation of the State and the Emerging of New Political Powers

The advent of the digitale age has significantly altered forms of interrelationship, not only in terms of private interactions, but also in the context of those between individuals and public power. The advent of the Internet has already marked the emergence of cyberspace, a new spatial dimension 'of a communicative and non-territorial nature' (Mangiameli 2000).

This new dimension is characterised, in fact, by the dislocation of every link between the individual and his physical space, which allows him to overcome the traditional natural and political limits imposed on his personal individual and social development. This leads, on the one hand, to the formation of an identity split from its historical and cultural roots; on the other, to the creation of communities without a stable place of reference. At the same time, the cyberspace does not admit any form of governance, insofar as it produces a mingling of centre and periphery through the circulation of the flow of data coming from each user. Consequently, the absence of a territory and an authority able to dominate the network's mare magnum seems to provide an absolutely limitless space in which human freedom can finally be realised. However, the constant presence of users and the massive input of data, which they carry out by surfing the net, poses the problem of a reconfiguration of the forms of control, no longer in a vertical sense but in a horizontal one. This means that in the digital world came out forms of structural control in which every user takes on the role of overseer and overseen simultaneously.[8]

In other words, cyberspace with its characteristics of de-centralisation, de-territorialisation and data-surveillance (Mangiameli and Campagnoli 2020) has completely revolutionised the sense of community and re-proposed in innovative forms the fundamental question of defining one's identity. The virtual destroys spatial and temporal distances, datalysing the human experience, which is no longer mediated by the body and sensory experiences but is cast into a non-place in which the global and the local mingle in the glocal (Mangiameli 2004), transcending space and time.

The subsequent redefinition of space inevitably impacts on the meaning and role of sovereignty. In fact, if traditionally the shape-making mechanisms of both individual and collective identities were delimited by the territorial space of the nation-state, today these processes cross the "national boundaries: sometimes they assert a global

---

[8] In this regard, one speaks of Synopticon insofar as "The act of looking releases the beholder from his or her own location, and transports him or her at least spiritually into cyberspace, where distance no longer matters, even if physically one has not moved. No longer does it matter whether the objects of the Synopticon, now transformed from the watched into the beholder, move or stand still. Wherever they are and wherever they go, they can and do connect to the Extraterritorial Network that allows the many to watch the few. The Panopticon forced people into a position where they could be watched. The Synopticon does not need to force anyone, it seduces people to watch" (Z. Bauman, *Dentro la globalizzazione. Le conseguenze sulle persone*, Laterza, Roma-Bari, pp. 59–60).

belonging, sometimes they are part of a *nomadic* culture, sometimes they open up to postmodern *monothematic* formations" (Mangiameli 2004). In this sense, the virtual world offers new possibilities for interaction that give rise to the formation of virtual communities, which make public mediation seemingly superfluous for the political cohesion of civil society.

The loss of the sovereign power of the national government apparatus and the consequent weakening of its connection with its citizens is thus evident. Precisely as a result of the modification of our 'being' within the new dimension, now freed from territorial constraints, no hierarchy or supervision is no longer possible at first sight.

So, if the essence of sovereignty is given by the schmittian synthesis of *Ordnung* and *Ortung* (ordering and localisation), by which the legitimacy of power required a primary rootedness in a territory (Schmitt 1991), the volatilisation of space has undoubtedly led to the disappearance of one of the preconditions of sovereignty, opening up to the crisis of the of the modern age and the loss of the state in the digital world. It is now well known that the increasing informatisation of existence has put the old nation states in a position of mutual interdependence, increasingly relativised within a global context where they are no longer the main actors.

Of the five disjunctures of sovereignty mentioned by Held (Held 1995), the second and fifth in particular play a leading role, because of the increasing computerisation of contemporary society. More specifically, the expression "second disjuncture" refers to the position of interdependence in which sovereign States are placed by the multiplication of inter-state actors—governmental and non-governmental—who are deputed to manage certain political spheres that have become transnational, leading to a modification and influence on traditionally state decision-making processes.[9] As for the "fifth disjuncutre", this is found in economic globalization: the internationalisation of productive systems and finance have caused the overturning of the relationship between economics and politics, turning the first into the engine and driver of the second. In fact, through the development of new technologies that allow the de-localisation of the entire productive cycle and the increase in trade on a global level, the need has been imposed for the crossing of state borders, thah has become obsolete in the way they limit the deployment of the new driving forces of politics (Held 1995). In other words, the phenomena of the internationalisation of the economy, carried out by the virtualisation of the human and social networked activities, have weakened the political autonomy of the old State-form (Carrino 2014). State power is thus relativised, passing from an ordering function to a regulating one that is expressed inside a space that largely oversteps its boundaries (Mangiameli 2004).

The retreat of state power thus reflects the growing expansion of a space that appears immune to any form of political dirigism, intangible to appropriation and

[9] "The development of international regimes and international organizations has led to important chances in the decision-making structure of world politics. New forms of multilateral and multinational politics have beem established and with them distinctive styles of collective decision-making involving governments, IGOs and a wide variety of transnational pressure groups and international non-governmental organizations (INGOs)" (Held 1995, p. 108).

settlement. In this sense, the reference to the contrast between land and sea in the schmittian theory of *nomos* appears pertinent. In his historical reconstruction of the international order of the *jus publicum europaeum*, Schmitt noted how the political equilibrium achieved by European states in the modern era was based on the opposition between land space, directly subject to the sovereign control of public power, and maritime space, insusceptible of occupation due to its elemental specificity. In this configuration of world order, the hostility between states could resume in the form of competition for control of trade patterns and with them of the world economy (Schmitt 2002).

If this was true in the modern era, it is evident that in the contemporary world the progressive evolution of technique has now made both *Landkrieg* and *Seakrieg* governable by the public authorities, due to the possibility of using means able to move rapidly from one continent to another one and to communicate in ways that were previously unimaginable (Mangiameli 2004). While this has allowed political domination over any physical space, technical progress has, at the same time, led to the formation of the cybernetic dimension that cannot be grounded in any way. In short: cyberspace could in this sense represent the anomic space of the post-modern era.

Therefore, technique requires a reflection on the evolution of political forms and sovereignty in front of the great spatial revolution of our century. After all, Schmitt was already wondering about the actual nature of technique and its future developments, facing the alternative between a definitive neutralisation of all political conflict or the enforcement of technique as a means able to open up new forms of conflict (Schmitt 1932). Far from interpreting technical evolution as the achievement of the movement of the hegelian Spirit in the perfect identity between reality and rationality, Schmitt on the contrary underlined the instrumental and political nature of tchnique. Consequently, he pointed out that "technology is always only an instrument and a weapon, and the very fact that it serves everyone is not neutral. From the immanence of the technical datum no single human and spiritual decision is derivable, least of all one in the sense of neutrality. Every civilisation, every people and every religion, every war and every peace can use technique as a weapon" (Schmitt 1932).

It is good to note that the withdrawal of the State does not mean the definitive emancipation of man from social restrictions within a digital society of aims, but rather the rise of new powers. These are *potestates indirectae* that are no longer public (Schmitt 1995),[10] capable of re-modelling forms of governance and re-orienting both public and private life, which are increasingly blurred and confused.

From the *tabula rasa* created by the unstoppable spread of the technique, what is left is only the new information space, an energy field on which different and new political powers, not only public but also and above all private, inevitably act. They operate by relativising the role of state power and leading to new conflicts, inequalities and vulnerabilities, so that "while it may be true that technological

[10] In his work, Schmitt identifies the emergence of private powers removed from the control of public power as the main cause of the crisis of the modern state which, losing its monopoly of the 'political', is destined to collapse in upon itself.

development facilitates connections and synergies, thus becoming a valuable tool of non-hierarchical coordination, the risk of a global society in which an elite rule over *electronic proletarians*, no longer masters of bodies and minds, is equally real" (Mangiameli 2004).

In the vacuum created by the widening of Held's disjunctures, new players have now infiltrated, providing Internet users with increasingly varied and personalised services that take on the function of satisfying every human need. On the net, we are observing the emergence of a genuine 'private governance' that 'guarantees' users the access to the new spaces of social life and to its services according to their own private regulations. The individual experience in the digital world is, in fact, now mediated by private platforms through which everyday activities are carried out, from work—increasingly *smart*—to private communications and expressions of thought, even political activity. And there is no one who cannot see how these private players—such as Google, Facebook (*rectius* Meta), Microsoft, Amazon, Apple—can take on the role of real political bodies able to condition the public life of millions of citizens with sometimes dysfunctional outcomes.

Over the last few years, we have experienced several episodes that, while on the one hand have highlighted the importance of platforms for the political life of citizens, on the other have figured out the risks of their possible instrumentalisation for economic-political purposes. For example, one thinks of the role played by social networks in the spread of the riots in the North African states during the so-called Arab Spring of 2011, which helped the spread of revolutionary waves.[11] Nevertheless, we can also remeber various episodes in which social networks were used to influence political contexts, such as the scandal of the Russian interference in the US political campaign in 2016 or the *Cambridge Analytica-Facebook* scandal in 2018. In fact, these large corporations, in the provision of their services, operate as legal bodies under private law. Nevertheless, they claim to completely replace public power with regulations of their services dressed up in ethical formalism, aimed at recreating in the virtual world a duplicate of the public space subject to their normativity and informational opulence.[12] This means that the decentralised acquisition and management of the data into which human experience is split in the digital world by new powers produces new dynamics of control, orientation and surveillance (Zuboff 2023).

It follows that there is a need to restore the relationship between public power and civil society in a way able to safeguard users from the dysfunctional situations that can

---

[11] Reference to Aa. Vv., *Il ruolo dei Social Network nelle Rivolte Arabe*, Approfondimento n. 40/2011, in *Osservatorio di politica internazionale*, (https://www.parlamento.it/application/xmanager/projects/parlamento/file/repository/affariinternazionali/osservatorio/approfondimenti/PI0040App.pdf).

[12] In this perspective, it is added that "it cannot be forgotten that we are dealing with economic operators of global importance, with financial resources greater than those of many medium-sized states, who have amassed an unimaginable amount of information and data, through covert profiling and discreet forms of surveillance, enabling them to exert influence over the needs and desires of individuals and their inclinations (including political ones)" (Saraceni and Mangiameli 2023). Cento e una voce di informatica giuridica. Giappichelli.).

arise on the net and to fully protect their information integrity on the net. "If, in fact, in the society of global communication it can be said that we are our information, what is most important is to govern the circulation so as to try to recover self-possession" (Mangiameli 2015). In fact cyberspace—despite its nature as a spontaneous and unconstructed order (Hayek 1986 *in* Mangiameli and Campagnoli 2020)—cannot be meant as an anomic space, but rather as a new "big space" (Schmitt and Maschke 1995).[13] in which the decline of the sovereign State to the role of mere regulator opens the door to the spread of new private powers that respond exclusively to the utilitarian logic of profit and are not. bound to the citizen by the reciprocal obligation of protection-obedience (Hobbes 1894).[14] Therefore, it is essential to reject the arguments of those who see in the virtual world an undominable and *nomos*-free smooth space, re-proposing by analogy that distinction between land and sea, according to which a space ordered by state regulation is necessarily opposed to an undomainable space left to de-regulated free trade, capable of providing global pacification (Schmitt 2006). On the contrary, it is opportune to emphasise how "for jurists, the entry into new spaces, as before into the sea and air and now into the virtual space, constitutes a challenge, since legal science, although born to regulate terrestrial relations and relationships, is perfectly capable of bringing the law everywhere, even into virtual spaces, provided that the law itself is supported by a sovereign power".

Far from being as close as ever to the "end of history" (Fukuyama 2020)[15] promised by the globalised world and neutralised by the strength of the techno-capitalist economy—capable of transforming itself from a means to an end and finally into an apparatus (Severino 1998)—we need to take up the challenge thrown down by the post-modern *Zeitgeist*. If this is the case, it is clear that this cannot be done exclusively at the level of the nation State, whose mediating capacities are fated to be increasingly regionalised. It is up to the European Union to become a global actor capable of engaging in a dialogue with those transversal powers that risk enslaving public space to their own economic interests. The European Union must represent more than just an economic and commercial union, rather it must recover its role of civilization (Huntington 2000)[16] that is at the core of its political essence. In the common origin of the European legal culture of the Christian and Romanistic tradition, the "last asylum of the legal conscience" (Schmitt 1950)

---

[13] In which the great space is defined as an operational space, an energy field in which new political forces deploy and assert their power.

[14] There is a clear reference to the *pactum subiectionis* theorised by Thomas Hobbes, according to whom individuals bound in the state of nature by a bellum omnia contra omnes evoke the modern state as a politic-legal form to which they submit in exchange for protection.

[15] The expression is taken from a work by F. Fukuyama, who believed that, following the victory in the Cold War of the single capitalist model and its spread throughout the world, also thanks to the technical developments of capital itself, it could be thought that we were actually at the last stage of development in human history. "It is possible that we have reached […] the end of history as such; that is, the end of the line of the ideological evolution of mankind and the universalisation of Western liberal democracy as the ultimate form of human governance".

[16] The expression is taken from the political model of S.P. Huntington, who, at the end of the Cold War, theorised the evolution of global society towards a multipolar setting characterised by the contraposition of new political aggregations based on the concept of civilisation.

is identified and the principles of justice of ontological parity between subjects, symmetry of positions, reciprocity, proportionality, and impartiality of judgement so that no one can rise to the status of *iudex in causa propria* (Cotta 1979). These structural elements of justice as a whole revolve around the common good, as "the good of that group, of that supra-individual identity, of that political we, and which nevertheless has an ulterior meaning: it is the consciousness of a co-partnership and is the very raison d'être of every grouping, of every community, as well as of every democratic rule of law" (Mangiameli 2004). This must be the *Weltanschauung* that must guide community action towards regulating the potential offered by the digital, in the awareness of its capacity to strengthen the process of political, economic, and cultural integration, but also of the inherent risk of its dysfunctional outcomes: *ab integro nascitur ordo.*

3 Open Data and Nudging of Public Utility. Insights into Freedom of Choice and Sustainability

Digitalization (with its signals, sensors and electronic pulses) is causing the circulation of an incredible amount of data, which we are interested in, that spreads us and that, quite simply, makes more about us than we imagine, to the point of being able to anticipate most of our daily decisions. A traffic of data not only precise, intimate, correlated and controllable, but also so extensive that it could "fill American libraries more than eight times [...] [by means of] a cycle that is self-sustaining" (Floridi, 2017) according to fragmentary logics (Barberis 2020). Just think that, to represent the amount of content currently available on the Web, it is necessary to resort to the zettabyte: a number followed by 21 zeros.

These figures are destined to grow quickly, without interruption due to the daily exchange of information, that spread in heterogeneous forms and contents, and that make people incredibly more exposed, since they show little ability to guard their secrets (Giovanni Ziccardi 2022, p. 81). What is more, people entrust their social representation to multiple and widespread data sets that modify its very knowledge and identity even being able to talk about *electronic bodies* (Rodotà 2015, p. 270) ideally opposed to the *physical bodies*. Besides, integrated telecommunications systems intensify large-scale transmission, storage and search for information, all of which have become potentially publishable, at relatively minimal cost (Granieri 2006, pp. 28–29), so that a continuous flow of information and communication shapes every level of planetary life, which is increasingly conditioned "by the speed and carelessness of hasty electronic word of mouth" (Campagnoli 2020).

Through ICT, therefore, individuals experience new existential and mental models that transform reality in its intrinsic nature, to the extent that they corrode the barriers between *online* and *offline* and make *being there* perfectly superimposable to *being connected*. As a result, technology ceases to be a mere tool (to calculate, write, store, inform, educate, etc.) and becomes "prosthesis that surpasses and perfects man and nature" (Dionigi 2019), as we live, grow and interact, with greater or lesser success and in a more or less healthy way, depending on the (knowledge-)information made available by the new devices. Laptops, apps and platforms, which "go beyond the dialectic of means to achieve the rhetoric of goals" (Mangiameli and Campagnoli 2020).

At the same time, however, all those machines that retrieve information and process data starting from his/her habits on the Net (from websites visited to emails exchanged, from conversations triggered in chats to orders and purchases made online) constantly challenge man. His/her habits, in fact, can be recorded and calculated with unprecedented precision, thanks to the action of software so sophisticated as to greatly overcome the intellectual and working limits of humans. The purpose is undoubtedly to store more and more numbers of data, and then produce further and valuable information, from the harvested raw masses.[17] Forasmuch—as Granger states in *Fahrenheit 451* with respect to surveillance activities in the context of an unidentified despotic society where reading or possessing books is considered a criminal offence—"you never know when being aware of certain data can be useful to you!" (Bradbury 1978). And this, today, is particularly useful to the superstar companies of Silicon Valley (Amazon, Apple, Google and other digital giants), whose economic-industrial model "aspires to transform every gesture, every breath, every relationship into an opportunity for profit" (Sadin 2018).

It is no coincidence, therefore, that in the face of the profound re-ontologization and re-stemologization (Floridi 2020) of the world caused by the advent of the Internet—the fastest, cheapest and most efficient (but not also the safest) means of communication exists—the big tech companies base their business systems on data and information. In addition, they make numerous efforts to secure the exclusive dominion of what is the key resource of the twenty-first century. The value of data, indeed, does not end with utilization, but unfolds using it over and over again, always creating different combinations, made possible by the unprecedented storage and analysis capabilities (or data mining techniques) their own algorithms (Ramge and Mayer-Schoenberger 2021). From this point of view, the frequent metaphor of data such as new oil—another important raw material that, however, is consumed as it burns—appears reductive, due to the fact that digital information—differs from the source from which it emanates—is modulates and multipliable in copies and is not lost (or destroyed) by making use of it.

Then, it is more correct to speak of non-rival goods, which not being consumed like oil, can be used simultaneously by several people. Consequently, it is possible to extract continuously from them—without reducing the surprising quality—new indications and perspectives, which currently translate into a competitive advantage for only consolidated digital monopolists, with consequent power imbalances between those who hold the data and those who intentionally or inadvertently provide it.

---

[17] With all the difficulties that derive from it in relation to the requirement of consent, which pursuant to the GDPR must be explicitly and liberating referring to specific processing purposes illustrated in a clear and precise way. In this regard, reference should be made to the *European Parliament resolution on fundamental rights implications of big data: privacy, data protection, non-discrimination, security and law-enforcement*, 14th March 2017 (2016/2225(INI)).

A disparity, which could be overcome by making it's flow free and open to all (to citizens, governments, international organizations, traditional businesses) (Mayer-Schönberger and Ramge 2018). In this way, data—especially that characterized by large volumes, velocity, variability and easy visualization (i.e. big data)—could increase, in addition to the profit of a few, also the well-being of many, configuring for the latter a safe investment in economic and social terms, too, given that:

the results [of data processing] which appear to be of no or little interest today could suddenly take on vital importance [...] due to unforeseeable future events—such as, for example, a pandemic, a natural cataclysm or a disruption of the stock markets—or further developments in information technology (Saraceni and Mangiameli 2023).

The possibility of obtaining sensible and statistically consistent forecasts from data processing, on which to calibrate the various decision-making processes, can be of stimulus to innovation and growth, both in the private and in the public sectors. In the first area, analytics systems would allow to optimize performance, to increase productivity, to lower costs and, more generally, to create more fruitful business forms. In the second case, however, the stakes go beyond mere economic power and concern, more closely, valuable aspects such as the security of citizens, the development of collective knowledge, the safeguarding of justice and equity, preventing and combating discrimination. This is because, by directing data towards a collective good, numerous public sectors (health, transport, environment, energy, etc.) could know real opportunities for change, certainly of an improving nature. They are linked to a more efficient and personalized provision of services, to the issuance of more accurate and timely measures (of which the effectiveness will also be verified), as well as a considerable tax savings.

For that reason, there is a need for much wider access to data (if not worldwide, then at least at European level), to try to reduce the current information asymmetry between organizations and companies, individuals and customers, the State and society, thus promoting a correct transition to digital based on open data for all. As Europe has been supporting politically for some years, too. This is the direction of the words—pronounced in February 2020, at the opening of work dedicated to digital strategy initiatives—by Ursula von der Leyen, president of the European commission:

We want that data to be available to all, whether public or private, big or small, startup or giant. [...] As part of this, big commercial digital players must accept their responsibility, including by letting Europeans access the data they collect.[18]

Only by conquering this universal sharing of data and resetting, consequently, power relations, state institutions, and non-profit associations and, in general, will civil society be able to really face the environmental, economic and humanitarian emergencies in progress. Vice versa, an unequal distribution of (knowledge-) information will always hinder the advancement of social, scientific and economic progress, understood in the perspective of a truly inclusive, democratic and sustainable development.

---

[18] https://ec.europa.eu/commission/presscorner/detail/en/ac_20_260

In addition to having intensified information asymmetries in a way that not even the pioneers of the Web could have foreseen, the digital revolution has also encouraged the emergence of new tools, based once again on information (and its representation), to promote—indirectly, but still significantly—certain behavior considered (under the guidance of the regulators on duty) desirable.

The reference is to all those techniques widely used in today's online decision-making environments, used by big tech companies to steer the conduct of individuals in certain directions, depending on how the information is shown on the screens of our devices. On the Net, in fact, our every choice is also the result of the designer-defined UI design. For example, the mobile payment application Square Point of Sale, particularly used in the United States, when it facilitated the release of tips to merchants with cleaner and immediate graphics, generated important repercussions on the number and extent of same tips (Carr 2013).

The effectiveness of this "new mass communication strategy" (Mangiameli 2017) is related to the fact that people are now used to making judgments or decisions (regarding the destination of a trip, the right partner for life, the best investment on the market, etc.) essentially on the screen. The latter has become "the scene, the stage of actions and relationships here and now [...] in which the subjects live and (rap-) present their stories" (Mangiameli 2017). On the screen, moreover, everything can be questioned and reconstructed from scratch an infinite number of times, in order to facilitate access to goods and services by the user(-consumer) or, more simply, to encourage their eagerness to share. From here, the user interface is enriched with design elements subservient to the logic of the so-called digital nudging (or digital persuasion) (Weinmann et al. 2016).

The reference is to banners, pop-ups and landing pages, aimed at creating targeted graphics; specific sections, such as consumer feedback; ambiguous configurations, as such capable of misleading Internet users in the expression of their actual preferences that are the so-called dark patterns. Just think of the default settings, which are often accepted passively, with significant consequences regarding the provision of personal data to Internet service providers. This, on the one hand, is representative of the common tendency of users to leave things as they are. On the other hand, it shows how the characteristics of virtual environments can alter behavior in a predictable way, without the need to rely on substantial economic incentives or, furthermore, to prohibit any choice, but only by implementing a sort of *libertarian paternalism* (Thaler and Sunstein 2022). It is sufficient, then, that the procedures for changing the default settings are purposely long and complex for users to desist.

The reason lies in an interference that operates at the subconscious level, thanks to the help of heuristics and biases (or cognitive deficits), because of which individuals are prone to inertia that leads to non-decision (or the continuous postponement of the same) and they often make choices based on emotions and/or feelings. They are also content with a partial information framework; reflect little on the long-term effects of their determinations; tend to imitate others, as they are judged (Kahneman et al. 1982). A way of proceeding, this, perfectly in line with the duality typical of thought processing processes, which in the course of daily activities (entrusted to System

1) are fast, automatic and guided by intuition, while they become slower, tiring and complicated when reason (or System 2) is called into question (Kahneman 2012).

The psychological effects related to the less rational part of the human mind (or System 1) sometimes, they can be exploited by the designer of human–machine interaction to manipulate individuals and groups according to the logic of profit maximization. The designer encourages them to purchase more products or services than necessary, to use certain functions rather than others, and, more generally, to increase the time spent on the Web, because the greater the time spent, for example, on social networks, the greater the economic benefit for the companies that manage them. This also operates the recommendation systems which, in order to produce high business value, automatically select the elements of interest to the user: those that he/she will most likely appreciate, because it is in line with his/her propensities. Then, the system makes them more visible and accessible (often in the form of an ordered list) and thus puts in place an excellent neuro-marketing strategy.

Now, considering that on the Net our ability to concentrate is continuously interrupted and distorted by an overwhelming amount of information, which is almost impossible to elaborate carefully, appropriate use of digital nudging tools could certainly help people make more satisfying choices, overcoming the vulnerability inherent in the formation of their will. In other words, these tools could try to correct the cognitive limitations inherent in decision-making processes since behavioral economics definitively removed the paradigm of absolute rationality of *homo œconomicus*, as a decision-maker always capable of wise choices, because he is totally indifferent to the count in which he operates (Simon 1955).

Besides, the implementation of digital nudges—i.e. relatively small changes to the user interface—it is fast, simple and cheap, yet very profitable, since the Internet provides specific features (such as profiling), that allow a perfect customization of choices. Nevertheless, the fact remains that technologies rarely combine such choices with the benefit of individuals, to whom is required, therefore, a greater awareness of their use.

Not only that, the design of devices, applications and websites could even be of public utility when it succeeds in encouraging citizens to engage in socially responsible behavior, such as, for example, leading a healthy life, reducing waste or energy consumption, making donations or participating in charitable activities. This, simply planning options so that the most advantageous—not only for digital monopolists, but also, and above all, for the community—become the most salient, convincing and easy to choose. For this purpose, however, the user interface should be designed in such a way that it is increasingly fair, protective and sustainable, placing man first at the center and as an end that qualifies progress, whose development must be directed towards the common good (Severino 2022).

The reason is easily said. Making good decisions is the most important skill of our life, private and professional, since the planning of the future both others and ours depends on it.

4 Between Threats, Attacks, and Possible Violations. Security and Protection of Rights in the Union's Digital Space, in the Name of a Reference to European Legal Science

To the two different but complementary critical guidelines outlined above—the first substantially focused on the examination of the provocations and challenges advanced by the post-modern *Zeitgeist*,[19] while the second more oriented to highlight the possible positive implications of open data[20] and the public nudging—a third must necessarily be added. This, also in accordance with the keywords (rights, freedom, equality, security) around which this essay unfolds. In fact, it is impossible not to pay particular attention to violations and attacks (public and / or *ad personam*) that, very often, take place in the folds of digital environments and that in various ways can threaten the rights of European citizens.

Decidedly wide and varied is the range of critical issues with which—especially in recent years—jurists (and *a fortiori* European jurists) have been forced to measure themselves (Cotta 1968), sometimes, in the search for new hermeneutics able to adapt to a context (such as that of cyberspace) (Mangiameli 2000) completely unprecedented, at times, in the attempt to develop more effective protection strategies able to reconcile the dual need: on the one hand, to open up to digital (which, from a certain point of view, proves to be a cornucopia of precious gifts) (Lévy 2002) and, on the other hand, to balance the area of freedom and that of security, trying to avoid the narrowing, compressions and possible lesions of both dimensions.

Proscenium in which many of our activities are now carried out (not only individual ones [Bauman and Lyon 2015; Thalera and Sunstein 2022; Dumouchel and Damiano 2019; Benasayang 2020], but also institutional ones [Macrì 2022]), cyberspace—in addition to having opened the door to what is unanimously defined as the infosphere society (Floridi 2017).—It has become, on the other hand, the privileged habitat within which attacks and violations of different orders and degrees can take place, moving transversely between the public and private dimensions, in a continuous coming and going of plans and positions.

From this point of view—and in partial continuity with the examination proposed in the first paragraph—an aspect that deserves to be emphasized here is undoubtedly the fact that, in recent years, an unprecedented and decidedly evanescent space of belligerence has also emerged, which has been added to the Land, the Sea and the Airspace; as if to mark a further passage in the bed of that acute narration of the evolution of spaces and conflict that Carl Schmitt has outlined with extreme foresight in *Land and Sea* (Schmitt 2002). Another factor worthy of attention (which, on closer inspection, constitutes a logical precipitate of the first) is represented by the entry on

[19] In which a techno-capitalist economy is imposed, new powers emerge that go beyond and transcend state sovereignty, and a renewed appeal to legal science and the European Union is gaining ground.

[20] Which, alongside the profit of a few, could also convey the well-being of many, not only in purely economic but also social terms.

the public scene of a new and somewhat heterogeneous category of combatants: state, para-state, non-state, non-recognized, individual agents. An element, this, that—from the point of view of the general theory of law—has led to a radical paradigm shift, due to the transition from symmetrical and regular conflict to irregular asymmetric belligerence: well known to history, but which, today, within the virtual space finds a significant ally in that new *ring of Gyges*[21] that is the Web.[22] It is, as is evident, a decisive paradigm shift which, moreover, is effectively witnessed using neologisms such as cyber-attack,[23] cyber-terrorism and cyber-war.[24] Beyond the structural differences between cyber-war, cyber-attack and cyber-terrorism (differences that refer to the fundamental categorical distinction between regularity/irregularity and symmetry/asymmetry), the fact remains that cyberspace—as a dimension that crosses, brings together and makes state borders spongy, as well as a privileged place where extremely different powers are compared and measured (Mangiameli 2004)—it has become to all intents and purposes one of the main (if not the main) front of belligerence, regular and otherwise. And it is from this awareness that in recent years—both on the part of the international community, as well as on the part of the European Union, as well as on the part of Italy—a path has been undertaken in the direction of cooperation aimed at guaranteeing security and digital peace.

It is significant to recall that, precisely in consideration of the highly fluid and permeable characteristics of cyberspace, NATO, for several years, has advocated the adoption of a shared and synergistic approach, suitable for ensuring a progressive and general improvement of the defense capabilities of what, to all intents and purposes, is considered as a further operational domain of the Alliance itself. Common cyber defence policy launched in 2008, when the conflict between Russia and Georgia highlighted the considerable risks of cyber warfare. It's from that period the *Policy on Cyber Defence* (aimed at defining the levels of protection of the Alliance's networks and establishing the minimum and essential security requirements of the networks

---

[21] Prodigious jewel, capable of "cloaking" the identity of the wearer, described by Platone nella *Repubblica.*

[22] In general, on the dynamics underlying the online attack, among many others.

[23] Formula with which we can refer to a multiplicity of behaviors carried out by agents that are quite disparate and that depending on the cases and situations can be substantiated: in the attack on critical infrastructures and essential services; in acts of digital vandalism; in obstruction of equipment; in espionage; in propaganda.

[24] In this case, these are real war actions that are conducted through the use of ICT and that: a) in some cases, can anticipate the military offensive (as, recently, happened in the Russian-Ukrainian conflict, characterized by a first IT phase of Denial of Service [DoS], during which all the sites of Ukrainian banks and government departments were literally blocked, becoming inaccessible); b) in other cases, they can serve as a tool to weaken enemy force (as happened with the use of the famous Stuxnet malware used to delay Iran's nuclear program); *c*) and, in still other cases, they can take on the most nuanced and larvate appearance of what is defined as a digital soft war (from secret surveillance of Internet users, to propaganda aimed at influencing public opinion and carried out through social media, as—in many respects—Zelens'kyj did with posts aimed at increasing his consent and discrediting the Russian government). On the other hand, criminal attacks by organizations, groups or even mercenaries, which—cloaked in the folds of the deep and dark web—can succeed in hitting the sensitive targets and resources of a State (altering communications and / or blocking operating systems of ministries, industries, banks, military bases, etc.).

of the member countries). Another fundamental step in the direction of greater digital security took place in 2014, with the adoption of the *Enhanced Policy on Cyber Defence*, which has consolidated the commitment to observe the principles of international law also in cyberspace, implementing the exchange of information between allies. During the Warsaw Summit in 2016—in view of the significant increase in cyber-attacks against NATO infrastructures (about 500 per month)—the *Cyber Defence Pledge*. Act, which was followed, in 2018, by the creation of the *Cyber Operations Centre* and, in 2020, the *Allied Joint Doctrine for Cyberspace Operations*. However, it is essential to remember that NATO's action—aimed at preventing, managing, and containing cyber threats—it always implies cooperation with partners and *in primis* and foremost with the European Union (as enshrined in the *NATO-EU Joint Declaration* and in *Technical Arrangement on Cyber Defence*), with the twin intent of *a*) increase own resiliency and *b*) encourage investment in new technologies.[25]

Looking at Italy (which has always participated in the Alliance's exercises on cyber-security(Saraceni and Mangiameli 2023), it must be said immediately that, compared to other states, such as France or Germany, our country has been slow to equip itself with an agency responsible for national cyber security. A delay, only recently filled with the establishment of the Agency for National Cybersecurity (ACN) (D.L. 14 June 2021, n. 82). The ACN's forecast, as well as the Cybersecurity Nucleus, represents a fundamental step forward in the rationalization and reorganization of cybersecurity governance. It is also appreciable that Parliament has decided to set up a technical-scientific committee (composed of qualified representatives of industry, research institutions, universities and sector associations), which is responsible for supporting and assisting the action of the ACN, with proposals and advice, in order to increase dialogue between all the actors involved and to identify the best strategies to raise the cyber security of our country. An intent reiterated, and then concretely supported, also by the National Recovery and Resilience Plan (PNRR) with the Fund for the implementation of the National Cybersecurity Strategy.

It is important to underline that in all the measures adopted so far—both at international level and at European and national level—there is an awareness of entering a space that, beyond the possible risks, is a bit like the sea (Mangiameli 2000). Described by Baudelaire (2015): unknown strength (and sometimes danger), but also seductive and irresistible appeal; A fruitful dimension, a harbinger of opportunities, relationships, riches and, in its own way, also an important opportunity for freedom. A dimension that, precisely for this reason, must continue to be regulated, pacified and, in a certain sense, saved by *law* (Cotta 1985; D'Agostino 2006). Hence too the appeal to a legal science and to an axiologically strong law—*jus quia justum!* (D'Agostino 2012)—because it can guarantee and always balance rights, freedoms, equality and security.

[25] A commitment, which was also reconfirmed by the NATO 2030 Agenda, which, identifying the Alliance's strategy for the next decade, has among its goals: (*i*) strengthening allied cyber defence capabilities; (*ii*) improving financing processes; (*iii*) internal Alliance recruitment and training; (*iv*) the provision of adequate political and legal apparatuses to deal with threats in the cyber domain.

After briefly summarized some of the main critical issues concerning the public sphere, let's move on to consider more closely the subjective sphere and the possible risks of digital for the fundamental rights of the individual. Meanwhile, as has already been partly said, we must start from the acknowledgment that we live immersed in a new context and in a new age, in which the so-called datism rages: a kind of religion based on the veneration of data, which in addition to having a particular importance (at a cognitive, economic, political, social level), are also shared continuously and as much as possible. It is a subtle mechanism that has been effectively illustrated by Harari:

Humanism believes that experiences happen within us, and that it is there that we should find the meaning of everything that happens [...]. Dataists [instead] believe that experiences are worthless if they are not shared [...]. We [...] need to record and connect our experiences [...]. Twenty years ago, Japanese tourists were the laughingstock of the global village as they always walked around armed with cameras and photographed any subject they came across. Now everyone is so [...] The new motto says: 'If you experience something—record it. If you record something—upload it. If you upload something—share it' (Harari 2018).

A decidedly realistic photograph, the one offered by the famous Israeli historian and essayist, which is inscribed in the bed of reflection—he advanced several years ago—by Bauman on the so-called confessional society, within which everyone (and, in particular, the youngest) no longer seemed to feel any desire to have secrets (Bauman and Lyon 2015).

Now, reconnecting to the observations developed in the second paragraph, it is certainly true that, when they are not exploited and distributed in an unequal and unequal way, but are shared and made accessible to all, data could act as a driving force for development, inclusion, equality and (why not) even greater sustainability. Which, in practice, would finally realize what was basically the hope of Tim Berners-Lee (2001): that is to say that the World Wide Web could improve the reticular existence of men in the world, allowing a profitable and equal exchange (*peer-to-peer*) of information between all people. Beyond the desirability of this type of approach to open data—substantially oriented to the common good and recently encouraged also at European level—the fact remains that, to date, within the digital universe, there are still several limitations and several traps that preclude an effectively widespread and free access to information. Just think, simply by way of example, of the algorithmic dynamics underlying filter bubbles (Pariser 2011), from the echo-chambers, but also to fake news (Saraceni and Mangiameli 2023).[26]

In addition, it is not at all rare that it is precisely the distorted and captious use of data (stolen, unduly manipulated, or completely counterfeited) that gives rise to

[26] "Altered, mystified and / or completely invented news, which, in various ways, alternate and overlap with respect to true information and authoritative content, fake news today represent one of the most pernicious forms of media pollution with which in the different digital environments (even if not simply in those) we are forced to confront and with respect to which, Almost continuously, we try to defend ourselves. A bit like what happened during the recent Covid-19 pandemic experience in the case of the much-talked-about Pandemic video (which invited people not to use masks and to be wary of the prescriptions imposed), then appropriately obscured by the platform managers".

compressions or real violations of the fundamental rights of the individual, among which, the most affected are the right to privacy, the right to image, but also the right to personal and sexual self-determination. Paradigmatic, in this sense, what happens with revenge porn (Paladino 2020), or with the undue dissemination of material (mostly images and videos) with sexually explicit content. Here—as in the case of other well-known computer crimes such as cyberstalking, cyberbullying, hate speech—the digitization and multimedia of data and content plays a primary role in implementing the harmful force of the conduct and amplifying the *vulnus* on the victim. This is essentially due to the fact that, due to the attitude of digitized data and information to permanency (i.e. permanence) and itinerancy (i.e. the ability to migrate from one platform to another), a kind of Doppler effect (i.e. a sort of autonomous wave of propagation and diffusion) of the contents themselves is produced within the ecosystem, which can easily imply the re-emergence in completely unexpected contexts and, consequently, the production of completely unforeseen and unpredictable repercussions.

Faced with the danger of a non-consensual dissemination of intimate content or that makes use of ICT to make persecutory, denigrating or discriminatory conduct even more penetrating, if, at national level, Law no. 69 of 19 July 2019 (so-called Red Code) (which led to the introduction of the ad hoc case referred to in art. 612-ter c.p.[27] and an increase in penalties for the offence referred to in Article 612-bis c.p.[28]), at European level, the *Proposal for a Directive of the European Parliament*

[27] Entitled—"Illicit dissemination of sexually explicit images or videos"—which reads: "1. Unless the fact constitutes a more serious crime, anyone who, after having made or stolen them, sends, delivers, assigns, publishes or disseminates images or videos with sexually explicit content, intended to remain private, without the consent of the persons represented, is punished with imprisonment from one to six years and a fine from € 5000 to € 15,000. 2. The same penalty shall apply to any person who, having received or otherwise acquired the images or videos referred to in the first subparagraph, sends, delivers, assigns, publishes or disseminates them without the consent of the persons represented with a view to causing them harm. 3. The penalty is increased if the acts are committed by the spouse, even separated or divorced, or by a person who is or has been linked by emotional relationship to the injured person or if the facts are committed through IT or telematic tools. 4. The penalty shall be increased from one third to one half if the acts are committed to the detriment of a person in a condition of physical or mental inferiority or to the detriment of a pregnant woman. 5. The crime is punished on complaint of the injured person. The deadline for filing a lawsuit is six months. The remission of the complaint can only be procedural. However, proceedings shall be taken ex officio in the cases referred to in the fourth paragraph, as well as when the act is connected with another offence for which proceedings must be taken ex officio".

[28] This is the conduct of "persecutory acts": "1. Unless the fact constitutes a more serious crime, anyone who, with repeated conduct, threatens or harasses someone in such a way as to cause a persistent and serious state of anxiety or fear or to generate a well-founded fear for one's own safety or that of a close relative or person linked to him by an emotional relationship or emotional relationship is punished with imprisonment from one year to six years and six months or to force the same to alter their habits of life. 2. The penalty is increased if the act is committed by the spouse, even separated or divorced, or by a person who is or has been linked by emotional relationship to the injured person or if the act is committed through IT or telematic tools. 3. The penalty is increased up to half if the act is committed to the detriment of a minor, a pregnant woman or a person with disabilities referred to in Article 3 of Law no. 104 of 5 February 1992, or with weapons or by a misrepresented person. 4. The crime is punished on complaint of the injured person. The

and of the Council on combating violence against women and domestic violence of 8 March 2022 deserves applause, with which—as part of the fight against gender-based violence—a specific space has been dedicated to combating online violence. In this sense, the article 7:

Member States shall ensure that the following intentional conduct is punishable as a criminal offence:

(a) make accessible to multiple end-users, through information and communication technology, images, videos or other intimate material depicting another person's sexual acts without his or her consent.
(b) to produce or manipulate and subsequently make accessible to multiple end-users, by means of information and communication technology, images, videos or other material in such a way as to give the impression that another person is engaging in sexual acts, without the consent of the data subject.
(c) threaten the conduct referred to in points (a) and (b) to force another person to, consent or refrain from, a particular act.

Mind you, the urgency of intervening to guarantee freedom, security, and protection of rights in cyberspace, in this case, is even more felt and perceived as a duty. The reason is due to the fact that, with the non-consensual dissemination of sexually explicit material, the intimacy of sexuality—a symbol of free, spontaneous, and gratuitous gift of oneself to the other—turns into an act of abuse, violence and domination over the other (D'agostino 2014). Pornographic nudity is exposed to anyone's view and without any filter or mystery. Hence, as a note Byung-Chul Han (2019), an authentic act of desecration not only of the relationship, but also and above all of the image and dignity of the person, with all the legal consequences (but also psychological and sociological) that can derive from it and that, alas, events that have risen to international prominence such as those of Anna Mayer, Marianna Taschinger, Tessa Komer and Tiziana Cantone have tragically highlighted.

5 Minimum Conclusions

The synergistic interweaving of the three perspectives proposed here, even in summary, has tried to offer a cross-section of the scenario that today's technological society places before the European jurist, with requests that, in some cases, are above all of understanding and support (I am thinking above all of digital citizenship, education and information, the exercise of democracy), in other circumstances, They are accompanying and adapting regulations (the discipline of e-commerce is

deadline for filing a lawsuit is six months. The remission of the complaint can only be procedural. The complaint is in any case irrevocable if the act was committed by repeated threats in the manner referred to in the second paragraph of Article 612. However, proceedings shall be taken ex officio if the act is committed against a minor or a person with disabilities referred to in Article 3 of Law no. 104 of 5 February 1992, as well as when the act relates to another crime for which proceedings must be taken ex officio.

emblematic), while, in other cases, they are prevention and protection (with particular attention to minors, the disabled, women and, in general, to all those vulnerable categories that may risk being exposed to dangerous situations).

Aware of the enormous potential offered by digital—which, to paraphrase Santyana's observations, is like a knife sunk into the future (Santayana 1905), from which it is not possible, nor rationally desirable, to escape—and, at the same time, aware of the risks and regulatory gaps, albeit through different perspectives, we wish to formulate our observations in the form of a renewed appeal to the jurist and the European legislator to remain faithful to what is their fundamental and inexhaustible mission: to juggle as best they can between *jus conditum* and *jus condendum*, in respect of what is the anthropological and socionomic attitude of law (Cotta 1985).

References

Barberis M (2020) Come internet sta uccidendo la democrazia (p. 159). Chiarelettere.

Baudelaire C (2015) Les Fleurs du Mal. Gallimard

Bradbury R (1978) Fahrenheit 451, trad. it. G. Monicelli, Mondadori, Milano

Bauman Z, Lyon D (2015) Sesto potere: la sorveglianza nella modernità liquida. Gius. Laterza & Figli Spa

Berners-Lee T (2001) L'architettura del nuovo Web. Dall'inventore della rete il progetto di una comunicazione democratica, interattiva e intercreativa. Feltrinelli Editore

Campagnoli MN (2020) Informazione, social network & diritto: dalle fake news all'hate speech online: risvolti sociologici, profili giuridici, interventi normativi

Carr A (2013) How square register's UI guilts you into leaving tips. Fast Company, 3

Carrino A (2014) Il problema della sovranità nell'età della globalizzazione. Rivista di Politica: Trimestrale di Studi, Analisi e Commenti 2(2014):151–174

Cotta S (1968) La sfida tecnologica, Bologna. Il Mulino, 80

Cotta S (1979) Perché il diritto (p. 106). Morcelliana

Cotta S (1985) Il diritto nell'esistenza: Linee di ontofenomenologia giuridica

D'Agostino F (2006) Elementi per una Teoria. Cinisello Balsamo

D'Agostino F (2012) Jus quia justum: lezioni di filosofia del diritto e della religione (vol 112). G Giappichelli Editore

D'agostino F (2014) Sessualità. Premesse teoriche di una riflessione giuridica. Torino, Giappichelli

Dionigi I (2019) Osa sapere. Contro la paura e l'ignoranza (p. 48). Solferino

Dumouchel P, Damiano L (2019) Vivere con i robot. Saggio sull'empatia artificiale

Floridi L (2017) La quarta rivoluzione: come l'infosfera sta trasformando il mondo. Raffaello Cortina Editore

Floridi L (2020) Il verde e il blu: Idee ingenue per migliorare la politica. Raffaello Cortina Editore

Fukuyama F (2020) La fine della storia e l'ultimo uomo. Utet

Giovanni Ziccardi (2022) Diritti digitali. Informatica giuridica per le nuove professioni (p. 81). Raffaello Cortina Editore

Granieri G (2006) La società digitale (pp. 28–29). Laterza

Han BC (2019) Eros in agonia. Nottetempo

Harari YN (2018) Homo Deus : a brief history of tomorrow. HarperCollins Publishers

Hayek FV (1986) Legge, legislazione e libertà: una nuova enunciazione dei principi liberali della giustizia e dell'economia politica. Milano: Il Saggiatore

Held D (1995) Democracy and the global order: From the modern state to cosmopolitan governance. Stanford University Press

Hobbes T (1894) Leviathan: Or, the matter, form, and power of a commonwealth ecclesiastical and civil (vol 21). G. Routledge and sons
Huntington SP (2000) The Clash of Civilizations and the Remaking of World Order (1996), trad. it. Lo scontro delle civiltà e il nuovo ordine mondiale, Garzanti, Milano
Lévy P (2002) L'intelligenza collettiva. Per un'antropologia del cyberspazio. Feltrinelli editore
Kahneman D (2012) Pensieri lenti e veloci. Edizioni Mondadori
Kahneman D, Slovic P, Tversky A (1982) Judgment under uncertainty: heuristics and biases Cambridge. MA: Cambridge
Macrì I (2022) Digitalizzazione, innovazione e sicurezza nella PA. IPSOA
Mangiameli ACA (2000) Diritto e cyberspace: appunti di informatica giuridica e filosofia del diritto
Mangiameli ACA (2004) Stati post-moderni e diritto dei popoli. RECTA RATIO
Mangiameli ACA (2015) Informatica giuridica (2nd ed., p. 320). Giappichelli
Mangiameli ACA (2017) Tecno-regolazione e diritto. Brevi note su limiti e differenze. IL DIRITTO DELL'INFORMAZIONE E DELL'INFORMATICA, 147–167
Mangiameli ACA, Campagnoli MN (2020) Strategie digitali.# diritto_educazione_tecnologie. RECTA RATIO
Mayer-Schönberger V, Ramge T (2018) Reinventare il capitalismo nell'era dei big data. EGEA spa
Paladino A (2020) Revenge porn e cyberbullismo. Alpes Italia
Pariser E (2011) The filter bubble: What the Internet is hiding from you. penguin UK
Ramge T, Mayer-Schoenberger V (2021) Fuori i dati!: Rompere i monopoli sulle informazioni per rilanciare il progresso. EGEA spa
Rodotà S (2015) *Il diritto di avere diritti* (p. 270). Laterza
Sadin É (2018) La silicolonizzazione del mondo. Giulio Einaudi Editore
Santayana G (1905) The life of reason: Introduction and reason in common sense. The MIT Press, 1
Saraceni G, Mangiameli AAC (2023) Cento e una voce di informatica giuridica. Giappichelli
Schmitt C (1932) Der Begriff des Politischen: mit einer Rede über das Zeitalter der Neutralisierungen und Entpolitisierungen. Duncker & Humblot
Schmitt C (1950) Die Lage der europäischen Rechtswissenschaft
Schmitt C (1991) Der Nomos der erde im Völkerrecht des Jus Publicum Euroapeum (1950), Duncker & Humblot, Berlin, 1974; tr. it. Il Nomos della Terra, 42–47
Schmitt C (1995) Der Leviathan in der Staatslehre des Thomas Hobbes: Sinn und Fehlschlag eines politischen Symbols. Klett-Cotta
Schmitt C (2002) Land und Meer: eine weltgeschichtliche Betrachtung. Klett-Cotta
Schmitt C (2006) The Nomos of the earth in the international law of the Jus Publicum Europaeum. Telos Press
Schmitt C, Maschke G (1995) Staat, Großraum, Nomos. Arbeiten aus den Jahren 1916–1969. Herausgegeben
Severino E (1998) Il destino della tecnica. Bur
Severino P (2022) Intelligenza artificiale: politica, economia, diritto, tecnologia (pp. 1–189). LUISS University Press
Simon HA (1955) A behavioral model of rational choice. Q J Econ 99–118
Thaler R, Sunstein CR. (2022) Nudge. La spinta gentile: La nuova strategia per migliorare le nostre decisioni su denaro, salute, felicità. L'edizione definitiva. Feltrinelli Editore
Weinmann M, Schneider C, Brocke JV (2016) Digital nudging. Bus Inf Syst Eng 58:433–436
Zuboff S (2023) The age of surveillance capitalism. In Social theory re-wired (pp. 203–213). Routledge

Which Data Governance for a Social Post-pandemic Recovery?

Maria Francesca De Tullio

1 Introduction

First, the research will consider how big data influences democratic processes, what connection exists between data protection and collective self-determination processes, as well as how data control affects inequalities within society. This first part will lay the backdrop to analyse, secondly, the EU regulatory framework for data governance, especially the *European Data Strategy* (European Commission 2020) and its follow up. Indeed, a series of regulatory proposals and acts were approved with the objective of creating European Data Spaces, able to foster competition along with human rights protection. The ultimate question, then, is whether these policies represent a way for the EU to improve its sovereignty through a social democratic accountability. Then, final remarks will be drawn about guiding principles for data policy to be oriented towards a more inclusive citizenship.

2 Data and Digital Sovereignty: Old and New Issues

Today, the concentration of online markets has questioned the illusion that the web could innovate politics by challenging the traditional structures and hierarchies of politics and information. Political studies (*ex multis*, Amoretti and Santaniello 2021, p. 63) show that new intermediate actors emerged in the Internet, not always committing to the protection of human rights and democracy. Nowadays, private ownership of immaterial goods, like source codes and big data, is critical for participation, as they represent—respectively—the procedures and informational ground for the exercise of political rights. Consequently, the exclusive domain of few economic

M. F. De Tullio (✉)
Federico II University of Naples, Naples, Italy
e-mail: mfdetullio@gmail.com

G. Enes et al. (eds.), *A Digital Europe for Citizens*,
https://doi.org/10.1007/978-3-032-02500-5_6

actors on these assets deprives communities of the possibility of controlling—and sometimes even knowing—decision-making modalities and phenomena on which political decisions are made.

While market dominations fall under the domain of antitrust law, as they concern the competition among private actors, they also affect fundamental freedoms in public sphere, making the digital a very specific entrepreneurial activity. In this context, offline rules on information, free speech, and electoral campaigns have little effect on the digital world; on the other hand, new rules, adequate to technological development, have yet to be enacted.

Informational assets are the core of these dynamics, as social media platforms use data-driven business models. A general description of these models will make it clear how such markets naturally generate dominance and oligopolies.

Platforms operate in a 'two-sided' market. On the one 'side', entrepreneurs provide a service—apparently free of charge—in exchange for the transfer of data concerning users' identity and behaviour. On the other 'side', these businesses profit from this data on a different market: e.g. they sell targeted advertising services to other economic actors or by creating artificial intelligence.

Such mechanisms systematically favour those who are already strong (Macchiati 2010, p. 478; Wang 2014, pp. 7–9; Newman 2014, pp. 411–420), as they produce 'indirect network effects'. Those who buy advertising space invest little in the newly established companies, because they have little information about surfers and are therefore less effective. Users are also more attracted to the dominant provider, since the latter has more data and more advertising revenue, therefore they have more resources to improve the service. This makes it impossible for the newcomers to collect data to finance the initial costs and start operations.[1]

Such dominance has an impact on fundamental rights and equality. Platform dominance affects the visibility of content, and thus freedom of expression. With regard to privacy, dominance allows platforms to impose their own conditions on the transfer of data by users, without users being able to find substantially different treatment from other competitors. The impacts on political participation are obvious: big players can thus monitor and direct the conduct of users while hiding their algorithms behind commercial secrecy.

This impact has also been recognised in the legal debate. For example, the District Court of Virginia has ruled that the behaviour of a politician with an institutional role who blocks a user on social media is unlawful because it restricts participatory rights.[2]

Moreover, the power of these platforms is not neutral, but based on individual profiling and on a majority criterion that gives more visibility to posts that receive more clicks, likes or shares. These parameters are linked to the economic needs of

---

[1] Autorité de la Concurrence, Bundeskartellamt (2016, pp. 11–13). Even more, this is true as high initial investments are required to conduct business in this sector: (Verhaert 2012–2013, p. 12).

[2] United States District Court for the Eastern District of Virginia—Alexandria Division, *Brian c. Davison, v. Loudoun County Board of Supervisors, et al.*, 1:16cv932 (JCC/IDD), 25/7/2017.

the platforms: the aim is to provide not correct information, but attractive content, so that the user stays as long as possible on the platform, leaving more data.

However, these criteria are sometimes critical. For example, in the case of Cambridge Analytica, candidates presented content profiled according to individual user-voters, with distorting effects on election campaigns. Equally critical is the formation of 'echo chambers', i.e. 'chambers' of conversation among 'similars', which strengthen the bonds between like-minded people and limit exposure to different thoughts (Flaxman, Goel, and Rao 2016, p. 307 ss.), thus fuelling the so-called hate speech. Moreover, privileging 'popular' contents has the defect of systematically favouring mainstream and majority ideas (Chandler 2007, pp. 1108–1109), as well as the so-called astroturfing, i.e. a set of techniques with which candidates create an apparent consensus from below, through the so-called 'coordinated inauthentic behaviours': the use of fake accounts, bots, people remunerated for the purpose, or other tools (Darmanin 2017).

In addition to the above risks for participatory rights, data-driven business models have also proven to generate concentrated markets that exclude newcomers (Visco Comandini 2018; Claussen 2018). Hence, market dominators have stronger negotiating positions, inducing users to systematically waiver fundamental rights as the only way to enjoy a given Internet service (Schermer et al. 2014).

In particular, this model is risky for antitrust law as it tends to stabilise the market power of already strong players. In this way, it puts them in a position to engage in independent behaviour with respect to consumers and competitors, which may also be aimed at abusively exploiting, maintaining or expanding the monopoly.[3] The sale of information for advertising purposes created, in particular, barriers to entry (Verband Deutscher Maschinen- und Anlagenbau 2016, p. 9) and closed markets that would otherwise have been wide open. Traditionally, technology was considered a contestable and competitive sector, where anyone could achieve a sales boom with an innovative stunt (Autorité de la Concurrence, Bundeskartellamt 2016, pp. 29–33; Lianos and Motchenkova 2014, p. 429). Today this is no longer the case, because no 'good idea' could improve the service to the same extent as the huge archives held by the already dominant player: it has been proven that the improvement of the algorithm does not give the same yield as the increase in the database on which it is applied. This circumstance puts new entrants at a disadvantage, as they do not have the means to purchase an information set comparable to that of the dominant.[4]

---

[3] Commissione Europea, Comunicazione della Commissione—Orientamenti sulle priorità della Commissione nell'applicazione dell'articolo 82 del trattato CE al comportamento abusivo delle imprese dominanti volto all'esclusione dei concorrenti, 2009/C 45/02, §§ 10–17; Corte di Giustizia dell'Unione Europea, Ditta Hoffmann-La Roche & Co. AG c. Commissione delle Comunità europee, C-85/76, 13/2/1979, http://curia.europa.eu/juris/showPdf.jsf?text=&docid=89251&pageIndex=0&doclang=IT&mode=lst&dir=&occ=first&part=1&cid=7535, punto 38. See Osti 2011; Floridia and Catelli 2003; Varhaert 2012–2013.

[4] Autorité de la Concurrence, Bundeskartellamt, pp. 11–13. As an alternative, data brokers can be involved, but this would have additional costs and would not allow to obtain the same results: *Ibidem*, pp. 36–41.

The value generated by the network giants through the proprietary acquisition of data has so far entirely remained in Silicon Valley. It has not trickled down to society,[5] nor to EU economy. In light of these remarks, data sharing has become a priority of EU policies. Protecting of consumers and human rights has been a legal obligation, but also the basic claim for the promotion of economic models alternative to and competitive with the US ones. Hence, the Commission with its data strategy has tried to unleash the potential of EU companies by urging them to move towards data sharing to improve their informational patrimony (Valero 2016). This strategy is an indication that the 'locking' of big data into few corporate repositories is hardly defensible even from the point of view of free competition and efficiency.

The above scenario of market concentration was even clearer with the outbreak of Covid-19. Indeed, individuals and organisations—but also public institutions themselves—found themselves having to transfer their activities to digital platforms (Bilancia, 2020). It was clearer, then, that public administrations and civil society had few alternatives to corporate software, due to the lack of previous public investments in open, fair and trustworthy technology, affordable for people with less literacy, with low performance devices and networks, and/or with limited economic resources. These circumstances were demonstrated by the overload of free/open services. For example, Framasoft—one of the leading actors of FLOSS solutions—in such a situation denounced the scarcity of resources for open services and paradoxically tried to discourage the use of its software by public institutions and other actors who could afford paid software.

De iure condendo, this situation would require a discipline capable of protecting human rights beyond the mere market competition considerations. Indeed, competition law is by nature designed to protect economic values, and therefore traditionally only punishes conducts that harm these interests, i.e. that causes harm to the user that is not adequately compensated by the efficiencies generated. However, *de iure condito*, it would be possible for the EU implementing authorities to consider evolutionary interpretation of these regulatory mechanisms, as market protection should be inseparable from the guarantee of fundamental rights, if not functionalised to it (Drexl 2016, p. 20 ss.).

For example, according to some scholars, even the infringement to privacy—deriving from a dominant position—can be considered a competitive abuse, as it diminishes product quality. In other words, dominations and mergers would allow the few firms in the industry not to compete with each other on product quality: consumers are forced to buy services that infringe on their privacy because they could not get better treatment from any competitor (De Minico 2019, p. 104). This solution would be fitting the technological world, considering that online markets often provide apparently priceless services where the transmission of individual data acts as a compensation; therefore, if only price abuses are taken into account, the

[5] «The law of the market seems to have won in the end. Because of that, the weaker parties do not receive the additional protection that they would deserve in accordance with the network promoted as the new lever of modern constitutionalism» (De Minico 2015, p. 29). Cfr. concerning data distribution (MacDonnell and Castro 2016, pp. 2, 12).

discipline fails to actually recognise anticompetitive behaviours. In this case, the issue of remedies also arises, considering that the regulation would protect not only the consumerist status, but also—and mainly—the fundamental rights infringed, through the restoration of sufficient conditions to ensure the protection of privacy.

In this evolutionary track there are also those theses claiming that today the anti-competitive nature of dominations and mergers should be assessed not only based on market share, but also on the possession of big data (De Minico 2017), entailing potential infringements of fundamental rights.

3 Data Governance and the Emergence of Privacy as a Collective Self-Determination Right

3.1 Information Control and Popular Sovereignty

The balancing rule between the exploitation of big data and fundamental rights related to data protection can only be identified starting from a legal framing of the two terms of the comparison: first, the interest in the use of data, then, data protection.

The first value, the use of data, does not always have the same weight in the balancing, as it does not always receive the same protection from the constitutional system: data is suitable to different uses, and therefore entitlements related to its collection derive their nature and rank from the purpose for which it is functionalised from time to time.

That being said, it can be noted that the purposes of the exploitation of big data, and hence the legal values involved in the balancing act, may be various. In fact, information repositories themselves can serve both individual profit and the fulfilment of fundamental rights. For instance, the data that Google collects for its own commercial interests could also benefit the right to health, as it allows the study of the spread of a disease. Thus, the interest in the exploitation of big data can be functional to economic freedoms, as well as serving inviolable rights and equality. This dual vocation must be taken into account.

Among the inviolable rights is also awareness as a cognitive prerequisite for the exercise of political and social participation rights. Indeed, the informational value of big data is also functional to the effectiveness of social control over governmental and economic elites. Thus, information, when distributed among members of society, makes it possible to 'profile' large actors and collect data on their actions, making these actors more responsive to the general will (Koops 2008, p. 6).

If, on the other hand, big data does not spread, but is centralised in few hands, a form of surveillance takes place, allowing a minority of privileged actors to learn about phenomena and people without being in turn observed by society. These information asymmetries, as such, are also an interference in collective freedoms, which transposed on a large scale creates powers antagonistic to popular sovereignty, equally strong or perhaps stronger, but oriented towards different ends (Federal Trade Commission 2016, pp. 8–11).

Surveillance in itself affects the self-determination of any controlled person or group, for at least three reasons. Firstly, collecting data on a person's life gives the possibility of influencing them with the threat of revealing compromising details (Schwartz 1999–2000, pp. 841–842; Solove 2006, pp. 539–541); so much so that in some cases governments have attempted to blackmail its main opponents in this way (Spencer 2002, p. 572). Secondly, as the testimonies from contexts of dictatorship show, espionage agents, if in a position to make decisions about the person under surveillance, may induce self-censorship, dictated by fear of the consequences that may result from certain behaviours or statements (Paye 2016; Solove 2006, pp. 493–498, 549–553).[6] Alternatively, self-censorship can also result from fear of social blame. Thirdly, those who control others can covertly influence their decisions, to the extent that according to some theorists States should learn the fallacies in the common citizen's reasoning and exploit them to influence their choices in the direction the administration deems most convenient and beneficial (Roberts 2013, pp. 17–26).[7] Consider, for example, a study showing that on average, the risk of a catastrophic but improbable event is more frightening than the risk of a minor but probable damage; in this case, those familiar with this research would have one more tool to create generalised alarm about a given phenomenon.

For the above reasons, data collection has an impact on individual and collective rights of people, both as individuals and parts of a broader society.

3.2 Privacy from Individual to Collective Entitlement

It has been noted so far that the use of big data presents a tension between potentiality and reality: information infrastructures may serve the general interest, but they are mostly a tool for exercising and maintaining economic or authoritarian power. It is now useful to analyse the other term of the balance, privacy, in order to understand whether it is sufficiently protected today in relation to the purposes pursued with the processing of information and, if not, to understand how its guarantee can become more effective.

Privacy and related rights are protected by Article 8 of the European Convention on Human Rights and Art. 8 of the Charter of Fundamental Rights of European Union. In particular, its main safeguard is given by Regulation 2016/679 (GDPR).

In such a system, privacy is constructed as 'informational self-determination', i.e. the right to full control over one's own information and not just secrecy: even when

---

[6] European Union Court of Justice, Digital Rights Ireland Ltd v. Ireland, C-293/12 and C-594/12, 8/4/2014, http://eur-lex.europa.eu/legal-content/EN/TXT/?uri=CELEX%3A62012CJ0293. Certain direct experiences are described in Turner (2016), Theoharis (2016), and Perlroth (2016).

[7] These opinions are also described in Koops (2008, p. 2). On libertarian paternalism, Sunstein (2005, ch. VIII).

data are no longer 'hidden'—because they have already been transferred to others, or to the same individual for different purposes—the individual can prevent any further use of them.[8] This choice is made by means of a contract by which the 'data subject' gives consent to specific processing, subject to prior information[9] and without prejudice to the rights of the data subject, including the right of access to information concerning him or her, and the right to rectification and erasure in the event of errors and violations.[10] This legal construction derives from the conception of privacy as an inviolable right, essential for the autonomous formation of the personality in the internal forum and in the relationship with others.

Precisely because privacy is a fundamental freedom of the person, its compression for economic needs poses certain problems in terms of respect for fundamental rights. The Court of Justice[11] explained that confidentiality, as an inviolable right, should in principle prevail over economic interests; instead, this good is currently being sacrificed by the legislator with the processing of huge masses of data for profit.

Despite this principle, it seems that fundamental rights struggle to prevail over economic interests. One of the reasons seems to be the current discipline of consent, which appears insufficient for its purpose of protection. In fact, on the one hand it entrusts the protection of privacy to an unfair negotiation between consumer and entrepreneur, and on the other it does not adequately take into account the collective interest that insists on informational self-determination.

Indeed, privacy today is also such an interest, collective as well as individual: *rectius* it can only be protected in the hands of each individual if it is guaranteed to all, because the dispositive act of one also has negative effects on third parties.[12] There are at least three arguments in support of this claim, which therefore justify a general regulation limiting individuals' rights.

The first argument lies in the contribution that each new consent to data processing makes to the domination of a few social-economic power centres (Morozov 2013) which place themselves in unfair competition with popular sovereignty. A second argument that manifests a collective dimension of privacy is related to the danger of discrimination inherent in data mining, which has potential repercussions on society as a whole. «The use of algorithmic profiling for the allocation of resources is, in a certain sense, inherently discriminatory: profiling takes place when data subjects are grouped in categories according to various variables, and decisions are made on the basis of subjects falling within so-defined groups» (Goodman and Flaxman 2016, p. 27). An immediate example is the investigation of jihadist terrorism: if statistics

[8] Art. 5, Regulation (EU) 2016/679 (hereinafter GDPR).

[9] On consent, in particular: *considd.* 32, 40, 42, 43, 47, 58, 60, Artt. 4, n. 11, artt. 6–7, Artt. 12-13 GDPR.

[10] *Considd.* 59, 63, 65-67, 70, artt. 16–18, 20–21 GDPR.

[11] Google Spain SL, Google Inc. contro Agencia Española de Protección de Datos (AEPD), Mario Costeja González, C-131/12, 13/5/2014, http://eur-lex.europa.eu/legal-content/IT/TXT/HTML/?uri=CELEX:62012CJ0131&from=HR, punti 97 e 99.

[12] In this sense, Hirsch (2005 § 2) compares infringements to privacy to environmental damage: the company damages a common good without bearing the costs. They capture at least a relational dimension of confidentiality, if not a collective one (Rodotà 1995, pp. 11–39).

reveal that the attackers are mostly young men from certain Arab countries and of the Islamic religion, then those who display these characteristics will be under special surveillance (Bignami 2007, p. 637).

A third and final argument is more structural: the output of data mining does not arise from an analysis of isolated data, but rather from a probabilistic investigation that results from crossing and combining as much information as possible, even from different subjects. In fact, data-driven choices are made not on the individual, but on the group in which the individual is placed according to statistics (Vedder 2000, pp. 14–18). Each person therefore has a legal interest in how much and what data others disclose and in the correctness of this information, because decisions are also made about the person itself on the basis of such group parameters (Mantelero 2016, pp. 12–14).

All these reasons highlight the need for a new discipline of data, capable of creating data spaces to foster fair competition. Moreover—and primarily—it becomes necessary to ensure a democratic governance of data assets, capable of safeguarding individual and collective self-determination. Here, in order to remedy these flaws in the system, a limitation of the individual's power to alienate his or her own data can be proposed, to be provided by law in combination with an instrument of 'collective bargaining' over information.

3.3 *Towards a Discipline of Open Public and Private Data*

The deeper meaning of collective informational self-determination, as described so far, is to allocate big data for the benefit of the community, for the enjoyment of fundamental rights and the exercise of popular sovereignty. To this end, we must move towards a general rule that, with some exceptions, contemplates the 'openness' of both public and private big data.[13]

In particular, the technical rule of 'openness' of data corresponds to a rule inherent in EU and Member States law, according to which information infrastructures and their monetary value must follow the same regime as inviolable freedoms, since they are an instrument of such values. Just as individual and collective fundamental rights must be exercised by all equally, so also big data must be managed in a non-dominant and participatory manner, for the use and benefit of the entire community (Evans 2016, pp. 8–11). For these reasons, the *Open Data Directive*[14] provides for wide possibility of reuse of public sector information; more recently, the *Data Governance Act*[15] provides for mechanisms to facilitate the reuse of certain public sector data that

[13] The scenary, together with alternative ones, is clearly explained in Wells and Scott (2016).

[14] Directive (EU) 2019/1024 of the European Parliament and of the Council of 20 June 2019 on open data and the re-use of public sector information (recast), PE/28/2019/REV/1, OJ 172 del 26 June 2019.

[15] Regulation (EU) 2022/868 of the European Parliament and of the Council of 30 May 2022 on European data governance and amending Regulation (EU) 2018/1724 (Data Governance Act) (Text with EEA relevance), PE/85/2021/REV/1, GU L 152 del 3 June 2022. Hereinafter DGA.

cannot be made available as open data. Therefore, it is crucial for governments to implement these prescriptions, by removing obstacles that prevent a certain number of EU citizens and inhabitants—especially disadvantaged ones—from actively using public open data to increase their democratic participation. Indeed, it is well known that there are still different forms of digital divide—concerning, for example, devices, alphabetisation, and networks—affecting European data spaces.

Moreover, it is necessary for the public sector to take actions against possible discriminatory outcomes of public data collection. Indeed, it has been observed that certain personal conditions entail a set of advantages—such as level of education, awareness of one's rights, availability of time, etc.—that facilitate frequent and effective contact with institutions. Conversely, there are people whose very existence is not even registered by the public administration, such as undocumented migrants or those living in extreme poverty. This means that discrimination is intertwined: the public administration has more data on the people with whom it most often comes into contact, i.e. those who are also privileged in other social spheres.

For these reasons, specific dispositives should be put in place in order to make public data collection a means to empower the voice of citizens and inhabitants, particularly the disadvantaged ones. A possible way could be for the public sector to support citizens science experiments (Evans 2016, pp. 11–16, 25–30), where individual persons and groups—in partnership with territorial, research or other institutions—can voluntarily produce their own data, with the aim of contributing to research identified by the community itself. A second example might be the data assemblies carried out in New York City,[16] which, on the model of the public debate, allow for the collective elaboration of some proposals regarding the questions that the administration should ask itself as a prerequisite for collecting data to formulate policies. In this case, values with a specific inclusive content were placed at the basis of the experimentation: increasing data and information literacy, equity and engagement, understood as the possibility for people to have a leading role in public policies.

Finally, it is crucial to address the issue of privately held data that are currently protected from public access, even if these databases contain important masses of information that can have a significant role in fostering general interest: «the status quo is that data are widely scattered in proprietary corporate databases, creating a tragedy of the anticommons that threatens to leave valuable stores of data inaccessible for research and other beneficial use» (Evans 2006, p. 15). Therefore, it becomes increasingly crucial for public sector to create a framework to accommodate and prioritise different interests on data, by allowing forms of disclosure of private data, able to liberate their value without disproportionately affecting economic rights.

For these reasons, the present discipline on consent to data processing shows limits in relation to its protective purpose. Indeed, the allegedly 'free' consent is actually entrusted to an unequal negotiation between consumers and entrepreneurs; therefore, data can be transferred even when data subjects are not fully willing to give them, but just accepting the transfer as a condition. Even if this act affects collective

[16] https://thedataassembly.org/.

interests—as shown before—there is no place where a collective will of netizens can be expressed and counterbalance the inequality of individual consent. Instead, it may be possible for a law provision to limit the data subject's power of alienating individual data, also with forms of 'collective negotiation' on information. This solution entails a compression of individual freedom, but not from an authoritarian and paternalistic perspective, according to which people would be incapable and in need of a 'tutor-State' (Maniaci 2014, pp. 675, 697). Oppositely, it responds to a physiologic balancing between constitutional values which would protect the alienating person and the community in their informational self-determination rights.

Normally, only entitlement, and not the exercise, of an inviolable right is not renounceable (Resta 2002, pp. 807–808, 816; Rose-Ackerman 1985, pp. 937–941, 960, 962–963). This is because the democratic order seeks to restrict freedoms as little as possible, since it considers that no one is more qualified than the person concerned to choose their own personality and life project, even when this self-determination results in the acceptance of negative effects in one's legal sphere.[17] It cannot be overlooked, however, that every freedom must be harmonised with the requirements of equal protection of rights that are inherent in the constitutional system. And in this sense, it will be noted that a wider unavailability of personal data is necessary to protect two goods of collective importance: substantive equality in the enjoyment of the right to privacy and the community's interest in privacy.

4 Post-Pandemic Recovery and Data Governance

In light of the above principles, it is possible to analyse EU digital policies, with special reference to data policies.

As mentioned above, pandemic created a real 'stress test' for the digitalization of our lives, as the majority of our everyday activities shifted online. This circumstance highlighted the need for a stronger public intervention in the online economy, using public funding to orient private actors' action towards the general interest (Mazzucato 2020).

In that sense, Covid-19 allowed the emersion of new regulatory needs concerning digitalization, hence it exacerbated a process that was already in place at the EU level. For this reason, notwithstanding the exceptional events, the post-pandemic digital strategy of the EU is designed in continuity with the efforts of the data strategy. However, it is important to observe the specific political options adopted in this period, translated by referring to two main policy documents: the Communication *Shaping Europe's Digital Future* and the *Digital Compass 2030: the European model for digital decade* (European Commission 2021).[18]

---

[17] Corte Europea dei Diritti dell'Uomo, *Case of Deweer v. Belgium*, Application no. 6903/75, 27/2/1980, in http://hudoc.echr.coe.int/eng?i=001-57469, § 49.

[18] The analysis of these documents is the outcome of an interdisciplinary work made with Adriano Cozzolino—from the legal and political science standpoint—in the development of the joint paper

In the two communications, two elements have a special role: the global projection of the EU and the idea of democracy that emerges from the documents. Concerning the first, through the instrument of 'international partnerships' the Commission aims at strengthening the global role of the Union and the digital has a special place. In the *Digital Compass*, the Commission states that «The degree of digitalisation of an economy or society has been shown not only to be a critical underpinning of economic and societal resilience, but also a factor in global influence. As the pandemic has highlighted the extent to which digital policy is never value-neutral, with competing models on offer the EU now has an opportunity to promote its positive and humancentric vision of the digital economy and society». Therefore, digital is clearly an essential element of a broader geo-political strategy to strengthen the EU in the global scenario.

The idea of democracy emerging from the document provides some social measures, namely the improvement of the access to the Internet, the alphabetisation, and the full accessibility of digital services. Nevertheless, the overarching model emerging from the *Digital Compass* is declared to be the 'government as a platform'. This paradigm is based on the 'thin state', where the public sector is supposed to provide only the backbone of the digital-administrative infrastructure, thus allowing a broad private intervention (O'Reilly 2010).

Underlying government as a platform is the idea that the government apparatus would no longer be able to fulfil all its performance duties and would therefore need a different strategy to fulfil its responsibilities. In particular, it should transform itself into a 'platform' where private individuals—who are endowed with the means and capabilities—can find all the necessary resources to develop services of general interest; at that point, the public entity should only produce directly those services that private individuals are not interested in providing.

In this sense, this strand gives a new technological twist to the theories of the 'small state', reducing—arguably excessively—the public presence and responsibility in the social and economic fabric.

The fundamental pivot of this view is that the government apparatus should become platform-like: it should not create sites and applications for the end user itself, but set up simple, available and publicly accessible infrastructures that 'expose' the underlying data (Robinson, Yu, Zeller, and Felten 2009, p. 161). In this way, private parties themselves could take charge of using data and infrastructure to implement the necessary services.

In effect, the government would come to have an open relationship with the private parties, through a division of roles that goes beyond the traditional concept of vertical administration: using the metaphor of a motorway, the public entity would be responsible for building the infrastructure and the 'rules of the road', stimulating the private parties—with their efficiency and creative capacity—to build the bus stops and junctions. In other words, the public entity cooperates, but does not mix, with

---

Digital and the commons in the EU. Critical reflections and possible alternative routes, presented at the RIODD (Réseau International de Recherche sur les Organisations et le Développement Durable) Conference (Paris, November 2022).

the operators, and plays the role of platform provider, while leaving the role of final service provider to the private parties. Inherent in this function is the prohibition of discrimination between downstream operators, in the sense that the public entity has the duty to establish clear, objective and transparent criteria for access to the infrastructure, and then to justify exclusion in the light of reasonable grounds, established in advance by the policy-making bodies.

The reference to this framework in post-pandemic policies clearly translate political choices that go towards the construction of public–private partnerships to make EU economy more competitive and sustainable. Conversely, the paradigm—still based on the idea of 'thin state'—does not adopt substantial equality as its framework.

Data governance policies are coherent with the same purposes. The *Data Act* proposal[19] is meant to favour pro-competitive alliances as an alternative to the US OTTs' data fortresses. In particular, it implements the *European Data Strategy*, with special reference to the creation of European Data Spaces. «In other words, the creation of a mixed public–private regulatory space will offer the infrastructural and regulatory framework within which data, including privately held datasets, will be voluntarily, or mandatorily when the required, exchanged for economic and societal benefit. This will effectively become what has been termed the European single market for data. By doing so, the EC aims to foster data sharing and re-use, which is expected to deliver growth and innovation, to support policy making and to preserve European values such as privacy, property, competition, consumer protection, pluralisms, safety, security, fairness, ethical standards and digital sovereignty» (Ducuing and Margoni 2022, p. 11).

The proposal creates a framework for data sharing, composed by obligations and guarantees for businesses and users. For example, Articles 3–4 provide obligations to make data generated by use of product and services accessible to users. Correspondingly, the conditions for data sharing are indicated, especially, on the one hand, the ban of abusive practices (Article 13) and the prescription of fair, reasonable, and non-discriminatory terms of sharing (Article 8); on the other hand, businesses are assured the right to receive a reasonable compensation to make data available.

The proposal has significant ambitions in terms of struggling against unfair market practices towards business users and consumers; moreover, it addresses the discipline of business-to-government data sharing,[20] related to the inequalities highlighted

[19] Proposal for a regulation of the European Parliament and of the Council on harmonised rules for fair access to and use of data (Data ACT), Brussels, 23.2.2022, COM(2022)68 final, 2022/0047 (COD). This manuscript has been submitted to review on August 12th, 2023.

[20] Commission Staff, Impact Assessment Report Accompanying the document Proposal for a Regulation of the European Parliament and of the Council on European Data Governance (Data Governance Act), Commission Staff Working Document, SWD/2020/295 final; European Parliamentary Research Service, Governing data and artificial intelligence for all: Models for sustainable and just data governance, 2022, in https://www.europarl.europa.eu/RegData/etudes/STUD/2022/729533/EPRS_STU(2022)729533_EN.pdf; Commission—Directorate General for Communications Networks, Content and Technology, Towards a European strategy on business-togovernment data sharing for the public interest: final report prepared by the High-Level Expert Group on Business-toGovernment Data Sharing', 2021, in https://op.europa.eu/en/publication-detail/-/publication/d96edc29-70fd-11eb-9ac9-01aa75ed71a1.

supra in this paper. The proposal appears to be only an initial step. Indeed, it creates hypotheses where data are shared for public interest not only through voluntary agreements—as provided by the *Data Governance Act*—but also on mandatory basis; however, Chapter V only makes data sharing mandatory in exceptional cases, like a public emergency or for absolute necessity in light of a specific public task.

This choice has been supported by those who believe that a general reference to 'public interest' or 'general interest' could have hindered the application of the proportionality principle, given that 'public interest' is a political concept, difficult to translate in appropriate legal definitions (Chu 2022, p. 12). However, the tight formulation of the current proposal goes even beyond this purpose, as it does not limit itself to ensure proportionality in the data disclosure; oppositely, the definition itself of the exceptional needs appears to be quite fluid. On the other hand, it is still possible, and necessary, to impose appropriate limitations, even in a general provision of data disclosure for public interest reasons, provided that these limitations are compatible with the prevalence that human rights should have over economic rights.

This is especially relevant since the Open Data Directive further promotes the sharing of Public Sector Information with private actors, thus creating an asymmetry of information between the public sector—that needs to disclose growing masses of data gathered with public resources—and private actors that can collect these data, by still keeping their repositories secret.

5 A Possible Alternative Route? on Digital and the Commons

In the above scenario, there is clearly a need to address concerns by both public and private sectors that hesitate to take action against online inequalities, particularly concerning data. In this field, direct participation of netizens can be a tool that—in the framework of representative democracy—might be able to innovate the state of the art of online citizenship towards a more equalitarian understanding of digital policies. Data can then be understood as commons that—beyond the traditional State and market devices—allow communities to collectively manage and maintain a resource, using it for its collective interest.

In a social State, the aim of representation is not only a practical one—the impossibility of gathering the whole constituency simultaneously—but also, and especially, a systemic one: to avoid an unmediated confrontation between unequal particular interests, which could lead to a predominance of those who are endowed with greater economic, cognitive, social or organisational capital (Innerarity 2015, p. 294). Indeed, participation is a costly activity, requiring time and capitals that are hardly affordable for some people. Therefore, participation is a social right: a right that can only be enforced with a material intervention of the public authority.

Representative regimes respond to this task by regulating institutional organisation and decision-making in order to aggregate and represent the interests of these categories through parties and parliamentary groups, thus levelling the different stakeholders' weight in public decision-making.

This theoretical justification of political representation is widely accepted in theory, but still one of the most controversial issues in practices. Indeed, the legal affirmation of universal suffrage did not tackle the inequalities that needed to be addressed for everyone to be able to concretely participate in the economic, political and social life of the State. This failure is a substantial part of the 'crisis of representation' that is currently affecting EU countries, which is also connected to the EU tendency—of which the above digital policies are an example—to involve private stakeholders as regulators and co-regulators through advanced legal mechanisms (Galgano 2009, p. 76, *contra* Cassese 2006).

Commons, and digital commons, try to address these contradictions by realising forms of participatory democracy that are created through the practice itself of participating and acting in mutual aid initiatives, especially with the direct involvement of marginalised categories. Similarly, civic technologies—i.e. technologies for participation and civic initiatives—become common technology when they result from open and horizontal cooperation between citizen-users of the platforms, in spontaneous actions of general interest or in collaboration with the public entity. Therefore, such experiments take over community interests through the development of production and management models alternative to vertical authority and the market. Usually, they avail themselves of FLOSS licenses, in order to allow the access to their source code, its modification and redistribution.

By now, such a participation is only feasible for narrow digital community, having time, political will, and technical capacity to develop and use such technologies. For instance, at least two obstacles to equality can be identified. The first is the availability of technological skills: the simple use of platforms requires digital literacy, which becomes even more advanced knowledge when it comes to processing open data or programming platforms. The second is the one common to the offline world: participation benefits those who have more time and resources to devote to it. Therefore, there is the need for public authorities, at all levels, to actively support these experiments, as required by the nature itself of participatory rights, that have to be considered as social rights.

In this sphere, the paradigm of 'government as a platform' used by the EU has the merit of identifying a specific guarantee and facilitation role for the State, but appears perhaps to go too far in restricting public tasks. In fact, the above issues cannot be resolved through the mere opening up of the infrastructure, under conditions of equal treatment, but require an active intervention of the public sector in support of bottom-up initiatives, such as open source platforms, citizens science, data assemblies, etc.

Concerning data governance, data can be resources capable of supporting grass-roots actions, even if this resource is currently appropriated by few actors and governmental authorities usually lack appropriate power to disclose this information for collective interest. In that sense, an interesting proposal might be to develop a new notion of data intermediaries for the purpose of multiplying the possibility for people to use open government data for general interest purposes—despite their unequal points of departure—and create a framework of trust in business-to-government sharing of data. Data intermediaries are third party actors regulated in the *Data Governance Act* that are supposed to act as facilitators to solve the practical issues that might impede the sharing of data. In this field, these actors can have the role of encouraging voluntary data sharing practices—regulated by DGA itself—and mediating mandatory sharing of data. However, in the latter case, further issues arise concerning the internal governance of these bodies, that should be able to balance the above inequalities.

6 Conclusions

The chapter provided a general analysis of the state of the art of data governance in the EU, in order to highlight its successes and challenges. Currently, it is clear that Euro-unitarian institutions are determined to question the power of Silicon Valley and platforms as they are. Across this path the European digital economy is now conceived as a market place which is convenient because it is attentive to both fundamental rights and competition. In the aftermath of the world pandemic, the recovery needs were an opportunity to accelerate across this path and give impulse to EU markets.

On the other hand, if citizenship is considered, there are reflections to be made concerning the democratic options behind this purpose. In that sense, democracy is still considered as a matter to be contended between governmental authorities and market powers, with forms of partnership between each other. What is lacking clarity is, consequently, a vision of technology as a resource that might transform this trend by nourishing collective self-organisation and decision-making power.

In conclusion, then, data governance reflects the idea of democracy that EU promotes, attentive to participation of relevant stakeholders, but unable to make technology a commons.

References

Amoretti F, Santaniello M (2021) Partecipazione politica e opinione pubblica online in tempo di crisi. In Iride 1. https://www.rivisteweb.it/doi/10.1414/101251

Autorité de la Concurrence, Bundeskartellamt (2016) https://www.autoritedelaconcurrence.fr/sites/default/files/Big%20Data%20Papier.pdf

Bignami F (2007) European Versus American Liberty: A Comparative Privacy Analysis of Anti-Terrorism Data-Mining. In BCLR 48. https://papers.ssrn.com/sol3/papers.cfm?abstract_id=955024

Bilancia P (2020) Il grave impatto del Covid-19 sull'esercizio dei diritti sociali. In: De Minico G, Villone M (eds) Stato di diritto—Emergenza—Tecnologia. Consulta OnLine, Milano

Cassese S (2006) Oltre lo Stato, Laterza, Roma-Bari

Chandler JA (2007) Right to Reach an Audience: An Approach to Intermediary Bias on the Internet. In Hofstra Law Rev 35. https://law.hofstra.edu/pdf/academics/journals/lawreview/lrv_issues_v35n03_cc5.chandler.final.pdf

Chu J (2022) Chapter V of the Data Act—Which should be the legal basis for B2G data sharing: 'exceptional need' or 'public interest'? In: Ducuing C, Margoni T, Schirru L (eds) White Paper on the Data Act Proposal. CiTiP Working Paper 2022

Claussen V (2018) Fighting Hate Speech and Fake News. The Network Enforcement Act (NetzDG) in Germany in the Context of European Legislation. In Media Laws 3. https://www.medialaws.eu/rivista/fighting-hate-speech-and-fake-news-the-network-enforcement-act-netzdg-in-germany-in-the-context-of-european-legislation/

Darmanin J (2017) Des internautes payés pour booster les clics sur le site de la primaire à gauche. In Buzzfeed.com, January 23, https://www.buzzfeed.com/fr/julesdarmanin/des-internautes-payes-pour-booster-les-clics-sur-le-site-de

De Minico G (2015) Towards an Internet Bill of Rights. In Loy LA L Rev 37(1). https://digitalcommons.lmu.edu/ilr/vol37/iss1/1

De Minico G (2017) Un nuovo modello per le Authority europee. In Sole 24 Ore, July 30th

De Minico G (2019) Big Data e la debole resistenza delle categorie giuridiche. Privacy e lex mercatoria. In Dir Pubb 1. https://www.iris.unina.it/handle/11588/759648

Drexl J (2016) Economic Efficiency versus Democracy: On the Potential Role of Competition Policy in Regulating Digital Markets in Times of Post-Truth Politics, Max Planck Institute for Innovation & Competition Research Paper No. 16–16, https://ssrn.com/abstract=2881191

Ducuing C, Margoni T (2022) Introduction. In: Ducuing C, Margoni T, Schirru L (eds) White Paper on the Data Act Proposal, CiTiP Working Paper. https://www.law.kuleuven.be/citip/en/Publications/citip-whitepaperdataact.pdf

Evans BJ (2016) Barbarians at the Gate: Consumer-Driven Health Data Commons and the Transformation of Citizen Science. In AJLM 42(4). https://papers.ssrn.com/sol3/papers.cfm?abstract_id=2750347

European Commission (2020) *Communication "A European Strategy for Data"*, COM/2020/66 final, https://eurlex.europa.eu/legal-content/EN/TXT/?uri=CELEX%3A52020DC0066

European Commission (2021) *Communication "Shaping Europe's Digital Future and the Digital Compass 2030: the European model for digital decade"*, Brussels, 9.3.2021, COM(2021) 118 final. https://eur-lex.europa.eu/legal-content/EN/TXT/HTML/?uri=CELEX:52021DC0118

Federal Trade Commission (2016) Big Data. A Tool for Inclusion or Exclusion? Understanding the Issues, FTC Report, https://www.ftc.gov/system/files/documents/reports/big-data-tool-inclusion-or-exclusion-understanding-issues/160106big-data-rpt.pdf

Flaxman S, Goel S, Rao JM (2016) Filter Bubbles, Echo Chambers, and Online News Consumption. In Public Opin Q 80. https://academic.oup.com/poq/article/80/S1/298/2223402

Floridia G, Catelli VG (2003) Diritto antitrust: le intese restrittive della concorrenza e gli abusi di posizione dominante, IPSOA, Milano

Galgano F (2009) La globalizzazione nello specchio del diritto. Il Mulino, Bologna

Goodman B, Flaxman S (2016) EU regulations on algorithmic decision-making and a "right to explanation", Paper presented at ICML Workshop on Human Interpretability in Machine Learning 2016, 28/6/2016, http://arxiv.org/pdf/1606.08813v1.pdf

Hirsch DD (2005) Is Privacy Regulation the Environmental Law of the Information Age? In Strandburg K, Stan Raicu D (eds) Privacy and Technologies of Identity: a Cross-disciplinary Conversation. Springer, New York. https://papers.ssrn.com/sol3/papers.cfm?abstract_id=799285

Innerarity D (2015) Democrazie di prossimità e distanza rappresentativa, in Iride, a. XXVIII, n. 75, maggio-agosto 2015

Koops BJ (2008) Some Reflections on Profiling, Power Shifts and Protection Paradigms. http://papers.ssrn.com/sol3/papers.cfm?abstract_id=1350584. Extract from Hildebrandt M, Gutwirth S (eds) Profiling the European Citizen. Springer, Dordrecht

Lianos I, Motchenkova E (2014) Market Dominance and Search Quality in the Search Engine Market. In J Compet Law Econ 2(9). https://academic.oup.com/jcle/article-abstract/9/2/419/1002541?redirectedFrom=fulltext

Macchiati A (2010) I motori di ricerca su Internet e il mercato delle news. Profili antitrust e regolamentari. In Merc Conc Reg 3. https://www.researchgate.net/publication/254432612_I_motori_di_ricerca_su_Internet_e_il_mercato_delle_news_Profili_antitrust_e_regolamentari

MacDonnell P, Castro D (2016) Europe Should Embrace the Data Revolution, Report of Center for Data Innovation, February 29th, http://www2.datainnovation.org/2016-europe-embrace-data-revolution.pdf

Maniaci G (2014) La dittatura dei diritti indisponibili. In Dir E quest Pub 14. https://www.dirittoequestionipubbliche.org/page/2014_n14/22-studi_Maniaci.pdf

Mantelero A (2016) Personal data for decisional purposes in the age of analytics: From an individual to a collective dimension of data protection. In CLSR 32(2). https://www.sciencedirect.com/science/article/abs/pii/S0267364916300280

Mazzucato M (2020) Non sprechiamo questa crisi, Laterza, Roma—Bari

Morozov E (2013) The Real Privacy Problem, in MIT Technology Review.com, October 22nd, https://www.technologyreview.com/2013/10/22/112778/the-real-privacy-problem/

Newman N (2014) Search, Antitrust and the Economics of the Control of User Data In Yale J Regul 31(2). http://digitalcommons.law.yale.edu/cgi/viewcontent.cgi?article=1389&context=yjreg

O'Reilly T (2010) Government as a platform. In Lathrop D, Ruma L (eds) Open Government. Collaboration, Transparency, and Participation in Practice, O' Reilly, Sebastopol, https://www.researchgate.net/publication/227627680_Government_as_a_Platform

Osti C (2011) Abuso di posizione dominante. In Enciclopedia del diritto, Giuffré, Milano

Paye JC (2016) France: An Algorithmic Power. In Monthly Review 67(9). http://monthlyreview.org/2016/02/01/france-an-algorithmic-power/

Perlroth N (2016) Governments Turn to Commercial Spyware to Intimidate Dissidents, in NewYorkTimes.com, May 2, http://www.nytimes.com/2016/05/30/technology/governments-turn-to-commercial-spyware-to-intimidate-dissidents.html?_r=0

Resta G (2002) La disponibilità dei diritti fondamentali e i limiti della dignità (note a margine della Carta dei diritti). In Riv Dir Civ 6:801–848

Roberts AJ (2013) A Republican Account of the Value of Privacy, University of Melbourne Legal Studies Research Paper No. 673, http://ssrn.com/abstract=2369680

Robinson, DG, Yu H, Zeller WP, Felten EW (2009) Government Data and the Invisible Hand, YJoLT, 11, https://papers.ssrn.com/sol3/papers.cfm?abstract_id=1138083

Rodotà S (1995) Tecnologie e diritti. Il Mulino, Bologna

Rose-Ackerman S (1985) Inalienability and The Theory of Property Rights, Faculty Scholarship Series. Paper 580, http://digitalcommons.law.yale.edu/fss_papers/580

Schermer BW, Custers B, van der Hof S (2014) The Crisis of Consent: How Stronger Legal Protection May Lead to Weaker Consent in Data Protection, February 25, https://papers.ssrn.com/sol3/papers.cfm?abstract_id=2412418

Schwartz PM (1999–2000) Internet Privacy and the State. In Conn L Rev, 32, https://paulschwartz.net/wp-content/uploads/2019/01/SCHWARTZ-CK1A-1.pdf

Solove DJ (2006) A Taxonomy of Privacy. In U Pa L Rev, 154(3), https://scholarship.law.upenn.edu/penn_law_review/vol154/iss3/1/

Spencer SB (2002) Security Versus Privacy: Reframing the Debate, in Denver Univ. Law Rev., 79(4), http://ssrn.com/abstract=2015040

Sunstein C (2005) Laws of fear: beyond the precautionary principle. Cambridge University Press, Cambridge

Theoharis J (2016) "I Feel Like a Despised Insect": Coming of Age under Surveillance in New York, in The Intercept, February 18, https://theintercept.com/2016/02/18/coming-of-age-under-surveillance-in-new-york/

Turner K (2016) Mass surveillance silences minority opinions, according to study, in WashingtonPost.com—The Switch, March 28, https://www.washingtonpost.com/news/the-switch/wp/2016/03/28/mass-surveillance-silences-minority-opinions-according-to-study/

Valero J (2016) Commission backs data sharing 'by default' to spur innovation, in EurActiv.com, April 27, https://www.euractiv.com/section/innovation-industry/news/commission-backs-data-sharing-by-default-to-spur-innovation/
Varhaert J (2013) The Challenges involved with the Application of Article 102 TFEU to the Market for Search Engines as part of the New Economy and the implications for the Google-case, Master Thesis in Intellectual Property Rights, August 30, http://papers.ssrn.com/sol3/papers.cfm?abstract_id=2340958
Vedder A (2000) Medical Data, New Information Technologies, and the Need for Normative Principles other than Privacy Rules. In: Freeman M, Lewis A (ed) Law and Medicine. (Series Current Legal Issues). Oxford University Press, Oxford, pp. 441–459. https://pure.uvt.nl/portal/files/368983/Ucl2.pdf
Verband Deutscher Maschinen- und Anlagenbau (2016) Industrie 4.0: Mastering the Transition, https://www.pac.gr/bcm/uploads/industrie-4-0-mastering-the-transition-december-2015.pdf
Visco Comandini V (2018) Le fake news sui social network: un'analisi economica, in Media Laws, 2. https://www.medialaws.eu/wp-content/uploads/2018/06/Visco-Comandini.pdf
Wang ML (2014) The Market Reality for an Ailing Democratic Institution: Why the Two-sided Market Theories Provide Inadequate Justification for Unrestricted Media Consolidation, Speech at IX IACL World Congress, Oslo, http://www.jus.uio.no/english/research/news-and-events/events/conferences/2014/wccl-cmdc/wccl/papers/ws14/w14-wang.pdf
Wells P, Scott A (2016) Comment: What would an open data future look like?, May 25, https://iniciativabarcelonaopendata.cat/ca/2016/05/comment-what-would-an-open-data-future-look-like/

Digital Markets, Positive Duties of Protection and the Freedom to Conduct a Business: How to Have Your Cake and Eat It Too

Inês Neves

Abstract The Digital Markets Act ('DMA') represents a significant legislative initiative within the European Union ('EU'), serving as the EU's flagship digital markets legislation. It seeks to promote fairer and more competitive markets within the framework of a social market economy. This chapter emphasises the necessity to reconsider the legitimacy of the DMA, both in terms of its textual content and its practical implementation, by giving due consideration to the freedom to conduct a business as a fundamental right. It is contended that the DMA should not be implemented on the basis of a reductionist perspective that perceives corporations as inherently malevolent or as manifestations of novel forms of power. This perspective is insufficient to consider all corporate subjects and situations. While digital companies and gatekeepers represent new forms of power that require regulation, it is essential to respect their autonomy and freedom under fundamental rights protection. After all, the freedom to conduct a business is one of the main reasons for the DMA, particularly when we consider business users. The text emphasises the role of duties of protection in favour of subjects of fundamental rights (companies), recognising that implementing them entails restrictions on other subjects of fundamental duties (companies). It also highlights the binding effect of these duties of protection on different actors, including the European Union, in place of the state. The chapter concludes that the DMA aims to reconcile the competing rights of gatekeepers and businesses and end users, thus illustrating the diverse nature of business entities and the possibility of mobilising the freedom to conduct business, as with other fundamental rights, as both a justification for interference and an interfered-with right. It

This chapter is founded upon sections of a text by the author, which was published on the Kluwer Competition Law Blog. See Neves, I. (2024), "A Reorientation of the European Commission's Discretion in the Digital Markets Act: Solutions From Digital Constitutionalism", 18 December, Kluwer Competition Law Blog, available at: https://competitionlawblog.kluwercompetitionlaw.com/2024/12/18/a-reorientation-of-the-european-commissions-discretion-in-the-digital-markets-act-solutions-from-digital-constitutionalism/

I. Neves (✉)
Faculty of Law of the University of Porto, Porto, Portugal
e-mail: ineves@direito.up.pt

CIJ—Centre for Interdisciplinay Research on Justice, Porto, Portugal

G. Enes et al. (eds.), *A Digital Europe for Citizens*,
https://doi.org/10.1007/978-3-032-02500-5_7

is therefore argued that reconciling the freedom to conduct business as a right of defence and a protection imperative is feasible. In order to achieve a right balance, it is believed that the flaws of the DMA text can be compensated for by a consistent and proportionate enforcement strategy.

Keywords Digital markets · Gatekeepers · Business users · Fundamental rights · Freedom to conduct a business

1 Introduction

The Digital Markets Act is a flagship piece of legislation within the European Union's ('EU') policy on digital regulation and digital markets. The interventionist approach on which it is based and its broader or cross-cutting normative nature—primarily due to its stated goals and the vast set of rights and interests that contestability and fairness seek to translate—are aligned with the spirit of European policies for this century. Two principal tenets must be taken into account: the protection versus freedom dichotomy and the rights versus innovation binomial.

It would be remiss to ignore important questions underlying the Digital Markets Act ('DMA'). Firstly, the DMA's promises regarding the fight against unfair practices and conditions of a special group of companies—gatekeepers—vis-à-vis their business and end users (see Article 1 DMA) are of particular interest. Secondly, the Regulation has been the subject of considerable debate due to doubts surrounding its true nature, its axiological anchorage, and its relationship with competition law (see, among others, Akman (2022), Beems (2022), Colangelo and Ribera Martínez (2024), Fernández (2021), Gryllos (2024), Komninos (2022), Mendelsohn and Budzinski (2023), Moreno Belloso and Petit (2023), van den Boom (2022), and Robertson (2023), not to mention the effectiveness of the expected Brussels effect Blockx (2023) and Drewes and Kirk (2024)). Finally, the criticism and suspicion surrounding the DMA, particularly from those who view it as an assault to innovation, must be considered (see, among others, Portuese (2022)).

Building on those discussions, the purpose of this text is to highlight the necessity to rethink the legitimacy of the DMA, both in terms of its status as a Regulation emanating from the European Union and in terms of its practical application. It is thought that a process of depuration is required in order to ensure that the DMA is not applied and enforced on the basis of a simplistic, universalised view of companies as inherently malevolent entities, or as manifestations of new forms of power, sovereignty or capitalism. Although it is accurate to assert that companies in the digital realm, and gatekeepers in particular, represent novel forms of power that necessitate regulation, the proposition that their autonomy, freedom and actions must be constrained at all costs and by all means ignores their status as subjects-holders of fundamental rights. This approach may ultimately undermine the rule of law.

The DMA's connection with fundamental rights and the freedom to conduct a business in particular provides us with the opportunity to recall fundamental principles of both the EU and Member States in a special context.

Fundamental rights represent an order of values that is closely aligned with the ideals of the rule of law. Any interference or impairment in a fundamental subjective position or freedom must comply with universally applicable requirements, which must be interpreted in a manner that avoids arbitrariness. It is imperative that both the legislative and the executive branches of government (either national or the EU) adhere to these principles. While these tenets are not novel, it is nevertheless crucial to reiterate them in the context of the present circumstances. As Jorge Pereira da Silva aptly observed, "History has shown that in societies politically organized as constitutional States, one shall not take for granted the achievements of civilization on which we set our lives. [...] Therefore, it is critical to revisit the different ideas that constitute the foundations of the constitutional State as a social and political paradigm, which rests on the crossover of three principles: the guarantee of fundamental rights, the separation of powers, and popular sovereignty. Righteously three principles that are very simple in their basic formulation, but very challenging legally and of enormous plasticity in their practical realization." (Silva 2024, p. 133).

There are several limitations imposed on the fundamental right set forth in Article 16 of the Charter of Fundamental Rights of the European Union ('CFR'). Concurrently, the EU legislator is obliged to safeguard fundamental rights, including the freedom to conduct a business. Indeed, in addition to other fundamental rights and interests (such as those pertaining to privacy and data protection, consumers' rights, the protection against fraudulent and deceptive commercial practices, or public order), the DMA also seeks to guarantee the fundamental right to conduct a business of business users, which, as businesses. Rather than perceiving their fundamental positions as being impaired, these users view their fundamental rights as being protected through legislation.

In short, the DMA strives to reconcile the competing fundamental rights of gatekeepers (whose scope of action is constrained by the DMA's positive and negative obligations—for an overview, Koenig (2024a, b)), on the one hand, and those of business and end users, often situated in a state of economic dependence. The power imbalance inherent to fundamental rights intervention gives rise to a corpus of regulatory interventionism aimed at ensuring a fair commercial environment and the contestability of the digital sector. In order for this to occur, the freedom of gatekeepers to determine the manner in which they provide their services, and the terms and conditions thereof, is constrained. With regard to companies in particular, the DMA serves as an illustrative example of the diverse nature of business entities and the multifaceted scope of their typical freedom—the freedom to conduct a business.

Consequently, it can be argued that the legitimacy of the Digital Markets Act is not undermined, but rather reinforced, by giving serious consideration to the freedom to conduct a business as a fundamental right. It is our contention that the DMA is attentive to the positive dimension of the freedom to conduct a business, linked with the duties of protection in favour of business users (and end users alike). Nevertheless, it is possible that the freedom to conduct a business of gatekeepers may not have been regarded as such.

In both domestic and European contexts, companies are holders of fundamental rights enshrined in constitutional and EU instruments. While the freedom to conduct a business (enshrined in Article 16 of the Charter of Fundamental Rights of the European Union and in national constitutions) does not guarantee success in the marketplace or an entitlement to unchanging competition conditions (as a result of the adoption of regulations), it nevertheless protects its holders (among whom companies) from obligations and requirements that impinge upon their freedom in the market and impair their competitive position. A pessimistic approach in general fails to recognise that fundamental rights do not cease to apply on the basis of status or the moral standing of their holders. Furthermore, this perspective fails to accept the diversity within the business community, which includes entities that require the same protection as other fundamental rights holders. Finally, it fails to acknowledge that companies, and platforms in particular, are typically required to satisfy a multitude of diverse, increasingly complex and often conflicting demands from a range of stakeholders, including users, civil society, advertisers and governments (Suzor 2018, p. 3). In conclusion, this limited perspective overlooks the fact that fundamental rights themselves are contextual in application and can provide suitable and proportionate solutions to scenarios of conflict.

We will conclude here that the required conciliation and harmonization between the freedom to conduct a business as a defence right (mainly perceived from the perspective of gatekeepers) and the freedom to conduct a business as an imperative of protection (from the view of business users) is a feasible objective. It is not implausible to suggest that the aforementioned desideratum is compatible with the demands of speed or effectiveness of the intervention. Indeed, these are also necessary in the context of a highly changeable reality and a context that is undoubtedly one of advantage for the gatekeepers. Although the text of the DMA is imperfect from the standpoint of the rule of law requirements, it is thought that this may be offset by an enforcement strategy that is consistent with fundamental rights and the rule of law.

It is not the intention of this text to set out the precise modifications that should be made to the text of the DMA. The author's intention is to recall the fundamental principles that must guide the enforcement of the new regulatory framework in order to ensure its legitimacy and acceptance. Furthermore, the text seeks to highlight the role that fundamental duties of protection now play in favour of new subjects (companies), with adverse implications for new subjects (companies), and in binding different actors (the European Union). In essence, how does the DMA guarantee the freedom to conduct a business (among other rights), while simultaneously imposing limitations on that same fundamental right? Furthermore, how can we guarantee that this equilibrium remains legitimate, fair and proportionate?

The text is structured into 3 (three) sections, in addition to the Introduction and its Conclusions. In Sect. 2 "The Need for a Framework of Governance for Digital Markets", we examine the rationale that could justify the legitimacy of the DMA as a governance framework for digital markets, despite the limitations it places on gatekeepers and their fundamental freedoms. In Sect. 3 "The Limitations of the DMA and its Agnostic Interventionist Normativism", we analyse some of the limitations of the DMA in order to highlight the necessity of compensatory enforcement. In Sect. 4 "Squaring the Circle: Reconciling the Positive and Negative Functions of the Freedom to Conduct a Business", we mobilize the multifunctionality and multidimensionality of fundamental rights, both as negative rights of defence and as positive duties to protect. This approach allows us to identify a fair balance between all the rights and interests underlying the DMA as a text and as implemented. It is assumed that a pessimist view of companies in general cannot negate their status as holders of fundamental rights and, most importantly, the objective requirements of the rule of law.

2 The Need for a Framework of Governance for Digital Markets

The insufficiency of existing regulatory instruments and competition rules (at least, as they currently exist) is typically cited as a rationale for advocating for a different approach. In particular, other legal domains are deemed inadequate or lacking the requisite dogmatic frameworks to (fairly) settle these controversies. The DMA represents a paradigm shift from a model of non-intervention, characterised by a hands-off approach or minimal regulation, to a proactive, preventive and responsible approach. In particular, it provides for a set of positive and negative obligations imposed on companies that are gatekeepers. In addition to their status as intermediaries or platforms, gatekeepers are qualified due to their position of supremacy and power over business users and end users, which depend on the former to provide their services and deliver their products in the digital sector or to satisfy their rights and interests as beneficiaries of the services being provided (see Article 3 DMA).

In the judgement in the case Bytedance v Commission, the General Court emphasised that "market processes were often incapable of ensuring fair economic outcomes with regard to CPSs and that existing EU law did not satisfactorily address the potential negative effects associated with some of the characteristics of CPSs. In particular, although Articles 101 and 102 TFEU remain applicable to the conduct of gatekeepers, the fact remains that the scope of those provisions is limited to certain instances of market power, for example dominance on specific markets and anticompetitive behaviour, enforcement of those provisions occurs only ex post and requires an extensive investigation of often very complex facts on a case-by-case basis. Moreover, the EU legislature found that existing EU law did not address, or did not address effectively, the challenges to the effective functioning of the internal market posed by the conduct of gatekeepers that are not necessarily dominant in competition law terms (see, to that effect, recital 5 of the DMA). It also noted that the DMA pursued an objective that is complementary to, but different from, that of protecting undistorted competition on any given market, as defined in competition law terms, which is to ensure that markets where gatekeepers are present are and remain contestable and fair, independently from the actual, potential or presumed effects of the conduct of a given gatekeeper covered by the DMA on competition on a given market (see, to that effect, recital 11 DMA)."

It is clear that the disputes and issues the DMA seeks to resolve (through preventive measures) extend beyond the mere assurance of fair and undistorted market competition. In contrast, the DMA was put forward as a means of addressing issues that have arisen from other legal fields, including data protection, consumer rights, copyright, and, most notably, constitutional law. The adjudication of fundamental rights between different holders—namely, the platform service providers or gatekeepers, its users, and, finally, the consumer—requires the intervention of constitutional law. It is only through the lens of constitutional law that a problematic balancing exercise can be framed, as the preference of one or more rights over others cannot be reduced to a mere hierarchical and abstract preference. It is only constitutional law that can overcome the disciplinary silos that exist. The DMA builds on this context.

In contrast to competition law, the theory of harm that underlies the prohibition or of certain practices or justifies the imposition of obligations on gatekeepers in the DMA is determined in a pre-emptive manner (*ex ante*). The legitimacy of the model is derived from the fact that the majority of the realities encompassed within its provisions are not novel. In contrast, they have been and continue to be subject to scrutiny under the auspices of competition law, primarily in accordance with the provisions set forth in Article 102 of the Treaty on the Functioning of the European Union ('TFEU'). A second source of legitimisation arises from the nature of the DMA as a harmonising law, which seeks to prevent and resolve a conflict between colliding fundamental rights or interests. In particular, the specific characteristics of digital markets give rise to a potential conflict between the prima facie content of the freedom to conduct a business of gatekeepers, and the fundamental rights and interests of business and end users that intersect with the former. The DMA aims to resolve intricate and challenging trade-offs, anticipating fundamental rights adjudication decisions and balancing exercises that are necessary in the context of evolving social realities. As a result, the impairment of the freedom to conduct a business, as observed in the case of the DMA, cannot be attributed to a casuistic fair balance in the light of the economic and legal context. Rather, it is the consequence of a harmonisation exercise by the EU legislator, whereby the prima facie content of the freedom to conduct a business is limited to a narrower scope of action and constrained by limits and requirements.

The ex ante nature of the Regulation does not negate the importance of an ex post dimension (see Blažo 2022), which derives, firstly, from a principle of self-assessment. It is incumbent on gatekeepers (those responsible for ensuring compliance with the DMA) to determine the efficacy of the technical, organisational and other measures they implement to this end (Carugati 2023; Fletcher and Vasas 2023). The fact that gatekeepers are permitted to determine the manner in which they comply with the DMA may be used to justify the respect for the essential core of the freedom to conduct a business. In accordance with Article 52(1) of the Charter of Fundamental Rights of the European Union, "Any limitation on the exercise of the rights and freedoms recognised by this Charter must […] respect the essence of those rights and freedoms".

The ex post nature of the DMA is also a consequence of the discretion afforded to the European Commission to enforce the DMA's provisions. Indeed, while the prohibitions and obligations set forth in the DMA appear to be clear and precise, they are, in fact, open to interpretation and implementation in a manner that is not easily discernible or definable in a strict and unique fashion. The Commission has considerable discretion in this regard and is empowered to open investigations into non-compliance with the DMA, should it deem the measures adopted by gatekeepers to be insufficient to meet the objectives of the DMA.

Whether at the *ex ante* or *ex post* stage, the DMA is, as previously stated, a game-changer. However, it must be understood in the context of a broader normative action. Indeed, although some may view the current situation as a revolutionary one, necessitating a shift in paradigm in the light of the emergence of new forms of power in algorithmic society (see de Gregorio 2022), it is important to recognise that such a paradigm shift is not a novel phenomenon in historical context. Conversely, it finds a close parallel in the same evidence of insufficiency that justified the transition from a minimal or liberal state to an intervening or supervisory state. The latter has also assumed an active role in ensuring the harmonisation of conflicting and colliding rights and interests. In a similar manner to how the state and the law were able to identify an inherent flaw in the concept of the private as a game, dialogue or relationship between equals, and were subsequently compelled to intervene in the physical market, the DMA is now reiterating and adapting this same finding to digital markets, where the issue of economic dependence and power imbalance is further exacerbated.

It is of no consequence whether the rights in question are threatened in an offline or online context, or whether the threat originates from a public authority or a private entity. The distinction lies in the fact that, as a consequence of the challenges posed by digitalisation and the specific characteristics of European integration, it is now incumbent upon the EU and its institutions to reform the existing frameworks, in order to guarantee the community of values that the EU strives to establish.

2.1 Fundamental Rights and the Rule of Law in the Digital Markets Act

The Digital Markets Act may be linked with two principal driving forces: fundamental rights and the rule of law.

While not negating the tenets of a market economy, the EU's endeavors to restrict the autonomy of gatekeepers are an affirmation of the fundamental rights enshrined in the Charter. The DMA represents a means of guaranteeing that the exercise of freedoms does not occur in a manner that exhausts the scope of the freedom of others. Its objective is to enable the EU to retain its role as an "arbitrator-moderator".

This is particularly relevant in the context of the application of a law of the strongest, which, in the digital context, is perceived by many as indicative of platform capitalism or surveillance capitalism.

In particular, the DMA aims to define a prima facie freedom that, in conjunction with the specific characteristics of the digital sector, allows certain businesses to leverage their advantages in ways that are unfair to other market actors and end users which rely on them. In essence, the EU legislator aims to guarantee that the freedom(s) at stake in this context can coexist in a manner that is mutually tolerable through the establishment of a governance framework that establishes the rules of a new digital society.

The traditional understanding of fundamental rights was that they were positions of the individual-citizen in relation to the state. The negative function of fundamental rights as prohibitions of intervention is insufficient to secure personal freedom. Fundamental rights also establish an objective order of values, which requires political actors to intervene in an adequate and sufficient manner.

As is clear from fundamental rights scholarship and the decisions of constitutional courts of the Member States, fundamental rights, in addition to being rights of the individual—the citizen—against the state (and other private individuals), also contain an objective dimension from which positive duties of protection derive, obliging the state and its organs to safeguard and defend the integrity of the protected interests deriving from fundamental rights. According to the case law of the German Federal Constitutional Court ('Bundesverfassungsgericht'), "Such duties of protection are only violated if no action is taken whatsoever, if the laws enacted and measures taken are evidently unsuitable or completely inadequate, or if they fall considerably short of the aim of protection". In short, there is a prohibition of insufficiency ('Untermaßverbot').

The competent authorities have a wide margin of appreciation, judgement, and decision in the fulfilment of these duties of protection. In particular, the legislator has the power to proactively harmonise conflicting rights and interests. According to the German Federal Constitutional Court "Particularly in cases of conflict between fundamental rights in their dimension as defensive rights against state interference on the one hand, and as rights giving rise to state duties of protection on the other, it is primarily for the democratically elected legislator to balance the conflicting constitutional interests against one another and to reconcile them using its margin of assessment and appreciation as well as its leeway to design".

The DMA acknowledges this and does not regard fundamental rights as mere shields or spheres immune to the intervention of powers. Rather, it perceives them as an "objective order of values" from which duties of protection arise for the state and, nowadays, for the EU itself. However, it must be borne in mind that ensuring the effectiveness of one's fundamental right might require an encroachment on conflicting and colliding rights and interests of third parties. As a result, in the event of an interference, the measure (whether statutory or in enforcement proceedings), must be appropriate and proportionate, in the sense that the aim(s) pursued and the likelihood of achieving it / them must not be disproportionate to the severity of the interference. In short, the conflicting fundamental rights (which may be restricted as a result of these duties) must be weighed carefully.

In addition to the prohibition of insufficiency, there is also a prohibition of excessive measures ('Übermaßverbot'). A fair balance ('praktischer Konkordanz') is needed to guide the evaluation of the scope of the duties of protection and the extent of the impairment. The prohibition of insufficiency guides the former, while the prohibition of excess guides the latter. In other words, the existence of a justification for interference—a duty to protect—does not, in and of itself, confer legitimacy upon public action.

In the context of a weighing up, the state is bound by the requirements of the rule of law and is thus precluded from making arbitrary decisions regarding the value of fundamental rights. The idea-principle of the rule of law gives rise to a set of imperatives, including the requirement that any action, regardless of its form or author, respects the limits set by law and abides by the values of democracy and fundamental rights. From a positive standpoint, it is postulated that the rule of law "creates additional obligations of the State to guarantee that individuals under their jurisdiction have access to effective legal means to enforce the protection of their human rights" and "creates a benchmark for the quality of laws protecting human rights: legal provisions in this field—and beyond—have to be, inter alia, clear and predictable, and non-discriminatory, and they must be applied by independent courts under procedural guarantees equivalent to those applied in conflicts resulting from interferences with human rights by public authorities". Consequently, the rule of law is regarded as a rationale for a governance structure that curtails specific liberties due to the necessity of safeguarding others. It will be demonstrated that the rule of law is sufficiently comprehensive to guarantee the due protection of subjects whose freedom is being constrained, as well as those whose freedom is being safeguarded or promoted.

2.2 The Digital Markets Act as a Harmonising Law

The Digital Markets Act represents an appropriate means of harmonising and arbitrating the important fundamental rights and interests that are protected. These include: (i) the guarantee of the contestability of digital markets and the fairness of the relationships established therein; (ii) the rights of consumers, (iii) data protection and the need to comply with privacy and security requirements; and finally, (iv) the safeguard of the very freedom of business, if not of gatekeepers, indeed of business users, which find themselves in a true status subjectionis to unfair behaviours, terms and conditions.

Indeed, among its legitimate objectives is the assurance of the freedom to conduct a business for companies that depend on gatekeepers to reach end users and operate in the market. This is achieved through a set of requirements, obligations and prohibitions imposed on gatekeepers. The objective is to ensure that other undertakings can "effectively overcome barriers to entry and expansion and challenge the gatekeeper on the merits of their products and services". Furthermore, the aim is to "prevent an imbalance between the rights and the obligations of business users where the gatekeeper obtains a disproportionate advantage, bearing in mind that, due to their gateway position and superior bargaining power, it is possible that gatekeepers engage in behaviour that does not allow others to capture fully the benefits of their own contributions, and unilaterally set unbalanced conditions for the use of their CPSs or services provided together with, or in support of, their CPSs".

The harmonisation of different rights and interests in digital markets presents a unique set of challenges, shaped by the idiosyncratic characteristics of these markets in comparison to more traditional exchange spaces (see Koenig 2024a, b). It is crucial to consider the characteristics of core platform services, including the significant economies of scale, substantial network effects, multilateral nature of the services, and the capacity to link numerous business users and end users. Additionally, the potential for blocking effects, lack of interoperability and vertical integration, as well as the advantages derived from data must be taken into account. These features cannot be ignored, especially when coupled with the potential for their exploitation by companies that, precisely because of those characteristics and the significant barriers to entry, exit, and expansion, tend to be limited in number and to have considerable economic power, generating severe imbalances of bargaining power or weak contestability in digital markets.

In light of the aforementioned considerations, it is our contention that the legislative margin of appreciation and conformation (either at the EU or national level) allows for the imposition of obligations and requirements on businesses that effectively reduce the scope of their freedom to conduct a business. The interventionist normativism that characterises the DMA, even if it may appear to be damaging to the freedom to conduct a business, is compatible with limits that allow the DMA to serve its purpose without annihilating, or, at the very least, reducing or side-lining the freedom to conduct a business. Although gatekeepers are not public entities, they are responsible for providing and ensuring access to essential services. Their nature and power, which resembles that of a state or public entity, allows for the imposition of obligations that limit the broader scope of their freedoms.

In conclusion, in view of the objectives pursued and the leeway afforded to the legislator in assessing the suitability of a regulatory framework, the DMA represents a justified and suitable framework for achieving the goals of contestability and fairness in digital markets. However, as will be discussed, the legitimacy of the DMA is not automatically ensured by this justification, primarily due to the unique regulatory framework that has been established. This framework has been designed with the intention of achieving effectiveness, which has resulted in the streamlining of various processes, leading to a situation where dialogue with gatekeepers is provided for only in specific and limited ways, at both the procedural and substantive levels. The following chapter will examine the limitations of the DMA's formal provisions.

3 The Limitations of the DMA and Its Agnostic Interventionist Normativism

The DMA's objective of addressing the deficiencies of market processes and existing EU law in guaranteeing fair economic outcomes has resulted in a normative architecture that is in contrast to the ex post enforcement and comprehensive case-by-case analysis typical of competition law. While the framework is justified and suitable for promoting the objectives underlying the notions of contestability and fairness, it must also not extend beyond what is necessary to protect those goals. This implies that, although we concur with those who highlight the insufficiency of a minimal state model—a critique justified, moreover, by the duties of protection arising from fundamental rights—we must nevertheless emphasise the necessity for a legal framework and a constitutionally legitimised discourse that is resilient to political and economic debates. The DMA's architecture ensures the speed and effectiveness of the protective intention of the DMA. Nevertheless, it may pose some problems from the perspective of the rights being restrained, namely those of gatekeepers.

The freedom to conduct a business is a fundamental right enshrined in Article 16 of the CFR, as well as in several national constitutions of Member States. Article 52 of the CFR establish the rules for the interpretation and limitation of rights. In addition to a justification, the principle of proportionality and respect for the essence of the rights in question serve to ensure that fundamental rights are not just rights in paper. Furthermore, it represents an important principle in the adjudication of fundamental rights: there is no formal, a priori, or abstract hierarchy between different fundamental rights or holders. By contrast, any conflict or collision must be resolved in a manner that ensures a fair balance, which must take into account the requirements of the rule of law.

Although the freedom to conduct a business is not an absolute shield against every legal provision affecting business activities, the DMA has an inherent regulatory effect, with several specific obligations imposed on gatekeepers (see Articles 5, 6, 11, 14 and 15 DMA). Non-compliance is punishable by fines (see Chapter V DMA), thus restricting the prima facie content of their fundamental freedoms. Furthermore, in addition to the direct restrictions imposed by the DMA, compliance with this legislation also entails costs that must also be considered. Ultimately, even users may be harmed as a result of a rigid list of assumptions and obligations, which, when combined with punitive enforcement, may lead to a disadvantageous battle in court.

It is believed that the legitimacy of the objectives and the margin of manoeuvre that is to be afforded to both the EU legislator and enforcer does not negate the necessity for consistent protection that not only (i) meets the requisite level of protection but also (ii) does not exceed what is demanded by the substantial danger or damage in question. In this regard, the DMA's text presents some shortcomings when viewed in the context of the rule of law principle.

The European Commission for Democracy through Law (Venice Commission), has stated that, "despite differences of opinion, consensus exists on the core elements of the Rule of Law as well as on those of the Rechtsstaat and of the Etat de droit, which are not only formal but also substantive or material (materieller Rechtsstaatsbegriff). These core elements are: (1) Legality, including a transparent, accountable and democratic process for enacting law; (2) Legal certainty; (3) Prohibition of arbitrariness; (4) Access to justice before independent and impartial courts, including judicial review of administrative acts; (5) Respect for human rights; and (6) Non-discrimination and equality before the law." With Pranvera Këllezi, "In the face of the trend towards market intervention, the rule of law must remain the pillar of the functioning of democratic societies and the free market itself" (Këllezi 2022, p. 2).

To illustrate the limitations of the DMA from this perspective, it is important to highlight the one-size-fits-all nature of the obligations imposed on gatekeepers, which fails to consider their diverse business models. Furthermore, the type, direction, and size of network effects, the concrete sources of economies of scale, the different incentives and anti-competitive potential, and the different "risks" depending on the type of market in question (monopolistic or oligopolistic) are not fully considered. We concur with Heike Schweitzer's assertion that "in any given setting, the rules set out in Art. 5 and 6 may be too broad, too narrow or simply miss the point. While it is true that the fundamental uncertainty of how digital markets will evolve requires robust rules and a certain range of errors is unavoidable, the "one size fits all" seems unsuitable to meet the DMA's primary goal: to effectively protect competition in gatekeeper-controlled markets wherever feasible" (Schweitzer 2021, p. 28). Ultimately, the Digital Markets Act may treat disparate subjects and services in a similar manner, equating entities that are not analogous. The DMA's agnosticism towards business models and the absence of proportional equality in the obligations and prohibitions it provides for represent a flaw that can undermine the requirement of equality before the law, as well as the prohibition of arbitrariness.

Secondly, the lack of "escape valves", which would allow businesses to justify prohibited behaviours or avoid imposed conduct, is also a cause of concern. This precludes any possibility of surmounting the presumption of harm associated with prohibitions or the presumption of the necessity of obligations. Although the use of presumptions and the imposition of obligations based on the presumed harm of certain behaviours appear to be a method or choice within the legislator's margin of conformation, the absence of mechanisms for dialogue-concretisation, together with the denial of a defence of efficiency and the restriction of the aforementioned escape valves (consecrated solely to certain obligations or particular cases of suspension or exemption) has prompted us to concur with the sentiments of those who perceive potential for enhancement and adaptation, particularly in the manner the DMA will be implemented (see Pablo and Fernández 2021).

Thirdly, there is a concern that the absence or limited participation of companies in the process may contravene the requirements of procedural legal certainty. Indeed, while the Regulation can be justified in light of the rights, values and interests at stake, it is important to bear in mind that the "fact that the DMA has a regulatory ambition does not imply by nature a relaxation of due process requirements" (Petit 2021, p. 9). In the view of Habermas, those whose legal situation may be affected by a particular result or normative solution must be afforded a realistic opportunity to present their view of the matter (Paunio 2009). It is imperative to guarantee that the demands for expediency and prompt intervention do not result in the silencing of the rights of gatekeepers, namely, companies, and the requirements of the rule of law against arbitrary or disproportionate intervention.

Finally, there are the risks associated with a model of a "a quasi-centralised enforcement system" (Ribera Martínez 2024a, b), with concentrated and exclusive competence of the European Commission. This has led some authors to express scepticism about whether the constraints of competition law are being replaced by "a "blank slate" that would free the Commission to shape the scope of the DMA's regulatory regime as well as the obligations of the gatekeepers" (Körber 2021, p. 4). The European Commission's leverage and discretion as the sole enforcer is not inherently problematic. However, the potential for undue interference is significantly heightened (Diez 2023, p. 13) in the absence of legal safeguards and an understanding of its discretion as being unlimited.

It is postulated that the intrinsic complexity of digital markets permits a greater margin of appreciation by the legislator and enforcer, but also necessitates the implementation of additional safety nets to ensure the definitive scope of the rights and freedoms of all relevant parties is clearly and fairly defined. It is beyond dispute that decisions pertaining to measures that restrict the freedom of citizens must not be left unilaterally to the discretion of public administration. After all, "any intervention by the public authorities in the sphere of private activities of any person, whether natural or legal, must have a legal basis and be justified on the grounds laid down by law, and, consequently, those systems provide, albeit in different forms, protection against arbitrary or disproportionate intervention. The need for such protection must be recognized as a general principle of Community law".

Notwithstanding the potential for companies, and in particular gatekeepers, to pose new sources of danger and threats to others' fundamental rights, it is of the utmost importance that the balance between the fundamental rights and interests at stake is perceived as fair. It is as important to protect companies (e.g., business users) from new sources of power and scenarios of imbalance and dependence as it is to protect companies (in particular, gatekeepers) from the old powers whose abuse and arbitrariness fundamental rights and the rule of law seek to constrain. In other words, while the freedom to conduct a business and the gatekeepers themselves must be understood in the light of an important social dimension of the services they provide and the overall context of digital markets, there is an important individual dimension that cannot be purely functionalised to other rights and interests. We are talking about gatekeepers as subjects of fundamental rights per se, and about the freedom to conduct a business in its dimension of subjective right. As a result, while it is true that part of the gatekeepers' position in the market may be grounded in the contributions also made by businesses and end users as members of the same digital markets community, there is a dimension of freedom, merit and property that is and must be protected by the EU legislator and enforcer. In short, while it is true that the legislator has prioritised the protection of vulnerable subjects—businesses and end users—vis-à-vis gatekeepers, this cannot be read as a carte blanche for the European Commission to exercise its discretion in all case-by-case assessments.

Any interpretation of the DMA that merely accepts the assertions made by the legislator regarding the proportionality of the legal framework and its obligations (see Recital 28 DMA) or is overly confident about the goodwill of the enforcer in respecting the principles of equal treatment, proportionality, and good administration (see Recital 65 DMA) is not a legitimate interpretation.

The obligations imposed on gatekeepers by the DMA and the strict normative framework, with several presumptions and few possibilities to rebut them, in the light of a high burden and standard of proof, require countermeasures capable of mitigating the weight of the interference and compensating for the burdens imposed (in the present case, by the textual provisions). It is our contention that the burden of the interference could be alleviated by a preference for dialogue and engagement with both gatekeepers and business and end users over punitive enforcement and coercive measures.

As a result, if the DMA is to remain in its current form, the Commission's discretion as the sole enforcer must be subjected to rigorous scrutiny to ensure that the DMA's shortcomings are not exacerbated by enforcement. In contexts characterised by change, metamorphosis or uncertainty, punitive enforcement should not be the default option (see Tzanaki and Nowag 2023). In contrast, mechanisms of dialogue and participation-intervention must be established to guarantee not only the predictability of the results, but also the acceptability of the solutions. It is crucial to ensure that the interventionist approach, whether in terms of discretion, opportunity, and efficiency; the preponderance given to speed and effectiveness of public action; or even in terms of liability and level of sanctions, does not result in outcomes that are contrary to its original intent: to control power and safeguard fundamental rights and democratic structures.

The following chapter aims to reconcile the two aspects of the freedom to conduct a business, namely its negative and positive functions. It is thought that a comprehensive grasp of the freedom to conduct business in its entirety will permit the enforcer to exercise discretion in awarding compensation for any shortfalls in the DMA's text.

4 Squaring the Circle: Reconciling the Positive and Negative Functions of the Freedom to Conduct a Business

The evolution of digital markets provides an illustrative example of the evolving scope of fundamental rights. Firstly, scenarios of conflict or collision, in which a specific fundamental right is in opposition to the fundamental right of another holder or with a public interest, are no longer confined to relationships between human beings. In contrast, novel scenarios are emerging, that pit different legal subjectivities against one another, such as the conflict between companies and companies and associations. While the Charter of Fundamental Rights of the European Union does not provide for a rule on the holders of fundamental rights, it is commonly accepted that, in addition to human beings, legal persons and other subjectivities are entitled to those fundamental rights which are compatible with their nature. This is a fundamental tenet of the rule of law and an inevitable consequence of a legal and social environment in which companies and other legal entities are regarded as subjects in their own right within the context of EU legal frameworks.

Secondly, while it is common to see fundamental rights as a shield, and thus from a negative perspective, they also entail important duties of protection on the part of states and political actors, requiring the adoption of measures (and in particular legislation) capable of anticipating and providing adequate responses to situations of risk in which the subjects of the legal community (which now includes companies as subjects per se) may find themselves. While positive duties to protect have been associated with the fundamental rights enshrined in the legal systems of the Member States, the moment the EU has adopted its own Charter, the objective dimension of these rights also becomes important in the European Union. If not as a result of an already established understanding, then certainly as a result of a principle or tradition common to the Member States.

A third aspect of metamorphosis is worthy of consideration. In light of the EU legislator and executive's prominent role in the digital regulatory landscape, there has also been a shift in the parties responsible for fulfilling duties of protection. Indeed, this protection is not limited to the dangers posed by state action; it also encompasses the threats that the exercise of liberties poses to other liberties. With the increasing importance of the European Union as a community of values, and in particular with a view to protecting the interests of European citizens and businesses, it is necessary to rethink the duties of the state. The duties of protection were initially justified as a counterbalance to the states' monopoly on the use of force and power. As sovereignty is being shared with the EU, and in an era where those normative, executive and judicial powers are transferred to the EU, it is believed that the duty to protect the fundamental rights and interests of both citizens and businesses must be a shared task of the EU and its.

Member States. In particular, the fact that the EU assumes the roles of legislator and enforcer in a specific domain requires that its institutions, agencies and bodies are also responsible for ensuring an appropriate response to the duties of protection arising from the fundamental rights enshrined in the Charter, as well as a fair balance in scenarios of potential conflict between them (see Article 52 of the Charter of Fundamental Rights of the European Union, 'CFR'). In short, the transfer or sharing of sovereign powers with supranational organisations has resulted in these same duties of protection now also binding the latter.

While the EU legislator bears the primary responsibility for designing and selecting measures that most effectively guarantee fundamental rights and those in need of special protection, the discretion afforded to the enforcer (the Commission) by digital regulations and the DMA in particular necessitates that it is also bound by positive duties. These are particularly relevant when the enforcer exercises its discretion.

4.1 Discretion in the Digital Markets Act

The discretion afforded to the European Commission is of central importance with regard to the implementation and enforcement of the DMA.

Firstly, there is the discretion to act which allows the relevant authorities to take action or refrain from doing so in response to a specific behaviour or request (Oliveira and Dias (2022), p. 137 ff). An illustration of this is the discretion afforded to the European Commission to engage (or not to engage) in a process to determine whether the efficacy of the measures implemented by the gatekeeper to ensure compliance with Articles 6 and 7 (see Article 8(3) DMA). An additional illustration can be found in Article 27(2) of the DMA, which grants National Competition Authorities ('NCAs') and the Commission full discretion to follow up on (or refrain from responding to) information received from third parties (including business users, competitors, or end users of a gatekeeper's core platform services).

Secondly, there is the discretion of choice, which allows the freedom to choose between two or more courses of action that are provided for in the legislation. In the context of the DMA, an illustrative example can be found in the relationship between the specification procedure set forth in Article 8 and the non-compliance procedure outlined in Article 29 of the DMA. Indeed, on the basis of the compliance reports submitted by the gatekeepers (see Article 11 DMA), the Commission has the discretion to either initiate a procedure to specify what is expected from the gatekeeper for effective compliance, thus favouring a cooperative and dialogical enforcement, or, alternatively, to proceed directly to a finding of non-compliance under Article 29 of the DMA. In this second scenario, the Commission is afforded a further degree of discretion in selecting an appropriate course of action. The Commission may elect to terminate the procedure without adopting a decision of non-compliance (see Article 29(7) DMA). An alternative course of action would be for the Commission to adopt a decision of non-compliance. This would entail ordering the gatekeeper to cease the infringement in question and to desist from further similar actions withing an appropriate deadline. Furthermore, the gatekeepers would be required to provide explanations as to how it plans to comply with the decision (see Article 29(5) DMA). Ultimately, the Commission may impose a fine on the non-compliant gatekeeper (see Article 30 DMA). In each of the aforementioned scenarios, the Commission exercises its discretion in the context of punitive enforcement. This approach appears to be consistent with the stance taken by the European Commission in relation to the initial compliance reports submitted by the gatekeepers.

Thirdly, creative discretion or the discretion to create provides the administration with the freedom to design concrete solutions within the applicable legal limits. In this instance, the law is thus limited to predicting and fixing a result, for which the administration is free to define the appropriate process or measures to achieve it. Although it may still be identified as a form of discretion of choice, it differs from the discretion to opt in that the options available to the administration are not predetermined or specified in legal provisions. Instead, they are the result of the administration's design. To illustrate this creative discretion, one might cite the interim measures which the EC is permitted to implement with the objective of preventing serious and irreparable damage for business users or end users of gatekeepers until the conclusion of an investigation. Article 24 of the DMA empowers the European Commission to exercise this competence in cases where it has prima facie established that gatekeepers have not complied with their obligations. However, a margin of creativity is permitted with regard to the design and choice of specific interim measures, as these are not defined nor specified in the DMA.

In contrast, technical discretion is employed primarily for the purpose of designing solutions that require a high level of specialised technical and professional knowledge and expertise. In this context, the reality to be regulated entails the formulation of technical judgements regarding the existence, value, or probability of a given situation. Although the complexity of the DMA authorises this type of discretion to be mobilised across the board, it is considered that it will mainly take place not in relation to the questions of 'if' or 'when'—often defined in the DMA in strict legal terms—but rather in relation to the 'how', i.e. the content or substance of the Commission's actions and decisions. Examples of this type of discretion can be found in the context of market investigations. It is noteworthy that companies may be designated as gatekeepers when the quantitative thresholds set out in Article 3(2) of the DMA are not met (see Article 3(8) DMA). Indeed, while the legislator defines the final objectives of the analysis and sets out elements that the Commission should consider for this purpose, the designation of a particular company as a gatekeeper requires the application of technical, scientific, and specialised knowledge, as well as a meta-legal assessment of the EC's suitability for conducting the task. The same is true of market investigations conducted for the purpose of introducing new services, practices, and obligations within the scope of the DMA (see Articles 12 and 19 DMA). In this regard, the Commission is acknowledged for its particular sapiential, particularly in light of its experience in relation to digital markets under Articles 101 and 102 of the TFEU.

One potential solution to the shortcomings of the DMA, or at the very least, to compensate for some of the blank interferences on the gatekeepers' subjective position, would be to ensure that the different moments of discretion afforded to the EC are used and exercised in a way that optimises the fundamental rights in question.

The DMA is mindful of the significance of exercising discretion within defined limits, upholding fundamental rights with a specific objective in mind: to guarantee the efficacy and optimisation of fundamental rights. In addition to references in the recitals, Article 34(1) of the DMA, entitled 'Right to be heard and access to the file', sets out the obligation for the Commission to provide the undertaking concerned with the opportunity to be heard before the adoption of a decision pursuant to Articles 8, 9(1), 10(1), 17, 18, 24, 25, 29 and 30 and Article 31(2) of the DMA. In accordance with the case law of the General Court, even decisions adopted under other Articles (for example, the decision in which the Commission designates an undertaking as a gatekeeper by rejecting its arguments seeking to call into question the presumptions laid down in Article 3(2) DMA) must respect the fundamental rights and observe the principles recognised by the Charter. This is precisely what results from Article 34(4) of the DMA, which makes reference to "any proceedings", as well as from Recital

109 of the DMA. The mention was, in any case, not essential, as it is inherent to the idea of fundamental rights. Indeed, as the General Court emphasises in Bytedance v Commission, "according to the case-law, the rights of the defence are fundamental rights forming an integral part of the general principles of law whose observance the Courts of the European Union ensure. That general principle of EU law is enshrined, in the context of the right to good administration, in Article 41(2)(a) and (b) of the Charter and applies where the authorities are minded to adopt a measure which will adversely affect an individual [...] Accordingly, observance of the right to be heard is required even where the applicable legislation does not expressly provide for such a procedural requirement [...] in accordance with Article 41 of the Charter, every person has the right to have his or her affairs handled impartially, fairly and within a reasonable time by the institutions, bodies, offices and agencies of the Union, which includes, inter alia, the right of every person to be heard, before any individual measure which would affect him or her adversely is taken. According to the case-law, that right guarantees every person the opportunity to make known his or her views effectively during an administrative procedure and before the adoption of any decision liable to affect his or her interests adversely".

In conclusion, it can be stated that discretion is not synonymous with either a monopoly in decision-making or arbitrariness. Discretion, in whatever form it may take or whichever actor it may be exercised by, is subject to external limits (such as the public interest or interests determined by the legislator and entrusted to the Commission) and internal limits. These include, first and foremost, fundamental rights, which, in the EU area, are not even limited to those enshrined in the CFR (see Article 6 TEU).

4.2 The Exercise of Discretion to Ensure the Protection of Fundamental Rights

Considering the discretionary authority vested in the Commission as the sole enforcer of the DMA (and the concentration of powers within its purview), and in consideration of the aforementioned shortcomings of the DMA for gatekeepers' fundamental rights, it is imperative that the DMA's implementation address these shortcomings. We put forward two countermeasures.

Firstly, it is possible to utilise the potential of administrative discretion in order to ensure the practical realisation and optimisation of the fundamental rights and interests at stake. It is proposed that the Commission's discretion to act and choose, as well as its creative and technical discretion, can address the flaws of the DMA in terms of rigidity and participation. To illustrate, in the event that compliance reports submitted by gatekeepers are deemed inadequate in light of the DMA's objectives, rather than automatically initiating non-compliance proceedings, the Commission could engage in specification (at least with respect to some of the obligations set forth in the DMA). In all cases, the EC is obliged to select the outcome that most respects and fulfils the positive duties that arise from fundamental rights. Following the entry into force and applicability of the DMA, the Commission appeared to pursue this course of action with regard to the right to be heard. Indeed, as is evident from the General Court ruling in Bytedance v Commission, "prior to the adoption of the contested decision, the applicant was heard on several occasions. Indeed, first of all, before the notification itself, four meetings, at the very least, were held between the applicant and the Commission [...] Next, after the notification was submitted on 3 July 2023, the Commission sent the applicant its preliminary views on 26 July 2023 and gave it the opportunity to state its position, which the applicant did by letter of 2 August 2023. Lastly, on 17 August 2023, another meeting between the applicant and the Commission took place."

Secondly, even if the Commission were to exercise its discretion in a manner that differs from the aforementioned interpretation, or even if a fair balance requires it to proceed with a solution, measure or decision that the gatekeeper deems to impair its rights disproportionately, judicial control over the discretionary adjacent binding zones is not only legitimate but also imperative.

It could be argued that, in a scenario where the Commission is afforded discretion, its decision-making process cannot be subject to judicial control. In such cases, the determining factors would be merit, convenience and/or expediency, and these are not susceptible to judicial review. Otherwise, the separation of powers, which is also a dimension of the rule of law and democracy—as values on which the Union is founded (see Article 2 of the Treaty of the European Union, 'TEU')—would be at stake.

Such an interpretation carries the risk of undermining the fundamental principles of the rule of law, namely the control of power and its subordination to the law. In conclusion, all power is ultimately subject to the law. All power is limited, regardless of the openness of the rule that translates into discretion. And all power is constrained by fundamental rights, serving both as a shield and a sword. Thus, it is reasonable to assume that if the legislature and the executive branch exercise Force and Will, the judiciary will be expected to exercise judgement.

Even if companies were not recognised as entitled to fundamental rights (which is not the position we are taking), procedural fundamental rights are considered to afford protection to any individual who is a party or is directly affected by administrative or other proceedings. In addition to their role as traditional cornerstones of individual subjective positions, they also serve as objective procedural standards and precipitates of constitutional values, common to both domestic and EU jurisdictions. When viewed in their objective dimension or even as principles, fundamental rights impose positive obligations on both to the legislature and the executive branch, independent of the subjects.

In order to ensure the effective protection of the law, the Court of Justice requires a fair trial that is independent of the executive branch. While this does not preclude the possibility of the enforcer's views influencing the judiciary's decision, it is essential that the courts maintain substantive independence, in the sense that executive decisions are not perceived as binding on the judiciary. It is only through this approach that those seeking justice and the general public can be assured of the continued confidence in the judicial system.

In addition to ensuring compliance with the relevant legislation (i.e., the control of all relevant questions of law), judicial review may extend to considerations such as the factual assumptions on which a Commission decision is based and the purpose that was actually pursued. Indeed, while the Commission is permitted a significant degree of discretion in making determinations of fact, these must be substantiated by evidence. In essence, it is the responsibility of the courts to delineate the scope of discretion granted to the authority by a specific statute. Moreover, the judiciary is able to determine whether the actions of the European Commission are impartial and proportional. Finally, with specific reference to fundamental rights, it is important to note that, in accordance with Article 52 of the Charter, any restriction on the exercise of the rights and freedoms recognised therein must be provided for by law, respect the essential content of those rights and freedoms, and comply with the principle of proportionality. This principle requires that any limitation on the rights and freedoms of individuals must be both appropriate and strictly necessary and proportionate in the strict sense. The principle and guarantee of judicial control also apply here. It is not policymaking; rather, it is fundamental rights adjudication.

This is how one can reconcile the fundamental rights and interests that require protection and effectiveness with those that the DMA is obliged to take into account as true fundamental rights.

5 Conclusions

The legitimacy of the Digital Markets Act is contingent upon a series of cumulative steps and underlying assumptions.Firstly, it is accurate to conclude that the specific demands and characteristics of digital markets give rise to novel or transformed dangers to the rights and interests of both end users and business users. It is vital to ascertain which rights and legal goods the Regulation's composite notions of contestability and fairness seek to safeguard. As has been previously indicated, these concepts cannot be reduced to a single right or interest. In contrast, they are appropriate for translating the legislator's purpose in anchoring the DMA in a set of "public interests", ranging from the safeguard of public order to the protection of privacy and the fight against fraudulent and deceptive commercial practices.

While there is a clear necessity for intervention by public authorities in this domain, it is imperative not to overlook the fact that such intervention ultimately represents an infringement upon the freedom to conduct a business. Consequently, when determining the reasons, methods and extent of intervention, the EU legislator and enforcer are obliged to comply with the requirements of the rule of law which include legal certainty and proportionality.

Conversely, the freedom to conduct a business of companies in a situation of danger may entail protective duties and positive actions, which, in the context of the Digital Markets Act, can be mobilised to emphasise the significance of the European

Commission's involvement in the design and enforcement of the DMA. Such protection duties cannot be anchored in any political-economic ideology, whether that be a strictly liberal, negative, or business-biased approach.

In short, the Digital Markets Act can be constitutionally justified by identifying a set of fundamental rights and values that are protected and pursued at the constitutional level. This set of protection obligations, which favour both business and end users and citizens, provides the justification for the obligations laid down in the Regulation. Furthermore, it offers a framework for evaluating the proportionality of the Regulation in its three dimensions: suitability, necessity, and prohibition of excess.

To return to the subject of the title, it is possible to reconcile what is seemingly irreconcilable, precisely if we recall that the freedom to conduct a business is presented as a right that is subject to a number of significant limitations, coupled with a social mission or responsibility. While the freedom to conduct business may be subject to limitations, linked with the rule of law, it possesses a minimum essential core. This core encompasses the following requirements: (i) legality; (ii) legal certainty; (iii) prohibition of arbitrariness; (iv) access to the law; and (v) non-discrimination or equality before the law.

It is at the level of proportionality that the various doubts raised regarding the Digital Markets Act must be highlighted and discussed (Dolmans et al. (2022), p. 8). While the DMA may be considered legitimate and proportionate on the surface, and while a formal reading of the Regulation would allow it to pass the rule of law test due to its "legal" nature, the justification on which it is based, or the exceptions and escape valves it provides, the text of the Digital Markets Act itself is flawed. The DMA is of concern due to its obligations of "automatic" application, its one-size-fits-all approach, the lack of opportunities to demonstrate efficiencies associated with prohibited behaviours, and the inability to prove the "impossibility" or excessiveness of the obligations imposed. From both the standpoint of the prohibition of excess (in terms of interference) and the prohibition of insufficiency (in terms of protection), the Digital Markets Act may prove to be unjustifiably detrimental to the freedom to conduct a business and, at very least, misaligned with the requirements of the rule of law.

In this text, we have put forth the hypothesis that enforcement may serve to ensure the fair balance required in all fundamental rights adjudication decisions, regardless of the institution responsible for making them. The Commission's discretion and judicial control by courts may provide the DMA with the necessary flexibility and fairness, thus ensuring that the hard law in its provisions does not obey only one master—effectiveness—and that other important fundamental rights, principles and values are not disregarded (de Streel et al. 2024).

In essence, the DMA is a vital instrument for safeguarding fundamental rights. However, it is crucial to recognise that these rights should not be interpreted as a licence for unbridled discretion. Instead, they must be viewed as cornerstones of a genuine and just system of governance. It is true that rights—and the freedom to conduct a business in particular—are not absolute prerogatives. They are, nonetheless, fundamental rights that must be taken seriously.

References

Akman P (2022) Regulating competition in digital platform markets: a critical assessment of the framework and approach of the EU Digital Markets Act. Eur Law Rev 47(1):85–114

Beems B (2022) The DMA in the broader regulatory landscape of the EU: an institutional perspective. Eur Compet J 19(1):1–29. https://doi.org/10.1080/17441056.2022.2129766

Blažo B (2022) The Digital Markets acts: Between market regulation, competition rules and unfair trade practices rules. Strani Prav Ziv 66(1):117–136

Blockx J (2023) The Digital Markets Act: Fostering Innovation 'Made in Europe'? SSRN. https://ssrn.com/abstract=4487366

Carugati C (2023) Compliance Principles for the Digital Markets Act. SSRN. https://ssrn.com/abstract=4738733

Colangelo G, Ribera Martínez A (2024) Vertical Interoperability in Mobile Ecosystems: Will the DMA Deliver (What Competition Law Could Not)? DEEP-IN Research Paper 2024. SSRN. https://ssrn.com/abstract=4826150

de Gregorio G (2022) Digital Constitutionalism in Europe: Reframing Rights and Powers in the Algorithmic Society. Cambridge University Press

de Streel A, Bourreau M, Feasey R, Fletcher A, Kraemer J, Monti G (2024) Implementing the DMA: Substantive and Procedural Principles. TILEC Discussion Paper. SSRN. https://ssrn.com/abstract=4700134

Diez F (2023) The DMA: A New Regulation for—or Against—Digital Markets in the EU? SSRN. https://ssrn.com/abstract=4321589

Dolmans M, Mostyn H, Kuivalainen E (2022) Rigid Justice is Injustice: The EU's Digital Markets Act Should Include an Express Proportionality Safeguard. Ondernemingsrecht issue 2–2022. SSRN. https://ssrn.com/abstract=3985562

Drewes H, Kirk A (2024) Extraterritorial Effects of the Digital Markets Act—The 'Elusive Long Arm' of European Digital Regulation. SSRN. https://ssrn.com/abstract=4763361

Fernández C (2021) A New Kid on the Block: How Will Competition Law Get along with the DMA? J Eur Compet Law & Prac 12(4):271–272. https://doi.org/10.1093/jeclap/lpab020

Fletcher A, Vasas Z (2023) Implementing the DMA: The Role of Behavioural Insights. SSRN. https://ssrn.com/abstract=4501429

Gryllos G (2024) The New Digital Landscape: Interaction between the DMA and Rules of national and EU law governing the conduct of gatekeepers. Concurrences—Revue des droits de la concurrence—Competition Law Review. SSRN. https://ssrn.com/abstract=4759968

Këllezi P (2022) Free Markets and the Rule of Law. J Eur Compet Law & Prac 1–2

Koenig C (2024a) Obligations for Gatekeepers. (Steinrötter / Heinze / Denga (eds), EU Platform Regulation, Beck Nomos Hart, Forthcoming). SSRN. https://ssrn.com/abstract=4715163

Koenig C (2024b) Introduction to the Digital Markets Act (DMA). (Steinrötter / Heinze / Denga (eds), EU Platform Regulation, Beck Nomos Hart, Forthcoming). SSRN. https://ssrn.com/abstract=4715147

Komninos A (2022) The Digital Markets Act: How Does it Compare with Competition Law? SSRN https://ssrn.com/abstract=4136146

Oliveira FP, Dias JEOF (2022) Noções Fundamentais de Direito Administrativo, 5th edn. Coimbra, Almedina

Ribera Martínez A (2024a) The Decentralisation of the DMA's Enforcement System. SSRN. https://ssrn.com/abstract=4857232

Ribera Martínez A (2024b) The Requisite Legal Standard of the Digital Markets Act's Designation Process. SSRN. https://ssrn.com/abstract=4681963

Mendelsohn J, Budzinski O (2023) Chapter 2 DMA: background, objectives, and its relationship to competition law. In: Schmidt JP, Hübener F (eds) New Digital Markets Act: A Practitioner's Guide. Nomos, Baden-Baden

Moreno Belloso N, Petit N (2023) The EU Digital Markets Act (DMA): A Competition Hand in a Regulatory Glove. European Law Review. 48. https://ssrn.com/abstract=4411743

Pablo AL, Fernández NB (2021) Why the Proposed DMA Might Be Illegal under Article 114 TFEU, and How to Fix It. J Eur Compet Law & Prac 12(7):576–589. https://doi.org/10.1093/jeclap/lpab059

Paunio E (2009) Beyond Predictability—Reflections on Legal Certainty and the Discourse Theory of Law in the EU Legal Order. Ger Law J 10(11):1469–1493. https://doi.org/10.1017/S20718322000183322009

Petit N (2021) The Proposed Digital Markets Act (DMA): A Legal and Policy Review. SSRN. https://ssrn.com/abstract=3843497

Portuese A (2022) The Digital Markets Act: A Triumph of Regulation Over Innovation. ITIF (Information Technology & Innovation Foundation). https://itif.org/publications/2022/08/24/digital-markets-act-a-triumph-of-regulation-over-innovation/

Robertson VHSE (2023) The Complementary Nature of the Digital Markets Act and Articles 101 and 102 TFEU. DMA working group (European Parliament's IMCO). Journal of Antitrust Enforcement. SSRN. https://ssrn.com/abstract=4458112

Schweitzer H (2021) The Art to Make Gatekeeper Positions Contestable and the Challenge to Know What is Fair: A Discussion of the Digital Markets Act Proposal. ZEuP 2021, Issue 3. SSRN. https://ssrn.com/abstract=3837341

Silva JP (2024) On the Origins of the Separation of Powers: Some Historical Remarks. In: Marques F, Albuquerque PP (eds) Rule of Law in Europe. Springer

Suzor N (2018) Digital Constitutionalism: Using the Rule of Law to Evaluate the Legitimacy of Governance by Platforms. Social Media + Society, 4(3). https://doi.org/10.1177/2056305118787812

Tzanaki A, Nowag J (2023) The Institutional Framework of the DMA: From Hybrid to Mature? (Christian Ahlborn, Pablo Ibáñez Colomo and William Leslie (eds.) The Law and Economics of the Digital Markets Act (Hart Publishing, Forthcoming). SSRN. https://ssrn.com/abstract=4574518

van den Boom J (2022) What does the Digital Markets Act harmonize?—exploring interactions between the DMA and national competition laws. Eur Compet J 19(1):57–85. https://doi.org/10.1080/17441056.2022.2156728

If I Could Have, I Would Have: Data Governance and Trust in the Implementation of Article 5(2) of the DMA

Alba Ribera Martínez

Abstract The Digital Markets Act (DMA) (Regulation (EU) 2022/1925 of the European Parliament and of the Council on contestable and fair markets in the digital sector and amending Directives (EU) 2019/1937 and (EU) 2020/1828 (Digital Markets Act) [2022] OJ L265/1.) is aimed to address contestability and fairness in the digital arena. The regulatory instrument encompasses the European Union's largest digital strategies in passing substantive legislation to ensure the right of every citizen to access a trustworthy digital environment (European Declaration on Digital Rights and Principles for the Digital Decade [2022] COM/2022/28 final.), as established by the European Declaration on Digital Rights and Principles for the Digital Decade. Trust as a standalone notion derived from effective enforcement and regulation has been analysed by the organization and management, sociology, or social capital literature. Economic exchanges have also been positively correlated with the existence of trust. Aside from these all-encompassing notions, trust remains widely understated to measure the effectiveness of regulation. The chapter identifies this gap in the literature and ties it in with the measurement of the DMA's effective enforcement. To do that, the chapter considers the DMA's impacts on end user trust in relation to its data-related provisions.

Keyword Digital Markets Act · Governance · Trust · Processing of Personal Data

1 Introduction

Article 1(1) of the DMA is a multi-tiered instrument aimed at the consecution of two main objectives: ensuring contestable and fair markets as well as tackling fragmentation between Member States when regulating digital markets from the regulatory perspective. The regulatory instrument applies to several economic operators that

A. Ribera Martínez (✉)
University Villanueva, Madrid, Spain
e-mail: riberamartinezalba@gmail.com

G. Enes et al. (eds.), *A Digital Europe for Citizens*,
https://doi.org/10.1007/978-3-032-02500-5_8

have been designated based on the core platform services that they cater for in the market (European Commission 2023c).

Both goals remain largely contested. Contestability and fairness are broad concepts that encompass the quasi-ethical and conflict-interest-driven problems that the main digital platforms cause in digital markets (Ribera Martínez 2023c). Those problems were first detected in the realm of competition law, but they have been brought to explain the rationale underlying the regulatory instrument. Some (and not all) of the DMA's provisions contained under Articles 5 to 7 pursue one or both goals from the regulatory perspective. Although the concepts have been defined under Recitals 32 and 33, the European Commission has delegated the addressees of the regulation to determine how contestability and fairness will look in practice (European Commission 2023a), without providing sufficient indicators for their compliance (Feasey and de Streel 2023). Moreover, the themes of contestability and fairness remain largely detached from the reality and economics of digital ecosystems, which is best depicted via the differentiation between intra and inter-platform competition (Bostoen 2023, Moreno Belloso and Petit 2023; de Steel et al. 2023; Teece and Kahwaty 2021).

With relation to the DMA's purpose of harmonisation, the DMA is construed upon this idea, since its legal basis is Article 114 TFEU. One of the reasons influencing the choice of this legal basis seems to point to the fact that no unanimity was required, whereas the practical consequences of its implementation are still to be seen, if at all (Ribera Martínez 2023d; Cappai and Colangelo 2023; Lamadrid de Pablo and Bayón Fernández 2021). Other instruments have been passed at the national level pursuing similar objectives to those of contestability and fairness such as the introduction of Section 19a to the German competition law regime (van den Boom 2023). The German newly introduced regime has produced its first results in prohibiting Google's processing activities from going further than the DMA's data-related obligations (Ribera Martínez 2023e).

However, less attention in the academic literature has been rendered to the analysis of the framework governing the effective implementation of the DMA's provisions. The DMA relies on a multi-level governance structure (Ribera Martínez 2023f). In other words, the regulatory instrument is not applied to one level of interacting agents, although it might be intuitive to depict that DMA in that way. Instead, the regulation builds up on a four-sided framework where the agents of the regulation interact with each other. These four sides are headed by the European Commission, the addressees of the regulation (gatekeepers), business users and end users. The multi-level governance structure entails idiosyncratic relationships take place as the DMA is being applied between these agents sporadically or via the procedural paths established by the regulatory instrument.

The multi-level governance structure is construed upon the myriad of mechanisms that crystallise compliance with the substantive content of DMA. First, the provisions of the DMA are to be considered by the gatekeeper as early as the technological design of its products and services in the same fashion as the GDPR's principle of data protection by design and by default (Recital 65). Second, the obligations set out in Articles 5 to 7 of the DMA follow a different governance structure. The obligations imposed on the gatekeeper in Article 5 are directly enforceable by the undertaking, whereas regarding the provisions in Articles 6 and 7, the gatekeeper may engage in a regulatory dialogue with the European Commission (EC) to specify the measures to ensure effective compliance (Article 8(3) DMA) (European Commission 2023b). The difference between the former and latter provisions does not stem from their enforceability -since they all apply 6 months later to the designation of the gatekeepers (Article 3(10) DMA)- but due to their clear-cut nature. The prohibitions under Article 5 DMA are presumed to be more straightforward than those surrounding Articles 6 and 7. Third, the gatekeeper bears the burden of demonstrating compliance with the DMA's provisions before the EC by reporting the detailed measures that it has implemented (Articles 8(1) and 11(1) DMA and European Commission 2023a). In this regard, third parties to the regulatory instrument, different to business users and end-users, are encouraged to provide comments to the EC regarding its preliminary findings on the DMA's compliance (Article 8(6) DMA).

The DMA is a governance-inspired regulatory instrument, insofar as compliance is not seen as a point on the horizon to reach and then maintain throughout the following years. Instead, compliance is ensured as a process, which may be tailored and fine-tuned throughout the years, depending on the relevant technological or commercial market developments (Recital 105).

Stemming from the substantive and institutional design of the DMA, the chapter revolves around the concept of governance as established by the regulatory instrument. Although governance is a moving-target-like concept which may capture a myriad of processes from the perspective of regulatory theory, the chapter comes to terms with the understanding of governance as a process in the hands of the authority, as a means used by an authority to guide, steer and regulate externalities through different mechanisms to maximise the public interest (Keping 2018; Fehr 2009, OECD 2014).

Governance, however, is not a self-supporting and self-enhancing tool in the hands of an authority operating in a vacuum. Instead, trust is, at least in theory, a prerequisite to securing a fully-fledged governance mechanism. When the processes to ensure an effective implementation are put into place by the Commission, there must be certainty on whether the enforcer of the DMA is competent and effective in delivering its goals and its capacity to operate consistently with a set of values that reflect the public's expectations of integrity and fairness. To this end, the chapter focuses on a definition of institutional trust based on the public's belief that the EC will act consistently with their expectations of positive behaviour (OECD 2017).

Against the backdrop of the interaction of the concepts of governance and trust with the DMA, the chapter seeks to respond to the question of whether the regulatory instrument is a sufficiently legitimate and effective tool in the hands of the European Commission. Legitimacy is explored from a procedural viewpoint as an element of legality as well as an expression of recognition conferred by others. The DMA's legitimacy relies not only on the fact that it should be fine-tuned correctly by the legislators in its procedures but also with regards to its regulatory justification, despite the fact that the latter feature of the regulatory instrument is largely contested due to its vaporous nature (Ribera Martínez 2023c; Colangelo 2023). Traditionally, the metrics to analyse legitimacy have been divided into input, throughput and output-oriented criteria (Bekkers and Edwards 2007).

Output-oriented criteria measure the effectiveness of regulations in solving the particular problems they wish to overcome (Scharpf 2009). Descending this perspective into the reality of the DMA, the chapter chooses to elucidate the links between the concepts of its multi-level governance structure with the enhancement of trust. To do that, the chapter considers the implementation of one of the most contested -and complex- provisions to implement by the gatekeepers: the prohibition set out in Article 5(2) DMA (Ribera Martínez 2023g). Even though the regulatory instrument is plagued with data-related obligations, Article 5(2) is the strictest provision from them all, since it outright prohibits the processing, combining, and cross-using of personal data across core platform services as well as into the gatekeepers' proprietary services and services of third parties. Article 6(2) prohibits the gatekeepers' use of any data that are not publicly available and that had been generated or provided by the business users in the context of their use of the relevant core platform services. As opposed to Article 5(2) DMA, Article 6(2) imposes a data-siloing obligation exclusively with regards to the B2B relationships of the gatekeeper, whereas the prohibition under Article 5(2) DMA is mainly directed at data defined as personal under the GDPR. The fact that Article 5(2) DMA engages with the prohibition of the processing, combination and cross-use of personal data (and not of non-public data) provides ample opportunity to narrow the gap between trust and governance since its immediate implications will be felt by end users, whereas the rest of the provisions are mainly engaged with the relationships between gatekeepers and their business users.

To perform this exercise, the chapter sets forth the case study of Article 5(2) of the DMA to future-proof its premises in light of the concepts of governance and trust. The gatekeeper-Commission's relations are considered as well as the gatekeeper's capacity to implement in full the prohibition laid out in Article 5(2) DMA (Section 1.2). Furthermore, end-user trust is examined in light of the DMA's governance structure and its ability to cushion institutional trust vis-à-vis the privacy paradoxes that are normally borne by consumers (Section 1.3). Finally, both aspects are brought together to draw out the inferences between end-user trust as a proxy to establishing whether good governance takes place in the context of the regulatory instrument (Section 1.4).

2 Data Governance in the Context of Article 5(2) of the DMA

Article 5(2) of the DMA prohibits the processing, combining, and cross-using of personal data across its core platform services. The prohibition de facto establishes a data-siloing obligation, insofar as the designated gatekeepers may not amalgamate their datasets containing personal data belonging to their core platform services unless the end user provides her consent within the meaning of Articles 4(11) and 7 of the General Data Protection Regulation (GDPR).[1] Article 5(2) DMA also points out that the gatekeeper may also continue relying on a number of the legal bases contained under Article 6(1) to continue processing personal data (Centre for Information Policy Leadership 2023).

The objective of the provision is to eradicate the exploitative conduct on the side of the gatekeepers which leverage their tight grip on the markets they operate in and transform it into a data advantage in relation to their competitors (Yan and He 2022). Recital 36 DMA concretises this broader objective as the need to lower barriers to entry posed by the competitive advantages in terms of the accumulation of data which play in favour of the gatekeepers when they are capable of accessing and processing larger troves of personal data as opposed to their business users and competitors.

2.1 *The Relationship Between Data Exploitation and EU Data Protection Regulation*

The DMA points out in its Recital 12 that its provisions apply without prejudice to the rules resulting from other acts of Union law regulating certain aspects of the provision of services covered by the regulation, notably the GDPR (Bania 2022). The GDPR is the legal framework which has aligned the interests of data subjects, data controllers and data processors regarding the processing, collecting and harvesting of personal data. The GDPR does not attribute legal ownership to data subjects over their personal data (Marinotti 2022). Instead, it permits the processing of personal data by data controllers and processors, considering that data subjects retain control over their personal data in light of the rights and attributions of the regulation. This retained control is the manifestation of the right to the protection of personal data enshrined in Article 8(1) of the Charter of Fundamental Rights of the European Union[2] (the Charter) and Article 16(1) of the TFEU. The legal requirements sustaining the alignment of the controller's economic interests with the effective protection of the data subject's fundamental rights are set out in Article 6 of the GDPR, namely via the legal basis that the data controller may justify his processing of personal data. Moreover, the data controller/processor retains responsibility for ensuring that the whole set of principles enshrined in Article 5 of the GDPR is complied with alongside the securement of the trove of rights enshrined by the GDPR in favour of data subjects (Chander et al. 2021).

Article 5(2) builds upon the experience of the interpretation of the GDPR regarding the concept of effective consent (Demircan 2023; Kerber 2022). Under the sphere

---

[1] Regulation (EU) 2016/679 of the European Parliament and of the Council on the protection of natural persons with regard to the processing of personal data and on the free movement of such data, and repealing Directive 95/46/EC (General Data Protection Regulation) [2016] OJ L119/1.

[2] Charter of the Fundamental Rights of the European Union [2012] OJ C326/391.

of the DMA, the interpretation of consent must be read in conjunction with the pre-emptive idea that consumers bear information asymmetries and the imbalances in bargaining power with regard to their position vis-à-vis that of gatekeepers (Ribera Martínez 2023b, Botta et al. 2023, Graef 2021). By this token, it is difficult to imagine a scenario where the interpretation of EU data protection regulation does not, at least, override or heavily influence the interpretation of Article 5(2).

The prohibition follows a long-drawn period in the field of data protection where the designated gatekeepers have systematically infringed the GDPR when processing their personal data. Data protection supervisory authorities have regularly fined these economic operators for acting in breach of data protection rules, especially in relation to the infringement of the purpose limitation and transparency principles. The Irish data protection supervisory authority has been especially active in this regard by sanctioning the processing activities of Meta or ByteDance (captured as gatekeepers by the DMA) due to infringements in the EU data protection regime. Simultaneously, the provision is also heavily inspired by the German competition authority's case against Facebook's processing activities where it considered that it had exploited consumers and caused anti-competitive harm by steering consumers to accept their terms and conditions (Ribera Martínez 2023c).

Against the yardstick of the GDPR's compliance, the DMA's intended objective to avoid interference with the data protection regulation under Recital 12 when applying its provisions seems far-fetched (Ribera Martínez 2023b). In light of Article 5(2) DMA, the gatekeepers will have to adapt their business models to the prohibition considering the existing framework for data governance and the GDPR's allocation of economic value over personal data.

The allocation of economic value is decimated from its underlying roots. Thus, the implementation of the provision cannot, in principle, be conflated with the attribution and legal responsibilities deriving from the GDPR. The most salient legal basis contained in Article 6(1)(a) GDPR (at least in terms of the scholarly debate triggered thereof) is construed on a notice-and-consent regime, even though the implications of this regulatory approach entail a one-time exercise of an informed and individual choice. This one-off exertion of choice may not always be realised in practice due to information and power asymmetries between data subjects and controllers (Bietti 2020). The same applies to the legal bases set out in Articles 6(c)-(e) of the GDPR, which may be applicable in the context of Article 5(2) DMA, effectively curtailing the implementation of the latter.

2.2 *Data Governance Under Article 5(2) DMA*

Stemming from the concept of governance, the prohibition contained in Article 5(2) of the DMA is contextualised into the framework of data governance. On top of the generalised notion of governance—as a process to maximise public interest –, data governance concretises the reality of data flows and amalgamates the methods by which private firms encompass their in-house policies and procedures to ensure that data are properly handled by default as well as while they are being used and retrieved from the gatekeeper's system (Viljoen 2021; Madison 2020).

These processes are based on the regulatory standards that align the interests of the different actors in play, namely the data protection regulations applicable in each corner of the World, as well as on the political and ethical necessities of stakeholders (Kim et al. 2013). Next to data governance, information governance is also relevant to the assessment of the perception of data as an asset but also as a means for value creation and capture in the hands of economic operators (Tallon et al. 2013).

Bearing in mind this context, compliance with Article 5(2) of the DMA may be factually impossible, given that the designated gatekeepers operate with great troves of data which they do not always categorise and segment correctly according to the requirements set out by the GDPR. In this regard, human rights organisations and academics have voiced their concern about the inadequacy of the configuration of the gatekeepers' internal data systems to satisfy the requirements set out by Article 5(2).

The main concern lies with the fact that gatekeepers themselves have little or no knowledge about the scope of their own data harvesting, processing and combining and its compliance with the existing standards under EU data protection regulation. Therefore, it will be hardly realistic to compel them to prohibit every operation relating to personal data if they do not distribute and combine their data in this same fashion. Even if they could, some analysts say, they would not know where to start from (Ryan 2022, Ribera Martínez 2023g).

Against this backdrop, one of the options at the European Commission's disposal in light of this complication would be to pre-emptively apply the exemption contained in Article 10 of the DMA. (European Commission 2023d, Ribera Martínez 2023h). The gatekeeper could be temporarily exempted from compliance through an implementing act issued by the Commission, issued as a consequence of the EC's initiative or upon the gatekeeper's request. Nonetheless, in practice, it would be difficult to articulate the exemption on these grounds. Article 10 of the DMA only provides an exemption of the prescriptions set out in Articles 5, 6 and 7 of the DMA on the grounds of public health or public security. The same limitation applies to those cases where the Commission may provisionally suspend the application of a specific obligation to one or more individual core platform services before the issuing of an implementing act (Articles 10(1)-(5) DMA). As a matter of fact, the European Commission has not granted such an exemption to any gatekeeper.

The second option which seems to pre-emptively satisfy the requirements of this scenario is Article 9 of the DMA, which allows gatekeepers to demonstrate that a specific obligation would endanger, due to exceptional circumstances beyond its control, the economic viability of its operation in the Union (European Commission 2023e, Ribera Martínez 2023g). If these circumstances are demonstrated by the gatekeeper, then suspension of compliance with particular provisions is granted. Although this possibility is open to the gatekeepers exceptionally, it cannot motivate the gatekeeper's utter lack of compliance towards a particular provision of the DMA indefinitely. In a similar vein to Article 10 DMA, the suspension of particular provisions is limited to a period deemed necessary by the European Commission to overcome the economic impossibility that was first alleged by the gatekeeper. No gatekeeper has sought to dodge the application of any of the DMA's obligations via this means.

Going back to the notion of data governance as the concrete expression of governance in the context of data flows, this notion pursues that firms are responsive to the risks associated with the unlimited amalgamation of personal data by ensuring visibility and processing traceability into their data systems whilst retaining the capacity to compete in the digital environment. Thus, the balance to strike is quite nuanced. On one side, the GDPR (despite the noble intentions of Recital 12 of the DMA) pursues the protection of personal data as a means to secure informational self-determination -an individual right of the data subject- (Thouvenin 2021). On the other side, the DMA pursues two main objectives deriving from Article 1(1), whereas Recital 36 concretises the rationale underlying the provision. From the perspective of data governance, these objectives must be aligned while preserving accountability and data integrity from an in-house perspective (Al-Ruithe et al. 2016, Demarquet 2015; McDowall 2017).

The potential trade-off when balancing the different interests in play faces two primary hurdles. First, the definition of the bounds of the specific intangible digital assets protected under Article 5(2) of the DMA (the personal data collected by a gatekeeper from its core platform services) may be quite a difficult task to perform. The gatekeepers' internal systems lack traceability and their digital assets do not abide by a concrete blueprint. They are driven by their amorphous nature (Marinotti 2021; Hayward 2016).

Datasets do not exist in a vacuum but in a greater relational landscape where different pieces of the same data may lie in distinct troves of data serving different purposes in the gatekeeper's business model (Halevy et al. 2016). The intersection of the GDPR and the DMA, although elusive, could play a major role in clarifying what the object of data governance is in the context of Article 5(2) DMA. Following the definition provided by the DMA, personal data is to be understood concerning its definition in the GDPR (Article 2(25) DMA). Thus, Article 5(2) DMA is concerned with data which may render the individual identifiable in line with the definition provided under Article 4(1) GDPR. The provision is not concerned, for instance, with non-personal data or inferred data in the hands of the gatekeeper, which may be equally attributed and produced due to a competitive advantage in scale caused by winner-takes-all dynamics caused by lack of contestability and fairness in the market.

The fact that the prohibition contained in Article 5(2) DMA is defined around the notion of personal data adds nothing to its technical implementation, even if it is useful from a legal perspective (Madison 2020). That is to say, gatekeepers' internal data systems may not be configured in line with the GDPR's requirements (even though they have not been found in breach of the data protection regulation), but instead, they may be constituted with limited codified information about their purpose, value, or origin from the internal perspective. In addition, extracting metadata from datasets to identify whether personal data is processed, combined or cross-used from them is not easy from a technical perspective, especially if Article 5(2) DMA is to apply *ex-ante*. Personal data are not static assets lying in one place at a time. They are produced daily by different teams -even involved in the catering of the same core platform service-, with different naming schemes as well as with different levels of granularity within each data configuration (Halevy et al. 2016).

Therefore, the technical implementation of the provision will only be feasible if an enterprise-wide opt-in is implemented to manage data in a standardised and secure manner, namely through the introduction of Enterprise Data Management (EDM) systems at every level of data extraction and at the level of each team responsible for collecting and processing data. In fact, some gatekeepers have crafted and fine-tuned their data infrastructures to such an extent as a consequence of the provision's implementation that they have, de facto, siloed data per each core platform service. This technical solution, however, does not seem proportionate to satisfy the DMA's compliance to applying the prohibition in Article 5(2) DMA exclusively regarding personal data derived from core platform services. Even if the technical solution would satisfy the requirement of data-siloing imposed by the prohibition, the legal requirements stand far off from the technical reality of the gatekeepers and their business models.

Second, the intrinsic rights related to the elements of those data troves may be complex to define, especially considering the European Union's strategies in enhancing alternative business models to those of the gatekeepers in the European sphere via the propulsion of data marketplaces (Botero Arcila and Groza 2023). Not only correctly identifying the assets by themselves, but differentiating personal from non-personal data may be quite complex, whereas other conceptualisations introduced into the business models of gatekeepers (for instance, third-party vis-à-vis first-party data) may complexify the process even further (Marinotti 2022).

Against this background, DG Comp and DG Connect (via their units in charge of enforcing the DMA) narrow the disconnect between the legal reality introduced by the DMA and the technical solutions which satisfy the compliance of Article 5(2) of the DMA. It is for the gatekeepers to assess how their data operations may continue (or what parts of them should be discontinued) in light of the provisions set out via the DMA as well as by the regulatory framework.

However, this will only happen if appropriate data governance mechanisms are progressively introduced or enhanced into the gatekeeper's business model on top of the existing requirements set out by the GDPR. Internal governance will have to closely measure the findings and progress made by gatekeepers in this regard, both by responding and analysing closely the reports issued by them on the measures implemented to ensure compliance in a detailed and transparent manner as well as by ensuring that oversight of the DMA's implementation is also pursued in-house through their compliance function (Articles 11 and 28 DMA).

Once these mechanisms are put in place, the European Commission's and gatekeeper's trust relationships will be sparked amid the DMA's compliance (Ribera Martínez 2023c), with the risk of regulatory capture and regulatory bias (Snoep 2023). These trust relationships and the reaction of the EC to the gatekeeper's proposed measures seeking compliance will serve as a yardstick to measure whether appropriate governance of the DMA is performed (OECD 2014).

3 The DMA's Capacity to Steer End-User Behaviour

The multi-level governance structure of the DMA places the locus of compliance on the interactions and iterations of four different intervening agents: the European Commission, the gatekeepers, business users and end users (Ribera Martínez 2023c). Trust relationships will be enhanced and carved out through these interactions. The most tangible effects will be those produced upon end users, in relation to their interaction with the European Commission, gatekeepers, and business users.

However, the exercise of measuring them may well be the most difficult to measure in practice (OECD 2017). In a similar vein to the intangibility and amorphous nature of data assets and the legal framework applicable to them, trust is also challenging to measure, but it is not an intractable metric.

3.1 Trust Relationships and Governance in the Abstract

The literature background around the concept of trust has analysed the matter in depth, as opposed to the nebulous concept of governance (OECD 2017). Trust may be measured both from the interpersonal and institutional perspectives. The interpersonal perspective is focused on the interactions between individuals, whereas the institutional viewpoint bears in mind the existing connections between citizens (consumers) and the institutions implementing rules to deliver a set of goals in the public interest. Regarding institutional trust, the interplay between the two groups will vary in degree and intensity depending on the type of institution concerned and the rules to be applied by that same institution, as well as by the goals pursued by these rules.

The pre-condition of the existence of trust between two or more economic agents in their transactions has been considered as a means to facilitate economic development (Arrow 1972; Williamson 1985; Dore 1983; Fehr 2009, Guiso et al. 2008). Even though the organisation and strategy literature have asserted that trust in economic exchanges is beneficial and can be a source of competitive advantage due to its resonance with efficient governance, these assumptions have not yet been translated towards the broader spectrum of the user's interactions and experience before the competitive dynamics presented by digital platforms (Arrow 1974; Bromiley and Cummings 1974). To be fair, the literature has not descended how their enhancement leads to an increase in economic welfare, either.

The uncertainty regarding the effects of both concepts has permeated their definition across these same fields of study. A sound conceptual and single agreed definition of trust has not been used across these disciplines, but they all have taken recourse to the same unifying themes. First of all, trust is defined against the yardstick of the expectations of an individual or a community regarding an institution (Hardin 2002; Uslaner 2002; Morrone et al. 2009; Zak and Knack 2001). These expectations may be reflected in a twofold manner: i) through the logic of consequences by establishing whether the institution's functioning matches the expectations of the outcomes desired by the rules steering them (trust in competence); and ii) through the logic of appropriateness by remarking whether the institution acts in a way that is perceived as ethical and fair (trust in intentions).

The second tenet of the conceptualisation around institutional trust revolves around the element of risk involved between the interactions of end users and the European Commission (OECD 2017). The theory goes that more risk involved leads to a greater elasticity of trust. In other words, institutional trust will be higher (and easier to assume) in those cases where the risk involved is minimal, and one dare say when the institution has a minor role to play in the minimisation of that risk via its discretion. Thus, a higher degree of institutional trust from the citizen to the institution will be harder to accomplish when the latter is provided more leeway to interpret how it should minimise risks.

3.2 Applying the Dichotomy to the Regulatory Framework of the Digital Markets Act

For the case of the DMA, and specifically concerning the implementation of the prohibition under Article 5(2), the objectives of fairness and contestability must be read in conjunction with the objective of bringing down the barriers to entry to the market derived from the harvesting and collecting of personal data vis-à-vis smaller players with a lower capacity to amalgamate great troves of personal data.

The Commission, that is, the authority in charge of its enforcement, does not derive its legitimacy from representative democracy but from the delegation and the conferral of powers provided by the Member States upon the Union. In the case of the DMA, its legitimacy is attributed to the output-oriented perspective. In other words, the Commission's role in monitoring the regulatory instrument's effective enforcement will be measured against its capacity to contribute toward remedying contestability and fairness of the digital arena (its intended outcome), and not producing unintended effects in the market by the inferred consequences of the imposition of its rules (Bekkers and Edwards 2007; Bellamy and Castiglione 2013, OECD 2021).

However, the DMA's provisions are sketched out through the translation of un-values to the applicable rules in the digital environment regarding gatekeepers (van Twist and Termeer 1991; Ribera Martínez 2023a). Experience in the enforcement of digital markets by competition authorities has demonstrated an incapacity to tackle these issues and has shown what ought not to be done, in terms of enforcement and the future gatekeeper's conduct (Recital 5 DMA). Hence, the ethical space of the regulatory instrument is sketched out from this blueprint (Ribera Martínez 2023a).

From the end-user perspective, this is the starting point from where the DMA's provisions are implemented and applied. In terms of trust, two alternative theories might apply to the particularly negative scenario described by the legislator.

Either end users mistrust gatekeepers in processing, combining and cross-using their personal data appropriately based on experience but have willingly accepted the reality due to a lack of alternative business models available in the digital arena, or end users implicitly trust gatekeepers with their personal data.

Bearing in mind the latter perspective, rational choice theory assumes that end users factored into their decision-making (for example, in disclosing data with the gatekeepers for their processing) the information asymmetries and imbalances in bargaining power they bore and decided, in any case, based on their self-interest, assume that the gains derived from the value derived by the gatekeepers are greater than the costs that they incur in via data harms and loss (Smith 1776; Chattopadhyay 2015; Lambert 2020).

However, if one stands to apply the more nuanced and substantive viewpoint that trust is not implied by the end users in the digital arena, then mistrust is the norm surrounding the operations of the gatekeepers. This starting point is key to understanding the construction of end-user trust through the DMA's provisions to ensure a trustworthy digital environment, as pointed out by the European Declaration on Digital Rights and Principles for the Digital Decade. Before this challenge, two alternative theoretical solutions may be proposed. On one hand, if mistrust is not irreversible, it can, thus, be restored so that end users recoup their former relationships with the economic agents they interact with online. On the other hand, if mistrust from the side of end users is categorical, then trust relationships must be construed under a different paradigm by the disintermediation of the direct relationships between the end user vis-à-vis the gatekeepers' interactions. This is the paradigm that the DMA is construed upon.

The enhancing (or re-building) of end user trust will depend on the European Commission's capacity -as a mediated figure between them- to narrow the gap between the end user's preferences and expectations regarding the gatekeeper's business models through the perception of how the institution is governing that situation towards its three-fold objectives (Bouckaert and van de Walle 2003).

The DMA is designed around the traditional double-interact steering mechanism. Future behaviour is re-evaluated in light of previous experience: an action performed by an agent (act), triggers a second agent to respond (interact), which finally forces the first agent to re-consider the behaviour that was triggered (double-interact) (van Twist and Termeer 1991). The DMA's provisions start to apply triggering an action on the gatekeeper (act), which the European Commission will respond to as the sole enforcer of the regulatory instrument (interact), and in the light of technological development and market trends, the European Commission may re-evaluate whether the requirements upon the application of the DMA should be interpreted with the same intensity or concerning the same gatekeepers and or core platform services (double-interact) (Ribera Martínez 2023a).

A myriad of consequences stems from this premise, insofar as end user preferences and experience towards disclosing their personal data may vary depending on a range of elements. Their expressed preferences online may not only manifest in the form of commercial transactions performed online as one-off transactions with the gatekeepers but also as repeated actions in their daily lives which may not change after all and may be difficult to capture in practice. The definition provided in the DMA for end users confirms that they are attributed a relevant role under the scope of the regulatory instrument even if they do not perform a commercial transaction, as long as they use a core platform service (Article 2(20) DMA).

Although a combination of transactional and non-transactional user behaviour may balance the market out from its tipping when end users move away from using a particular gatekeeper's service, a prolonged increase or decrease in one of these metrics does not necessarily imply that end user trust has directly increased or decreased in favour of the use of that same service. It does seem wise to sustain that the DMA is covertly directed to steer the digital arena by favouring practices which are inspired by the principles of ensuring contestability and fairness (Ibáñez Colomo 2021).

The inferred consequence of this motion, however, does not seem that straightforward. If the DMA is based on un-values, then the alternate multiverse is to imagine that fairness and contestability may prevail in a digital environment where anti-competitive conducts do not truffle the competition authority's pipeline of work. Hence, the immediate result of the DMA may not necessarily derive to dethrone the designated gatekeepers in favour of levelling the playing field to gain a greater pool of competitors in the provision of core platform-services-alikes (Ribera Martínez 2023f; Cennamo and Santaló 2022; Cennamo 2023). End user trust in the digital arena may be triggered as a consequence of increasing trust in the (seldom monopolistic-like) gatekeepers from a position of mistrust due to their anti-competitive conduct as well as by a generalised trust in the European Commission to monitor compliance of their conducts closely, as opposed to their response thus far in the field of antitrust.

Furthermore, expressed preferences online are also an elusive concept, because end users may be deceived into making choices which do not necessarily align with their preferences (Acquisti et al. 2017). Going back to Article 5(2) DMA, given that end users may provide their consent to enable gatekeepers to process, cross-use and combine their personal data across their core platform services, this 'expressed preference' may not always reflect an increase in end-user trust for that gatekeeper vis-à-vis that of other gatekeepers (assuming that the former increases whilst the latter remains the same). The presence of trust relationships may be deceptive in the digital arena, given that data subjects tend to trust larger players as opposed to smaller competitors when disclosing their personal data, reinforcing the idea that larger competitors ride on their economies of scale and scope to obtain their data advantages (Rubinfeld and Gal 2017).

Empirical research performed among end users of platform services has also demonstrated that gatekeepers may utilise behavioural science inspired by mechanisms such as hyper-nudging to steer end-users away from exercising their rights relating to their data protection and in favour of enhancing information sharing and data flow across their services (Morozovaite 2021, Condorelli and Padilla 2020). Heuristics also pose a main challenge in this context, insofar as privacy and economic experts have not been able to overcome the disconnect between end users' expressed preferences online and the actual behaviour that they manifest as far as their privacy is concerned (Akman 2022, Lorenzo et al. 2020). End users could well grant their consent to the gatekeeper to exempt it from the prohibitions contained under Article 5(2) of the DMA whereas they might assign high importance and value and, thus, possess a high expectation of their personal data to remain protected.

Following the rationale of the elasticity of institutional trust, end users have conferred upon the EC a margin of discretion (via the indirect Member States' conferral of powers) to affect their interests surrounding the digital environment, by trying to reign in the power of gatekeepers when they operate and cater for their core platform services online. The encapsulation of the end users' expectations is conditional upon the first defining element of trust: their knowledge and beliefs regarding the DMA's implementation and the role it will play in transforming the digital environment. The margin of discretion granted by the end users has been filled and occupied with the DMA's prescriptions and prohibitions which will apply to the designated gatekeepers, to counter the risk of anti-competitive conduct.

The question is whether the logic of consequences rationale will apply and whether the EC as the DMA's sole enforcer will be able to causally derive its desired outcomes without any unintended consequences. This is a bold question to formulate, given that end users' interests, needs and expectations may also change over time in light of technological development and enhanced connectivity across countries in the world.

4 The Apparent Disconnect Between End User Trust and Good Governance

The last element surrounding the interplay between end user trust and good governance is concerned with narrowing the gap in the disconnect between the end user's expectations when navigating and transacting online and the European Commission's capacity to govern appropriately its monitoring and enforcement to pursue its intended purposes. Causality surrounding end user trust as a proxy to good governance on the side of the EC is not straightforward.

The EC, through the provisions of the DMA, stimulates citizens to change their demands or, at least, points out the conflicting nature of their current demands. For instance, end users may be encouraged to use services online which are not as data intensive as those that preceded and dominated the market in the last few years as a consequence of the prohibition of Article 5(2) DMA (Bouckaert and van de Walle 2003). This may lead end users to receive less personalised services as a consequence of their interaction with a DMA-compliant regulatory framework, which may not always coincide with their preferences vis-à-vis their privacy concerns.

Although some end users may value the regulation-led change, individual expectations do not remain static across different Member States and are not monistic in nature (Bouckaert 2012, Falk and Beckert 2015). Thus, end user trust may suffer as a consequence of the DMA's implementation, even though the regulatory instrument forbids gatekeepers from degrading the conditions or quality of any of its core platform services (Article 13(6) DMA). The management of their expectations throughout the DMA's progressive implementation plays a key role in accommodating their preferences into a fair and contestable paradigm in the context of digital commoditisation.

From this perspective concerning the administration of public competence and authority, the link between governance and trust has been mainly portrayed in the negative. That is to say, bad performance caused by institutional overload cannot meet the rising demands of the citizens or, simply, institution's and the citizens' demands are contradictory in nature and cannot be attained simultaneously. By this token, bad governance is associated with low levels of trust. However, the opposite paradigm has been seldom portrayed. Increased user trust might be a misleading proxy for assessing the regulatory instrument's good governance. In sum, the fact that the DMA is governed correctly and satisfactorily may lead to increased end user trust, but the disconnect between the institution's desired regulatory outcomes and the end-user's expectations may still prevail in practice.

Governance is measured against the normative implications of the DMA. However, end user trust is assessed in the face of expectations and preferences expressed online, with the inherent limitations of behavioural sciences and heuristics. Therefore, the latter cannot be an appropriate proxy for good governance. They capture different dimensions of the same phenomenon. Nonetheless, both concepts share common traits regarding the same phenomenon (the process concerning the DMA's implementation, enforcement, and monitoring) under different lenses. Governance is defined stably and externally relating to what purposes are placed prominently by the DMA. The appropriate benchmark to measure governance against relates to the regulatory instrument's goals of fairness and contestability. Trust may be defined differently due to its changing nature, and it is expressed internally relating to the expectations of an individual or a group of end users with common interests and expressed preferences (Bouckaert and van de Walle 2003). The yardstick to navigate the DMA as a trust-building measure will involve a score of societal and psychological factors which may not be relevant to the notion of governance nor correspond with reality after all (Bouckaert and van de Walle 2003).

The apparent disconnect between both concepts does not necessarily imply that good governance is completely oblivious to end user trust, and vice versa. In the absence of end trust, governance may act as the last recourse to ensure that, at least, regulatory and democratically ridden outcomes are obtained.

Even though the DMA has been largely criticised for interfering with the existing business models of the main digital platforms, the regulatory instrument is construed to ensure governance with a double-tiered mechanism in mind: (i) the EC ensures that regulatory outcomes are met according to the objectives set out in the DMA; and (ii) the functioning of the digital markets will satisfy the needs and preferences of the end users from the regulatory outcomes to the better and informed outcomes which will take place as a consequence of economic transactions where the economic operators and the end users will be directly concerned. The logic of consequences is balanced in the DMA to satisfy and provide for the appropriate discretion upon gatekeepers' economic decisions to cater for their core platform services in line with the regulatory aims surrounding fairness and contestability.

The operationalisation of trust in the context of the DMA is quite abstract in nature and it may be captured in relation to governance regarding each one of the provisions set out in the regulatory instrument and concerning the groups of individuals sharing the same expressed preferences. Even within these groups, their response towards the DMA's implementation and further governance may be scattered and non-linear as far as end user trust is concerned, given its malleable and individualised nature.

5 Conclusions

Good governance is purported as one of the main concepts that justify the legitimacy of a set of rules. The chapter explores the two sides of the coin as far as governance is concerned relating to the particular application of Article 5(2) of the DMA. First, the gatekeeper's capacity to implement the prohibition is assessed under the lens of data governance. Second, the end users' reaction towards its application is also considered, insofar as trust goes hand in hand with governance to ensure that at least regulatory outcomes are met according to the DMA's proposed objectives.

Against this background, the chapter reviews the disconnect between the former and the latter expressions of governance, given that trust does not always imply satisfactory governance or vice versa. Although a complex exercise, the chapter shows that the gap between governance in the hands of the European Commission and an increase in end user trust as a result of applying the DMA's provisions may be narrowed by considering the differentiated correlations of the Commission's capacity to regulate a particular tenet of the gatekeeper's business model and the discretionary space open to gatekeepers to operating in the market in compliance with the regulatory instrument in the fashion of end users' trust in the EC's competence.

References

Acquisti A et al (2017) Nudges for privacy and security: Understanding and assisting user's choices online. ACM Comput Surv 50(3):44–85

Akman P (2022) A Web of Paradoxes: Empirical Evidence on Online Platform Users and Implications for Competition and Regulation in Digital Markets. Va L & Bus Rev 16(2):217–292

Al-Ruithe M, Benkhelifa E et al (2016) A Conceptual Framework for Designing Data Governance for Cloud Computing. Procedia Comput Sci 94:160–167

Arrow K (1974) The Limits of Organizations. Norton, New York

Arrow K (1972) Gifts and exchanges. Philos Public Aff 1(4):343–362

Bania K (2022) Fitting the Digital Markets Act in the existing legal framework: the myth of the 'without prejudice' clause. Eur Compet J 19(1):116–149

Bellamy R, Castiglione D (2013) Democracy by Delegation? Who Represents Whom and How in European Governance. Gov Oppos 46(1):101–125

Bekkers VJJM, Edwards AR (2007) Legitimacy and Democracy: A Conceptual Framework for Assessing Governance Practices. In: Bekkers V, Dijkstra G, Fenger M (eds) Governance and the

Democratic Deficit: Assessing the Democratic Legitimacy of Governance Practices. Routledge, pp. 35–60
Bietti E (2020) Consent as a Free Pass: Platform Power and the Limits of the Informational Turn. Pace Int Law Rev 40(1):310–398
van den Boom J (2023) What does the Digital Markets Act harmonize? Exploring interactions between the DMA and national competition laws. Eur Compet J 19(1):57–85
Bostoen F (2023) Understanding the Digital Market Act. Antitrust Bull 68(2):268–306
Botero Arcila B, Groza T (2023) The New Law of the European Data Market: Demystifying the European Data Strategy. Available via SSRN. https://doi.org/10.2139/ssrn.4580036
Botta M, Da Costa Leite Borges D (2023) User's consent under Art. 5(2) Digital Markets Act (DMA): Exploring the complex relationship between the DMA and the GDPR. Robert Schuman Centre Working Paper: in file with author
Bouckaert G (2012) Trust and public administration. (2012) Administration 60(1):91–115
Bouckaert G, van de Walle S (2003) Comparing measures of citizen trust and user satisfaction as indicators of 'good governance: Difficulties in linking trust and satisfaction industries. Rev Adm Sci 69(3):329–343
Bromiley P, Cummings LL (1974) Transaction Costs in Organizations with Trust. In: Lewici RJ, Bies RJ, Sheppard BH (eds), Research on Negotiation in Organizations. JAI Press, pp. 219–247
Cappai M, Colangelo G (2023) Applying Ne Bis in Idem in the Aftermath of bpost and Nordzucker: The case of EU competition policy in digital markets. Common Mark Law Rev 60(2):431–456
Cennamo C (2023) The EU Digital Markets Act: It is Not About Markets but Ecosystem Failures! Available via Network Law Review. https://www.networklawreview.org/dma-ecosystems/
Cennamo C, Santaló J (2022) Value in Digital Platforms: The Choice of Tradeoffs in the Digital Markets Act. Available via SSRN. https://doi.org/10.2139/ssrn.4152113
Centre for Information Policy Leadership (2023) Limiting Legal Basis for Data Processing Under the DMA: Considerations on Scope and Practical Consequences. CIPL Discussion Paper. Available via CIPL. https://www.informationpolicycentre.com/uploads/5/7/1/0/57104281/cipl_dma_limiting_legal_basis_may2023.pdf
Chander A, Kaminski ME et al (2021) Catalyzing Privacy Law. Minn L Rev 105:1733–1802
Chattopadhyay S (2015) Rational Choice Theory Applied to the Modern Digital Economy. Available via Prospus. https://prospus.com/blog/rational-choice-theory-applied-to-the-modern-digital-economy/
Colangelo G (2023) In Fairness We (Should Not) Trust: The Duplicity of the EU Competition Policy Mantra in Digital Markets. The Antitrust Bulletin: forthcoming
Condorelli D, Padilla J (2020) Harnessing Platform Envelopment in the Digital World. J Compet Law Econ 16(2):143–187
Demarquet G (2015) Five Key Reasons Enterprise Data Governance Matters to Finance… and Seven Best Practices to Get You There. J Corp Account Finance 27(2):47–51
Demircan M (2023) The DMA and the GDPR: Making Sense of Data Accumulation, Cross-Use and Data Sharing Provisions. In: Bieker F, Meyer J, Pape S, Schiering I, Weich A (eds) Privacy and Identity Management. Privacy and Identity 2022. Springer, 148–164
Dore R (1983) Goodwill and the Spirit of Market Capitalism. Br J Sociol 34:459–482
European Commission (2023a) Template form for reporting pursuant to Article 11 of Regulation (EU) 2022/1925 (Digital Markets Act) (Compliance Report). Available via European Commission official website. https://digital-markets-act.ec.europa.eu/system/files/2023-10/Article%2011%20DMA%20-%20Compliance%20Report%20Template%20Form.pdf
European Commission (2023b) Template relating to the reasoned request for a specification process pursuant to Article 8(3) of Regulation (EU) 2022/1925 (Digital Markets Act). Available via European Commission official website. https://digital-markets-act.ec.europa.eu/system/files/2023-10/Article%208%283%29%20DMA%20Template%20%28request%20for%20specification%20dialogue%29_1.pdf

European Commission (2023c) Commission designates six gatekeepers under the Digital Markets Act. Available via European Commission official website. https://digital-markets-act.ec.europa.eu/commission-designates-six-gatekeepers-under-digital-markets-act-2023-09-06_en
European Commission (2023d) Template relating to the submission of a reasoned request pursuant to Article 10 of Regulation (EU) 2022/1925 (Digital Markets Act). Available via European Commission official website. https://digital-markets-act.ec.europa.eu/system/files/2023-10/Article%2010%20DMA%20Template%20%28exemption%20request%29.pdf
European Commission (2023e) Template relating to the submission of a reasoned request pursuant to Article 9 of Regulation (EU) No 2022/1925 (Digital Markets Act). Available via European Commission official website. https://digital-markets-act.ec.europa.eu/system/files/2023-10/Article%209%20DMA%20Template%20%28suspension%20request%29.pdf
Falk A, Beckert A et al (2015) The nature and predictive power of preferences: Global evidence. IZA Discussion Paper. Available via SSRN. https://doi.org/10.2139/ssrn.2696302
Feasey R, de Streel A (2023) DMA Output Indicators. CERRE Draft Issue Paper. Available via SSRN. https://cerre.eu/wp-content/uploads/2023/07/CERRE-Draft-Issue-Paper-DMA-Output-Indicators.pdf
Fehr E (2009) On the Economics and Biology of Trust. J Eur Econ Assoc 7(2):235–266
Graef I (2021) Why End-User Consent Cannot Keep Markets Contestable. Verfassungsblog. Available via Verfassungsblog. https://verfassungsblog.de/power-dsa-dma-08/
Guiso L, Sapienza P et al (2008) Trusting the stock market. J Financ 63(6):2557–2600
Halevy A, Korn F et al (2016) Managing Google's Data Lake: An Overview of the GOODS System. IEEE Engineering Bulletin 39(3):5–14
Hardin R (2002) Trust and Trustworthiness. Russel Sage Foundation, Washington
Hayward B (2016) What's in a Name? Software, Digital Products, and the Sale of Goods. Syd Law Rev 38(4):441–462
Ibáñez Colomo P (2021) The Draft Digital Markets Act: A Legal and Institutional Analysis. J Eur Compet Law Pra 12(7):561–575
Keping Y (2018) Governance and Good Governance: A New Framework for Political Analysis. Fudan J Hum Soc Sci 11(1):1–8
Kerber W (2022) Taming Tech Giants: The Neglected Interplay Between Competition Law and Data Protection (Privacy) Law. Antitrust Bull 67(2):280–301
Kim KK, Browe DK et al (2013) Data Governance Requirements for Distributed Clinical Research Networks: Triangulating Perspectives of Diverse Stakeholders. J Am Med Inform Assoc 21(4):714–719
Lamadrid de Pablo A, Bayón Fernández N (2023) Why the Proposed DMA Might Be Illegal Under Article 114 TFEU, and How to Fix It. J Eur Compet Law & Prac 12(7):576–589
Lambert TA (2020) Rent-Seeking and Public Choice in Digital Markets. University of Missouri School of Law Legal Studies Research Paper. Available via SSRN. https://ssrn.com/abstract=3728990
Lorenzo P, Padilla J et al (2020) Consumer Preferences for Personal Data Protection in Social Networks: A Choice Modelling Exercise. Available via SSRN. https://doi.org/10.2139/ssrn.3716206
Madison MJ (2020) Tools for Data Governance. University of Pittsburgh School of Law Legal Studies Research Paper Series. Available via SSRN. https://ssrn.com/abstract=3653209
Marinotti J (2022) Data Types, Data Doubts & Data Trusts. New York University Law Review Online 97:146–172
Marinotti J (2021) Tangibility as Technology. Ga St U L Rev 37(3):671–738
Masson J (2023) Gatekeeper rivals cannot use DMA to obtain market advantages, EU official says. Available via Global Competition Review. https://globalcompetitionreview.com/article/gatekeeper-rivals-cannot-use-dma-obtain-market-advantages-eu-official-says
McDowall RD (2017) Understanding Data Governance. Part II. Spectroscopy 32(4):12–18
Moreno Belloso N, Petit N (2023) The EU Digital Markets Act (DMA): a Competition Hand in a Regulatory Glove. Eur Law Rev 48(4):391–421

Morozovaite V (2021) Two sides of the digital advertising coin: putting hypernudging into perspective. Market and Competition Law Review 5(2):105–145
Morrone A, Tontoranelli N et al. (2009) How Good is Trust? Measuring Trust and its Role for the Progress of Societies. OECD Statistics Working Papers. Available via OECD Library. https://www.oecd-ilibrary.org/economics/how-good-is-trust_220633873086
Organisation for Economics Co-Operation and Development (2014) Best Practice Principles for Regulatory Policy: The Governance of Regulators. OECD Publishing, Paris
Organisation for Economics Co-Operation and Development (2017) OECD Guidelines on Measuring Trust. OECD Publishing, Paris
Organisation for Economics Co-Operation and Development (2021) Ex post evaluation. OECD Publishing, Paris
Ribera Martínez A (2023a) The Steering of End-User Behaviour in the Digital Markets Act: The Intrinsic Value of Trust for Governance. North East Law Review 9(2):8–19
Ribera Martínez A (2023b) The Circularity of Consent in the DMA: A Close Look into Articles 5(2) and 6(10). Concorrenza e Mercato: forthcoming
Ribera Martínez A (2023c) The DMA's Ithaca: Contestable and Fair Markets. World Competition 64(4):1–30
Ribera Martínez A (2023d) An Inverse Analysis of the Digital Markets Act: Applying the Ne Bis in Idem Principle to Enforcement. Eur Compet J 19(1):86–115
Ribera Martínez A (2023e) The Appropriation of Article 5(2) DMA: Google's Commitments under Section 19a of the German Competition Act. Kluwer Competition Law Blog. Available via Wolters Kluwer. https://competitionlawblog.kluwercompetitionlaw.com/2023/10/09/the-appropriation-of-article-52-dma-googles-commitments-under-section-19a-of-the-german-competition-act/
Ribera Martínez A (2023f) Rocking the Contestability and Fairness Foundations: Multi-Level Governance and Trust Relations for Futureproofing the DMA's Effectiveness. European Yearbook of International Economic Law, 1–35
Ribera Martínez A (2023g) Fourth Workshop on the DMA – This is not a Blueprint for the DMA: The Unknown Knowns of Data-Reliant Business Models. Kluwer Competition Law Blog. Available via Wolters Kluwer. https://competitionlawblog.kluwercompetitionlaw.com/2023/05/08/fourth-workshop-on-the-dma-this-is-not-a-blueprint-for-the-dma-the-unknown-knowns-of-data-reliant-business-models/
Ribera Martínez A (2023h) A Three-Ring Template: How to Get Away with Exemption, Suspension and Specification under the DMA. Kluwer Competition Law Blog. Available via Wolters Kluwer. https://competitionlawblog.kluwercompetitionlaw.com/2023/10/16/a-three-ring-template-how-to-get-away-with-exemption-suspension-and-specification-under-the-dma/
Rubinfeld DL, Gal MS (2017) Access Barriers to Big Data. Ariz Law Rev 59:339–381
Ryan J (2022) Meta's internal use of data and the DMA. Irish Council for Civil Liberties. Available via ICCL. https://www.iccl.ie/wp-content/uploads/2022/11/ICCL-to-Commission-17-November-2022.pdf
Scharpf FW (2009) Legitimacy in the multilevel European polity. Eur Polit Sci Rev 1(2):173–204
de Streel A, Bourreau M et al (2023) Effective and Proportionate Implementation of the DMA. CERRE Working paper. Available via SSRN. https://cerre.eu/wp-content/uploads/2023/01/DMA_Book-1.pdf
Smith A (1776) An Inquiry into the Nature and Causes of the Wealth of Nations. Methuen, London
Snoep M (2023) Follow-up to Panel 1: forward-looking remarks and insights. At 4th workshop on the DMA and app store related provisions, European Commission, Brussels, March 2023
Tallon PP, Ramírez RV et al (2013) The Information Artifact in IT Governance: Toward a Theory of Information Governance. J Manag Inf Syst 30(3):141–178
Teece DJ, Kahwaty HJ (2021) Is the Proposed Digital Markets Act the Cure for Europe's Platform Ills? Evidence from the European Commission's Impact Assessment. Berkeley Research Group Institute working paper. Available via Lisbon Council. https://lisboncouncil.net/wp-content/uploads/2021/04/TEECE-AND-KAHWATY-Dynamic-Digital-Markets1.pdf

Thouvenin F (2021) Information Self-Determination: A Convincing Rationale for Data Protection Law? JIPITEC 12:246–256
Uslaner EM (2002) The Moral Foundations of Trust. Cambridge University Press, Cambridge
Van Twist M, Termeer CJAMK (1991) Introduction to Configuration Approach: A Process Theory for Societal Steering. In: Veld RJTL, Schaap L, Katrien Termeer CJAM, van Twist M (eds) Autopoiesis and Configuration Theory: New Approaches to Societal Steering. Kluwer Academic Publishers, Amsterdam
Viljoen S (2021) A Relational Theory of Data Governance. Yale Law Journal 131:573–654
Williamson OE (1985) The Economic Institutions of Capitalism. The Free Press, Minnesota
Yan X, He H (2022) Fine-tuning the Ex Ante Approach to Regulating Data Combination Practices. J Compet Law Econ 18(4):881–904
Zak PJ, Knack S (2001) Trust and growth. Econ J 111(470):295–321

Online Marketplaces in the Digital Services Act

Esther Arroyo Amayuelas

Abstract The developments in the DSA regarding provisions on online platforms that allow consumers to conclude distance contracts with traders (B2C) are to be welcomed. Nevertheless, Art. 6.3 DSA deals with liability exemptions and it is up to the Member States to decide when and under what conditions non-neutral platforms (those that have control or create the appearance of being the provider of the underliying service) should be liable for the seller's non-performance. The following pages provide a comparison between the legislation and case law in Portugal and Spain, showing to what extent or under what circumstances these Member States acknowledge the contractual liability of a third party not involved in the contract between the trader and the consumer.

1 Introduction

Regulation (EU) 2022/2065 of the European Parliament and of the Council of 19 October 2022, on a Single Market for Digital Services,[1] deals with the protection of citizens' fundamental rights in the online platform environment, and also addresses consumer protection issues in Art. 6.3 (online marketplace safe harbours), Art. 14 (transparency of contractual clauses), and Section 4 of Chapter III, Arts 30 ff. (Schulte-Nölke 2023, pp. 705–714).

[1] OJ L 277, of 27 October 2022.

The text of the lecture delivered on 16 April 2023 at the Universidade do Porto is reproduced here, with only a few essential footnotes. This contribution is based on the author's article "Consumer Protection in Online Marketplaces", previously published in Rev. Fac. Direito UFMG, Belo Horizonte, 2024, 83, 183–195 and falls within the scope of the R+D+I Project PID2024-157907NB-I00 funded by MICIN/AEI/https://doi.org/10.13039/501100001033 and ERDF 'A Way of Making Europe'.

E. Arroyo Amayuelas (✉)
University of Barcelona, Institute TransJus, Barcelona, Spain
e-mail: earroyo@ub.edu

G. Enes et al. (eds.), *A Digital Europe for Citizens*,
https://doi.org/10.1007/978-3-032-02500-5_9

In this paper, I am mainly interested in focusing on Art. 6.3 DSA. The aim of this rule is to provide protection to consumers in the event that the seller using the platform to provide its services breaches the contract with the consumer, as long as certain requirements are met. The following pages will analyze whether or not the rule does indeed fulfil this goal.

2 Online Trading and Intermediation Platforms

For the analysis of Art. 6.3 DSA, it is essential to establish the role played by the intermediary and the consequences linked to its involvement in the contract's conclusion.

2.1 Control and Appearance Are Indications of Non-neutrality

When examining the role of collaborative platforms, the European Commission considered certain criteria that could provide insight into the role played by the platform. The Commission considered that some elements could indicate that the platform had a high level of control and influence over the provision of the underlying service and, therefore, that this could suggest that it also performed the underlying service in addition to providing an information society service. For example, if the platform established the price, set mandatory instructions on the underlying service, put the service provider in an employment relationship, owned key assets to perform the activity, or bore the costs and assumed all the risks associated with the supply of the underlying service.[2]

According to this approach, the CJEU held that Uber was a transport undertaking and not merely an intermediary providing information society services.[3] By contrast, the CJEU admitted that in the ancillary services offered by Airbnb (receipt of payment, assessment of the service, damage guarantee and, optionally, liability insurance), it is not possible to appreciate the same level of control as in Uber.[4] Airbnb does not directly or indirectly set the rental price, nor does it select the tenants or the

---

[2] COM (2016) 356 final, p. 6–7.

[3] CJEU C-434/15, of 20 December 2017, *Asociación Profesional Élite Taxi* (EU:C:2017:981), paras 39–40; CJEU C-320/16, of 10 April 2018, *Uber France* (EU:C:2018:221), paras 20–26.

[4] CJEU C-390/18, of 19 December 2019, *Airbnb Ireland* (EU:C:2019:1112), paras 56–64. Shortly before, the STJ Catalunya of 13 December 2019 (ES: TSJCAT:2019:8266) similarly did not deny Airbnb's role as an intermediary, but held that it was responsible because it could identify which housing should be offered as tourist accommodation (only those that were registered). On Homeaway (now Vrbo España), on the other hand, see STS 30 December 2020 (ES:TS:2020:4484), against STJ Catalunya of 5 October 2018 (with criticism, ÁLVAREZ MORENO, Mª Teresa, *La contratación electrónica mediante plataformas en línea*, Madrid, Reus, 2021, pp. 256–263) and, more recently, STS

accommodations offered on the platform (de Miguel Asensio 2022, p. 3).[5] Therefore, the higher the level of control and organisation in the selection of content providers or the way in which content services are delivered (e.g. if intermediary service providers verify quality and/or set the price), the more obvious it becomes that the platform itself may also be considered as a content provider and/or does not deserve to qualify as an information society service provider.[6]

However, another way of looking at things is to understand that the intermediary does not lose that role, even though it is clear that "intermediation + control" is something fundamentally different from "mere intermediation" (Hacker 2018, pp. 85–86, 93; Busch 2021, p. 38). Thus, the lack of neutrality is a criterion for attributing liability to the platform, which is something that US courts have also had occasion to affirm in the context of product liability (Podszun and Offergeld 2022, pp. 244–271; García-Micó 2022, pp. 6–12; Fernández Chacón 2022, pp. 711–718).

There is another element to be considered when analysing the role of the intermediary, which was initially pointed out by Advocate General SPUZNAR. The AG considered not only the functions or services provided by the platform, but also the appearance with which users perceived that rendering of services. As he stated:

> "[...] Uber's activity comprises a single supply of transport in a vehicle located and booked by means of the smartphone application and [...] this service is provided, from an economic standpoint, by Uber or on its behalf. The service is *also presented to users, and perceived by them, in that way*. When users decide to use Uber's services, they are looking for a transport service offering certain functions and a particular standard of quality. Such functions and transport quality are ensured by Uber".[7]

Previously, the CJEU C-149/15, of 9 November 2016, *Wathelet*, had already ruled, in a case that had nothing to do with marketplaces, that the consumer must be protected by the rules of consumer law when it is not disclosed to them that the other party is acting on behalf of a natural person who does not have the status of a trader but appears to be acting as such. According to the judgment, the protection of appearance is crucial when the buyer believes that the seller is a trader, because there

---

07 January 2002 (ES:TS:2022:6). On the housing portal *El Idealista*, see Juzgado de lo Contencioso-administrativo n° 1 de Barcelona, judgment of 11 October 2022 (La Ley 236,209/2022). On the role of platforms in short-term accommodation rental services, see now Proposal for a Regulation COM(2022) 571 final, Brussels, 7 November 2022.

[5] CJEU C-390/18, of 19 December 2019, *Airbnb Ireland* (EU:C:2019:1112), paras 66–68. For the transport sector, see CJEU C-62/19, of 3 December 2020, *Star Taxi App* (EU:C:2020:980), para 55, which holds that the platform operator does not select taxi drivers, nor does it fix or charge the price of the journey, nor does it exercise control over the quality of the vehicles or their drivers, nor over the behaviour of the latter. It follows that such a service cannot be considered as part of an overall service whose main element is the provision of transport. However, if this were the case, the intermediation service would still be subject to the rules of the DSA, in accordance with Recital 6 and Art. 2.2.

[6] SWD(2020) 348 final. Part 2/2, pp. 160–161.

[7] Opinion of Advocate SZPUNAR delivered on 11 May 2017, in Case C-434/15, *Asociación Profesional Élite Taxi*, (EU:C:2017:364), para 53.

is nothing that suggest that she/he is acting on behalf of another consumer.[8] If the reasoning of that judgment is extended to platforms, what would matter is how the platform presents itself to the buyer. In other words, despite the fact that the platform is not an agent of the trader or seller, as was the case in the latter judgment, the allocation of liability to the platform for the trader's breach of contract would result from the fact that it created the impression for the consumer that the contract was concluded with the platform and that it was the platform's responsibility to perform the contract.

2.2 A Soft Law *Model of Liability*

Building on these reflections, a group of academics, under the auspices of the European Law Institute (ELI), drafted model rules (Busch et al. 2020), which, taking up the ideas set out above, provided some examples to determine when the platform can be understood to have influence or control over the service provider (over the seller or trader) and what consequences should flow from the fact that the platforms display the information relating to the transaction in a way that suggests to consumers that it is the platforms or traders acting under their authority or control who are providing such information (Podszun and Offergeld 2022, pp. 259–263). These soft law provisions clearly call for liability to be imposed on the platform for the trader's breach, as long as the platform breaches its duty to disclose its role as a mere intermediary, or induces the consumer to reasonably rely on its predominant influence over the trader, without prejudice to the right of redress or recourse against the actual breaching party. Of course, in parallel, the platform may also be liable for damages if it provides misleading information, and in particular for breach of the duty to inform the consumer whether the supplier offers its goods, services or digital content as a trader, or of the duty to warn the consumer that consumer law does not apply to the contract between supplier and customer, where this is the case.[9]

[8] CJEU C-149/15, of 9 November 2019, *Wathelet* (EU:C:2016:840). On the possible extension of this judgment to platforms, see Communication from the Commission: Guidelines on the interpretation and application of Directive 2011/83/EU of the European Parliament and of the Council on consumer rights (OJ C, 525, 29 December 2021), pp. 27–28.

[9] See in particular Art. 13–14, 19–24, 25 ELI Model Rules.

3 Intermediation Platforms that Allow Consumers to Conclude Distance Contracts in the Digital Services Act

Art. 6.3 DSA is a rule specifically aimed at platforms acting as online marketplaces, which the provision defines as the intermediation service between a trader and a consumer for the conclusion of a contract. Only contracts between traders and consumers (B2C) are covered, so contracts between peers (B2B or C2C) are excluded.

3.1 What Art. 6.3 DSA Says

According to Art. 6.3 DSA, online marketplaces should not enjoy the safe harbour privilege where they present the specific piece of information or otherwise enable the specific transaction in question in a way that would lead a consumer to believe that the information, or the product or service which is the subject of the transaction, is provided by the online platform itself or by a recipient of the service acting under its control. It should be determined objectively, on the basis of all relevant circumstances, whether the presentation could lead an average consumer to believe that the information in question was provided by the online platform itself or by traders acting under its authority or control (Fernández Chacón 2022, pp. 737–742; Cauffmann and Goanta 2021, p. 9).[10]

This is a well-intentioned rule which, however, surely does not provide sufficient protection for consumers. Firstly, the criterion of the "average consumer" refers to one who is reasonably well-informed and reasonably observant, which opens the door to legal uncertainty and discussions on how the scenario should be interpreted. Secondly, the rule is vague, as will be explained below.

3.2 What Art. 6.3 DSA Does not Say

What does it mean to act under the authority or control of the platform? Only the Recitals of the Regulation can help to understand the undefined wording of Art. 6.3 DSA. Thus, Recital 23 refers to the fixing of the price of the goods or services offered by the provider, as a sign of the platform's predominant influence over the essential elements of the economic transactions. Moreover, Recital 24 describes other significant behaviours that may lead consumers to make erroneous assumptions about the identity of the supplier: failure to clearly display the identity of the trader

[10] Recital 24 DSA.

(Fernández Chacón 2022, pp. 683–690),[11] withholding the identity or contact details of the trader until after the conclusion of the contract between the trader and the consumer,[12] or marketing the product or service in the platform's own name.[13]

3.3 Provisional Assessment

An initial assessment of Art. 6.3 DSA requires considering that such platforms retain their status as intermediaries, even though they do not perform a "mere or simple" intermediary function. A distinction can thus be made between platforms providing goods and services which act as a contractual party in the sense of Recital 18 DCD;[14] other platforms which are mere intermediaries, not involved in the contractual relationship between customer and supplier; and finally, intermediary platforms which also have control of the underlying service (Díez Soto 2023, pp. 203–206, p. 210; Guimarães 2023, pp. 474 ff). The latter two categories of platforms are covered by the DSA.

Indeed, according to Art. 2.2 DSA, the DSA is only aimed at platforms acting as intermediaries. This also means that even if the intermediation service provided is part of an overall service whose main element is not remote (e.g. transport), the intermediation service is still subject to the rules of the DSA (Art. 2.2 and Recital 6 DSA). This changes the previous orientation of European case law.

Additionally, the DSA breaks with the idea that an active role of the platform amounts to having control of the contents or that it amounts to a presumption of knowledge of wrongdoing. Recital 18 still refers to services playing an active role, but this concept is rather built on notions such as "editorial functions", "knowledge"

---

[11] See Communication from the Commission: Guidance on the interpretation and implementation of Directive 2005/29/EC of the European Parliament and of the Council concerning unfair business-to-consumer commercial practices in the internal market (OJ C 526, 29 December 2021), p. 89: "In fact, if the failure by the marketplace to inform about the identity of the actual trader creates the impression that the marketplace is the actual trader, this may result in it being liable for the obligations of the trader". Regarding the obligation to display such information, see Art. 30.1 DSA and Art. 3.4 (a) (ii) and Art. 4.5 of Directive (EU) 2019/2161, of 27 November 2019, on modernisation of Union consumer protection rules (OJ L 328, 18 December 2019) inserting a new Art. 7.4 (f) in Directive 2005/29/EC and a new Art. 6a in Directive 2011/83, of 25 October 2011, on consumer rights, respectively. See also Art. 30.7 DSA and Art. 3.5 of Regulation (EU) 2019/1150, of 20 June 2019, on promoting fairness and transparency for business users of online intermediation services (OJ L 186, 11 July 2019) in relation to the visibility of the identity of the professional user offering goods or services.

[12] Art. 20.2 (b) ELI Model Rules.

[13] Art. 20.2 (f) ELI Model Rules.

[14] Directive (EU) 2019/770 of the European Parliament and of the Council, of 20 May 2019, on certain aspects concerning contracts for the supply of digital content and digital services (OJ L 136, 22 May 2019).

and "(intellectual) control".[15] What is important in the context of online markets is to analyse the way in which platforms design their information society services in order to find out whether they actually act as true hosting intermediaries. It is indeed generally the case that the role of platforms today always involves some degree of activity, either by optimising the presentation of user content, promoting it, tagging or indexing it, or providing search functionality, among other activities. Therefore, if "control" is to be identified with an active role of the platform, it must refer to intellectual control of the activity (Wimmers 2021, p. 384).[16] and, additionally, the relevant indicators must be established to define when platforms are to be understood as having control over and participating in the underlying business. The problem is that there is a lack of clear indicators in the DSA. As mentioned above, Recitals 23 and 24 provide some clues, but they are not enough and it is not certain that a single parameter is sufficient to interpret that the platform plays a role that goes beyond mere or simple intermediation.

4 The Effect of the Safe Harbour on Platforms that Do not Act as Simple Intermediaries

What happens when a platform is not simply an intermediary, but also has control and/or otherwise gives the consumer the impression that it is the other party to the contract? At this point it is necessary to refer to another novelty of the DSA, which consists of maintaining the safe harbours, previously regulated in Directive 2000/31, of 8 June 2000, on electronic commerce,[17] in exchange for imposing duties of care on intermediary companies (regardless of whether or not they qualify as platforms). The DSA establishes a scenario with differentiated duties of care, tailored to the nature and size of intermediary undertakings, including hosting businesses and content distribution platforms and search engines, with a particular focus on very large platforms and search engines (Díez Soto 2023, pp. 159–220; Arroyo Amayuelas 2025, pp. 716 ff).

The DSA continues to focus the exemption from liability on the concept of illegality (of content, products, services, activities), which must be defined in accordance with European law or national law in accordance with European law [Art. 3 (h) DSA]. The concept refers to what, under the applicable law, is illegal in itself or is related to activities that are illegal. Recital 12 provides illustrative examples, which broadly reflect existing rules in the offline environment.

[15] Significantly, CJEU C-682/18, of 22 June 2021, *Frank Peterson/YouTube* and C-683/18, *Elsevier/Cyando* (ECLI:EU:C:2020:586), paras 79–80, 105–106, 108, 114–115, 117, has ruled that an active role of the provider amounts to control of the activity or a presumption of knowledge of the activity.

[16] Opinion AG Saugmandsgaard Øe of 16 July 2020, delivered in C-682/18, *Frank Peterson/Youtube* and C-683/18 (*Elsevier/Cyando*) (ECLI: EU:C:2020:586), para 152.

[17] OJ L 178, 17 July 2000.

Once the safe harbour no longer applies, the intermediary is only liable for the infringement if the conditions laid down in the respective Member State for doing so are fulfilled. Therefore, not being exempted from liability (under EU law) does not imply a correlative and automatic imposition of liability (under national law). It is the case, however, that the loss of immunity can be considered as an indication from which it might be to deduced that the provider was aware of or contributed in some way to the wrongful act or the infringement, which is, at the same time, an indication that due diligence was not exercised, and therefore an element that would allow liability to be charged on this ground (Arroyo Amayuelas 2020, pp. 809–810).

It can be assumed that in all cases where the intermediary should have had knowledge that the content it hosts is illegal, but does not obtain such knowledge because it breaches certain duties of care, e.g. does not establish contact points, does not have a mechanism for notice and action, or does not clearly explain how the notification should be made, the benefit of the exemption from liability should be lost (De Miguel Asensio 2022, p. 16). However, Recital 44 states that the due diligence obligations are independent of the question of the exemption of intermediary service providers from liability. It would seem, on the contrary, that Art. 6.3 DSA starts from precisely the opposite premise, i.e. that the exemption from liability does not apply when the platform infringes certain duties of care, such as the duty to inform about the trader (Art. 30.1 DSA), notwithstanding the fact that, in addition, the infringement of this duty entails liability ex Art. 54 DSA.

It does not seem appropriate to rely on the loss of the safe harbour to hold platforms liable when they fail to fulfil duties for which they themselves are solely responsible. Indeed, platforms are liable for non-performance of ancillary services they may offer (e.g. car rental insurance or airport transfer to hotels) and/or for breach of their own duties of transparency, e.g. by providing misleading information or otherwise failing to comply with their information duties under national and EU law.[18] Liability also arises for breach of obligations relating to the contract that have been shared with the online marketplace provider.[19] The safe harbour is only intended to exempt intermediaries from liability for illegal content/infringing conduct of third parties (Schulte-Nölke 2023, pp. 705–714). When the platforms breach their own duties the

[18] Art. 6 and 7 of Directive 2005/29, and Art. 3.7 of Directive (EU) 2019/2161 on modernisation of Union consumer protection rules, amending Annex I of Directive 2005/29. See Guidance on the interpretation and implementation of Directive 2005/29/EC of the European Parliament and of the Council concerning unfair business-to-consumer commercial practices in the internal market (OJ C 526, 29 December 2021), pp. 87–89.

[19] According to Art. 6a of Directive 2011/83, as amended by Art. 4.5 of Directive (EU) 2019/2161 on modernisation of Union consumer protection rules, obligations related to the contract can be shared between the third party offering the goods, services or digital content and the online marketplace provider. As per CJEU C-536/20, of 24 February 2022, *Tiketa* (ECLI:EU:C:2022:112), para 53, the information referred to in Art. 6.1 of Directive 2011/83 can only be provided to the consumer, prior to the conclusion of the contract, in the general conditions for the provision of services on the intermediary's website, which that consumer actively accepts by ticking the box provided for that purpose, provided that such information is brought to the consumer's attention in a clear and comprehensible manner.

liability for this is direct and cannot be derived from the fact that a safe harbour (that applies in different scenarios) has been lost.

But what about otherwise? It is up to the Member States to decide when and under what conditions non-neutral platforms (those that have control or create the appearance of being the provider) should be liable for the seller's non-performance of its duties. Art. 6.3 DSA merely states that they will not enjoy the (conditional) exemption from liability that other platforms (hosting intermediaries in general) can benefit from for infringements committed by third parties using their services.

5 Which Liability for Intermediation Platforms?

5.1 On the Identification of the Seller

The DSA seeks to ensure that traders improve compliance with consumer legislation. Thus, the marketplaces referred to in Chapter II, Section 4 (excluding micro or small enterprises) must ensure that the trader offers products that comply with applicable EU consumer law and product safety legislation, although for this purpose self-certification by the trader her/himself is sufficient [Art. 30.1 (e) DSA], who is solely responsible for the information s/he provides, without detriment to the platforms making every effort to assess whether this information is reliable, complete and accurate (Art. 30.2 DSA).[20] Indeed, imposing a duty on the platform to provide information on the trader, as well as ensuring that the design of the online interface facilitates this (Art. 31 DSA), aims to make it clear with whom the consumer is contracting, to ensure traceability and/or to suspend the provision of their service to certain traders who do not comply with the request to provide reliable, complete and up-to-date information (Art. 30.3, 31.3 DSA).

However, the duty to require this prior identification or information is of limited use to consumers if it turns out that they cannot sue traders, for example, because they live in another country or because they are not creditworthy. In addition, platforms

[20] See Regulation (EU) 2023/988 of the European Parliament and of the Council of 10 May 2023 on general product safety (OJ L 135, 23 May 2023), Recital 58: "Building on the provisions of Regulation (EU) 2022/2065 concerning the traceability of traders, providers of online marketplaces should not allow a specific product offer to be listed on their platforms unless the trader has provided all information related to product safety and traceability as specified in this Regulation. Such information should be displayed together with the product listing so that consumers can benefit from the same information made available online and offline. However, providers of online marketplaces should not be responsible for verifying the completeness, correctness and the accuracy of the information itself, as the obligation to ensure the traceability of products lies with the relevant trader". On traceability of products, the obligations of economic operators in case of distance selling and, specifically, the obligations of online marketplace providers related to product safety, see Art. 18, 19 and 22 of Regulation 2023/988. In particular, Art. 20.10 (b) stresses that it is the self-certification of traders that commits them to offer only products that comply with the provisions of the Regulation 2023/988 and additional identification information, in accordance with Art. 30.1 DSA.

are only required to check randomly whether products offered by third parties have been identified as illegal (Art. 31.3 DSA). Art. 32 DSA is particularly noteworthy in the sense that, while it obliges the platform to explain to the consumers concerned—or publicly in the online interface—that it has identified the illegality of the goods or services offered through its services, this duty is limited to transactions made within the last six months from the moment the platform becomes aware of such illegality. The platform is not liable for having made the illicit behaviour possible; it must simply warn deceived consumers of the identity of the trader and of the remedies available to them against the latter.

5.2 On the Seller's Breach of Contract

5.2.1 The Portuguese Example

Portugal is the only country, to my knowledge, that has addressed the liability of non-neutral platforms in accordance with the proposed ELI Model Rules on Online Platforms (Morais Carvalho 2023, pp. 541–542). Thus, if the requirements foreseen in art. 44 Decreto-Lei n. 84/2021 are met, online marketplaces are jointly and severally liable with traders for non-compliance:

1. The online marketplace provider who, acting for purposes related to her/his activity, is a contractual partner of the professional who makes the digital good, content or service available is jointly and severally liable to the consumer for the latter's lack of conformity under the terms of this decree-law.
2. For the purposes of the provisions of the previous paragraph, the online marketplace provider shall be considered the contractual partner of the professional if he exercises a predominant influence on the conclusion of the contract, which shall be the case in the following cases:

    a) The contract is concluded exclusively through the means made available by the online marketplace provider;
    b) the payment is executed exclusively through the means made available by the online marketplace provider; or
    c) the terms of the contract concluded with the consumer are mainly determined by the Online Marketplace Provider or the price to be paid by the consumer may be influenced by the Online Marketplace Provider; or
    d) the associated advertising is focused on the Online Marketplace Provider and not on professionals.

3. Without prejudice to the provisions of the previous paragraph, for the purposes of assessing the existence of dominant influence in the conclusion of the contract, any facts which may give rise to the consumer's confidence that the online marketplace provider exercises a dominant influence over the professional supplying the digital good, content or service may be considered.

5.2.2 And in Spain?

The platform's liability for breach of a contract that it has not entered into and from which no obligation arises for it is a complex issue. Certainly, assigning liability to it is contrary to the principle of the relativity of contracts, and yet, if the European legislator decided to do so, it would not be the first time that this would have happened (Díez Soto 2023, pp. 211 ff; Podszun and Offergeld 2022, p. 261; Martínez Espín 2023, pp. 473–474).[21] Without referring specifically to platforms, the Consumer Code in Catalonia had already provided (not necessarily in a representative action scenario), for the joint and several liability of the traders and the intermediary who offers goods or services to consumers (Art. 231–1, Art. 231–5.2), for the breaches of the latter, though the consequences are not limited to private law. According to this rule, the trader is also liable to the consumer for breaches of duties that are only incumbent on the intermediary with whom he has a contractual relationship. This is not what is being discussed here, but the example illustrates well how relative the very relativity of contracts ends up being when the legislator imposes it for the sake of greater consumer protection.

It is reasonable to impose liability on platforms, at the very least if they are not neutral and play a role of predominant control, if one considers that they do not merely facilitate transactions but, beyond that, have the power to transform market relations and to influence the contract between their users (Arroyo Amayuelas 2023, pp. 545–547). There is an economic link between contracts concluded on and with platforms that should also be considered. Moreover, if the consumer enters into a contract with the supplier of goods and services through the platform, it is precisely because of the trust that the platform merits. In Spain, the confidence or good faith placed in third parties is an argument that has been particularly considered in the *Dieselgate* judgments. The Spanish Supreme Court Judgement of 11th March 2020 allows the consumer to claim damages from the manufacturer, on the understanding that this is a basic consumer right that could be frustrated by the difficulty in claiming damages from a seller who could be insolvent, or which could be affected in the event that the seller was in good faith and, on the other hand, the manufacturer was fraudulent (art. 1107 CC). Thus, if the car does not meet the characteristics with which it was offered, with respect to the ultimate consumer, there is not only a breach by the seller, but also by the manufacturer who placed it on the market and advertised it; the damage suffered by the buyer corresponds directly to the breach attributed to the manufacturer. Therefore, if such a direct action is possible against the manufacturer, with a scope that goes beyond the provisions of art. 125 TR-LGDCU, why should it be ruled out that this same (contractual) action could be brought against the platform, when it is the platform that, in the end, creates the risk of contracting with it? These risks—when they exist—should be borne by them, jointly and severally with the seller, without prejudice to the actions that they could

[21] See Recital 46 and Art. 13, 23 of Directive (EU) 2015/2302, of 23 April 2008, on package travel and linked travel arrangements (OJ L 326, 11 December 2015).

later bring against the latter, given that the platform is in the best position to hold the defaulting supplier liable (Cauffmann and Goanta 2021, p. 10).[22]

Therefore, it is reasonable that such platforms are contractually liable, not only for the breach of the duties incumbent on them—because they have so assumed in the contract with the seller or because professional diligence so requires—but also when the third party, i.e. the seller (who fails to supply, supplies late, or supplies improperly), is in breach of its obligations. In Spain, until now, platforms have been held jointly and severally liable only when they could be understood to have implicitly taken on the role of guarantor with respect to the suppliers' fulfilment of their contractual obligations, for example, by providing misleading information about the quality standards of the underlying service. In particular, this is the view of the SAP Cuenca of 8 May 2018 (Álvarez Moreno 2021, pp. 208–210). Nevertheless, some of the reasoning in this judgement is not consistent, since it cannot be said that the platform should have informed the consumer that the service provider was not legal, and/or neither did it have the required liability or accident insurance. If the platform had been aware of this situation, the liability would not derive from the lack of information in this respect, but from the failure to immediately withdraw the offer of the hosted services.

6 Conclusions

The new features of the DSA regarding the liability of certain platforms that allow online contracts to be concluded with consumers are to be welcomed. However, the regulation is still too dependent on how Member States decide to impose such liability in their domestic legislation. It is necessary to be very expectant of the evolution, in particular, of the Portuguese regime and, in other countries, to wait until the legislator undertakes a reform of domestic legislation, waiting for national jurisprudence to lead the way, as has already happened in other areas in which there has been no hesitation in recognising the contractual liability of a third party not involved in the contract.

References

Álvarez Moreno T (2021) La contratación electrónica mediante plataformas en línea (pp. 208–210). Reus

Arroyo Amayuelas E (2023) A Redefinition of the Principles of the Acquis Communautaire. In The Future of European Private Law (pp. 523–547). Hart-Nomos

[22] See European Parliament resolution of 20 October 2020 with recommendations to the Commission on the Digital Services Act: Improving the functioning of the Single Market (Section VI); Draft IMCO I report (2020/0361 (COD)). Amendment 73 with a proposal for a new Art. 5 (a).

Arroyo Amayuelas E (2020) ¿Puertos seguros a prueba de futuro? Cuadernos de Derecho Transnacional 12(1):808–837

Arroyo Amayuelas E (2025) Comments to arts. 4–8 DSA. 2nd ed. In EU Digital Law (pp. 711–769). Hart-Beck-Nomos

Busch C, Dannemann G, Schulte-Nölke H, Wiewiórowska A, Zoll F (2020) The ELI Model Rules on Online Platforms EuCML 9(2):61–70

Busch C (2021) Rethinking Product Liability Rules for Online Marketplaces: A Comparative Perspective. In SSRN Journal (pp. 1–43). https://doi.org/10.2139/ssrn.3784466

Cauffmann C, Goanta C (2021) A new order: The digital services act and consumer protection. In https://www.researchgate.net/publication/348787835

De Miguel Asensio PA (2022) Obligaciones de diligencia y responsabilidad de los intermediarios: El Reglamento (UE) de Servicios Digitales. La Ley Unión Europea (109) Diciembre 1–47

Díez Soto CM (2023) Responsabilidad de los proveedores de mercados en línia por incumplimiento del contrato subyacente. In Contratación en el entorno digital (pp. 159–220). Aranzadi

Fernández Chacón I (2022) Caracterización contractual y régimen de responsabilidad aplicable a los e-marketplaces. In Estudios de Derecho Contractual Europeo: Nuevos problemas, nuevas reglas (pp. 665–763). Aranzadi

García-Micó T (2022) Platform Economy and Product Liability: Old Rules for New Markets. *IDP*. Revista de Internet Derecho y Política 35:1–24. https://doi.org/10.7238/idp.v0i35.378523

Guimarães R (2023) As plataformas "colaborativas" enquanto "prestadoras de serviços da sociedade de informação": reflexões à luz da Lei do comércio electrónico e desenvolvimentos recentes. In Economia colaborativa (pp. 467–498). UMinho Editora

Hacker P (2018) UberPop, UberBlack, and the regulation of digital platforms after the Asociación Profesional Elite Taxi judgment of the CJEU: judgment of the Court (Grand Chamber) 20 December 2017, Asociación Profesional Elite Taxi (C-434/15). ERCL 14(1):80–96

Martínez Espín P (2023) Productores, proveedores, plataformas, intermediarios, guardianes de acceso. In Derecho de consumo: materiales, fundamentos, aplicaciones (pp. 459–486). Aranzadi

Morais Carvalho J (2023) Portugal. In Harmonising Digital Contract Law (pp. 533–545). Hart-Beck-Nomos

Podszun R, Offergeld P (2022) Plattformregulierung im Zivilrecht zwischen Wissenschaft und Gesetzgebung: Die ELI Model Rules on Online Platform ZEuP 2, pp. 244–272

Schulte-Nölke H (2023) The EU Digital Services Act and EU Consumer Law. In Harmonizing Digital Contract Law (pp. 705–714). Hart-Beck-Nomos

Wimmers J (2021) The Out-of-court dispute settlement mechanism in the Digital Services Act: A disservice to its own goals. JIPITEC 12:381–401

Consumer Protection in the Digital Age: A Reflection on Regulation 2022/2065 (Digital Services Act—DSA) and Agenda 2030

Fernanda de Araujo Meirelles Magalhães and Irene Merino Calle

Abstract The European Union made digital transformation one of its priorities to be achieved by 2024, through the objective of a "Europe fit for the digital age. Empowering people through a new generation of technologies". Twenty years after the adoption of Directive 2000/31/EC of the European Parliament and of the Council on information society services and intermediary services, new and innovative business models and services have emerged, such as social networks and online platforms allowing consumers to conclude distance contracts with traders, giving business users and consumers new ways to communicate and access information. Most EU citizens now use such services in their daily lives. However, the digital transformation and the increasing use of these services also entail new risks and challenges for individual recipients of these services, businesses, and society as a whole. For this reason, the European Parliament adopted a few months ago, Regulation 2022/2065 of 19/10/2022 on the single market for digital services. It is not only the European Parliament that is acting in this area of digital transformation, though. Member States are also developing, or are in the process of developing, national legislation to accommodate the matters covered by the Regulation, in particular by imposing due diligence requirements on intermediary service providers as regards how they should deal with illegal content, misinformation and other risks to society (in particular to consumers, the weaker party in contractual relationships). At the same time, by working on these national rules, possible divergences between national rules and European law,

This chapter was supported by FCT – Fundação para a Ciência e Tecnologia, I.P. (DOI: https://doi.org/10.54499/2023.00397.BD). It also acknowledges the project "It's a Wonderful (Digital) World: Law in a Digital and Technological Society", developed at CIJ—Centre for Interdisciplinary Research on Justice, Faculty of Law, University of Porto. Additional funding was provided through the Margarita Salas programme (2021–2023) for the requalification of the Spanish university system, University of Valladolid, funded by the European Union—NextGenerationEU.

F. de Araujo Meirelles Magalhães (✉)
Faculty of Law, University of Porto, Porto, Portugal
e-mail: up201710250@edu.direito.up.pt

I. M. Calle
University of Valladolid, Valladolid, Spain
e-mail: irene.merino.calle@uva.es

G. Enes et al. (eds.), *A Digital Europe for Citizens*,
https://doi.org/10.1007/978-3-032-02500-5_10

which negatively affect the achievement of a true internal market, can be eliminated. Finally, the authors will discuss the 2030 Agenda and the Digital Services Regulation from a Portuguese and Spanish perspective, seeking to identify whether the regulation has considered the Agenda's sustainable development goals. In essence, although the issues are not directly related, it is essential to approach them, since the 2030 Agenda, in its objective of digital transformation, may have an impact on the protection of consumer rights in the digital environment, and Regulation 2022/2065 may be relevant to ensure the adequate protection of these rights in the digital era, such as, for example, those related to the protection of personal data and information.

Keywords Consumers · Digital Europe · Regulation of Digital Services · Spain · Portugal

1 Introduction

The way people live their lives is being transformed by digital technology. To ensure that this transformation benefits both individuals and businesses contributing to the goal of achieving a climate neutral Europe by 2050, the EU has implemented (and continues to implement) a digital strategy. The European Commission is committed to making this decade Europe's "Digital Decade", which requires consolidating its digital sovereignty and setting standards focused on data, technology, and infrastructure, rather than following the rules of others.[1]

The Commission has committed to updating the horizontal rules setting out the responsibilities and obligations of digital service providers, in particular online platforms, in its Communication "Shaping Europe's Digital Future".[2] In the Treaty on the Functioning of the European Union, the European Parliament adopted two resolutions containing two proposals for regulations: the "Digital Services Act: improving the functioning of the single market" and the "Digital Markets Act: adapting commercial and civil law rules to commercial entities operating online".[3] A resolution was also adopted under the non-legislative procedure: "Digital Services Act and fundamental rights issues".[4] These complementary resolutions, which will avoid fragmentation of national transposition rules, strongly call for the basic principles of the e-commerce

[1] European Comission (2023). *A Europe Fit for the Digital Age Empowering people with a new generation of technologies*. https://commission.europa.eu/strategy-and-policy/priorities-2019-2024/europe-fit-digital-age_en.

[2] Proposal for a Regulation of the European Parliament and of the Council on a Single Market for Digital Services (Digital Services Act) and amending Directive 2000/31/EC. *Comisión Europea, Bruselas, 15.12.2020 COM (2020) 825 final 2020/0361 (COD)*. https://eur-lex.europa.eu/legal-content/EN/TXT/?uri=CELEX%3A52020PC0825.

[3] *Idem.*

[4] *Idem.*

directive to be maintained and for fundamental rights to be protected in the online environment, as well as for online anonymity where technically possible.[5]

Since the E-Commerce Directive was adopted, new digital services have emerged that have transformed the daily lives of EU citizens and changed ways of communicating, connecting, consuming, and doing business. While these services have greatly contributed to the social and economic transformations that have taken place in the EU and globally, they have also produced new risks and challenges both for users and for society in general.[6]

The European Parliament resolutions set transparency, information and accountability obligations for digital Service Providers and call for effective obligations to act against illegal content online in order to provide effective protection for users and consumers of digital services. Efforts are also called for public scrutiny at national and EU level, as well as cooperation among competent authorities in different jurisdictions to enforce the law, especially on cross-border issues.

Moreover, digital services can support the Sustainable Development Goals by contributing to economic, social, and environmental sustainability.

The Covid19 pandemic similarly highlighted the importance of digital technologies in all aspects of modern life. It highlighted the dependence of our economy and society on digital services, as well as the benefits and risks arising from the current framework for the functioning of digital services.[7]

Following the relevant legislative procedures, the proposed resolutions were adopted in October 2022, published in the Official Journal of the EU on 27 October 2022 and entered into force on 16 November 2022, becoming known as Regulation (EU) 2022/2065 of the European Parliament and of the Council of 19 October 2022 on a single market for digital services and amending Directive 2000/31/EC (Directive on electronic commerce)—hereafter referred to as the E-commerce Directive (ECD); and Regulation (EU) 2022/1925 of the European Parliament and of the Council of 14 September 2022 on fair and contestable markets in the digital sector and amending Directives (EU) 2019/1937 and (EU) 2020/1828, Digital Markets Regulation.[8]

[5] Directive 2000/31/EC of the European Parliament and of the Council of 8 June 2000 on certain legal aspects of information society services, in particular electronic commerce, in the Internal Market ('Directive on electronic commerce'), *Official Journal of the European Communities, L178,* of 17 July 2000. https://eur-lex.europa.eu/legal-content/EN/TXT/PDF/?uri=CELEX:32000L0031. This does not imply that the rules of the E-Commerce Directive should be ignored but integrates them into its articles with a few editorial changes. De Miguel Asensio, P. A. (2021). Servicios y mercados digitales: modernización del régimen de responsabilidad y nuevas obligaciones de los intermediarios. *Revista La Ley Unión Europea,* 88, enero, 1–18, especialmente p. 2.

[6] Proposal for a Regulation…, *op. cit.*

[7] *Idem.*

[8] Regulation (EU) 2022/2065 of the European Parliament and of the Council of 19 October 2022 on a Single Market for Digital Services and amending Directive 2000/31/EC (Digital Services Act). *Official Journal of the European Union L 277/1,* of 27 October 2022. https://eur-lex.europa.eu/legal-content/EN/TXT/PDF/?uri=CELEX:32022R1925;

Regulation (EU) 2022/1925 of the European Parliament and of the Council of 14 September 2022 on contestable and fair markets in the digital sector and amending Directives (EU) 2019/1937

2 Regulation (EU) 2022/2065 of the European Parliament and of the Council of 19 October 2022 on a Single Market for Digital Services and Amending Directive 2000/31/ec (Digital Services Act)

2.1 General Aspects

Firstly, it is noted that the regulation in question, known as the Digital Services Regulation or Digital Services Act (hereafter DSA), is characterized by the fact that it establishes obligations and responsibilities for digital service providers, without changing the origin or internal market criterion established in the E-Commerce Directive (ECD) in relation to the provision of intermediary services. However, it must be observed that the unification inherent in the DSA will erode the practical scope of this approach with respect to the liability regime for intermediaries.

On the other hand, the DSA's connection with the internal market is different from that of the E-Commerce Directive, since its objectives are not limited to facilitating the smooth functioning of the internal market, but also seek to establish uniform rules to ensure a secure digital environment that protects users' fundamental rights.[9]

The Regulation is organized into five chapters and starts with a series of general provisions and definitions. As regards the spatial scope, Article 2(1) of the DSA states that it applies to the provision of intermediation services to recipients of intermediation services whose residence or establishment is within the Union, irrespective of whether the service provider is in a Member State or in a third country. However, the wording of this article is questionable as it is not precise enough, leaving room for different interpretations (De Miguel Asensio 2021). In contrast, recital 7 of the DSA emphasizes that what is important in relation to the territorial scope of its rules is that the intermediary provides its services in the Union, in circumstances where there is a substantial link with the Union.[10] A connection is deemed to exist where the provider has an establishment in the Union or has a considerable number of users in the Union or directs its activities to one or more Member States.[11] Similarly, where the regime of limitations of liability for intermediaries is relevant for civil liability claims, the application of those rules will be conditioned by the law applicable to

and (EU) 2020/1828 (Digital Markets Act). *Official Journal of the European Union L 265/1*, of 12 October 2022. https://eur-lex.europa.eu/legal-content/EN/TXT/PDF/?uri=CELEX:32022R1925.

Due to the length of the text, the authors will concentrate on what is known as Digital Services Act.

[9] Digital Services Act…, *op. cit.*

[10] *Ibidem*, 5.

[11] With regard to the subjective scope of application, the author mentions that doubts arise in relation to referring as an alternative to the specific activities' criterion to the fact that there is a significant number of users of the service in one or more Member States. It may be more appropriate to understand that where there is a significant number of users in one or more Member States, the activities of the service provider are directed to the Union or to some of its Member States. *Ibidem*, 5. Digital Services Act…, *op. cit.*, p. 5 et seq. Art.3.d) and e). pp. 42.

civil liability under the relevant conflict rules. In general, these rules will lead to the application of the DSA to the extent that the intermediary service provider directs its activity to an EU Member State.

Chapter II deals with the liability of intermediary services and is similar to Section 4 of Chapter II of the ECD, with some modifications, for example, with respect to virtual hosting (Leitão 2023).The purpose of these rules is to provide for exemptions from liability (safe harbor) in favor of intermediaries in relation to the content disclosed by their users. The DSA reproduces the rules contained in articles 12 to 15 of the ECD (repealed) in articles 4 to 8 of Chapter II, and it is no longer an obligation of the MS to exempt service providers from liability, as they are laid out directly in the Regulation. The liability of intermediary service providers is determined according to the applicable law. Article 5 of the DSA introduces an addition regarding liability arising from the consumer protection rules of online platforms. This addition does not seem questionable, but a similar result could be imposed in relation to the non-application of the exclusion of the hosting service provider's liability in other situations where liability arising from other torts is required. Under Article 14 ECD (Article 5 DSA), it is decisive to assess whether the intermediary has exercised due diligence in order to establish whether it benefits from the liability exemption.[12] In future, the service provider's compliance with the due diligence standards of the DSA will play an important role in this context. In order to assess whether the hosting service provider has acted with due diligence, it is necessary to evaluate the risks posed by the business model chosen by the service provider with respect to the dissemination of illegal content provided by its users in order to benefit from the safe harbor. Indeed, the DSA defines the term "illegal content" as any information that infringes EU or Member State law.[13]

On the other hand, Chapter III establishes due diligence obligations for different types of digital service providers.

Chapter IV establishes a public enforcement regime and sanctions for non-compliance. In particular, Article 40 empowers states to enforce the rules in Chapters III and IV. Finally, articles 50 to 66 contain the supervisory and control regime for large platforms.[14]

The disparity of risks arising from the different business models conditions the assessment of the measures that the intermediary should take in order to be verified as having exercised due diligence, so as to benefit from the limitation of liability

---

[12] Furthermore, where the system of limitations of liability of the intermediaries are relevant in the context of tort claims. In case of tort or delict, the application of these specific rules (Articles 3 to 7) may be understood as the application of the PSRD will normally be conditioned by the law applicable to non-contractual liability under the relevant conflict rules (see Article 15 of Regulation 864/2007 on the law applicable to non-contractual obligations or Rome II Regulation), without prejudice to the fact that these rules will normally lead to the application of the PSRD insofar as the intermediary service provider directs its activity to an EU Member State (as follows e.g. from Articles 6, 8 and even 4 of the above-mentioned Rome II Regulation). De Miguel Asensio, P. A. (2021). Servicios y mercados digitales…, *op., cit.*, p. 5.

[13] Digital Services Act…, *op. cit.*, p. 42.

[14] *Ibidem, 79 et seq.*

in the absence of actual knowledge of the irregularities. This approach is based on recital 48 ECD, which provides that Member States may require service providers hosting data provided by recipients of their services to apply a duty of care in order to detect and prevent certain types of illegal activities. This text needs to be revised to reduce national fragmentation (De Miguel Asensio 2021).

Similarly, the legal text refers to a possible gap in the regulation of the liability of online service providers (DSAs) in relation to the liability regime applicable to intermediary service providers. The problem lies in the lack of clarity in defining what is considered an intermediary service, which is key to determining whether an online service provider can benefit from the limitation of liability. The DSA states that only intermediary services can be regulated by law, and defines the category in terms of transmission, caching and hosting of data. However, the definition is not exhaustive and the characterization of a service as an intermediary is decisive for the limitation of liability to apply.

In this regard, the case law of the Court of Justice of the European Union (CJEU) has established that a hosting service provider can only be qualified as an intermediary within the meaning of Article 14 of the E-Commerce Directive (ECD) if it limits itself to the neutral provision of the service by a purely technical and automatic processing of data provided by its clients, and does not play an active role enabling it to acquire knowledge or control of the data.[15]

There are certain practices of social networks and platforms that host and manage content submitted by their users may require detailed examination before concluding that their activity is that of a neutral hosting service provider. For example, if the content is suggested by the platform or social network itself as a result of the activity of its own algorithms, it may be necessary to determine whether the online service provider is acting as an intermediary.

The question of whether the activity of an internet video platform operator falls within the scope of Article 14 ECD has been examined in the CJEU cases.[16] The Advocate General argues that the ECD must be interpreted considering the changes that have occurred in the market since its adoption.[17]

---

[15] CSTJ of 23 March 2010, Google France and Google, C-236/08 to C-238/08, ECLI:EU:C:2010:159, and of 12 July 2011, L'Oréal, C-324/09, ECLI:EU:C:2011:474. Proposal for a Regulation…, *op., cit.*

[16] Court Joined Cases C-682/18 and C-683/18, YouTube and Cyando. De Miguel Asensio, P. A. (2021). Servicios y mercados digitales…, *op., cit.*, p. 9 et seq. According to the judgment, Article 14 "of Directive 2000/31/EC of the European Parliament and of the Council of 8 June 2000 on certain legal aspects of information society services, in particular electronic commerce, in the Internal Market (Directive on electronic commerce) must be interpreted as meaning that the activity of the operator of a video-sharing platform or of a file-sharing and hosting platform falls within the scope of that provision in so far as that operator does not play an active role such as to give it knowledge of, and control over, the content uploaded onto its platform". STJEU C-682/18 and 683/18, YouTube and Cyando, paras 103 et seq.

[17] *Idem.*

2.2 The Regulation's Relation with Spain and Portugal

As we have been stating throughout this chapter, the Directive 2000/31/EC was an important milestone in the regulation of e-commerce in Europe, but over time, it has become outdated and inadequate to face the new challenges of modern e-commerce, for several reasons.

Firstly, we can mention that technological advancement has profoundly transformed the Internet landscape, with the emergence of new platforms and business models that did not exist when the Directive was created. This has made the ECD regulation insufficient to deal with the new online business practices.

In addition, over the years, consumer behavior has changed significantly. Today, consumers expect an easy and convenient online shopping experience, as well as adequate protections regarding aspects such as the privacy and security of their personal data.

Another important factor is the role that digital intermediary platforms now play in the exploitation of content, no longer being mere passive hosts of other people's content, as has been seen in case law, such as the Judgment of the Court of Justice of the European Union, concerning the eBay platform, in case no. C-324/09 (Leitão 2023).

In view of all these digital transformations in recent years and the emergence of new and innovative (digital) information society services, changing the way European citizens live their daily lives and the way they communicate, connect and share, the Digital Services Regulation (DSA) was adopted. The DSA's main objective is to update the liability regime for intermediary service providers for the transport and storage of illegal content (Farinha 2022). In essence, the DSA, instead of recreating the principles of intermediary liability and content moderation, addresses rather the "codification and normative deepening of practices that were already part of interventions with the main stakeholders".[18] To this end, it has harmonized rules on the provision of intermediary services in the internal market.

Based on the basic principles of the existing e-commerce directive, the text ensures the best conditions for the provision of innovative digital services on the national market and contributes to online safety and the protection of fundamental rights. The DSA maintains liability rules for intermediary service providers set out in the E-Commerce Directive. It also establishes clear responsibilities for MS, which must supervise compliance with the obligations stipulated in the Regulation by service providers located on their territory, ensuring maximum speed and efficiency in applying the rules. It sets clear responsibilities, including liability, for intermediary service providers, especially online platforms such as marketplaces and social media; imposing clear due diligence obligations on certain intermediary services, such as notice and action procedures in relation to illegal content and the possibility to challenge platforms' content moderation decisions, seeking to improve the safety of online users across the Union and enhancing the protection of their fundamental rights. It also imposes obligations on certain online platforms to receive, retain and

---

[18] *Idem.*

partly verify and publish information about the traders using their services in order to ensure a safer and more transparent online environment for consumers. Recognizing the particular impact that the largest online platforms have on our economies and societies, this proposal calls for a greater level of control over content moderation, advertising and algorithmic processes used by providers of such platforms.

In both Portugal and Spain, the Regulation is also directly applicable, pursuant Article 288 TFEU. That is, the DSA is binding and mandatory in all EU member states, without the need for transposition into domestic law. It becomes a law automatically in all EU countries as soon as it comes into force, without the need to be incorporated or adopted by national authorities. This ensures uniform application of the rules throughout the European Union and helps to avoid divergences or contradictions between the national laws of different member states.

Nevertheless, with regard to digital services, according to information contained in the diploma itself, in recitals 9, 10 and 11, the regulation does not exclude the application of the diplomas dealing with the following subjects: other national legislation applicable to intermediary service providers, which is in conformity with Union law; other acts of Union law regulating the provision of information society services in general, regulating other aspects of the provision of intermediary services in the internal market or specifying and complementing the harmonized rules laid down in this regulation; Union law on consumer protection, on the protection of personal data, on private international law and on copyright and related rights.[19]

2.2.1 Spain

Looking at Spanish Law, the Regulation is directly applicable, without the need of any other legal act for it to become valid.[20] However, and as provided in its guidelines, in Spain, it would be necessary to consider not only what is contained in this regulatory text, but also what is contained in other legal frameworks, such as Regulation (EU) No. 1215/2012, in terms of which courts will have jurisdiction to judge a hypothetical conflict, such as the Rome I and Rome II regulations, concerning the law applicable to contractual and non-contractual obligations. Similarly, together with the Digital Services Regulation, the rules contained in the General Data Protection Regulation (EU) 2016/679 (GDPR) and the rules on specific regimes relating to the provision of certain information society services should also be considered.[21] This is the case with the Audiovisual Media Services Directive and in particular its

[19] Regulation (EU) 2022/2065 of the European Parliament…, *op. cit.*

[20] According to Article 288 of the Treaty on the Functioning of the European Union (TFEU), regulations are legal acts of general application which are binding in their entirety and directly applicable in the EU member states. EUR-Lex-114522-PT-EUR-Lex (europa.eu) (27 March 2023).

[21] Regulation (EU) 2022/2065 of the European Parliament…, *op. cit.* p.4. Spain enacted a LO 3/ 2018 on the protection of personal data and guarantee of digital rights, to achieve the adaptation of the Spanish legal system to Regulation (EU) 2016/679 of the European Parliament and of the Council of 27 April 2016, General Data Protection Regulation, and to complete its provisions. *Boletin Oficial del Estado, 294*, December 6, 2018, pages 119,788 to 119,857 (pp. 70).

regime on video-sharing platforms. The Audiovisual Media Services Directive 2010/13/EC (AVMSD), following its amendment by Directive (EU) 2018/1808, includes specific provisions applicable to providers of "video-sharing platform services" or "video-sharing platform" in its Articles 28a and 28b.[22] The DSA will also be applied considering Article 17 of Directive (EU) 2019/790 on copyright and related rights in the Digital Single Market. As is well known, this rule establishes a specific liability exemption regime for a category of hosting service providers in relation to a specific matter, the protection of copyright and other protected subject matter, which replaces the horizontal rules of the ECD and whose application is not affected by the DSA rules in principle (De Miguel Asensio 2021).

In addition, and as stated in the DSA, this regulation is an update of the 2000 Directive on digital services, so in Spain the provisions of the regulations that transposed the Directive must also be considered. In particular, the provisions of Law 34/2002 on information society services and electronic commerce,[23] and the subsequent laws that have amended and updated this law, must be taken into account. We refer to the partial modernization carried out by the Telecommunications Law 9/2014.[24]

2.2.2 Portugal

Regarding the internal legal system, Directive 2000/31/EC was transposed in DL 7/2004 (Electronic Commerce Law—LCE), concerning certain legal aspects of information society services, in particular electronic commerce, in the internal market. Therefore, the modification of the Directive by the DSA also has some repercussions on Portuguese legislation.

In this context, we can refer to Article 15 of the Portuguese Electronic Commerce Law, which deals with intermediate storage (Article 13 of the ECD). From the revocation of the corresponding article in the Directive by the DSA, it is understood that this change also has repercussions in domestic law. In this sense, in an analysis of the DSA made by Menezes Leitão, the author regrets that there is this substitution, since he believes that article 15 does not differ substantially from article 5 of the DSA and, furthermore, believes that the provision of the LCE is much more complete (Leitão 2023), an argument with which we agree.

On the other hand, some provisions of the DSA, such as the one regarding the notification of suspicion of crime, article 18 (19-A and 19-B of DL 7/2004), were

[22] Directive (EU) 2018/1808 of the European Parliament and of the Council of 14 November 2018 amending Directive 2010/13/EU on the coordination of certain provisions laid down by law, regulation or administrative action in Member States concerning the provision of audiovisual media services (Audiovisual Media Services Directive) in view of changing market realities. *Official Journal of the European Union L 303/69*, of 28 Novembr 2018.

[23] Ley 34/2002, de 11 de julio, de servicios de la sociedad de la información y de comercio electrónico. *Boletín Oficial del Estado, n.º 166*, de 12 de Julio de 2002. https://www.boe.es/eli/es/l/2002/07/11/34/con.

[24] Ley 9/2014, de 9 de mayo, General de Telecomunicaciones. *Boletín Oficial del Estado, nº 114*, de 10 de mayo de 2014. Ley 9/2014, de 9 de mayo, General de Telecomunicaciones. (boe.es).

already foreseen in the LCE, due to the transposition of the Directive.[25] This provision means that intermediaries are not completely exempt from investigations and decisions to act, in case of suspicion of illegal content,[26] immediately reporting the suspicions to the competent authority, in the case of Portugal, the Public Prosecution Service.

Note, therefore, that although they are different laws, the DSA, the LCE and the ECD are related to the regulation of economic activities and aim to protect consumers and ensure the safety of the services offered. While the Directive 2000/31/CE establishes the bases for electronic commerce in the EU, the Decree-Law 7/2004 adapts these specific rules to the Portuguese reality. Regulation (EU) 2022/2065 seeks to harmonize the rules for digital services across the EU, with the aim of creating a more secure and efficient digital single market.

Another important point to be mentioned is that the DSA prevailing over Portuguese law in case of conflict or contradiction between the two, companies offering digital services in Portugal must comply with the rules and obligations established by the regulation, regardless of Portuguese laws and regulations. However, it is important to note that the Portuguese LCE is still valid and applicable in Portugal, as the DSA does not repeal existing national laws that are compatible with its provisions. Therefore, companies operating in the Portuguese market must comply with both the EU regulation and the relevant national laws, the former prevailing over the latter.

That said, the publication of the DSA in the Portuguese legal system has several impacts, especially for companies offering digital services in the country. Among them, we can highlight:

i. Clearer rules for businesses offering digital services: the regulation sets clearer and more specific rules for businesses offering digital services, including online platforms, social networks, cloud computing services and online advertising services. This should help promote fairer and more transparent competition, as well as protect the rights of consumers and users.
ii. Greater protection for users of digital services: the regulation requires companies offering digital services to implement measures to protect users' privacy and personal data, as well as measures to combat misinformation and hate speech online. This should help make the internet a safer and more trusted environment for users.
iii. Clearer Corporate Liability: The regulation includes the liability that has already been understood in EU jurisprudence, and while it includes the exemption of liability for companies offering digital services, it sets out the conditions and cases in which they do not apply. It also addresses liability for removal of illegal or harmful content within a specific timeframe and obliges companies to provide clear information about their personal data collection and use practices.

[25] *Ibidem*, 30 e 31.

[26] *Ibidem*, *Loc. Cit.*

2.3 Consumer Protection and Regulation 2022/2065

The Digital Services Act is not exactly a regulation directed at consumer law, nor does it prevent the application of existing consumer law, as stated in the text of the regulation[27] itself, but its provisions are designed, in a way, to protect consumers. The DSA is a horizontal regulatory framework proposed by the European Commission to regulate digital services in the EU, which aims to complement existing EU directives and focus on fundamental rights, which consequently includes consumer protection (Farinha 2022).

The relationship between the DSA and consumer protection can be seen in several provisions of the Regulation, such as, for example, Article 22, which deals with confidence flags. The article states that the platform operator must monitor the reliability of the information contained and request that it be corrected, in case of inaccuracy. Furthermore, according to paragraph 5 of the aforementioned article, this information must be available "in a publicly accessible database in a readily accessible and machine-readable format"[28] and kept up to date at all times.

In this regard, Morais Carvalho, J. (2021) in an analysis of the proposed regulation, argues that this can be considered the rule that has the closest relationship with the issue of consumer protection, among the various regulations, since it imposes on platform operators the duty to verify content and information. Guimarães (2023) also considers the provision of this article important in relation to consumer protection, considering that anonymity could facilitate illegal activities of the service provider and the provision of this information is fundamental for the safety of contracting by the consumer. In the Spanish context, Fernández Hernández, C. (2020) shares the opinion of his Portuguese counterparts. Online platforms are also required to organize their interface to allow traders to comply with EU consumer and product safety legislation.

On the other hand, in a reflection made by Farinha, M. (2022) the most relevant is the rule contained in article 6(3), which deals with virtual accommodation. In this provision, the exclusion of liability contained in paragraph 1 does not apply, "with regard to the liability under consumer protection law of online platforms which allow consumers to conclude distance contracts with traders, where those platforms display the specific element of information or otherwise enable the specific transaction in question to mislead an average consumer into believing that the information, product or service which is the subject of the transaction is provided by the online platform itself or by a recipient of the service acting under its authority or control".[29] That is, the exclusion of liability of the intermediary platform does not apply, whenever a relationship is identified between the intermediary platform and the contract concluded with the consumers.

This is a well-observed provision, as in some cases the platform is no longer just a simple digital platform for intermediation, as it involves, in a sense, exploitation

[27] Recital 10 and Article 2, 4, f) of the DSA.

[28] Digital Services Act…, *op. cit.*

[29] Digital Services Act…, *op. cit.*

and control over that service, and is outside the scope of the DSA.[30] That is, in some cases, the contact between the service provider and the consumer only exists because it is made through that platform, and those services provided are often inseparable from the intermediation service. In this context, Raquel Guimarães mentions, and we agree, that "the identification of the platform, or its inseparability with the service provided by a third party, leads to equating the business model of bipartite or tripartite business platforms with that of platforms providing direct services, devaluing the intermediation service provided" (Guimarães 2023).

The provisions of paragraph 3 of the aforementioned article ultimately address the criticism that consumers often rely on the platform's brand image and even consider the platform as their contracting party rather than the party that uses the platform to market their products and services, but it is unclear whether this is sufficient to ensure consumer protection (Cauffman and Goanta 2021).

Once again, it is observed that, even if in the initial proposal of the Regulation there was not so much care in relation to the consumer, today, thanks to the recommendations given by the European Parliament, the DSA, speaks of unfair practices and platform liability, for example. Thus, regardless of which rule is more relevant in this regard, the fact is that there is, albeit indirectly, a focus on their protection, in order to complement the Directives and safeguard the rights of those consumers who often find themselves harmed by abusive practices online.

However, we must point out that the DSA is not complete and fails to observe some aspects related to platforms, such as those related to the collection and processing of personal data and the use of artificial intelligence, increasingly present in this type of digital platforms (Guimarães 2023). It is indeed noticeable a legislative evolution, regarding the creation of the DSA, however, as the Regulation relates to any user, including consumers, due to the rapid evolution of the way these platforms and auxiliary technologies work, the consumer may still remain unprotected regarding some specific matters. In the opinion of authors Caroline Cauffman and Catalina Goanta, the DSA seems to be more concerned with providing legal protection and security to intermediary service providers than to the consumers who use their services (Cauffman and Goanta 2021).

3 Consumer Protection in Digital Services and the Sustainable Development Goals of Agenda 2030

Since the beginning of the DSA discussion, it has been argued that the creation of the Regulation aims to complement the Sustainable Development Goals by better regulating digital services. This is because digital services can contribute to economic, social, and environmental sustainability. That is why the DSA aims to regulate the operation of digital platforms in the EU to ensure greater transparency, safety, and

[30] In this sense, see CJEU Judgment, Case No. C-434/15 (Asociación Profesional Elite Taxi vs. Uber System Spain, SL).

consumer protection in a more targeted way, as well as to promote the sustainable development of the digital market.

As we know, the 2030 Agenda for Sustainable Development was signed in 2015 at the United Nations by the highest representatives of the institution's member countries. Although it is not mandatory for countries to comply with it, this agenda symbolizes the international pact, commitment, and responsibility to address the social, economic and environmental challenges caused by the phenomenon of globalization and the homogenization it entails, focusing its attention on people, the planet, progress and well-being, and peace, bringing everything together under the emblem of "leaving no one behind".[31]

The sustainable development agenda seeks to meet the needs of today's social groups without harming or threatening the future of the next generation. Moreover, it seeks to shape societies where there is inclusive fiscal growth, where there is progress toward greater community cohesion and justice, and where there is harmony with the environment. To this end, it seeks to bring together three dimensions of social reality—economic, collective, and environmental, promoting a strengthening and balance between them.[32] These three pillars are articulated through seventeen Sustainable Development Goals (SDGs), setting goals for the next decade that are destined to be intensely transgressive. All SDGs are universal in nature, meaning that they apply equally and equitably to all countries—developing or not—and address diverse issues, such as the roots of poverty, inequality, or the erosion of the planet.

As mentioned above, the EU Regulation on Digital Services is closely related to Agenda 2030 and the Sustainable Development Goals adopted by the UN in 2015.[33] Among the objectives directly or indirectly related, we can point out:

a) SDG 8: which seeks to ensure a level playing field for businesses and protect workers on digital platforms. Decent work and economic growth are also located. This goal seeks to promote sustainable economic growth and decent work for all. To achieve SGD 8, it is necessary to adopt policies that support economic growth, including investments in infrastructure, innovation, and technology. On the other hand, consumers can contribute to this goal by choosing products produced in an ethical and sustainable way and by supporting companies that promote decent work.
b) SDG 9: recognizes the importance of investing in infrastructure, innovation and technology for sustainable development, as well as promoting inclusive

[31] The Spanish Council of Ministers approved the Action Plan for the Implementation of the 2030 Agenda for Sustainable Development on June 29, 2018, and submitted it to the United Nations in support of the Voluntary National Review that Spain underwent on July 18, 2018, in New York. Available in.

http://www.exteriores.gob.es/Portal/es/PoliticaExteriorCooperacion/Agenda2030/Paginas/Inicio.aspx

[32] Paper on the EU's approach to the implementation of the UN 2030 Agenda for Sustainable Development together with its member countries. Available in.

https://ec.europa.eu/info/strategy/international-strategies/sustainable-development-goals/eu-approach-sustainable-development_es

[33] Proposal for a Regulation…, *op. cit.* p. 1.

and sustainable industrialization. on Industry, Innovation and Infrastructure. In this regard, since regulating digital platforms and promoting innovation can contribute to the development of a resilient and inclusive digital infrastructure. The DSA also seeks to promote fair competition and transparency in digital platforms, which can help promote inclusive and sustainable industrialization.

c) SDG 12: ensures that companies are responsible for their digital activities and reduce their environmental impact. In addition, it establishes the need to ensure sustainable and responsible consumption and production patterns. This means that it is necessary to promote the production and consumption of goods and services that are produced in a sustainable and responsible manner in order to reduce environmental impact, promote social and economic justice, and protect the health and welfare of consumers. To achieve this goal, it is necessary to adopt measures that ensure transparency, safety and fairness in business, as well as to promote consumer awareness about the importance of their consumption choices and how they affect the environment and society in general.
d) SDG 16: establishes clear and transparent rules for better competition in the digital marketplace.[34] Since regulating digital platforms and promoting transparency and accountability can contribute to building effective, responsible and inclusive institutions at all levels, the DSA can relate to this goal by protecting the rights of online users, including privacy, freedom of expression and access to information, helping to promote fairness and social inclusion. In addition, the DSA seeks to promote fair competition and transparency on digital platforms, which can help prevent corruption and promote corporate responsibility.

Among all these objectives, we consider that SDG 9 and 12 are the ones that give special emphasis to consumers in the Regulation. Thus, SDG 12 focuses on educating consumers to make informed choices about the products they consume and to promote sustainable consumption (Saumier 2021). On the other hand, SDG 9 focuses on industry, innovation and infrastructure and seeks to improve the quality and affordability of products and services, foster competition and diversity in markets and ensure access to infrastructure and services for all consumers, including those in vulnerable situations.[35] Although SDG 9 is not specifically focused on consumers, it has a direct relationship with them, since it seeks to improve their quality of life and well-being through better products, services, and access to infrastructure.[36]

The efforts that have been focused on users/consumers in digital platforms and in the digitalization process can thus be observed. In this context, both the 2030 Agenda and the DSA were designed, albeit indirectly, to protect consumers, since effective

[34] United Nations (2015). Resolution adopted by the General Assembly on 25 September 2015. *Transforming our world: the 2030 Agenda for Sustainable Development* A/RES/70/1. https://sdgs.un.org/2030agenda

[35] Framework of global indicators for the Sustainable Development Goals and Targets of the 2030 Agenda for Sustainable Development, Resolution adopted by the General Assembly on the Work of the Statistical Commission on the 2030 Agenda for Sustainable Development, UN Doc A/RES/71/313, Annex A, 21. Bath, V. (2021). SDG 9: Industry, Innovation and Infrastructure.

[36] *Ibidem*, 3.

consumer protection contributes to a more inclusive and balanced society, which is a goal of the 2030 Agenda.[37]

As regards the DSA, it seeks to ensure the protection of users in relation to digital services, including consumers. This protection includes protecting users' privacy, preventing the dissemination of illegal or harmful content, ensuring transparency in the commercial practices of digital platforms, and creating effective mechanisms for resolving disputes between companies and consumers. The DSA also requires companies to provide clear and accessible information about their terms and conditions, and to treat all users fairly and in a non-discriminatory manner.

In addition, the regulation also provides for companies to be held liable in the event of defective or harmful products or services to consumers, making it easier for consumers to seek redress or compensation for damages caused. In addition, Regulation 2022/2065 requires companies to provide clear and accurate information on how consumer data is collected, used and shared, thus ensuring that consumers' privacy is protected.

Regarding the 2030 Agenda for Sustainable Development, among its goals and strategies to achieve them, we see that it is necessary to ensure that products and services are produced and consumed responsibly, considering the needs of present and future generations.

As we reiterated at the beginning of this section, the fulfillment of these SDGs depends on the voluntary nature of the member states; i.e., it will be up to the member states to comply with their national legislation in the achievement of these goals. Since both Spain and Portugal are, in addition to being signatories to the UN Agenda, EU Member States, however, they are countries to which, by virtue of EU law, the 2022 Digital Services Regulation[38] will be directly and bindingly applicable. Since this regulation includes assistance to meet these Sustainable Development Goals, *ergo*, it will be a goal to be achieved by both Spain and Portugal.

---

[37] *Ibidem*, 27. Access to the courts can support Target 12.6 in other ways. The growth of producer sustainability claims regarding consumer goods and services opens up the option of judicial review under laws governing unfair trade practices. See Anna Beckers, Enforcement of Corporate Social Responsibility Codes: On Global Self-Regulation and National Private Law (Hart Publishing 2015) and Borko Mihajlović, 'The Role of Consumers in the Achievement of Corporate Sustainability through the Reductionof Unfair Commercial Practices' (2020) 12(3) Sustainability 1. Since unfair commercial practices are typically remedied through injunctions, this approach ties companies to their unilateral sustainability claims or subjects them to the risk of serious reputational damage and loss of market share. The current EU Injunctions Directive, while underutilized, is an example of one type of instrument that could be developed regionally or globally to police producers' sustainability claims in the consumer market. This is a positive aspect of consumer sovereignty and empowerment that could translate into support for SDG 12. Directive 2009/22/EC of the European Parliament and of the Council of 23 April 2009 on injunctions for the protection of consumers' interests (codified version) [2009] OJ L110/30. This Directive is likely to be replaced in the near future under the "New Dealfor Consumers" initiative. *Idem.*

[38] Regulations are binding legislative acts. They must be applied in their entirety throughout the EU, without the need for transposition into national law. It is precisely regulations that seek to avoid national fragmentation through transposition. European Union. (2023). *Types of legislation.* Types of legislation | European Union (europa.eu).

To this end, there are still challenges to be faced, such as the lack of transparency by a large number of companies; algorithmic discrimination, which can lead to unfair commercial practices; dissemination of harmful content, such as illegal content, hate speech, harassment and misinformation; and the lack of education of consumers, who, for the most part, do not have sufficient knowledge about their rights and about sustainable consumption practices, which hinders the promotion of fair and responsible commercial practices.

4 Conclusions

Regarding consumer protection in the digital age, it is important to consider that technology has transformed the way people consume, making e-commerce increasingly present in everyday life. In this context, it is important to ensure that consumers are also protected in the online environment. To this end, several laws have been created around the world to regulate consumer protection in e-commerce, establishing clear rules for the advertising and promotion of products and services, ensuring consumers' right to information, privacy, and security.

Additionally, technology also enables the use of tools that assist consumers in making decisions, such as price comparison and product and service evaluation applications. These tools can contribute to increase transparency in the market, empowering consumers in their relationship with companies.

In summary, consumer protection is a relevant and present theme in several goals of the 2030 Agenda, and it is important to consider its protection also in the digital age, through the creation of legislation and tools that ensure transparency, privacy and safety of consumers in the online environment.

With the increasing digitalization of the economy and the rise of e-commerce, it has become necessary to develop strategies and measures to protect consumers in online transactions, since in the digital age consumers face a number of risks, including deceptive commercial practices, privacy violations, data security, and security flaws of digital products, as we listed above. In addition, online transactions can be complex and present challenges for consumers, such as assessing product quality, selecting a supplier, and resolving disputes.

The European Union has taken measures to protect consumers in the digital age, including the implementation of the General Data Protection Regulation (GDPR), the E-Commerce Regulation, and the DSA itself. These measures aim to ensure transparency, protect consumers' privacy, and ensure the security of digital products and services. On the other hand, in the context of Agenda 2030, consumer protection in the digital age is important for achieving the sustainable development goals. This includes ensuring that consumers have access to safe, high-quality products and services in the digital economy, as well as ensuring that consumers are protected against deceptive commercial practices and privacy violations.

However, while efforts are focused in this area, due to constant technological developments, legislation and regulations need to be kept up to date and flexible to deal with new threats and challenges in consumer protection in the digital age. In addition, it is crucial that companies are also responsible for consumer protection and comply with the established standards. It is necessary to foster a culture of respect for consumers and to promote education about consumer rights in the digital age, so that consumers can make informed and safe choices. Consumer protection in the digital age is an ongoing process that requires the collaboration of all sectors of society, including governments, businesses, and consumers, to ensure a fair, safe and sustainable digital environment for all.

References

Bath V (2021) SDG 9: Industry, Innovation and Infrastructure. In: Michaels R, Ruiz Abou-Nigm V, Loon Hv (eds) The Private Side of Transforming our World—UN Sustainable Development Goals 2030 and the Role of Private International Law. Cambridge: Intersentia Online

Beckers A (2015) Enforcing Corporate Social Responsibility Codes: On Global Self-Regulation and National Private Law. Hart Publishing, UK

Carvalho JM (2021) A proteção dos consumidores no Digital Services Acte, Nova Consumer Lab. https://novaconsumerlab.novalaw.unl.pt/a-protecao-dos-consumidores-no-digital-services-act/

Cauffman C, Goanta C (2021) A New Order: The Digital Services Act and Consumer Protection. Cambridge University Press, pp. 758–774. https://www.cambridge.org/core/journals/european-journal-of-risk-regulation/article/new-order-the-digital-services-act-and-consumer-protection/8E34BA8A209C61C42A1E7ADB6BB904B1

Digital Markets Act. OJ L 265 of 12.10.2022

Digital Services Act. OJ L 277 of 27.10.2022

Directive 2000/31/EC of the European Parliament and of the Council of 8 June 2000 on certain legal aspects of information society services, in particular electronic commerce, in the Internal Market ('Directive on electronic commerce'), OJ L 178 de 17.7.2000

European Comission (2023) A Europe Fit for the Digital Age Empowering people with a new generation of technologies. https://commission.europa.eu/strategy-and-policy/priorities-2019-2024/europe-fit-digital-age_en

Farinha M (2022) Finalmente, o novo Regulamento dos Serviços Digitais (Digital Services Act DSA)!, Nova Consumer Lab https://novaconsumerlab.novalaw.unl.pt/finalmente-o-novo-regulamento-dos-servicos-digitais-digital-services-act-dsa/

Fernández Hernández C (2020) La Comisión presenta la Digital Services Act, su propuesta de regulación de los Servicios Digitales en la Unión, Diario La Ley, N.º 46. diariolaley - Documento relacionado (laleynext.es)

Guimarães MR (2023) As plataformas "colaborativas" enquanto "prestadoras de serviços da sociedade de informação": reflexões à luz da Lei do comércio electrónico e desenvolvimentos recentes, Economia colaborativa, Carvalho. M. M.; Gonçalves, A. S. de S. (coordenadoras). Braga, UMinho Editora 2023:467–498

Leitão de LMTM (2023) Digital Services ACT (DSA)—O Regulamento Europeu 2022/2065 Sobre os Serviços Digitais. Coimbra, Almedina

Miguel Asensio de PA (2021) Servicios y mercados digitales: modernización del régimen de responsabilidad y nuevas obligaciones de los intermediarios, Revista La Ley Unión Europea, N. 88, Janeiro 2021

Mihajlović B (2020) The Role of Consumers in the Achievement of Corporate Sustainability through the Reduction of Unfair Commercial Practices. Sustainability 12(3):1009–1029

Proposal for a Regulation of the European Parliament and of the Council on a Single Market for Digital Services (Digital Services Act) and amending Directive 2000/31/EC. https://eur-lex.europa.eu/legal-content/EN/TXT/?uri=CELEX%3A52020PC0825

Saumier G (2021) SDG 12: Sustainable Consumption and Production. In: Michaels R, Ruiz Abou-Nigm V, Loon Hv (eds) The Private Side of Transforming our World—UN Sustainable Development Goals 2030 and the Role of Private International Law. Cambridge: Intersentia Online. https://www.intersentiaonline.com/permalink/7a005f4c216430beb9b333db9279e2b5

United Nations (2015) Resolution adopted by the General Assembly on 25 September 2015, Transforming our world: the 2030 Agenda for Sustainable Development A/RES/70/1. https://sdgs.un.org/2030agenda

Digital Services Act: Towards the *Digital Rule of Law*

Tiago Morais Rocha

Abstract This chapter analyses the link between the Digital Services Act (DSA) and the *rule of law* principle, arguing that the new Regulation contributes to the affirmation and development of a *digital rule of law* in the European Union. Some of the obligations set forward in the DSA materialise the principles arising from the *rule of law* applied to the digital ecosystem and departing from the need for a strong "digital constitutionalism" in the algorithmic society. While formally private, digital giants manage materially public spaces, that form to the new "digital public sphere", in which private actors perform functions and exercise powers that traditionally belong to public authorities. The intervention of constitutional law is required considering the primary function of the *rule of law*: to temper power wherever it is and regardless of who exercises it. Focusing on the new procedural obligations introduced by the DSA, the article describes how the DSA is articulated with the *digital rule of law*.

Keywords Digital Services Act · Rule of law · Digital rule of law

1 Introduction

In the wake of the 6 January 2021 attack on the US Capitol by a group of Donald Trump supporters, two social networks—Twitter (now X), Facebook, and Instagram—decided to suspend the account of the President of the United States of America (Buchanan et al. 2021). At the time, Donald Trump had 88 million followers on Twitter (Collins and Zadrozny 2021), often using that social network as a megaphone for his political positions, as a means of political and electoral campaigning, and as a privileged form of outreach to his supporters and the general public. The suspension, decided by Twitter on 8 January, was permanent and justified by the

T. M. Rocha (✉)
University of Porto, Porto, Portugal
e-mail: trocha@direito.up.pt

Centre for Interdisciplinary Research On Justice, Porto, Portugal

G. Enes et al. (eds.), *A Digital Europe for Citizens*,
https://doi.org/10.1007/978-3-032-02500-5_11

digital platform with two tweets published by the former President[1] and how they were «being received and interpreted on and off Twitter».[2] Said content allegedly violated the platform's terms and conditions regarding the "Glorification of Violence Policy". Notwithstanding, both tweets invoked by the social network do not in themselves contain any direct appeal to violence or, using the words of the platform's terms and conditions, glorify violence in such a way as to «inspire others to replicate violent acts», so much so that Twitter felt the need to explain the reasons and factors that led the social network to interpret those tweets as a form of glorification of violence and, consequently, a violation of its policies, which led to the permanent suspension of Donald Trump's account.

As for Facebook and Instagram, where Trump had respectively 35 million and 24 million followers,[3] the platforms started to suspend the former President's account for 24 h and then moved to suspend it «indefinitely and for at least the next two weeks until the peaceful transition of power is complete».[4] META's Oversight Board eventually reviewed Facebook's decision. This Board, which began operating in 2020, seeks to be an independent body replicating a "high court" that reviews the social networks' decisions on content moderation and issues recommendations regarding platform policies (Wong and Floridi 2023), while is considered to be in a «twilight zone between being a decisionmaker exercising immensely consequential power, and being a made-up body that exists at the whim of its creator» (Douek 2024), with no state-given mandate to adjudicate on the interpretation or application of fundamental rights, especially the right to freedom of expression.

The Oversight Board, albeit recognizing that «Facebook has become a virtually indispensable medium for political discourse, and especially so in election periods», maintained that Donald Trump's posts violated the social network's terms and conditions but severely criticized the sanction imposed by Facebook, even going so far as to say that «in applying a vague, standardless penalty and then referring this case to the Board to resolve, Facebook seeks to avoid its responsibilities».[5] In its findings, the body stressed the lack of provision for an «indefinite suspension» sanction in the platform's terms and conditions, which renders that restriction on freedom of expression vague and uncertain, possibly violating the prohibition of arbitrariness. In a nutshell, META's Oversight Board, if it were a judicial body, took the view that the social network's decision had violated the *rule of law*, namely, but not exclusively,

---

[1] On January 8, 2021, former President Trump tweeted the following: "*The 75,000,000 great American Patriots who voted for me, AMERICA FIRST, and MAKE AMERICA GREAT AGAIN, will have a GIANT VOICE long into the future. They will not be disrespected or treated unfairly in any way, shape or form!!!*". Shortly afterwards, Donald Trump also tweeted this: "*To all of those who have asked, I will not be going to the Inauguration on January 20th*". See the blog posted by Twitter on January 8, 2021. Available in https://blog.x.com/en_us/topics/company/2020/suspension.

[2] See above.

[3] See the META's Oversight Board Case Decision 2021-001-FB-FBR. Available in https://www.oversightboard.com/decision/fb-691qamhj/.

[4] See above.

[5] META's Oversight Board Case Decision 2021-001-FB-FBR.

the legality principle (in the sense of *nullum crimen, nulla poena sine lege*[6]) and the prohibition of arbitrariness, both essential elements of the *rule of law* principle (Dias 2019). As a result, Facebook revised its initial decision and ordered the suspension of Donald Trump's account for a period of two years. Meanwhile, in January 2023, the suspension was lifted. Ironically, the announcement of the end of the suspension was accompanied by a statement in which META claimed that, as a general rule, it does not seek to hinder public and democratic debate, especially in the electoral context, the more so because the public should be able to hear what politicians have to say, which includes the «good, the bad and the ugly» so that they can make informed choices (Clegg 2023).

More curious and significant, however, is the social network's statement from 21 January 2021, when it referred to the Oversight Board the decision to 'deplatform' Donald Trump:

> Every day, Facebook makes decisions about whether content is harmful, and these decisions are made according to Community Standards we have developed over many years. It would be better if these decisions were made according to frameworks agreed by democratically accountable lawmakers. But in the absence of such laws, there are decisions that we cannot duck. (Clegg 2021)

In its statement, META appears to agree that private companies and tech giants should not make decisions that significantly impact the public sphere, particularly regarding content moderation. META wisely adds that it would be better if decisions on content moderation were made according to rules adopted by democratically elected legislators accountable to citizens. However, in META's vision at the time of those comments, no public laws regulate and restrict the content moderation activity carried out by digital platforms. Meanwhile, perhaps responding to the implicit invitation laid out by the digital platform in 2021, the European Union adopted the Digital Services Act (DSA),[7] intending to ensure a safe, predictable, and trustworthy online environment that facilitates innovation and in which fundamental rights enshrined in the Charter of Fundamental Rights of the European Union are effectively protected.[8]

This chapter explores the DSA as a regulatory step by the European Union towards a *digital rule of law* in the context of the emergence and consolidation of "digital constitutionalism". The chapter proceeds as follows: Sect. 2 explores the notion of digital constitutionalism and its articulation with the *rule of law*. Section 3 delves into an overview of the DSA and how it is based on a "platform realism" logic that moves from liability to responsibility, due care, risk management, and transparency. Finally, Sect. 4 argues that one of the most critical contributions of the DSA is the

---

[6] The *rule of law* principle implies, *inter alia*, that strict limits must be set on the arbitrary and excessive actions of power, to uphold citizens' rights and freedoms. Thus, in a bid to prevent arbitrariness and excess, the exercise of power must be strictly subject to a legality principle, the essential content of which is, in this context, the idea that there can be no negative consequence in a citizen's legal sphere that is not based on a prior, written, strict and certain rule.

[7] Regulation (EU) 2022/2065 of the European Parliament and of the Council of 19 October 2022 on a Single Market For Digital Services and amending Directive 2000/31/EC (Digital Services Act) PE/30/2022/REV/1, *OJ L 277, 27.10.2022, p. 1–102.*

[8] Article 1(1) DSA.

mitigation of arbitrariness of digital platforms in the relations established with users, which is a fundamental feature of the *rule of law* applied in the digital realm. We then present some examples that show how the obligations laid down in the DSA effectively implement some of the principles of the *digital rule of law* framework in the European digital ecosystem. We conclude that the DSA is a legal instrument that affirms the *digital rule of law* in the European Union.

2 The *Digital Rule of Law* and 'Digital Constitutionalism'

Over the last 20 years, the Information Age has become a Digital Age in the context of an algorithmic society, dependent on and driven by algorithms—an "algocracy", i.e., «a particular kind of governance system, one which is organized and structured on the basis of computer-programmed algorithms» (Danaher 2016). The algorithmic society is dominated by multinational giants, who manage digital platforms on which citizens are increasingly dependent and who stand between the nation-state and individuals, using algorithms and artificial intelligence as mediating agents to shape public discourse and, to a large extent, human action itself (Celeste 2023). In doing so, "digital giants" de facto govern vast communities of people (Simoncini and Longo 2021), having a «quasi-state status» (Savin 2022). Today, digital platforms, inserted in "digital empires" (Bradford 2023), are actors that create, shape, and amplify the dominant grand narratives of our time. Such platforms are often virtual places without *state* and *law* and, therefore, without the *rule of law*.

Since the end of last century, the allure of the enormous promises of technological development—many of which have come true—has led to neglect and oblivion of the role of constitutionalism, constitutional law, and the *rule of law* in limiting the consolidation of uncontrolled private powers and in the protection of fundamental rights (Gregorio 2022). For a long time, the prevailing discourse was essentially optimistic ("cyber-utopianism") and relatively deified of technology, associated with liberal positions or non-intervention by public authorities in the online environment (Morozov 2011). This "constitutional neglect" has allowed the growth and consolidation of massive digital platforms that accumulate powers beyond public supervision and play "quasi-constitutional" roles that compete with traditional public authorities (Bassini and Pollicino 2023). These powers can either be delegated as a result of indirect transfers and conscious dismissals by public authorities in favor of private companies, sometimes due to a lack of technological or financial capacity, sometimes due to political convenience, or can arise autonomously as a result of the very architecture of the network and the market power of these private actors (Gregorio 2021). Although exercised by multinational private companies, the powers in question may frequently be equivalent to legislative, administrative, executive and judicial functions traditionally performed by public authorities.

The powers of the large digital platforms are evident in the context of online content moderation activities. According to Article 3(t) DSA, content moderation refers to the activities, whether automated or not, undertaken by digital platforms that are aimed at detecting, identifying, and addressing "illegal content" or information incompatible with terms and conditions, including measures taken that affect the availability, visibility, and accessibility of that "illegal content" or that information, such as demotion, demonetization, disabling of access to, or removal thereof, or that affect the ability of users to provide that information, such as the termination or suspension of a user's account. Let us be clear: freedom of expression is a core feature of any democratic state under the *rule of law*, as the European Court of Human Rights (ECHR) has consistently recognized in its decisions. ECHR considers freedom of speech as «one of the essential foundations of such [democratic] society, one of the basic conditions for its progress and for the development of every man».[9] Regarding the possibilities that the digital environment poses to freedom of expression, the Court stated in the landmark case *Delfi v. Estonia* (Kaur 2023) the following:

> [...] the Internet provides an unprecedented platform for the exercise of freedom of expression. [...] However, alongside these benefits, certain dangers may also arise. Defamatory and other types of clearly unlawful speech, including hate speech and speech inciting violence, can be disseminated like never before, worldwide, in a matter of seconds, and sometimes remain persistently available online.[10]

Guaranteeing the conditions upon which it is possible to exercise one's freedom of expression is among the main tasks that citizens in liberal democracies endow to legislators, governments, and courts, all bound by the *rule of law*. There is no reason for the digital realm to be any different, even though the private sector's role in the digital age appears pervasive. In fact, «the contemporary exercise of freedom of opinion and expression owes much of its strength to private industry, which wields enormous power over digital space, acting as a gateway for information and an intermediary for expression» (United Nations 2016). As "gatekeepers",[11] digital platforms can impose numerous restrictions on online freedom of expression in violation of users' fundamental rights. Such tremendous capabilities demand new regulatory approaches and "constitutional counteractions" that adequately address the challenges of the Digital Age (Celeste 2023). Gone are the days of cyberspace demanding to be left alone and rejecting any claim of sovereignty or authority by elected legislators and governments (Barlow 1996). And the promise that a (cyber)world was being created where «anyone, anywhere may express his or her beliefs, no matter how singular, without fear of being coerced into silence or conformity» was, at best, disappointing. Cyberspace is not and cannot be a space free of law and (fundamental) rights; emphasizing that citizens enjoy the same rights online as they do offline (United Nations

---

[9] Decision from the ECHR Handysed v. The United Kingdom [Plenary], n.º 5493/72, § 49, 7 December 1976.

[10] Decision from the ECHR Delfi AS v. Estonia [Grand Chamber], n.º 64569/09, § 110, 16 June 2015.

[11] In EU law, a 'gatekeeper' is an undertaking that has a significant impact on the internal market, provides a core platform service which is an important gateway for business users to reach end users, and enjoys an entrenched and durable position, in its operations, or it is foreseeable that it will enjoy such a position in the near future. See Regulation (EU) 2022/1925 of the European Parliament and of the Council of 14 September 2022 on contestable and fair markets in the digital sector (Digital Markets Act), PE/17/2022/REV/1, OJ L 265, 12 October 2022, p. 1–66.

2016) is no longer enough, although the constitutional values that need to be upheld do not vary.[12]

The "digital constitutionalism" framework, which has received considerable attention in recent years, allows us to deal with the array of matters posed by the emergence of uncontrolled digital powers and their challenges to fundamental rights and democratic processes, from online speech and platform governance to data protection, non-discrimination, property, cybersecurity, and artificial intelligence (Duarte et al. 2024). As Terzis puts it, digital constitutionalism addresses «the fear that constitutional principles and protections are quickly crumbling under the obscure forces of novel digital technologies and the private entities wielding technological power», being an «umbrella term that seeks to encompass a diverse array of legal instruments and political *desiderata*» (Terzis 2024). The role of digital constitutionalism is not to regulate technology itself but to limit the threats that result from the growth of private, global, and plural (Golia 2023) powers that affect modern democracies, shifting the emphasis from the "empire of government" to the "empire of digital platforms" (Koskenniemi 2013). Notwithstanding the criticism (Terzis 2024; Golia 2023; Costello 2023),[13] digital constitutionalism is both a «form of reaction» and a «normative strategy» to protect fundamental rights and democracies while limiting the emergence of powers outside any public and democratic control or oversight (Gregorio 2022). In doing so, as Sirota observes, digital constitutionalism entails «the empowerment of the state or of supranational entities as the European Union [...] to bring commercial actors to heel and so protect individuals» (Sirota 2023). This is no easy task, as digital constitutionalism requires

> consensus about how power over the internet should be shared and limited, how those limits may be imposed, and by whom. Unlike regular constitutions, which just have to articulate how power is shared between different parts of a single government, digital constitutionalism requires us to develop new ways of limiting abuses of power in a complex system that includes many different governments, businesses, and civil society organizations. (Suzor 2019)

Constitutionalism is traditionally understood as a «fundamental set of principles» and the «correlative institutions arrangement» (Sartori 1962) aimed at countering the arbitrary power of the state, ensuring a "limited form of government" (*idem*). This

---

[12] See Opinion from the Supreme Court of the United States Moody v. NetChoice, LLC, 603/1, 1 July 2024. This case, brought before the US Supreme Court, concerns two statutes adopted in Texas and Florida, which curtail the capacity of large social media companies to engage in content moderation and make those platforms give reasons to a user if they remove or alter the uploaded content. In its Opinion, the Court found that the curation and content moderation activity of social media networks, insofar as it results in an «expressive product», is protected by the First Amendment. Albeit expressing sympathy for those who believe that «modern media empires» had gained ever greater capacity to «shape» and even «manipulate popular opinion», going as far as affirming that digital platforms «unabashedly control the content that will appear to users, exercising authority to remove, label or demote messages they disfavor», the Court asserts that government cannot interfere with «editorial choices—say, by ordering the excluded to be included», even when the government invokes an interest «in improving, or better balancing, the marketplace of ideas», despite the importance of having a «well-functioning sphere of expression, in which citizens have access to information from many sources».

[13] For a detailed account of the critiques regarding digital constitutionalism.

«negative» understanding of constitutionalism (Barber 2015) highlights the need for a defense mechanism against the interference of public powers and authorities vested with the so-called *ius imperium*. But constitutionalism does more than watch against oppression. On the «positive» side, constitutionalism requires from the state a set of «effective and powerful institutions» that can act in order to achieve its primary purpose: «advance the well-being» of the community (*idem*). Constitutionalism, to advance the public interest, instructs politicians to adopt measures to protect and promote fundamental rights, which they do even in horizontal relations between private individuals, as is the case of the Portuguese Constitution[14] and some provisions of the Charter of Fundamental Rights of the European Union (Prechal 2020; Brkan 2019), as the Court of Justice of the European Union (CJEU) decided.[15]

According to Zürn, «the exercise of power includes all instances in which an actor A brings an actor B to think or do something they would not thought or done otherwise» (Zürn 2018). In its nature, power isn't exclusive to the state. Indeed, in an algorithmic society, the primary sources of threats to fundamental rights and democratic processes are not public authorities but new private actors who govern digital spaces (Duarte et al. 2024). Despite being formally private, these digital spaces are de facto public spaces, corresponding to the new "digital public sphere", which is necessarily more polarized and where professional journalism and traditional mass media are «increasingly bypassed as gatekeepers of public communication» (Seeliger and Sevignani 2022). In these materially public spaces, private actors exercise functions that traditionally belong to public authorities (Belli et al. 2017). When the exercise of these powers that mimic public authority is carried out without constitutional safeguards and controls, we have a problem that concerns us collectively, requiring the intervention of constitutional law and the *rule of law*.

Above all, the *rule of law* principle translates the normative ideal that all public powers are subject to limits derived from the law itself. In a nutshell, the *rule of law* stands for «tempering power» (Krygier 2016). Caunes emphasizes the relationship between law and power by pointing out the following:

> Law, ruling alone, is a force confining and power, unattended, is a flame that burns to its own destruction. The rule of law thus constitutes an anchoring nexus or connecting bond between law and power. It is both channeling and ordering their interrelations. It represents the legal mantle of power in a democratic society. (Caunes 2022)

Undoubtedly, the *rule of law* arose as a defense against the arbitrariness of state power. However, the main problem that the *rule of law* seeks to address is power itself, wherever it may be and regardless of the form in which it is exercised. Thus, if we

---

[14] Article 18(1).

[15] See Judgment of the CJEU of 17 April 2018, Vera Egenberger v Evangelisches Werk für Diakonie und Entwicklung e.V. (*Egenberger*), C-414/16, EU:C:2018:257; Judgment of the CJEU of 11 September 2018, IR v JQ (*IR*), C-68/17, EU:C:2018:696; Judgment of the CJEU of 22 January 2019, Cresco Investigation GmbH v Markus Achatzi (*Cresco Investigation*), C-193/17, EU:C:2019:43; Judgment of the CJEU of 6 November 2018, Stadt Wuppertal v Maria Elisabeth Bauer and Volker Willmeroth v Martina Broßonn (*Bauer*), C-569/16 and C-570/16, EU:C:2018:871; Judgment of the CJEU of 6 November 2018, Max-Planck-Gesellschaft zur Förderung der Wissenschaften eV v Tetsuji Shimizu (*Max-Planck*), C-684/16, EU:C:2018:874.

recognize that digital platforms, although private, exercise quasi-public functions or mimic the powers of public authorities, it is not unreasonable to demand that their activity be subject to defined constitutional and legal limits, always to protect citizens' fundamental rights and uphold democratic societies. In fact, it's just a matter of applying to the digital realm the idea that «wherever there is power there ought to be constitutional limits» (Maduro 2012), which can be encapsulated in the formula *ubi potestas, ibi constitutione.*

In Tom Bingham's formula, the *rule of law* presupposes that «all persons and authorities within the state, whether public or private, should be bound by and entitled to the benefit of laws publicly made, taking effect (generally) in the future and publicly administered in the courts» (Bingham 2011). It must be acknowledged that digital platforms effectively perform roles or functions that are traditionally public functions. In fact, regarding content moderation, digital platforms often act as legislators by defining the content that can legitimately be shared on their platforms through their terms and conditions. They act as judges, deciding the legitimate content in specific cases and determining the appropriate sanctions. They act as administrative bodies, applying the sanctions they have decided and undertaking activities to detect, identify, and combat illegitimate content (Perel and Elkin-Koren 2016). If we recognize that (public) powers in the modern "agoras" and forums are being handed over to a handful of private digital giants, constitutional mechanisms must be put in place to restrict the exercise of these powers in order to ensure respect for fundamental rights and the *rule of law*. In this sense, «principles such as transparency, accountability, representation, or due process, should be observed *whenever* organised power threatens fundamental rights, irrespective of the power's nature» (Duarte et al. 2024).

Today, intermediary service providers, especially digital platforms, are living in a regulatory paradox, expressing two contradictory concerns regarding content moderation: over or under-blocking or filtering illegal and harmful content. In either case, citizens' fundamental rights are potentially at stake, namely the right to human dignity, freedom of expression, and information, including freedom and pluralism of the media, the right to privacy, the right to data protection, the right to non-discrimination, and children's rights. When moderated excessively, the operation of digital platforms can have significant impacts on freedom of expression and information, often giving rise to the so-called "chilling effect" or "deterrent effect" of freedom of expression and, as Jack Balkin puts it, to problems of «collateral censorship» and «digital prior restraint» (Balkin 2018a, b). When not sufficiently moderated, digital platforms can be a place for online crime, the dissemination of illegal and harmful content, including hate speech, the distribution of child pornography, human trafficking operations, the promotion of terrorism and terrorist recruitment, the amplification of disinformation, the facilitation of internal and external interference operations in democratic processes, and for the manipulation and abuse of users' personal data (De Streel et al. 2020).

In addition to the implications for the fundamental rights of citizens, Ekin-Koren and Perel argue that content moderation efforts carried out by intermediary service providers, namely digital platforms, entail four major challenges for the *rule of law* principle (Elkin-Koren and Perel 2020): they mitigate the distinction between private interests and public responsibilities; they delegate the power to make normative choices about the legitimacy of content to opaque algorithms; they circumvent the constitutional safeguard of the separation of powers; and they undermine the constitutional guarantees of *due process* and *fair trial*.

Taking a closer look at each of these sources of concern:

2.1 Mitigation of the Distinction between Private Interests and Public Responsibilities

According to Ekin-Koren and Perel, digital platforms are in a dual position as private companies and as facilitators or intermediaries of civic discourse in the public sphere (Elkin-Koren and Perel 2020). These two roles are not always reconcilable: on the one hand, as commercial players, digital platforms seek to maximize their profits and satisfy their financial interests in all the activities they perform, including content moderation. From a business model viewpoint, it is convenient for online platforms, often self-described as "communities", to proclaim themselves as champions of freedom, diversity, and openness insofar as that message builds and sustains trust for their users to keep seeing, creating, uploading, reacting, or sharing content in the network: the "attention economy" demands it.

Practically since their birth, and especially in the European Union with the e-Commerce Directive,[16] digital platforms have benefited from a safe harbor privilege and a conditional exemption from liability for content uploaded and shared by users (Spindler 2017). This conditional exemption from liability originally had a twofold purpose: to empower technological companies in the early days of their development by not burdening them economically with the costs of responsibility for third-party content and, on the other hand, to be an effective way of protecting citizens' fundamental rights, namely against interventions that could excessively restrict freedom of expression, opinion, and information, causing unintended censorship or deterrent effects (Gregorio 2022). However, the role of platforms in the digital economy has evolved and is no longer strictly passive or neutral.[17] In fact, while increasing the number of users and exploiting the "attention market", digital platforms started to intervene algorithmically in prioritizing and recommending content (Weitzenboeck 2023), placing themselves not precisely as arbiters of truth but certainly as arbiters of visibility. Thus, in addition to private and commercial interests, digital platforms have also come to govern the public discourse of their users, but with questionable and contestable criteria or without paying full attention to the public interest and responsibilities behind that task. Therefore, digital platforms are consequently

[16] Directive 2000/31/EC of the European Parliament and of the Council of 8 June 2000 on certain legal aspects of information society services, in particular electronic commerce, in the Internal Market ('Directive on electronic commerce'), *OJ L 178, 17.7.2000, p. 1–16.*

[17] See Judgment of the CJEU of 12 July 2011, L'Oréal SA et al. v eBay International AG et al. (*L'Oréal*), C-324/09, ECLI:EU:C:2011:474.

hostage to a conflict of interests: they must moderate those who sustain their business model or, as Ekin-Koren and Perel put it, «guard against those who potentially tend their garden» (Elkin-Koren and Perel 2020).

Albeit this conflict, one of the requirements at the heart of the *rule of law*, within the framework of the legality principle, is that private entities performing public functions should be subject to the *rule of law* and can be held accountable in terms comparable to public entities. As the Venice Commission asserts:

> [...] individual human rights are affected not only by the authorities of the State, but also by hybrid (State-private) actors and private entities which perform tasks that were formerly the domain of State authorities, or include unilateral decisions affecting a great number of people, as well as by international and supranational organisations. The Commission recommended that the Rule of Law principles be applied in these areas as well. § The Rule of Law must be applied at all levels of public power. *Mutatis mutandis*, the principles of the Rule of Law also apply in private law relations. (European Commission for Democracy Through Law (Venice Commission) 2016)

2.2 Delegating the Power to Make Normative Choices about the Legitimacy of Content to Opaque Algorithms

Whether we like it or not, online content moderation activities involve normative and frontier choices, especially regarding harmful content not considered illegal ("lawful but awful"), as with disinformation. Even regarding illegal content, content moderation requires applying and interpreting legal provisions that often give rise to doubts and interpretative issues. The use of automated content filtering processes frequently contributes to the violation of users' fundamental rights and freedoms. It transforms the inherent human nature of normative, judicial, and executive functions (Frosio 2023), potentially leading to the arbitrariness that the *rule of law* principle seeks to avoid.

2.3 Bypassing the Constitutional Safeguard of the Separation of Powers

Traditionally, the substantive criteria of what does or does not constitute legitimate, protected, or unprotected speech are set out in the law, and decisions adopted based on those laws are subject to judicial scrutiny as part of effective judicial protection. However, the content moderation decisions adopted by digital platforms are not, as a rule, subject to traditional control mechanisms, especially since these private actors are not necessarily obliged to respect fundamental rights, given the lack of horizontal effect of these provisions. Democratic regimes have taken advantage of this state of affairs to enlist, co-opt, or cooperate with private actors to restrict or limit citizens' freedom of expression in the face of constitutional guarantees and the *rule of law* (Elkin-Koren and Perel 2020).

2.4 Undermining the Constitutional Guarantees of Due Process and Fair Trial

Due process and *fair trial* presuppose that all defendants have the right, for example, to an independent and impartial court of law, that they can present their arguments and evidence on an equal footing ('equality of arms'), and that they can receive a duly reasoned and appealable decision (Monsen and Willumat 2024). Pasquale explains that *due process* rights, "while flexible, should include four core features in all but the most trivial or routine cases: the ability to explain one's case, a judgment by a human decisionmaker, an explanation for that judgment, and an ability to appeal" (Pasquale 2021).

However, the content moderation mechanisms on digital platforms are far from complying with these standards. If the platform itself decides on the content it stores and displays, independence and impartiality are not guaranteed, especially since decisions can be automated and obscure, without human intervention, rarely reasoned, adopted without prior contradiction, and not subject to review by an independent and disinterested body. On the other hand, using automated and algorithmic mechanisms in decision-making and balancing the interests and fundamental rights at stake raises serious concerns about transparency, accountability, and the contestability of decisions (Elkin-Koren and Perel 2020).

3 The Digital Services Act and "Platform Realism"

As we are witnessing at an increasing pace (Rogero 2024),[18] intermediary services operations, namely online platforms, raise a significant number of ethical, political, economic, legal, and societal challenges «due to their reach, in particular as expressed in the number of recipients of the service, in facilitating public debate, economic transactions and the dissemination to the public of information, opinions and ideas and in influencing how recipients obtain and communicate information online».[19] There is no doubt that the activities of online platforms, especially the large ones, are prone to impact fundamental rights protected by the Charter of Fundamental Rights of the European Union, mainly freedom of expression and information, freedom to

[18] Among other possible examples, see the recent decision of the Brazilian Supreme Court to suspend X in Brazil following the failure of the platform to appoint a legal representative in the country.

In response to the court's decision, Elon Musk, X's owner, launched a public crusade against the judge of the case, not only revealing the court proceedings subject to secrecy but also adding that "the people of Brazil have a choice to make—democracy, or Alexandre de Moraes". See: https://x.com/GlobalAffairs/status/1824819053061669244.

[19] Recital 75 DSA.

conduct a business, the right to non-discrimination, and the attainment of a high level of consumer protection.[20]

Recognizing the transformative power of digital technologies both in terms of opportunities and dangers, the European Commission set out in February 2020 its ambition to create a «Europe Fit for the digital age» (European Commission 2020), focusing on three overarching objectives: technology that works for people, a fair and competitive economy, and an open, democratic and sustainable society. In this context, the Commission announced that, in the last quarter of that year, it would propose a Digital Services Act Package to implement *ex ante* risk-based rules designed to guarantee fair and contestable markets in the digital sector and review the liability regime of intermediary services laid down in the e-Commerce Directive from 2000, reinforcing the «oversight over platforms' content policies in the EU» (*idem*).

The step to present a horizontal legislative framework for digital services in the European Union follows the introduction of several «sector-specific legislative and soft law instruments» (Schwemer 2023), like the revision of the Audiovisual Media Services Directive,[21] the Directive on Copyright in the Digital Single Market,[22] the Regulation on promoting fairness and transparency for business users of online intermediation services,[23] the Regulation on addressing the dissemination of terrorist content online,[24] the European Union (EU) Code of Conduct on Countering Illegal Hate Speech Online,[25] and the Code of Practice on Disinformation (strengthened in 2022 and integrated into the DSA in 2025).[26] Despite these EU regulatory interventions, and in the same period, some Member States (e.g., Germany, Austria, and France) have not shied away from adopting or considering adopting legislative measures to contain the growing power of digital platforms in areas non-harmonized by EU law (e.g., illegal content and online disinformation) (Pitruzzella and Pollicino

---

[20] Recital 3 DSA.

[21] Directive (EU) 2018/1808 of the European Parliament and of the Council of 14 November 2018 amending Directive 2010/13/EU on the coordination of certain provisions laid down by law, regulation or administrative action in Member States concerning the provision of audiovisual media services (Audiovisual Media Services Directive) in view of changing market realities. PE/33/2018/REV/1. *OJ L 303, 28.11.2018, p. 69–92.*

[22] Directive (EU) 2019/790 of the European Parliament and of the Council of 17 April 2019 on copyright and related rights in the Digital Single Market and amending Directives 96/9/EC and 2001/29/EC. PE/51/2019/REV/1. *OJ L 130, 17.5.2019, p. 92–125.*

[23] Regulation (EU) 2019/1150 of the European Parliament and of the Council of 20 June 2019 on promoting fairness and transparency for business users of online intermediation services. PE/56/2019/REV/1. *OJ L 186, 11.7.2019, p. 57–79.*

[24] Regulation (EU) 2021/784 of the European Parliament and of the Council of 29 April 2021 on addressing the dissemination of terrorist content online. PE/19/2021/INIT. *OJ L 172, 17.5.2021, p. 79–109.*

[25] Available in: https://commission.europa.eu/strategy-and-policy/policies/justice-and-fundamental-rights/combatting-discrimination/racism-and-xenophobia/eu-code-conduct-countering-illegal-hate-speech-online_en.

[26] Available in: https://digital-strategy.ec.europa.eu/en/library/2022-strengthened-code-practice-disinformation.

2020). The risk that diverging national laws would negatively affect the digital single market was one of the reasons that led to the adoption of the DSA.[27]

As service intermediaries have grown out of their infancy, the dominant strategy of the beginning of the century, based on a shield against liability for third-party content and the absence of a general obligation to patrol platforms aimed at promoting the growth and development of the internet and lowering compliance costs (Kosseff 2019), has ceased to stand up to scrutiny. As Savin points out, from 2015 onwards, we have witnessed a «change in values or attitudes» in the EU regarding intermediaries, from non-liability to responsibility and minimalism and non-intervention to care and duty (Savin 2022). This change of heart was immediately apparent in the Commission's announcement of the Digital Services Act Package, given that one of the key actions was the adoption of «new and revised rules deepen the Internal Market for Digital Services, by increasing and harmonizing the responsibilities of online platforms and information service providers» (European Commission 2020).

Proposed by the European Commission in December 2020 and passed by the European Parliament and the Council in a record time (less than two years), the DSA, in conjunction with the Digital Markets Act (DMA), is a «paradigmatic example showing the shift of paradigm in the Union towards more accountability of online platforms to protect European democratic values» (Duarte et al. 2024), seeking to «foster responsible and diligent behavior by providers of intermediary services to ensure a safe online environment, which allows Union citizens and other parties to freely exercise their fundamental rights» (European Commission 2020b). Adopted on 19 October 2022, the DSA took full effect on 17 February 2024,[28] allowing the European Commission to designate the Very Large Online Platforms (VLOP) and Very Large Search Engines (VLOSE) under Article 33 DSA—Zalando, Wikipedia, XVideos, Temu, X, TikTok, Stripchat, Snapchat, Pinterest, XNXX, Bing, Instagram, Facebook, LinkedIn, Shein, YouTube, Google Shopping, Google Maps, Google Play, Google Search, Booking.com, Pornhub, App Store, Amazon Store, and AliExpress.[29]

The DSA, which has already been said to be a "digital constitution"[30] or a "digital civil charter" (Husovec 2023) for the EU, «can be seen as a milestone» in the path to European digital constitutionalism based on transparency and accountability in line with European values (Gregorio 2022). Although the constitutional aura associated with the new regulation can be disputed (Wilman 2022), the truth is that the DSA is a significant effort to regulate digital services, or, more correctly, intermediary services ('mere conduits' (infrastructures), temporary storage services ('cashing'), and 'hosting services', including online platforms and social networks), i.e., «services that involve the transmission and storage of user-generated content» (*idem*).

---

[27] Recital 2 DSA.

[28] Article 93(2) DSA.

[29] Updated list of VLOP and VLOSE designated by the European Commission under DSA available in: https://digital-strategy.ec.europa.eu/en/policies/list-designated-vlops-and-vloses.

[30] The Greens/EFA in the European Parliament (2022) European Parliament Votes on Constitution for the Internet. Press Release. Available in: https://www.greens-efa.eu/en/article/press/european-parliament-votes-on-constitution-for-the-internet.

The DSA aims to provide a safe, predictable, and trusted online environment that facilitates innovation and where users' fundamental rights are respected (Article 1(1) DSA). To this end, a «second generation» (Husovec 2023) of harmonized rules that apply horizontally and «asymmetrically» (Savin 2022) to intermediary services are adopted, signaling a shift away from sector-specific regulation. In fact, the DSA intends to be a general legal instrument without prejudice to other legal acts adopted by the EU that also apply to intermediary service providers, namely those listed in Article 2(4) DSA. Twenty years later, the DSA replaced the e-Commerce Directive regarding the liability regime for intermediary service providers. Notwithstanding, the e-Commerce Directive will remain in force as it has a broader scope of application, apart from the rules on the liability of intermediary service providers, which have been transferred to the DSA's Chapter II.

Regarding intermediary services provider's liability, the DSA maintains the fundamental framework of conditional exemption from liability (the «negligence-based model» (Turillazzi et al. 2022) laid down in the e-Commerce Directive. However, it introduces some surgical changes to adapt the rules following technological developments and the CJEU case law on the matter (Schwemer 2023). To protect citizens' fundamental rights against over-blocking and to avoid placing excessive burdens on intermediary service providers, the DSA also maintains the ban on Member States introducing obligations to patrol or police user-generated content (Article 8 DSA). However, innovatively, a so-called "Good Samaritan principle" is introduced for non-neutral roles played by intermediaries: they can now proactively adopt voluntary patrolling actions and take measures on illegal content without this affecting their exemption from liability, provided they adopt these measures (detecting, identifying and removing, or disabling access to, illegal content) in good faith and diligently (Article 7 DSA). The use of vague concepts in this context is to be criticized (Schwemer 2023), despite the attempt at clarification in recitals, which specifies that the condition of acting in good faith and in a diligent manner «should include acting in an objective, non-discriminatory and proportionate manner, with due regard to the rights and legitimate interests of all parties involved, and providing the necessary safeguards against unjustified removal of legal content».[31]

From another angle, the DSA also standardizes the minimum procedural rules and the obligations of intermediaries in the context of decisions by judicial and administrative authorities against illegal content (Article 9 DSA). Notably, and perhaps explaining the relative speed with which the Act was adopted, the Regulation does not define what constitutes illegal content, leaving that task mainly to national legislation and EU law (Article 3(h) DSA). In other words, the DSA does not provide an autonomous legal basis for decisions on illegal content, which must be found in different national or European laws.

Given that the DSA does not imply a rupture with the liability regime provided by the e-Commerce Directive, some might assume this is not a cutting-edge regulation. However, the new regime's main feature is the focus shift from liability to platform diligence, accountability, and transparency in two main pillars: content moderation

---

[31] Recital 26 DSA.

and risk management. According to Frosio, the DSA «attempts to govern these widespread private ordering practices via their constitutionalization, regulation and institutional governance» (Frosio 2023). It does so not by intervening on the boundaries of what is considered to be illegal or harmful content (regarding 'lawful but awful' content, it is still up to the platform, when drawing up their terms and conditions, to decide what user-generated content may or not circulate), but rather by introducing substantive and, most importantly, procedural safeguards that "constitutionalize" and harmonize the content moderation practices around the EU, protecting users fundamental rights as laid down in the Charter of Fundamental Rights of the European Union (Frosio and Geiger 2023). In this regard, Pollicino goes so far as to say that the DSA (alongside the DMA) represents a "second season" for European digital constitutionalism, marked by a move towards «procedural digital constitutionalism» (Pollicino 2023). As we later show, this procedural dimension of digital constitutionalism is anchored in the *digital rule of law* and the *digital due process.*

In the digital age, as Fisher would say (Fisher 2009), it is easier to imagine the end of the world than to imagine the end of digital platforms, which calls for a sort of "platform realism". Given that the existence of some immunities from liability related to third-party content is a prerequisite for the viability and flourishing of intermediary services as we know them, the 'realistic' regulatory option in the DSA was to decouple liability from an array of substantive and procedural rules aimed at solving a «wide range of societal problems that emerged» from the platform dominance (Husovec 2023). As stated in Recital 41 DSA «the due diligence obligations are independent from the question of liability of providers of intermediary services which need therefore to be assessed separately», caving in a separate set of rules on sanctions and enforcement (Chapter IV) and cementing the «accountability-but-not-liability» (Husovec 2023) design of the DSA.

These due diligence obligations imposed in the DSA on intermediary service providers are structured in proportion to the type and size of the intermediary and the nature of the service provided[32] in a sort of regulatory pyramid with four cumulative levels of obligations (Husovec and Laguna 2022): (a) universal, applying to all intermediary service providers; (b) basic, applying only to hosting services; (c) advanced, applying only to online platforms, including social networks; (d) special, applying only to VLOP and VLOSE, as summarized in Table 1[33]:

The special obligations to VLOP and VLOSE focus, as said, on systemic risk management stemming from the design, functioning, and use of platforms. The basic idea behind these additional obligations is 'the bigger the power, the bigger the responsibility'. As large online platforms and search engines can «strongly influence safety online, the shaping of public opinion and discourse, as well as online trade»,[34] they must periodically assess the systemic risk deriving from their activities in areas

[32] Recital 41 DSA.

[33] Inspired by Husovec, M. and Laguna, I. R. (2022).

[34] Recital 79 DSA.

Table 1 DSA's due diligence and transparency obligations

Type of obligation—cumulative	Type of service	Size of the service	Obligations under the DSA
Universal obligations (L1)	**Providers of intermediary services**	All sizes	• Designation of a single point of contact—Art. 11 and 12; • Obligations regarding terms and conditions—Art. 14; • Making publicly available annual transparency reports related to content moderation (except micro or small enterprises)—Art. 15
Basic obligations (L2)	**Hosting services**	All sizes	• Implement notice and action mechanisms—Art. 16; • Provide a statement of reasons—Art. 17; • Notification of suspicious of criminal offenses—Art. 18
Advanced obligations (L3)	**Online platforms**	All sizes except micro or small enterprises that aren't VLOP	• Creation of an internal complaint-handling system—Art. 20; • Making available out-of-court dispute settlement—Art. 21; • Give priority to trusted flaggers notifications—Art. 22; • Adopt measures and protection against misuse—Art. 23; • Making publicly available annual transparency reports—Art. 24; • Obligations and prohibitions regarding online interface design and organization—Art. 25; • Obligations related to advertising on online platforms—Art. 26; • Obligations concerning recommender systems transparency—Art. 27; • Adopt measures to ensure the online protection of minors—Art. 28

(continued)

Table 1 (continued)

Type of obligation—cumulative	Type of service	Size of the service	Obligations under the DSA
Special obligations (L4)	**Very large online platforms and very large online search engines**	Online platforms that have a number of average monthly active users equal to or higher than 45 million	• Risk assessment—Art. 34; • Put in place mitigation measures to the specific systemic risks identified—Art. 35; • Take concrete actions in the context of a crisis response mechanism—Art. 36; • Promote independent annual audits—Art. 37; • Give an opt-out option for recommender systems based on profiling—Art. 38; • Addition online advertising transparency obligations—Art. 39; • Provide access to data—Art. 40; • Establish a compliance function ('Chief compliance officer')—Art. 41; • Making publicly available semesterly transparency reports—Art. 42; • Pay a supervisory fee—Art. 43

such as the dissemination of illegal content, and the impact on fundamental rights, democracy, civic discourse, electoral processes, public security, gender relations, public health, minors, and physical and mental well-being (Article 34 DSA). They must not only assess the risks but also take concrete, reasonable, proportionate, and effective measures to mitigate the identified risks (Article 35 DSA). The approach of the DSA to societal risks does not rely on a substantive scheme, where public authorities dictate to digital platforms the 'does and don'ts', instead demanding platforms to identify the potential risks and come up with the solutions to address them better, always protecting users. Suppose an argument can be made that digital platforms are the "architects" of modern public spaces (Gillespie 2018). In that case, it is only correct to demand that when planning, building, and maintaining those spaces, intermediary service providers intervene when needed to ensure that online tools' societal benefits greatly surpass the harms.

4 Digital Services Act: Towards the *Digital Rule of Law*

All things considered, we tend to believe that one of the most critical contributions of the DSA is to reduce the discretion and arbitrariness of digital platforms' behavior in the relations established with users and citizens. Indeed, surrounding the exercise of power with guarantees against discretion and arbitrary action is one of the key features of the *rule of law* that should be extended to the digital realm. As Suzor argues:

> The rule of law requires that decisions of those who have power over us are made according to law, defined in opposition to the arbitrary or capricious exercise of human discretion. The values of the rule of law—consent, predictability, and procedural fairness—are core liberal values of good governance. (Suzor 2018).

When we refer to the *digital rule of law* in the context of digital constitutionalism, we refer to the application and (where necessary) adaptation of the traditional *rule of law* rulebook to the digital environment. The Council of Europe Venice Commission has contributed enormously to the densification of the *rule of law,* which can be considered a multifaceted principle. Departing from Tom Bingham formula, the Venice Commission finds that the *rule of law* «is accepted as a fundamental ingredient of any democratic society» (European Commission for Democracy Through Law (Venice Commission) 2011), and a consensus can be found for a set of elements of the *rule of law* «which are not only formal but also substantial or material» (*idem*). The six elements or ingredients that make the *rule of law* principle are as follows:

- Legality (supremacy of the law);
- Legal certainty;
- Prohibition of arbitrariness;
- Access to justice before independent and impartial courts;
- Respect for human rights;
- Non-discrimination and equality before the law.

The definition and the list of elements promoted by the Venice Commission have an advantage linked to the interdependence between the *rule of law*, democracy, and the promotion of fundamental rights.[35] Thus, the *digital rule of law*, in addition to limiting the powers of private actors in the digital sphere, placing them under the aegis of the law, and making their decisions and actions subject to control, also leads to the promotion of democracy and respect for fundamental rights. These aspects

[35] Such interdependence is also a feature of the definition of the *rule of law* in EU legal system. Indeed, the *rule of law* «refers to the Union value enshrined in Article 2 TEU. It includes the principles of legality implying a transparent, accountable, democratic and pluralistic law-making process; legal certainty; prohibition of arbitrariness of the executive powers; effective judicial protection, including access to justice, by independent and impartial courts, also as regards fundamental rights; separation of powers; and non-discrimination and equality before the law. The rule of law shall be understood having regard to the other Union values and principles enshrined in Article 2 TEU». Article 2(a) of the Regulation (EU, Euratom) 2020/2092 of the European Parliament and of the Council of 16 December 2020 on a general regime of conditionality for the protection of the Union budget. *OJ L 433I, 22.12.2020, p. 1–10.*

(the *rule of law*, protection of democracy, and respect for fundamental rights) are all present throughout the DSA, leading us to believe that the new Regulation is a legal instrument that affirms the *digital rule of law* in the European Union.

We can now point out three examples of how the obligations laid down in the DSA effectively implement some of the principles of the *digital rule of law* framework in the European digital ecosystem:

4.1 Terms and Conditions

Terms and conditions are the 'constitutions' of digital platforms governing the contractual relationship between the provider of intermediary services and the users.[36] Derived from private law, terms and conditions are unilaterally defined, modified, and imposed on users in an arbitrary, obscure, 'take it or leave it' logic (Suzor 2018). Terms and conditions are a fundamental element of power distribution in digital platforms, often tipping the balance disproportionately in favor of digital platforms and their commercial interests.

Against this background, the DSA introduces procedural obligations for all providers of intermediary services when drafting, modifying, and implementing their terms and conditions. The Regulation does not interfere with the substantive content of platforms' terms and conditions, which is left to the contractual liberty of the parties. However, in applying the *rule of law* elements, Article 14(1) DSA requires that intermediaries include in their terms and conditions all «policies, procedures, measures and tools used for the purpose of content moderation, including algorithmic decision-making and human review, as well as the rules of procedure of their internal complaint handling system».

This provision materializes the *rule of law* in its legal certainty dimension. This element presupposes that the texts in which rules are laid down are easily accessible. Moreover, legal certainty entails a duty to respect and apply the existing regulations in a foreseeable and consistent manner. Foreseeability demands the rules are proclaimed in advance, have predictable effects, and are formulated with sufficient precision and clarity to enable individuals to regulate their conduct (European Commission for Democracy Through Law (Venice Commission) 2011). On the other hand, the principles of *nullem crimen sine lege* and *nulla poena sine lege* are also part of the *rule of law* (Article 49 of the Charter of Fundamental Rights of the European Union).

In this context, the DSA demands from digital platforms the *ex ante* or previous definition of the users' rules of conduct, the sanctions ('restrictions') they may impose, and the procedure leading to the decision on those sanctions. For the benefit of clarity and precision, terms and conditions should be set out in «clear, plain,

[36] Article 3(u) DSA.

intelligible, user-friendly and unambiguous language, and shall be publicly available in an easily accessible» format (Article 14(1) DSA). Against long and unreadable texts, VLOP and VLOSE are also obligated to provide users with a «concise, easily-accessible and machine-readable summary of the terms and conditions, including the available remedies and redress mechanisms, in clear and unambiguous language» (Article 14(5) DSA). Albeit digital platforms maintain their rule-making power, they are now «indirectly constrained by the limits placed on the procedure» (Husovec 2023); they are prevented from having hidden rules, retroactively changing their policies, or applying restrictions that have no basis in preexisting rules. Indeed, digital platforms are now obligated to inform users of «any significant change» to terms and conditions (Article 14(2) DSA).

In addition, Article 14(4) DSA seems to impose on intermediaries the effective enforcement, in a diligent, objective, and proportionate manner, of their terms and conditions, always respecting the rights and legitimate interests of the parties involved, including fundamental rights of users. Legal certainty and supremacy of the law, both elements of the *rule of law*, imply that rules are implemented in practice and don't just live in the books.

Also steaming from the *rule of law* is the prohibition of an arbitrary and discriminatory application of the existing rules, which is likewise banned for digital platforms. Given the platforms' obligation to respect fundamental rights and apply their terms and conditions in an equal and non-discriminatory fashion, they are prevented from treating differently users who break the same rules, depending, for example, on their visibility or other criteria of opportunity.

4.2 Notice and Action Mechanisms and Statement of Reasons

The conditional exemption liability regime for hosting services provided in the e-Commerce Directive and transferred to the DSA is based on the 'notice and takedown' model. Insofar as a hosting service obtains knowledge of any legal activity or illegal content, it must act expeditiously to remove or disable access to said content (Article 6(1) and Article 16(3) DSA).

Without changing this paradigm, the DSA introduces harmonized procedural rules regarding the reception and treatment by providers of hosting services of notifications on illegal content, especially the notice formal requisites. Article 16(6) DSA stipulates that providers of hosting services shall process all (not just some) notifications they receive and make their decisions promptly, diligently, non-arbitrarily, and objectively. Given that it prohibits arbitrariness, these norms materialize the *rule of law* principle. According to the Venice Commission, unfair, unreasonable, irrational, or oppressive decisions are inconsistent with the *rule of law* (European Commission for Democracy Through Law (Venice Commission) 2011). By requiring that any notification is handled in a timely, non-arbitrary, and objective manner, the DSA imposes on digital platforms the rationalization of their decisions regarding content moderation, which cannot be discretionary but based on existing and enforceable policies with respect for equality and non-discrimination.

Article 16(5) and Article 17 DSA establish a basic procedural duty of notification of the platforms' decision to the person who submits the claim, and the person affected by it. If the platform's decision on content moderation gives rise to a restrictive measure (removal, disabling access, demotion, suspension, termination, or restriction of the service or monetary payments), Article 17(1) DSA imposes an obligation on hosting services providers to give reasons for their content moderation decisions to the affected users. The statement of reasons must indicate the (a) restrictive measures adopted and, where relevant, its scope of application and duration, (b) the facts and circumstances in which the decision was based, (c) the information on the use made of automated means in taking the decision, (d) the legal or contractual ground on which the content is prohibited, (e) the information on the possibilities for redress available to user, in particular, where applicable through internal complaint-handling mechanisms, out-of-court dispute settlement and judicial redress (Article 17(3) DSA). The statement of reasons imposed by the DSA is, after all, very similar to the rationale that a public authority's decision, including a judicial one, must include under the *rule of law* and *due process*. Under the DSA's new rules, platforms' decisions on content moderation that adversely affect users cannot be based on secret and obscure criteria; instead, to legitimize them, they must be transparent and explainable using clear and prior criteria. From the point of view of the *rule of law*, this is about respect for fundamental rights, particularly procedural rights. As referred by Pasquale, however flexible, *due process* must include the explanation of the decision that adversely affects an individual in all cases (Pasquale 2021).

The *rule of law* also implies fundamental rights such as the right of access to justice and the right to an effective remedy (Article 47 of the Charter of Fundamental Rights of the European Union). Considering this framework, the DSA imposes on digital platforms the duty to inform users negatively affected by content moderation decisions on their rights on internal, extrajudicial (Article 21 DSA), or judicial redress. As a result, digital platforms cease to have the final word on content moderation decisions, which can be reviewed.

4.3 Internal Complaint-Handling System

Finally, and closely related to the previous topic, Article 20 DSA imposes on online platforms (excluding micro and small enterprises) the provision of an internal complaint-handling system. For a minimum period of six months, users have the opportunity to lodge complaints against decisions that have been adopted in the context of content moderation (suppression, blocking, or restriction of visibility of content; suspension or termination of the provision of the service; suspension or termination of accounts; suspension, termination or restriction of the ability to monetize content).

Symmetrically to Article 16(6), Article 20 DSA also stipulates that online platforms handle complaints in a timely, non-discriminatory, diligent, and non-arbitrary manner. The online platform may uphold or revoke its decision. However, if the complaint contains sufficient grounds for the online platform to consider that its decision not to act upon the notice is unfounded or that the information to which the complaint relates is not illegal and is not incompatible with its terms and conditions or contains information indicating that the complainant's conduct does not warrant the measure taken, it shall reverse it without undue delay (Article 20(4) DSA). In any case, the provider must inform the complainant of the decision and give reasons, also explaining the remedies available (Article 20(5) DSA). Lastly, Article 20(6) DSA imposes on online platform providers the human oversight of the complaints decision process.

From the viewpoint of the *rule of law*, these rules are, as explained, features related to the prohibition of arbitrariness and the respect for fundamental rights, such as procedural rights, the right of access to justice, and the right to an effective remedy. Suzor explains: «As minimally applied to governance by platforms, we might expect due process to have two main components. First, that before a regulatory decision is made, it is made according to valid criteria and processes. Second, once a decision has been made, due process then requires that users who are adversely affected have some avenue of appeal and independent review» (Suzor 2018). As demonstrated, the DSA accomplishes both components.

5 Conclusion

In the digital age, the activities of online platforms raise a significant number of societal challenges that require solutions. These challenges go to the heart of liberal democracies' features, threatening their flourishing. The internet's unique characteristics («lack of editorial approval, low barriers of entry (including omnipresent zero cost of service), incredible speed and scale of distribution, broad social and geographical inclusiveness, and resilience of communications» (Husovec 2023)) exacerbate the problems. Legislators everywhere act as funambulists, trying to articulate competing interests to better protect citizens' fundamental rights and the workings of democracies.

In the European Union, the DSA marks a critical turning point in the ongoing struggle to create a more transparent, accountable, and rights-respecting digital landscape. In a world where online platforms wield unprecedented influence, the DSA offers a regulatory framework that tempers this power, aligning it with the *rule of law* principles. Cyberspace is not and cannot be a space free of (fundamental) rights and the *rule of law.* We must apply to the digital realm the idea that constitutional limits follow power wherever it may be (*ubi potestas, ibi constitutione*).

There is an argument to be made that the primary function of the DSA is to fight against platforms' discretion and arbitrariness, a struggle that is an inherent feature of the *rule of law* principle. «By enlisting online intermediaries as watchdogs, governments would de facto delegate online enforcement to algorithmic tools» (Frosio 2023), which, in return, requires strong procedural safeguards introduced by the DSA. Even if digital platforms are not liable for illegitimate content their users post, they must still be held accountable for content moderation (Elkin-Koren and Perel 2020) through the *digital rule of law.* The DSA ends the «fragmented» and discretionary voluntary remedies provided by online platforms (Gregorio 2022), introducing a set of harmonized, horizontal, and asymmetric obligations related to content moderation and risk management.

The *rule of law,* protection of democracy, and respect for fundamental rights are all present throughout the DSA, leading us to believe that the new Regulation is a legal instrument that affirms the *digital rule of law* in the European Union. The DSA is a cornerstone in the EU's effort to ascertain the *digital rule of law* and the *digital due process.* It places vital constraints on digital platform operations while reinforcing the values of democracy, transparency, and the protection of fundamental rights through the *digital rule of law.* Although the DSA may not resolve every challenge posed by the digital age, it is a bold step toward ensuring that the *rule of law,* long the guardian of unchecked power, is upheld in the online sphere. As digital platforms evolve, so must the frameworks that regulate them. The DSA is a strong foundation upon which to build a more accountable and transparent digital future.

References

Balkin JM (2018a) Free Speech in the Algorithmic Society: Big Data. Private Governance, and New School Speech Regulation, UC Davis Law Review 51:1149–1210

Balkin JM (2018b) Free Speech is a Triangle. Columbia Law Rev 118(7):2011–2056

Barber NW (2015) Introduction: Constitutionalism, Oxford Legal Studies Research Paper No. 7/2015, Available via SSRN. https://papers.ssrn.com/sol3/papers.cfm?abstract_id=2565721

Barlow JP (1996) A Declaration of the Independence of Cyberspace. Available in https://www.eff.org/cyberspace-independence

Bassini M, Pollicino O (2023) The reshaping of the freedom of expression in the digital environment in light of the role of social networks. In: Savin A, Trzaskowski J (eds) Research Handbook on EU Internet Law, 2nd edn. Edward Elgar Publishing, Cheltenham, pp 429–468

Belli L, Francisco PA, Zingales N (2017) Law of the Land or Law of the Platform? Beware of the Privatisation of Regulation and Police. In: Belli L, Zingales N (eds) Platform Regulations: How Platforms are Regulated and How They Regulate Us. FGV Direito Rio, Rio de Janeiro, pp 41–64

Bingham T (2011) The Rule of Law. Penguin Books, London

Bradford A (2023) Digital Empires: The Global Battle to Regulate Technology. Oxford University Press, New York

Brkan M (2019) Freedom of Expression and Artificial Intelligence: On Personalisation, Disinformation and (Lack Of) Horizontal Effect of the Charter. Available via SSRN. https://papers.ssrn.com/sol3/papers.cfm?abstract_id=3354180

Buchanan L, Gamio L, Kelso C, Khavin D, Leatherby L, Parlapiano A, Reimhard S, Singhvi A, Watkins D, Yourish K (2021) How a Pro-Trump Mob Stormed the U.S. Capitol. The New York Times

Caunes K (2022) #IAmPetra; Prologue: The paradoxes of the rule of law in EU context—with special emphasis on the Polish RRP and EAW sagas. In This Issue. European Law Journal 27(1–3):2–38
Celeste E (2023) Digital Constitutionalism: The Role of Internet Bills of Rights. Routledge, Oxon
Clegg N (2021) Referring Former President Trump's Suspension from Facebook to the Oversight Board. Available in https://about.fb.com/news/2021/01/referring-trump-suspension-to-oversight-board/
Clegg N (2023) Ending Suspension of Trump's Accounts with New Guardrails to Deter Repeat Offenses. Available in https://about.fb.com/news/2023/01/trump-facebook-instagram-account-suspension/
Collins B, Zadrozny B (2021) Twitter permanently suspends President Donald Trump. NBC News
Costello RA (2023) *Faux ami?* Interrogating the normative coherence of 'digital constitutionalism.' Global Constitutionalism 12(2):326–349
Danaher J (2016) The Threat of Algocracy: Reality, Resistance and Accommodation. Philos. Technol. 29:245–268
De Streel A, Defreyne E, Jacquemin H, Ledger M, Michel A, Innesti A, Goubet M, Ustowski D (2020) Online Platforms' Moderation of Illegal Content Online. Study for the committee on Internal Market and Consumer Protection, Policy Department for Economic, Scientific and Quality of Life Policies, European Parliament, Luxembourg, 2020
Dias JF (2019) Direito Penal. Parte Geral. Tomo I. Gestlegal, Coimbra
Douek E (2024) The Meta Oversight Board and the Empty Promise of Legitimacy. Harvard Journal of Law & Technology 37 Forthcoming
Duarte FA, Gregorio G, Golia A Jr (2024) Perspectives on digital constitutionalism. In: Brozek B et al (eds) Research Handbook on Law and Technology. Edward Elgar Publishing, Cheltenham, pp 315–329
Elkin-Koren N, Perel M (2020) Guarding the Guardians: Content Moderation by Online Intermediaries and the Rule of Law. In: Frosio G (ed) Oxford Handbook of Online Intermediary Liability. Oxford University Press, Oxford, pp 669–678
Commission E (2020) Communication: Shaping Europe's digital future. Publications Office of the European Union, Luxembourg
European Commission (2020b) Proposal for a Regulation of the European Parliament and of the Council on a Single Market for Digital Services (Digital Services Act) and amending Directive 2000/31/EC. Brussels, 15.12.2020. COM(2020) 825 final
European Commission for Democracy Through Law (Venice Commission) (2016) The Rule of Law Checklist. Adopted in the 106th Plenary Session (Venice, 11–12 March 2016). Available in https://www.venice.coe.int/images/SITE%20IMAGES/Publications/Rule_of_Law_Check_List.pdf
European Commission for Democracy Through Law (Venice Commission) (2011) Report on the rule of law—Adopted by the Venice Commission at its 86th plenary session (Venice, 25–26 March 2011) CDL-AD(2011)003rev. Available in: https://www.venice.coe.int/webforms/documents/?pdf=CDL-AD(2011)003rev-e
Fisher M (2009) Capitalist Realism: Is There No Alternative? O Books, Hants
Frosio G (2023) Platform responsibility in the Digital Services Act: constitutionalising, regulating and governing private ordering. In: Savin A, Trzaskowski J (eds) Research Handbook on EU Internet Law, 2nd edn. Edward Elgar Publishing, Cheltenham, pp 253–270
Frosio G, Geiger C (2023) Taking fundamental rights seriously in the Digital Services Act's platform liability regime. Eur Law J 29:31–77
Gillespie T (2018) Regulation of and by platforms. In: Burgess J et al (eds) The SAGE Handbook of Social Media. SAGE Publications Ltd., London, pp 254–278
Golia A (2023) The Critique of Digital Constitutionalism. Global Constitutionalism. Max Planck Institute for Comparative Public Law & International Law (MPIL) Research Paper No. 2022–13:1–31

Gregorio G (2021) The rise of digital constitutionalism in the European Union. International Journal of Constitutional Law 19(1):41–70
Gregorio G (2022) Digital Constitutionalism in Europe: Reframing Rights and Powers in the Algorithmic Society. Cambridge University Press, Cambridge
Husovec M (2023) Rising Above Liability: The Digital Services Act as a Blueprint for the Second Generation of Global Internet Rules. Berkeley Technology Law Journal 38:883–920
Husovec M, Laguna IR (2022) Digital Services Act: A Short Primer. Availabe in: https://papers.ssrn.com/sol3/papers.cfm?abstract_id=4153796
Kaur M (2023) Social media before higher courts in Estonia: *Delfi* says it all. In: Casarosa F et al (eds) Social Media, Fundamental Rights and Courts: A European Perspective. Routledge, Oxon, pp 73–88
Koskenniemi M (2013) Globalization and Sovereignty. Rethinking Legality, Legitimacy and Constitutionalism. International Journal of Constitutional Law 11(3):818–822
Kosseff J (2019) The Twenty-Six Words That Created the Internet. Cornell University Press, New York
Krygier M (2016) The Rule of Law: Pasts, Presents, and Two Possible Futures. Annual Review of Law and Social Science. 12:199–229
Maduro MP (2012) Three Claims of Constitutional Pluralism. In: Avbelj M, Komárek J (eds) Constitutional Pluralism in the European Union and Beyond. Hart Publishing, London, pp 67–84
Monsen C, Willumat M (2024) Due Process and Fair Trial. In: Caeiro P et al (eds) Elgar Encyclopedia of Crime and Criminal Justice. Available in https://www.elgaronline.com/display/book/9781789902990/b-9781789902990.due.process.fair.trial.xml
Morozov E (2011) The Net Delusion: How Not To Liberate The World. Penguin Books, London
Pasquale F (2021) Inalienable Due Process in an Age of AI: Limiting the Contractual Creep toward Automated Adjudication. In: Micklitz HW et al (eds) Constitutional Challenges in the Algorithmic Society. Cambridge University Press, Cambridge, pp 42–56
Perel M, Elkin-Koren M (2016) Accountability in Algorithmic Copyright Enforcement. Stanford Technology Law Review 19:473–533
Pitruzzella G, Pollicino O (2020) Disinformation and Hate Speech: a European constitutional perspective. Bocconi University Press, Milano
Pollicino O (2023) The quadrangular shape of the geometry of digital power(s) and the move towards a procedural digital constitutionalism. Eur Law J 29(1–2):10–30
Prechal S (2020) Horizontal Direct Effect of the Charter of Fundamental Rights of the EU. Revista De Derecho Comunitario Europeo 66:407–426
Rogero T (2024) Brazilian court orders suspension of Elon Musk's X after it missed deadline. The Guardian
Sartori G (1962) Constitutionalism: A Preliminary Discussion. The American Political Science Review 56(4):853–864
Savin A (2022) Designing EU Digital Laws. Copenhagen Business School, CBS LAW Research Paper No. 22–13. Available in https://ssrn.com/abstract=4293314
Schwemer SF (2023) Digital Services Act: a reform of the e-Commerce Directive and much more. In: Savin A, Trzaskowski J (eds) Research Handbook on EU Internet Law, 2nd edn. Edward Elgar Publishing, Cheltenham, pp 232–252
Seeliger M, Sevignani S (2022) A New Structural Transformation of the Public Sphere? An Introduction. Theory Cult Soc 39(4):3–16
Simoncini A, Longo E (2021) Fundamental Rights and the Rule of Law in the Algorithmic Society. In: Micklitz H et al (eds) Constitutional Challenges in the Algorithmic Society. Cambridge University Press, Cambridge, pp 27–41
Sirota L (2023) What is the Constitution of Cyberspace Like? Diritto Pubblico Comparator Ad Europeo 1(2023):249–278
Spindler G (2017) Responsibility and Liability of Internet Intermediaries: Status Quo in the EU and Potential Reforms. In: Synodinou T et al (eds) EU Internet Law. Springer, Cham, pp 289–314

Suzor N (2018) Digital Constitutionalism: Using the Rule of Law to Evaluate the Legitimacy of Governance by Platforms. Social Media + Society 4(3):1–11

Suzor NP (2019) Lawless: The Secret Rules That Govern Our Digital Lives. Cambridge University Press, Cambridge

Terzis P (2024) Against digital constitutionalism. European Law Open. Available via Cambridge University Press. https://www.cambridge.org/core/journals/european-law-open/article/against-digital-constitutionalism/CDD6DD1071C7CC8C5EA0E62DB4BE39DC

The Greens/EFA in the European Parliament (2022) European Parliament Votes on Constitution for the Internet. Press Release. Available in: https://www.greens-efa.eu/en/article/press/european-parliament-votes-on-constitution-for-the-internet

Turillazzi A et al (2022) The Digital Services Act: An Analysis of Its Ethical, Legal, and Social Implications. Available in: https://papers.ssrn.com/sol3/papers.cfm?abstract_id=4007389

United Nations (2016) Report of the Special Rapporteur on the promotion and protection of the right to freedom of opinion and expression. A/HRC/32/38. Available in https://www.ohchr.org/en/documents/thematic-reports/ahrc3238-report-freedom-expression-states-and-private-sector-digital-age

Weitzenboeck EM (2023) User empowerment in the age of algorithms: two steps forward, one step back? In: Savin A, Trzaskowski J (eds) Research Handbook on EU Internet Law, 2nd edn. Edward Elgar Publishing, Cheltenham, pp. 389–411

Wilman F (2022) The Digital Services Act (DSA)—An Overview. Available in: https://papers.ssrn.com/sol3/papers.cfm?abstract_id=4304586

Wong D, Floridi L (2023) Meta's Oversight Board: A Review and Critical Assessment. Mind Mach 33:261–284

Zürn M (2018) A Theory of Global Governance: Authority, Legitimacy, and Contestation. Oxford University Press, Oxford

Who Moderates the Moderators?: A Brief Overlook into How the Digital Services Act Impacts the Economics of Content Moderation Against "Over-Blocking"

Martim Farinha and Diogo Brandão

Abstract This chapter tackles the intricacies surrounding the subject of content moderation in online platforms, concerning the problem of "over-blocking", the chilling effects it causes on the freedom of speech of users and how it affects user empowerment. It does so by analysing the evolution of the legal framework on content moderation of the last twenty years, focusing the Atlantic dialogue between European Union Law, the e-Commerce Directive, and the Content Decency Act and Digital Millennium Copyright Act. Concretely, it demonstrates the previous framework's pitfalls in ensuring the fundamental rights of freedom of expression and right to information, and how the economics of content moderation allowed for a "false positives" phenomenon ("over-blocking"). It then argues that the more pernicious effect of this comes in the form of chilling effects on users being weaponized for commercial and or political means. It concludes by scrutinizing the recent Digital Services Act's provisions regarding the viability of the procedural mechanisms of redress for users and the accountability of the platforms and third-party stakeholders for misuse of content moderation, whether through algorithmic or individual means. The chapter resorts to a methodology of doctrinal research focused on primary and secondary sources of law.

Keywords Content Moderation · Fundamental Rights · Digital Services Act · Law and Economics · Over-blocking

M. Farinha (✉) · D. Brandão
Nova School of Law, Lisbon, Portugal
e-mail: martim.farinha@novalaw.unl.pt

D. Brandão
e-mail: diogo.brandao@novalaw.unl.pt

G. Enes et al. (eds.), *A Digital Europe for Citizens*,
https://doi.org/10.1007/978-3-032-02500-5_12

1 Introduction

Recent years have been marked by an enhanced public perception of the proliferation of illegal content online (from violations of intellectual property rights (IPR), to child pornography, hate speech, terrorist propaganda, misinformation, etc.) and its undesirable impact[1] in society. This has prompted a wider reflection across political lines, on the roles of online content-sharing platforms, their practices on content moderation and their responsibilities on the harms caused by their (in)action.

While there are several possible business models, most online content sharing platforms adopted a "freemium model", deriving most of their profits (Desjardins 2019) from the activities connected to the processing of personal data of their users, which allows them to create detailed profiles for personalized targeted advertising and to tailor their recommender systems, to continuously promote user activity in the service. It is understood that while these platforms act as intermediaries, assuming a passive stance towards user content unlike traditional publishers and editors, they still derive value from this content, which may not always be lawful. They may not promote such illegal activities, or are even fully aware of them, they nevertheless benefit from them.

Whether the damages from these activities are caused to singular private parties (rightsholders, victims of defamation, etc.), groups or to society as a whole (hate speech, child pornography, terrorism propaganda), tackling illegal content online has been framed as a matter of determining the most optimal model for the attribution of liability or safe harbour to these platforms (designing the exemption of liability or the liability itself may yield similar results in practice) (Nordemann 2018; Husovec 2017).

Determining the appropriate liability rule for these online hosting platforms requires an analysis of the incentives to detect and remove illegal content. A liability rule should be designed to minimize the combined costs of harm and of detection and removal, considering both the private costs and social costs. This rule should also consider the role of each actor in this matter, since there may be other parties than platforms, such as users of third party-victims or public bodies, that may have better information available to them to detect illegal content and its harm. Therefore, it is a difficult exercise to determine which policy is most proportionate and effective.

This chapter purports to provide a brief overlook on the way in which these concerns have been tackled by the European Union's legislature and judges and on the role the recent Digital Services Act (DSA)[2] plays in mitigating the "over-blocking" phenomenon. The analysis is conducted under the lens of user empowerment, with each section demonstrating how each specific aspect impacts the control users have over their own content and the mechanisms they have to react to content moderation. Additionally, given the horizontal character of the DSA as an asymmetric regulation,

[1] An example of this pertains to Molly Russel's suicide in 2017, following exposure to graphic content in Instagram. See < https://www.bbc.com/news/uk-england-london-54307976 >.

[2] Regulation (EU) 2022/2065 of the European Parliament and of the Council of 19 October 2022 on a Single Market For Digital Services and amending Directive 2000/31/EC (Digital Services Act).

with a wide subjective and objective scope of application, the analysis will be focused on how effective its provisions will be when applied to the very large online platforms (VLOP) and very large search engines (VLSE).[3]

The second section of this chapter provides a legal context of relevant policies and court decisions on content moderation to highlight the European Union's (EU) key motivations and concerns regarding the phenomenon under analysis.

The third section of the chapter analyzes the "over-blocking" phenomenon at a conceptual level and assesses how it has been fueled by platforms growing use of algorithms. Moreover, this part of the chapter describes the chilling effect that has concerned scholars and policy makers over recent years and frames some of the key concerns that the EU legislator purported to mitigate through the DSA. These considerations are fueled by practical examples of online platforms' content moderation systems, particularly that of Youtube.

In turn, the fourth section of the chapter offers a brief examination of the economics of content moderation law and provides palpable outcomes and behaviors stemming from the prior regulation on the topic. It does so by providing both a user and platform perspective.

The fifth and final section of the chapter focuses on the DSA per se and assesses its prospective merits in combatting the chilling effect of the "over-blocking" phenomenon. It specifically emphasizes the transparency obligations imposed by the DSA regarding action and notice and redress mechanisms, while also focusing on the functioning of the mechanisms per se. The analysis is also supported by occasional analogies with the current EU legislation on personal data protection, especially regarding the role of regulators, given the General Data Protection Regulation's (GDPR) connection to the DSA's goals and its standing in the Digital Single Market.

The research conducted is theoretical and doctrinal in nature, having been conducted through the analysis of primary and secondary legal sources in the form of scholar articles, court decisions, policies and other legal documents.

2 Brief Legal Context of Content Moderation: The Road until Now

It is relevant to assess the way legislators have tackled the topic of content moderation to give a comprehensive notion of the phenomenon under discussion and to justify the need for tackling it. For purposes of this section, emphasis is to be given to an EU

[3] The DSA is a "layered" or "pyramidal" regulation: as the "size" of the service provider increases, so do the sets of obligations applicable. At the very top, the VLOP and VLSE have to comply to the entirety of the DSA. G'sell, Florence (2023) The Digital Services Act: a General Assessment. In: Antje von Ungern-Sternberg (ed.), Content Regulation in the European Union—The Digital Services Act, Schriften Des Irdt—Trier Studies On Digital Law, Vol. 1, Verein für Recht und Digitalisierung e.V., Institute for Digital Law (IRDT), Trier April 2023, available on SSRN, p.5.

context, focusing particularly on the E-Commerce Directive (ECD)[4] and Directive 2019/790 (DSMD)[5] from a policy perspective, as well as on relevant European Court of Justice (CJEU) jurisprudence.

2.1 Policy

From the late 90s, lawmakers on both sides of the Atlantic established the principle of "safe harbour" for online intermediary service providers (OSP), to protect these entities from secondary liability that could arise due to the unlawful activities of their users, namely the hosting of unlawful content.

These policy decisions were justified on several concerns, namely:

1. The common understanding that if these OSP performed a passive role of transmission, caching and hosting of content, they should not be directly responsible for it.
2. The notion that due to the anonymous, probable insolvent and jurisdictionally unreachable character of the actual primary infringer, OSP would be the preferred target of lawsuits by third parties seeking reparations. Intermediaries act as "choke points", where this strategy allows claimants to secure relief in a single procedure against multiple infringements from several perpetrators.
3. The understanding that, without these "shields" shifting some of the liability, these activities would be so risky as to, either resulting in over-enforcement (also known as "over-blocking") by overtly cautious intermediaries, silencing the legitimate users (Dinwoodie 2017); or
4. The conclusion that, when considering the factors mentioned above, the provision of these services risks becoming commercially unviable or overburdened, stunting the development of information society services and overall technological progress. These fears of stagnation could culminate in the inability of American/European companies to be competitive in global markets.

Considering these risks, many legislators adopted provisions in those early days of the Internet, that either established a "positive" (circumstances that establish liability) or "negative" (actions and standards that immunize intermediaries against claims) definitions of safe harbour (Dinwoodie 2017).

[4] Directive 2000/31/EC of the European Parliament and of the Council of 8 June 2000 on certain legal aspects of information society services, in particular electronic commerce, in the Internal Market ('Directive on electronic commerce').

[5] Directive (EU) 2019/790 of the European Parliament and of the Council of 17 April 2019 on copyright and related rights in the Digital Single Market and amending Directives 96/9/EC and 2001/29/EC.

In the EU this was established with the ECD,[6] which defined the conditions intermediaries that provide online services required for an horizontal liability immunity regarding the goods, services, and contents they provide.[7] For hosting services, the requirements hinged on the service not having actual knowledge of the illegal activity, and upon obtaining such awareness, acting expeditiously to remove or disable access to the infringing information.[8] The ECD also enshrined the principal of "no general obligation to monitor", which would preclude Member-States from creating such obligations.[9] In summary, the ECD's liability regime requires intermediaries to assume a liability stance regarding their content and to also commit to eliminating illegal contents, as well as the access to said contents upon notification.

However, the ECD displays a visible difficulty in accompanying the evolution of tech services as well as in harmonising a legal framework between the EU Member-States in what concerns the monitoring and supervision of digital service providers' activity, as well as combatting data asymmetries. These difficulties are worsened by the power imbalances between platforms and users, which in turn stem from a lack of transparency over how user data is processed and monitored. Indeed, despite the guarantees created by the e-Commerce Directive, studies conducted by BEUC indicated that about two thirds of a significant number of digitally acquired products did not display proper safety guarantees regarding the monitoring and notification of their contents.[10] This situation became more severe during the Covid-19 pandemic, in which the illegal acquisition of digital goods and services registered a significant increase, in line with growing dissatisfaction with platforms' reporting mechanisms for their content.

At the time, these conditions were considered an open invitation to self-regulation due to the belief that the removal of strict obligations to monitor—while leaving some room for liability -would incentivize hosting services to impose some measure of control upon the content which they receive (Hornik and Villa Llera 2017) The framework also promoted the implementation of "notice-and-takedown" mechanisms for third parties to notify OSP and complaint-and-redress schemes for users whose content had been taken down. Public consultations conducted by the European Commission further demonstrated a general predisposition from market players towards creating simple, transparent, and harmonized standards for purposes of reporting illegal content in the context of the Digital Single Market.[11]

---

[6] Directive 2000/31/EC of the European Parliament and of the Council of 8 June 2000 on certain legal aspects of information society services, in particular electronic commerce, in the Internal Market ('Directive on electronic commerce').

[7] Arts. 12–15 ECD.

[8] Art. 14 ECD.

[9] Art. 15 ECD.

[10] BEUC (2020) "Two-thirds of 250 products bought from online marketplaces fail safety tests, consumer groups find", BEUC Press Release, < https://www.beuc.eu/press-releases/two-thirds-250-products-bought-online-marketplaces-fail-safety-tests-consumer-groups > .

[11] This public consultation, which preceded the proposal for a Digital Services Act, collected the answers of two hundred and eleven companies (ranging from conglomerates to "start-ups") that provide digital services, as well as one hundred and fifty-nine Non-Governmental Organizations

2.2 A Joint Policy and Jurisprudential Analysis

Through the years, the CJEU was "called" several times to interpret these provisions (Quintais et al. 2022), namely the character of an "active" or "passive" host and the scope and matter of the prohibition of general monitoring obligations, in relation to several national laws in different fields, from the protection of intellectual property rights (IPR) to defamation. On the latter, the case law focused itself on whether certain provisions or injunctions concerned general or specific monitoring obligations, where the threshold was located (from a single copy of specific unlawful file on a URL, to all copies of that file, subsequent reposting of copies, variations, etc.). Through the years, the CJEU failed to provide a precise criterion to distinguish permissible specificity from prohibited generality, rather deciding each individual case on proportionality assessments, weighting primarily the impact on fundamental rights and social values (Sartor and Loreggia 2020).

This is most noticeable on various copyright cases, such as C-275/06 Promusicae,[12] C-275/06 Scarlet Extended,[13] and C-360/10 SABAM,[14] in which it was decided that injunctions to filter all copyrighted content were general in scope, infringing on the fundamental rights of users (Art. 8 and 11 of the EU Charter of Fundamental Rights), and thus inadmissible. *Au contraire*, in a defamation case, C-18/18 Glawischnig-Piesczek,[15] the CJEU allowed an injunction to block and prevent the reposting of equal or equivalent content, since the host would not be required to carry out independent assessments and the measured was required to protect the interests at stake (Sartor and Loreggia 2020).

The CJEU found that video-sharing and file-hosting platforms could not be directly liable in C-682/18 and C-683/18 (Youtube, Cyando),[16] and that (in relation to secondary liability) would only have actual knowledge if properly notified of a specific illegal act, "where the application of an exception is not automatically precluded". As many pointed out, on the matter of the right of communication to the public of EU copyright law, the CJEU slowly eroded the paradigm of traditional strict liability, by incorporating elements typical of intermediary, secondary or accessory liability (Quintais and Schwemer 2022).

While the CJEU was "carefully" building its case-law on the interpretation of the Arts. 14 and 15 ECD and Art. 3 of the InfoSoc Directive,[17] the Commission began

(NGOs) and fifty-nine public authorities. European Commission (2020) Summary Report on the open public consultation on the Digital Services Act Package. In < https://digital-strategy.ec.europa.eu/en/library/summary-report-open-public-consultation-digital-services-act-package > .

[12] Judgment of the Court of 29 January 2008, Promusicae, C-275/06, ECLI:EU:C:2008:54.

[13] Judgment of the Court of 24 November 2011, Scarlet Extended, C-275/06, ECLI:EU:C:2011:771.

[14] Judgment of the Court of 16 February 2012, SABAM, C-360/10, ECLI:EU:C:2012:85.

[15] Judgment of the Court of 3 October 2019, Glawischnig-Piesczek, C-18/18, ECLI:EU:C:2019:821.

[16] Judgment of the Court of 22 June 2021, Youtube & Cyando, C-682/18 and C-683/18, CLI:EU:C:2021:503.

[17] Directive 2001/29/EC of the European Parliament and of the Council of 22 May 2001 on the harmonisation of certain aspects of copyright and related rights in the information society.

the process of re-balancing the roles of intermediaries and the problem of tacking illegal content online. This occurred first soft law instruments, such as the 2018 Commission Recommendation,[18] and with hard law proposals such as the DSMD on 2015, and later, with the DSA in 2020 (recently approved in late-2022).

The DSMD and its Art. 17 are the biggest reform in the recent years on platforms' liability (Quintais et al. 2022), concerning IPR. It acts as *lex specialis* of the ECD, by stating that online content-sharing service providers (OCSSPs) carry out acts of communication to the public when they give access to work/subject matter uploaded by their users and that the hosting safe harbour is not applicable (Quintais 2020). OCSSPs may now be held directly liable for their users infringing content, if they cannot prove their best efforts to either:

a) Secure appropriate authorisations from rights holders; or
b) to ensure the (i) unavailability of specific works for which they have been provided with information, (ii) act expeditiously after notices to take down infringing content, and (iii) prevent their future re-upload.

These conditions seem to impose, as it widely criticized in the legislative process, both an upload filtering obligation and a notice-and-stay-down (or re-upload filter) obligation (Quintais 2020). Due to many criticisms from civil society,[19] academia, Non-Governmental Organisations (NGOs)[20] and courts on the matter of upload filters constraining users' fundamental rights of freedom of expression and of accessing information, the DSMD includes some safeguards in this regard.[21]

Platforms must ensure that their measures do not prevent users from uploading their lawful content, including when it relies on exceptions and limitations (E&L), such as parody and quotation, which became mandatory across the EU. Following the Commission's guidance and the AG opinion on C-401/19, under Art. 17, platforms should only filter ex-ante manifestly infringing content, based on a highly probable quantitative assessment (Geiger and Jütte 2021).

Finally, the CJEU's decision on C-401/19[22] cemented the understanding that in Art. 17 of the DSMD there is a clear hierarchy, where the obligation to ensure the availability of lawful content is a obligation of result, that supersedes the (best efforts obligation) to ensure the unavailability of unlawful content (Quintais and Schwemer 2022). It is insufficient for users to merely rely on ex post complaint and redress mechanisms to ensure the accessibility of their user generated content (a

[18] Commission Recommendation (EU) 2018/334 of 1 March 2018 on measures to effectively tackle illegal content online C/2018/1177.

[19] #SaveYourInternet, "The #SaveYourInternet fight against Article 17 [ex Art. 13] continues", at < https://saveyourinternet.eu/ > .

[20] EDRi (2019) Upload filters: history and next steps. in < https://edri.org/our-work/upload-filters-status-of-the-copyright-discussions-and-next-steps/ > , OpenDemocracy (2018) The EU call it copyright, but it is massive Internet censorship and must be stopped. In < https://www.opendemocracy.net/en/can-europe-make-it/civilised-societies-don-t-call-it-censorship-but-copyright/ > .

[21] Art. 17(7)(9) DSMD.

[22] Judgment of the Court of 26 April 2022, Poland v European Parliament and Council of the European Union, C-401/19, ECLI:EU:C:2022:297.

position that was held by France, Spain and Portugal). OCSSPs are required to have ex ante safeguards to avoid "over-blocking" of users' content due to the usage of filtering technologies, "upload filters", which were recognized as implicitly required (Quintais and Schwemer 2022). Only filtering/blocking systems that unequivocally can distinguish lawful from unlawful content without the need for "independent assessment" by OCSSPs are admissible (so, only manifestly infringing content as in *Glawischnig-Piesczek*), without infringing the prohibition of general monitoring obligation under Art. 17(8) DSMD (and the ECD) (Quintais and Schwemer 2022). Users' have (fundamental) rights, not mere defenses.

Still, while both the AG and the CJEU aimed to uphold Art. 17 in balance with the prohibition of general monitoring obligations and the fundamental rights if users, by emphasizing the objective of avoiding "over-blocking" in combination with good redress mechanisms, in practice, some matters were left unresolved. In practice, there is no concrete definition of what acceptable error rates for content filtering are. Many "key" details regarding these "redress" procedures and how they look like in practice were not explored in the decision, nor transparency obligations or compliance instruments for the OCSSPs. Additionally, the directive and the case concerned only copyright infringement, leaving many doubts persisting in relation to other types of illegal content and even "harmful" content,

3 The Chilling Effect of "Over-Blocking"

Despite the context presented above, worries persist and are fueled by various factors—both legal and technical -, out of which this chapter highlights the chilling "over-blocking" effect caused by algorithmic content moderation. The next section will focus on describing the phenomenon and highlighting its pernicious effects for the topic of the chapter. For these purposes, it is relevant to clarify the role algorithms (Hill 2016)[23] play in fueling "over-blocking" and how the chilling effect affects users and content moderation.

3.1 The Role of Algorithms in Content Moderation

Although protected by safe harbors in both side of the Atlantic, many of the most influential content-sharing platforms suffered pressures to self-regulate, leading to major investments in technological measures aimed at proactively detecting and removing illegal content. As these mega-platforms grew (and the controversial incidents multiplied), the need to turn to AI for moderation became undeniable. In turn, the task to

[23] For purposes of the research, we follow the simplified definition of algorithms as a "finite, abstract, effective, compound control structure, imperatively given, accomplishing a given purpose under given provisions".

monitor all content uploaded for illegal activity became humanly impossible. This context led to the adoption of algorithms trained to detect illegal content using several techniques, such as matching, hash-matching, perceptual-hashing, classification, and prediction (using natural-language-processing).

In the current state of the art, depending on the type of illegality pursued, each OSP may employ different combinations of these systems to monitor user content (Gorwa et al. 2020). However, even with the major breakthroughs in their capabilities, evidence shows that these systems still have major problems at understanding many caveats of human language, especially concerning context-dependent nuances. A notable example of this is that of Youtube's Content ID which, while highly advanced at creating and detecting quality fingerprints of copyrighted content, is not actually adept at evaluating actual infringements, due to not understanding the applicability of E&L.

Concerns have arisen over the deployment of fully automated moderation resulting in systematic "over-blocking" when applied to more context-dependent judgments, such hate speech or misinformation, the fears that the deployment of fully automated moderation will result in systematic over-blocking become exacerbated. On this note, scholars (Quintais et al. 2022) have highlighted how the European Commission's guidance[24] on OCSSP clarifies that automated filtering and blocking measures should be reserved for what the EC classifies as "manifestly infringing" and "earmarked" content.

Due to these concerns, platforms usually (claim to) include a "human-in-loop" to review the decisions of their algorithms, but these do not necessarily confer neither security nor legitimacy to these systems (Gorwa et al. 2020). Once again, Youtube's Content ID exemplifies this conundrum, since the automated decision are confirmed by rightsholders, which have an interest in concluding on the inapplicability of fair-use standards or E&L (Kaye and Gray 2021). In other cases, the "human" in these procedures lacks the appropriate tools, formation and time to adequately decide on the matters under review. In opposite sides, these "content moderators" may suffer psychological damage from the exposure to violent material (Newton 2019)[25] or help train the automated filtering with bias against certain people, groups, political orientations (Haimson et al. 2021).

Despite a growing number of controversial takedowns decisions and recent empirical studies which report that automated copyright enforcement systems incur in substantial over-blocking of legitimate content (Bar-Ziv & Elkin-Koren 2018; Erickson & Kretschmer 2018; Urban et al. 2017) on the regulatory trend of promoting *ex ante* decisions has persisted, as it was referred in regarding the DSMD.[26]

[24] European Commission (2021) Communication from the Commission to the European Parliament And The Council—Guidance on Article 17 of Directive 2019/790 on Copyright in the Digital Single Market, COM/2021/288 final.

[25] https://perma.cc/GD4C-U8AE.

[26] See Sect. 2 of this chapter.

3.2 The Chilling Effect of Takedowns

Empirical studies indicate that takedown notices produce a chilling effect against users. This occurs with both formal notices and through internal alternative dispute resolution (ADR) systems in these online services. After receiving a DMCA notice (for copyright infringement), it has been reported that 66% of users would not even attempt to challenge it, even "when they believed it to be wrong or inaccurate". This position was justified on the concerns regarding "legal costs (81%) and avoiding additional risks (legal or otherwise) (53%) and a lack of legal knowledge (34%)" (Penney 2019).

A similar effect can be observed in Youtube's Content ID system. This automated system not only detects the fingerprint of copyrighted material in users' content, but also informs rightsholders and allows them to either: block the video, monitor the statistics or claim it (the video is monetized, and the ad-revenue reverts to the rightsholder). Users may dispute the claim. Afterwards, rightsholders have 30 days to decide whether to release the claim, uphold it or issue a removal request. If they choose the latter two, they automatically win the dispute, and the uploader receives a strike. If a user receives three strikes, whether legitimate or not, their account (which may be their livelihood) is terminated (Kaye and Gray 2021). Youtube's own transparency report reveals that over-blocking is real and that users are highly discouraged from fighting it (Kaye and Gray 2021).

If a user wishes to learn more on how these systems work, under what rules they are operating under when uploading content, they will quickly be "submerged" when trying to study the T&C regarding content moderation. Platforms have, over time, published longer T&C, more documents, more add-ons (on more URLs), with more (kinds of) rules, which have become more intricate, vague and complex. They have essentially created an ever-updating opaque web of legal documents that the normal user cannot adequately understand (Quintais et al. 2022).

Regular users do not engage with content moderation redress mechanisms when their content is blocked/filtered, even they believe that the decisions were wrong. Instead, they seem to take the notices as warnings, resorting to self-censorship in the future. "Content creators" in Youtube and other OCSSPs, either resort to tactics to trick the systems into not erroneously flagging their content (Kaye and Gray 2021), or just "surrender" and accept the loss of revenue due to the licensing system in Art. 17. The pre-DSA framework does not prevent the chilling effect of "over-blocking". It seems to allow it.

4 The Economics of Platforms' Liability and Content Moderation

To provide a better understanding of the phenomenon under analysis, it is relevant to assess the economics of platforms' liability and content moderation from the standpoint of both the platforms and of the users. This analysis will contextualize some of the goals of the DSA, which will be analyzed in the next section of the chapter.

4.1 The Platforms' Perspective

The platforms themselves have several incentives to monitor and remove illegal content, as they can be negatively affected by its proliferation. Much of this content can result in the deterioration of the user-experience, which can lead to a reduction in customers' participation or activity. OSP risk losing users to more trustworthy and less "toxic" competitors (Buiten et al. 2019). Indeed, the presence of illegal content may cause harm to the reputation and credibility of a platform with its users, customers, and commercial partners. Obscene or highly problematic content can scare off advertisers, who do not wish to see their products placed alongside terrorist propaganda, xenophobic or pornographic videos (Gillespie 2017).

The initiative in implementing content moderation measures may also be driven for the purpose of preventing legislators from enacting new regulations, by convincing them that their self-regulation suffices (Husovec 2017). As their influence in society expands, monitoring may also be motivated out of a sense of "public obligation", or as means of answering to criticisms form activists and journalists (Gillespie 2017). Beyond the purely profit-maximising incentives, these platforms may also be committed to nurturing a healthy and creative online community as a goal by itself (Buiten et al. 2019), or at least, to appear to do so.

In terms of costs, platforms will need to deploy several measures for detection, removal, and sanctioning, which will be affected by different factors. These measures can be automated to varying degrees depending on the concrete case. They will include the development and maintenance of detection and flagging software, as well as notice and takedown systems, with varied degrees of human-reviewer intervention. These will be affected by the size of the platform (larger OSP may benefit from data-drive economies of scale, which will increase efficiency and lower costs), type of harmed party, the business model (freemium vs payment-for-access, social media) and the type of illegal material (automation is less prone to error if the illegality is not context dependent) (Buiten et al. 2019).

4.2 The Users' Perspective

When approaching this matter from a third-party perspective, the costs and incentives differ across the type of victim. In the case of IPR violations, rightsholders may have the means to notify OSP about infringements and may leverage their position so that content is proactively detected and removed. Some platforms, such as Youtube, offer rightsholders a third option besides just accepting or removing: monetising the infringing content in their favor. Victims of hate speech have little means to prevent this kind of harm against the primary infringers and must rely of notifying the platforms (Buiten et al. 2019).

As previously referred, there is also content which harms society, without clear individual victims, such as terrorist propaganda. If no private parties act, unless public law enforcement acts, this material could stay up. Both users and third parties have no means of removing illegal content once detected if platforms do not provide those means. Platforms often lack the relevant information to detect said content, even if motivated to remove it. There is a clear link between the costs of each party in this relationship. Users are a heterogeneous group, sensible to different interests and incentives. Some may just consume content while others produce and share. For the latter, there is a wide range between amateurs and professional creators, motivated by profit, who are also interested in the removal of unlawful and toxic content.

The problem here lies on whether the platforms consider that the costs of implementing said infrastructure (user-friendly notice-and-takedown systems), and acting upon it, do not go beyond the incentives to do so (Buiten et al. 2019). Therefore, a liability regime[27] for OSP is necessary to internalize these externalities. Two solutions should be avoided: full exemption and strict liability, as the latter would inevitably promote excessive over-blocking.

5 The Digital Services Act's Role in Combatting "Over-Blocking"

The context provided above contextualizes some of the key concerns that motivated the drafting and development of the DSA which, alongside the Digital Markets Act (DMA), assumes a key position[28] (Kaiser and Ratcliff 2022) in the European Commission's strategy to tackle data processing by massive online platforms and

---

[27] European Commission (2017) Working Document on the free flow of data and emerging issues of the European data economy COM(2017) 9 final. https://eur-lex.europa.eu/legal-content/EN/TXT/HTML/?uri=CELEX:52017SC0002&from=EN.

[28] https://www.europarl.europa.eu/RegData/etudes/BRIE/2022/703347/IPOL_BRI(2022)703347_EN.pdf.

better respond to the challenges of a 'data driven economy'.[29] From the start of its discussions (Morais Carvalho et al. 2021) the DSA (European Commission 2020) focused on revising the liability framework for the actors partaking in the collection, storage, and transmission of data and content in the context of intermediary services (G'sell 2023), aiming to improve the functioning of the Digital Single Market (G'sell 2023).[30] On this note, the DSA's scope encompasses not only service providers that are based in EU Member-States, but also those based in countries outside the EEA and whose activities affect the EU internal market.[31] This greater territorial reach aims to not only protect the users whose data will be processed, but also to keep service providers headquartered in the EU from being at a competitive disadvantage regarding service providers headquartered outside the EU.[32]

The DSA as a piece of legislation, tackles many of its objectives through a "meta-regulation" approach (Zingales 2023), which include several elements of hard and self-regulation. Many provisions establish regulatory principles and obligations that give businesses a significant amount of discretion in their implementation (with standards and codes of conduct) which then are coupled with other obligations for continuous monitoring and evaluation of results, by the businesses themselves (risk assessments, risk mitigation measures, compliance function), authorities (enhanced transparency and access to data by the Digital Coordinators and Commission) and certified third parties (enhanced transparency obligations, independent audits, access to data by vetted researchers). The DSA follows a recent trend of risk-based regulation—or risk-based compliance—(Savin 2022) in European Law, which can also be found in the GDPR (with the Data Protection Impact Assessment and Data Protection Officer as mere examples) and the Artificial Intelligence Act, its proposal and subsequent amendments (Calvi and Kotzinos 2023).

One of the key changes that the DSA promotes is a greater set of responsibilities for intermediary service providers, while maintaining the core principles of exemption of liability for intermediary service providers from the previous e-Commerce Directive. Among these reforms, it includes the "Good Samaritan Principle" and the development of user-friendly notice and take-down mechanism that allow for third parties to notify illegal content. With these mechanisms, third parties must be able to submit detailed notices on the content that they deem to be illegal and incompatible with the service provider's Terms and Conditions (T&C). The service

[29] European Commission (2014) Communication from the Commission to the European Parliament, the Council, the European Economic and Social Committee and the Committee of the Regions towards a thriving data-driven economy. https://eur-lex.europa.eu/legal-content/EN/TXT/PDF/?uri=CELEX:52014DC0442&from=EN.

[30] European Parliament (2020) European Parliament resolution of 20 October 2020 with recommendations to the Commission on the Digital Services Act: Improving the functioning of the Single Market (2020/2018(INL). https://www.europarl.europa.eu/doceo/document/TA-9-2020-0272_EN.pdf.

[31] Art. 1(3) DSA.

[32] These concerns are in line with the Impact Assessment conducted on the DSA itself; European Commission (2020) Impact assessment of the Digital Services Act SWD(2020) 348 final. https://digital-strategy.ec.europa.eu/en/library/impact-assessment-digital-services-act.

provider will then decide on whether to remove or restrict the notified content, and then inform the notifier of its choice. Equally relevant for purposes of this chapter are the redress mechanisms developed by the DSA regarding content moderation. (Savora 2022). Concretely, the DSA lays down obligations for online platforms to provide users with an internal complaint-handling systems[33] for decisions taken over content. Moreover, it adds a second layer of redress for content moderation by obliging platforms to engage with certified out-of-court dispute settlement bodies,[34] while also requiring transparency enhancing practices from online platforms over how they moderate content.[35]

It is, therefore, clear that the DSA actively purports to empower users by endowing them with the proper tools to handle restrictions on the content they share online, while also creating mechanisms and procedures that aim to prevent OSP from engaging in the "over-blocking" phenomenon. Theoretically, with the DSA comes a framework of greater accountability for OSP and of greater flexibility in terms of how users might exercise their rights over their content. However, despite the legislator's efforts, one of the main reservations highlighted during the DSA's discussion pertained to the pernicious effects of automated decision-making regarding the monitoring of content in digital platforms. The main concern stemmed from how automated decision-making could exacerbate the power asymmetry[36] between users and platforms, rather than mitigate said asymmetries.[37] On this note, scholars (Quintais et al. 2022) have pointed out that automated platforms can unilaterally follow decision patterns and be opaque regarding the factors weighed into consideration. In response to these reservations, some the final revisions[38] on the DSA proposal prior to its approval included endowing users with redress mechanisms for any damages incurred due to platforms' monitoring practices.

Focusing on DSA's wording of service providers' transparency obligations regarding content moderation, on the resources required to implement an effective notice, action, and redress mechanism and on the mechanisms per se, this chapter will aim to assess these measures' purported effectiveness. The assessment to be conducted will also be impacted by the role Digital Services Coordinators (the

---

[33] Art. 17 DSA.

[34] Art. 18 DSA.

[35] Art 23. DSA.

[36] C-401/19 CJEU para 85 and 86, in which filtering systems that cannot distinguish lawful from unlawful content are incompatible with the right of freedom of expression. See also the thoughts of the Advocate General on this case, concretely 64, 165 and 191 to 193 of his Opinion, in which he tackles the limits of automatic recognition and filtering tools for content moderation purposes.

[37] A notorious example of such an asymmetry pertains to Youtube's content moderation system, based on which users are strongly discouraged from contesting automated decisions over their own content. See http://copyrightblog.kluweriplaw.com/2021/12/09/youtube-copyright-transparency-report-overblocking-is-real/.

[38] European Commission (2021) Report on the proposal for a regulation of the European Parliament and of the Council on a Single Market For Digital Services (Digital Services Act) and amending Directive 2000/31/EC. https://www.europarl.europa.eu/doceo/document/A-9-2021-0356_EN.html?redirect.

primary national authorities designated to ensure the consistent application of this Regulation) might play in the tackling of the "over-blocking" phenomenon. The topic is approached in a manner that clarifies the role played by users, moderators and regulators. Considering that the practical implications of the DSA have yet to be documented, these considerations are purely theoretical.

5.1 On the Effectiveness of the Mechanisms Per Se

This part of the chapter specifically focuses on assessing the practical effectiveness of the DSA's mechanisms for content moderation, considering the context presented thus far, as well as all the considerations presented during the chapter. Specifically, it aims to demonstrate each mechanism's role in promoting user empowerment.

5.1.1 Counter-Notice Mechanisms

Upon assessing the provisions set forth by the DSA regarding redress mechanisms on notice and action, scholars have identified a common "missed opportunity"in the lack of provisions that would entitle users to issue counter-notices (De Streel et al. 2020). An immediate consequence of this is the inherent vulnerability of users, who are put into a more reactive position regarding their rights, seeing how they can only lodge claims following an intermediary's decision.

A strong framework ensures user empowerment by making users able to not only flag content that is illicit, but also to properly defend their own content from automated decisions. This can only be achieved if both service providers and service recipients are able to proactively contribute to creating the intended robust framework. Considering that one of the main concerns that has been pointed out regarding the DSA is the uncertainty of some of its dispositions when put to practice, it is curious that the legislator precluded the opportunity to give users additional motivation in being more active in the regulation of content.

Whether or not the legislator's final decision reflected reservations on internal and external channels being flooded with complaints remains unclear, but the current formulation of the DSA does not properly mitigate these concerns either, as discussed in the previous parts of this section. Thus, from the perspective of empowering the service user, the cost/benefit relation at hand indicates that a counter-notice provision might prove to have been more beneficial in the long run.

5.1.2 Internal Redress Mechanisms

The more recent drafts of the DSA before its approval raised concerns (Zeybek et al. 2022) on how the broadened internal complaint-handling systems risk compromising the functionality of the redress mechanism itself, a statement that merits a critical assessment. Concretely, Art 20(4) DSA states that platforms should handle complaints in a timely, non-discriminatory, diligent, and non-arbitrary manner, which is a very abstract disposition, regardless of Recital 58 DSA mentioning that systems should promote fair outcomes. The very abstract dispositions of Art. 20 DSA risk incurring in a high degree of unpredictability when it comes to the resolution of complaints, which does not allow for a uniform application of the Regulation's norms, even when admitting different terms and conditions for different service providers.

Therefore, OSP concerns that hosting proper dispute resolution channels might prove to be too costly (Kuczerawy 2022) raises reservations in the sense that these providers can be inclined to make their policies and terms and conditions overly restrictive. Perhaps more concerning than this is the incentive that OSP might have to actively push for external resolution methods that users end up being unable to afford, which can prove most pernicious for purposes of users' interests and their right to redress.

5.1.3 Measures to Tackle Misuse of the Notice Mechanism

Art. 23 of the DSA aims to tackle the problem of "misuse" of the online platform, by recipients of the service that frequently provide manifestly illegal content, and by individuals or entities that frequently submit notices or complaints that are manifestly unfounded—which is at the core of over-blocking. The provision mixes two different opposing issues and seems to solve neither. The article merely establishes an ill-defined bottom floor for both problems, with soft consequences for each. Concretely, it prescribes an obligation to suspend "for a reasonable period of time and after having issued a prior warning", which while it may be welcomed, it can reveal itself insufficient and be considered to constitute a *"loophole"*. By mixing both problems—users uploading illegal content vs. abuse of the notice mechanism—the article actually ensures that the online platforms have enough discretion to treat both problems very differently.

As such, the provision merely establishes that service providers must suspend users that frequently upload manifestly illegal content[39] but does not disallow harsher measures. The service provider may suspend for longer periods or even terminate the provision of the service for uploading content that, while illegal, is not necessarily manifestly illegal. The standard for how frequently those violations need to occur may also "play" against the recipient. Additionally, it is also unclear how the "prior warning" system can be implemented in practice for instances of simultaneous detection of several violations.

On the other hand, service provides may adopt a higher standard to consider a notice "manifestly unfounded" for the purposes of applying this article, allowing the submission of notices and claims that are "just" incorrect or "partly" unfounded. Much content could be unlawfully blocked if doubts arise about its legality (see the problems with exceptions and limitations to copyright protection previously alluded

[39] Fn 68 (2022).

to). Additionally, while well intentioned, Art. 23(3)(b) could also be used to temper with the system in favor of whoever is abusing the notice mechanism: if enough correct notices are made, the mechanism that punishes for misusing the system is not triggered.

Nevertheless, Art. 23(3)(d) is a positive inclusion. If applied correctly, this provision could be a game-changer. Individuals or entities which abuse the notice and claim system with an agenda would be suspended thanks to this criterion. Nevertheless, some skepticism can persist, given that while some may see a pattern of abuse with a clear intention (harassment, censorship, whether economic, political, or ideological), others could conclude that such a malicious intention does not exist. Therefore, a joint application of Art. 23(4) with Art. 14 DSA will be crucial in cases in which there is uncertainty regarding the practical implications of many provisions of the DSA, particularly on how intermediary service providers will comply with them.[40] This is yet another measure that aims to tackle the opaqueness of online platforms by prescribing transparency obligations via the inclusion of clear and detailed policies regarding "misuse" in the terms and conditions. This obligation of transparency is further enhanced with the obligatory inclusion of examples of facts and circumstances that will be considered in the assessment of misuse, providing much necessary legal certainty to users and third parties.

As a conclusive note, this system needs to receive the appropriate attention by OSP or it is bound to fail in its objectives. Many notice and complaint systems are notorious for being abused against users due to lax consequences for misuse and or lack of oversight and enforcement (Appelman 2023). If faux complaints are submitted are followed through, users can be the subject of harsh penalties and damages, while the "complainant" can only be temporarily suspended. One may find this sort of imbalance in the similar issue in the practice of SLAAP lawsuits.

5.1.4 The Out-of-Court Dispute Settlement Mechanism

Out-of-court dispute settling bodies are to be designated by the Digital Services Coordinators[41] which are, in turn, designated by the European Commission.[42] In this regard, there are doubts as to the harmonization of practices throughout the EU, considering that there does not seem to be any indicator that there will be uniform choice criteria for each Member-State's coordinator. In this regard, a lack of uniformity in designating out-of-court dispute settling bodies indicates some frailties in the DSA's harmonization aims, considering its purposes as a regulator, which adds to the legal uncertainty already present in terms of the internal dispute resolution criteria mentioned above.

---

[40] Art. 14 as a provision mandating the codification of the Terms and Conditions will have an important on tackling discretionary and abusive content moderation practices, protecting fundamental rights.

[41] Art. 18(2) DSA.

[42] Art. 38 DSA.

Still on the topic of out-of-court dispute settlements, the DSA makes it clear that dispute settlement bodies do not have the power to impose a binding settlement on the involved parties.[43] This disposition constitutes a noticeable change from initial proposals of the DSA,[44] in which dispute resolution bodies' decisions on this topic were to be considered binding. The change stemmed from concerns of bad actors using these mechanisms to arbitrate every content removal decision at a company's expense and due to the risk of legal fragmentation.[45] While the legislator's concerns are legitimate for the purposes of the mechanism's effectiveness, it is relevant to question whether the change does not risk turning the mechanism more performative. Indeed, the changes raise the question of how effective this redress mechanism can be, considering how platforms can simply disregard any decisions reached out of court whenever they prove too unfavorable for them. Moreover, it puts the very functionality of the entire redress system into question, in the sense that platforms might deliberately opt to exhaust all available mechanisms until only judicial redress is left. Though users are theoretically able to resort to courts, in practice, the costs associated with legal proceedings can prove to be a barrier for content creators to go through with challenging removals or restrictions that they consider unfair.

There is an inherent power imbalance between hosting service providers and users, particularly in what concerns to resources. This imbalance only becomes more prevalent in the case of VLOPs which, despite the numerous obligations they are subject to by the DSA, seem to still have broad leeway in terms of their content control, regardless of how broad or restrictive their terms and conditions might become. Furthermore, these vulnerabilities raise concerns on the effectiveness of the DSA's efforts to combat whitelisting practices, which favor high-profile accounts with large numbers of followers when it comes to the protection of their speech (Gorwa et al. 2020). Indeed, considering what has been exposed, it is not far-fetched to consider that these accounts and their respective users will be the only ones monetized enough to be able to exercise the mechanism of judicial redress, not to mention that they might continue to benefit from greater leeway.

Overall, despite the changes made to ensure that dispute resolution bodies' decisions are not to be binding, the very validity of the inclusion of out-of-court dispute settlement processes in the DSA raises severe concerns. Scholars Wimmers 2021 have pointed out how this procedure is both unnecessary and counter-productive for the goals of the DSA and how its very theoretical conception undermines the value of normative decision usually reserved for the judiciary (Wimmers 2021).

[43] Art. 21(2) DSA.

[44] European Parliament (2022) Proposal for a Digital Services Act. https://www.europarl.europa.eu/doceo/document/TA-9-2022-0269_EN.html.

[45] This choice also is in line with the European Commission's initial goal of avoiding legal fragmentation through the DSA. See the Explanatory Memorandum (n 1) in European Commission (2020) Proposal for a Regulation of the European Parliament and of the Council on a Single Market For Digital Services (Digital Services Act) and amending Directive 2000/31/EC COM(2020) 825 final.

5.1.5 Collective Actions

The last resort for solving disputes surrounding illegal content in these platforms is, naturally, judicial. The DSA does not attempt to subvert or change this fundamental principle. It aims to implement many instruments and mechanisms that should be used first (by third parties, users and even administrative authorities), from internal complaint systems to out-of-court dispute resolution. Nevertheless, as shown in the previous paragraphs, many of their provisions have several cracks through which problems may arise. Art. 54 provides that users can always request compensation for damages and damages caused by OSP that have breach obligations under the DSA.[46]

Unfortunately, the DSA does not include measures that aim to facilitate access to court for individuals or weaker parties when all else fails. Access to justice in these matters will still be regulated by national law, in compliance with the Charter of Fundamental Rights, namely art. 47.[47] It could be argued that these instruments were largely not designed for this kind of problems and in practice may not be sufficient to ensure the principles of effectiveness and equivalence.

Nevertheless, the DSA does include two provisions that aim to strengthen the position of individuals by promoting collective action, in different models: Arts. 86 and 90. Both provisions have the objective of allowing organisations, associations and other entities to exercise the rights of recipients of intermediary services conferred by the DSA in their representation. By pulling resources together and similar complaints of non-compliance and infringement, these entities may be able to pursue the interests of larger amounts of recipients that otherwise could not do it.

Art. 86 is broader in its subjective scope, allowing for any "type" of recipient of intermediary services to be part of these bodies. They may include natural persons such as consumers and other individual users (that do not qualify as such) and legal entities, from non-profit organisations, universities, businesses, act. However, the entities that are mandate for representation in accordance with Art. 86 cannot themselves be profit motivated and must pursue a legitimate interest that the DSA is complied with. This restriction is welcomed to ensure that this representation is not subverted, as it happened in past (Alexander 2019; Geyser 2022).[48] Recital 149 refers that the primary purpose of these entities will be the exercise of rights related with the submission of notices, challenging decisions by intermediaries and lodging complaints, while Art. 86(2) reinforces this, by stating that complaints submitted by these entities will be processed with priority and without undue delay.

Art. 90 represents a true final effort regarding the matter of access to justice in the DSA. It is an amendment that adds the DSA to the annex of Directive (EU) 2020/1828

---

[46] See Fn68: 13.

[47] See Fn68: 12.

[48] As it happened in the past with Multi-Channel Networks (MCN) on Youtube. MCN were organisations that were created to represent many individual youtubers when dealing with Youtube, but many became infamous due to predatory practices (such as revenue theft and perpetual contracts) against the people that they were supposed to represent. Additionally, many were sold to large media conglomerates.

on representative actions for the protection of consumers.[49] This simple provision allows private qualified entities to pursue injunctions and reparation for damages against OSP for violations of the DSA in behalf of large groups of consumers.

While it has a lot of distinctions from the American class-action model and it does not intend to promote the emergence of a litigation industry—which prioritizes the litigator's financial gains over consumer interests (Agulló 2022), this Directive aims to strengthen collective action with the clear objective of tackling concerns regarding the principle of effectiveness, access to justice and enforcement of European (consumer) law. It requires all Member States to incorporate representative actions for redress and injunctions in their legal systems, for national and cross-borders cases, but it allows for much discretion in the transposition, including in more controversial matters, such as the choice of opt-in or opt-out system.

In summary, despite Art. 90 being a welcomed addition to the DSA, its effectiveness is yet to be assessed. While in certain Member States with a more active civil society, it may provoke useful externalities by indirectly promoting compliance with the DSA; in in others it may have little to no effect. It is also necessary to refer that Directive 2018/1828 is limited to protect consumers, which leaves out of its subjective scope many individuals and entities which still require protection.

5.2 *On the Topic of Transparency under the DSA*

The very effectiveness of the mechanisms mentioned prior depends on a proactive approach from users. Indeed, creating specific bodies and rules to combat the "over-blocking" phenomenon is unlikely to effectively combat unjustified and excessive content restriction practices by itself if users do not actively resort to the proper mechanisms. This is only made possible if the users are cognizant of how their content is being affected by the moderation tools, which demonstrates the key role transparency plays in the DSA's goals of empowering users and in allowing for a proactive and meaningful (Mylly 2023) exercise of rights. It is therefore relevant to assess the role the DSA's transparency obligations play in empowering users and combatting "over-blocking", if at all.

In theory, the DSA obliges providers of intermediary services to fulfill minimum transparency and fairness requirements[50] in their T&C, in the sense that they are required to include information on any policies, measures, procedures and tools used for content moderation. Alongside the statement of the reasons for the content's removal—which include the legal or contractual ground behind the decision -, hosting service providers are to also include information on the available redress mechanisms. Depending on the specific case, affected recipients of the server may have access

[49] Directive (EU) 2020/1828 of the European Parliament and of the Council of 25 November 2020 on representative actions for the protection of the collective interests of consumers and repealing Directive 2009/22/EC (Text with EEA relevance).

[50] Examples of this are Recitals 50 to 54 and Arts. 15 and 16 DSA.

to internal complaint-handling mechanisms,[51] an out-of-court dispute settlement,[52] and/or judicial redress.[53]

All these measures towards transparency are in line with the DSA's obligations for all intermediaries to publish a yearly report detailing their content moderation operations,[54] further demonstrating an effort to distribute power through the internet more evenly (Genç-Gelgeç 2022). Moreover, online platforms must include information on their internal complaint handling systems in the form of reports, in which they must identify the number of disputes referred to out-of-court dispute settlement bodies, alongside the average time needed to complete said proceedings.[55] Indeed, whether these reporting obligations end up originating reports with strategically structured information remains to be seen, though there is an understandable risk that service providers can feel inclined towards embellishing their results to avoid scrutiny. The effectiveness of the transparency obligations for providers of intermediary services and of the impact of the annual transparency obligations regarding the report of their content moderation actions is still to be assessed in practice. For this purpose, the first year of the DSA in effect being essential to later enrich the following assessment.

The fact that the DSA provides for this type of specific transparency obligation on behalf of hosting service providers demonstrates the legislator's commitment to empower users regarding content moderation that might affect them. Given that the exercising of rights depends on people being aware that they are being affected by another agent, the legislator aids users in challenging decisions that might affect them in a timelier and more effective manner. In theory, by having affected recipients be told of the specific reasons for the removal or restriction of the content and on the available means of redress, the DSA allows them to specifically challenge the removal's reasoning in the route specifically projected for said purpose. It also constitutes an attempt at minimizing "shadow bans" to a certain degree, though the extent of this minimization with be very dependent on the practical application of the Regulation.

In practice, however, the obligations mentioned above do not necessarily ensure that users will be clarified on the criteria that providers resort to when blocking or removing content. Indeed, the DSA requires providers to inform users regarding the existence of their means for content moderation, but not on how they operate. Similarly, though providers must inform users on the reasons for the content's removal, they are not obliged to indicate how they reached their decision, how the reasons presented influenced the decision, nor on the amount of automation involved in said

[51] Art. 20 DSA.

[52] Art. 21 DSA.

[53] Though the DSA does not provide for this route in its articles, it recalls that it must be made available. Moreover, judicial redress is subject to specific national legislation and procedures, and as such, the affected recipients should resort to said national norms to challenge any decisions that might impact them.

[54] Art. 13 DSA.

[55] Art 23(1) DSA.

decision.[56] On that regard, the level of transparency of provider's T&C can be brought into question, and in turn, raise concerns on how well users can oppose decisions and the fairness (or lack thereof) of the criteria used to remove or restrict content.

Despite these concerns, the DSA does demonstrate a commitment to avoid performative transparency by always requiring disclosure of crucial information, which did not always happen under the ECD. If anything, even under the risk of subversive reporting, there is an inherent increment of the information that must be disclosed to users. Though these measures' practical implications have yet to be verified, this exercise, in theory, promotes broader knowledge of the decisions made about user content and, consequently, demonstrates an effort in empowering users.

5.3 On the Role of Digital Services Coordinators: An Analogous Comparison with Data Protection Authorities

Alongside the concerns presented above, it can be said that DSA proposal's formulations suggest that the regulation perceives content blocking as an interim measure, rather than a last resort. This is made clear in how the Digital Services Coordinators[57] are endowed with the capacity to order the blocking of websites, which can have a global impact for all users.

The lack of specific dispositions in what constitutes a violation risks making Digital Services Coordinators engage in the "over-blocking" phenomenon, rather than adopting a truly case-by-case approach in mitigating it. Indeed, for all intents and purposes, the Digital Services Coordinators' priorities, strategies, and stances are yet to be verified in practice. Moreover, one must not ignore that the various Member-States each hold varying legal traditions and doctrines that necessarily impact the way each Coordinator will perform its monitoring duties. This degree of uncertainty may prove disconcerting for OSP, who face fines of up to six percent of their annual global turnover upon eventual failures to comply with the DSA, and who may be over restrictive in their T&C to avoid these hefty fines.

Though it is difficult to predict how Digital Services Coordinators might exercise their monitoring powers, it can be possible to do so. Furthermore, in the context of digital platforms, it is relevant to look at the context of personal data protection supervisory authorities (DPAs) and on their specific fines towards big tech companies and platforms that constitute intermediaries and Very Large Online Platforms (VLOPs).[58] This analogy is relevant considering the relation between the DSA and

---

[56] Art. 15(1)(b)(e) DSA.

[57] Art. 38 DSA.

[58] On this, see Chapter IV, Sect. 4 DSA. VLOPs are a relevant focus of the DSA and are defined in Art. 33(1) of the DSA as being "online platforms which have a number of average monthly active recipients of the service in the Union equal to or higher than 45 million".

the General Data Protection Regulation (GDPR),[59] given that the DSA is meant[60] to be articulated with and complement the GDPR's dispositions.[61] Therefore, it can be interesting to assess how DPAs exercise their competences regarding non-conformity with the GDPR, in order to predict what might be expected from Digital Services Coordinators, given the DSA and the GDPR's close relation. As it stands, the highest GDPR fines applied to date mostly pertain to the practices of digital platforms, with companies and groups like Amazon,[62] WhatsApp[63] and Meta[64] being some of the most frequently sanctioned actors. Considering that all of these sanctioned actors are also intermediaries and VLOPs as per the DSA's definitions, it is not unfair to muse that the same level of scrutiny and high fines is to be expected from the recently appointed Digital Coordinators, who are likely to align with DPA's stances and practices towards certain actors.

With this context in mind, and as stated previously, intermediaries and other service providers (whether they are VLOPs or not) are unlikely to be willing to risk more hefty fines and reputation damage, based on which a more radical approach of defining very strict T&C simply removing or restricting content without many criteria is more likely. From a practical standpoint, it is technically simpler and safer for platforms to just wait for users to trigger redress mechanisms and only then handle the take-down's particularities. This may hinder the accuracy of the notice and action mechanisms and the creation of balanced moderation criteria. Indeed, the vast number of resources required to assess allegations under a notice-and action makes it unlikely that intermediaries other than VLOPs will be able to properly devote time and effort to effectively assessing notifications. These reservations also extend to internal redress mechanisms. It is, therefore, more likely for intermediaries to simply remove or restrict all notified content to save resources and avoid scrutiny rather than risk a lackluster attempt at rigorous moderation in the face of reduced resources.

Should the prior considerations turn out to be true, users might be disempowered due to being discouraged from even resorting to the redress mechanism both due to overly strict T&C and to no expectations of success in overturning decisions over

---

[59] Regulation (EU) 2016/679 of the European Parliament and of the Council of 27 April 2016 on the protection of natural persons with regard to the processing of personal data and on the free movement of such data, and repealing Directive 95/46/EC (General Data Protection Regulation).

[60] European Commission (2022) Questions and Answers: Digital Services Act. https://ec.europa.eu/commission/presscorner/detail/en/qanda_20_2348.

[61] Recitals 10, 34, 67, 68, 69, 71, 94 and 98 of the DSA clarify some of these complementarities.

[62] Amazon Europe was fined € 726 M in Luxembourg, though the execution of this fine has since been partially suspended by order of the president of the Administrative Court of Luxembourg. See Tribunal administratif du Grand-Duché de Luxembourg (2021) Audience publique du 17 décembre 2021 < https://justice.public.lu/content/dam/justice/fr/actualites/2021/46630ord.pdf.

[63] Irish Data Protection Commission (2021) Data Protection Commission announces decision in WhatsApp inquiry. https://www.dataprotection.ie/en/news-media/press-releases/data-protection-commission-announces-decision-whatsapp-inquiry.

[64] Bryant, Jennifer (2023), Irish DPC fines Meta 390 M euros over legal basis for personalized ads, available at https://iapp.org/news/a/irish-dpc-fines-meta-390m-euros-over-legal-basis-for-personalized-ads.

their content. Naturally, the validity of these considerations greatly depends on the practical application of the DSA and of the Digital Services Coordinators' practices in their first years of existence, but as it stands, the current transparency obligations for content moderation do not appear to bode well for a fair content moderation framework. On this note, it will be easier to perform a more thorough assessment of the practical implication of Digital Services Coordinator's practices through the analysis of their respective annual reports, which are mandatory, as stated by the DSA.[65]

6 Conclusion

An effective liability framework needs to acknowledge the interdependence between all parties in this matter. It needs to carefully consider the underlying economic and social trade-offs. There are three essential elements.

1. The liability framework needs to encourage the participation of users, injured parties and OSP. It is structural requirement, aimed at reduction of the asymmetry of information, and coercing each to "do their part". OSP should have a duty of care to monitor and subsequently reduce expected harm. This can be further promoted through a "Good Samaritan clause". Rating, notice-and-takedown and flagging systems are essential, and third parties and users should be motivated to use them.
2. A liability rule should incentivize the diligent monitorization and removal of illegal content by OSP, with minimal errors. Strick one-sided liability will inevitably coerce OSP to engage in over-blocking and censorship. Rightsholders need to be held accountable for abuse and error, while users need a certain level of protection to mitigate chilling effects. If OSP detract themselves from the dispute process, leaving rightsholders to preside over it, the results will seriously harm fundamental rights and social welfare (Buiten et al. 2019).
3. Therefore, this liability regime should protect the OSP only when certain procedural obligations are implemented that ensure the transparency and accessibility of these systems. OSP should be required to be regularly audited and produce detailed reports to the public, about all the relevant statistics, from takedown-notices to complaints about over-blocking (such as the model in the German Network Enforcement Act). Moreover, it is "no one-size-fits-all" liability rule for all types of harm and OSP. Attempting it would likely amplify current asymmetries, creating serious market barriers which would ultimately promote the large incumbents, and would generate substantial inefficiencies (Lefouli et al. 2021).

[65] Art. 44 DSA.

The ECD's model does not need to be completely reinvented, but rather reformed towards an adaptable principle-based framework, that efficiently shares the responsibility of detection and removal among the many actors, with adequate checks-and-balances and enhanced transparency (Buiten et al. 2019). The DSA attempts to codify some of these ideas, though its success in practice remains to be assessed.

Efforts to mitigate the pernicious effects of disinformation[66] and hate speech tread a fine line with the protection of users' fundamental rights,[67] and any imbalance[68] in this exercise risks enlarging the risk of power asymmetries between users and the platforms that monitor their content. Legal initiatives should combat the growing lack of incentives users have to contest decisions made over their content. On this note, it remains to be seen whether the DSA's dispositions provide an improvement in the current state of the art. However, the DSA's dispositions prove to be both broad and ambiguous, which, when paired with the impacts of an out-of-court settlement in the redress procedure for content moderation, raise serious doubts on the effectiveness of this legislation in combating the asymmetries mentioned above and the chilling effect of the "over-blocking" phenomenon.

The DSA's goal should align with creating a framework that promotes the exercise of fundamental rights and free, democratic discourse, for which there are reservations as to how the legislator's choices will actually fulfill these purposes (Reda and Selinger 2021). Mitigating these concerns is key to fulfill the goal of making the DSA a global standard-setter[69] in terms of consumer protection, and as such, time will tell what the practical repercussions of the DSA will truly look like.

References

Agulló D (2022) The interplay of data, consumer and Private International law rules in the area of collective access to justice in the European Union, available at https://repositorio.comillas.edu/jspui/bitstream/11531/74625/1/Lainteraccionentrelasnormasdeproteccion.pdf

Alexander J (2019) These YouTubers are owed $1.7 million, and they're probably never going to get it/Ally Bank responds to concerns from creators. The Verge. https://www.theverge.com/2019/1/29/18202131/matpat-defy-media-youtube-ally-bank-ryland-adams-multi-channel-network. Accessed 29 Aug 2025

---

[66] These efforts are in line with the European Commission's European democracy Action Plan. See European Commission (2020) Communication from the Commission to the European Parliament, the Council, the European Economic and Social Committee and the Committee of the Regions On the European democracy action plan COM(2020) 790 final. https://eur-lex.europa.eu/legal-content/EN/TXT/HTML/?uri=CELEX:52020DC0790&from=EN.

[67] On this topic, the Advocate General's statements regarding freedom of expression in Case C-401/19 are essential to consider.

[68] On this topic, see Joined Cases C-682/18 and C-683/18 Frank Peterson v Google LLC, YouTube LLC, YouTube Inc., Google Germany GmbH (C-682/18) and Elsevier Inc. v Cyando (C-683/18) (Opinion of Advocate General): 151.

[69] European Parliament (2020) Digital Services Act: Improving the functioning of the Single Market. https://www.europarl.europa.eu/doceo/document/TA-9-2020-0272_EN.html.

Appelman N (2023) Research Report on Disparate Content Moderation—DSA Observatory. DSA Observatory. https://dsa-observatory.eu/2023/10/31/research-report-on-disparate-content-moderation/

Bar-Ziv S, Elkin-Koren N (2018) Behind the scenes of online copyright enforcement: Empirical evidence on notice & takedown. Conn Law Rev 50:339

Buiten M, de Streel A, Peitz M (2019) Rethinking liability rules for online hosting platforms. Discussion Paper Series – CRC TR 224. 074:10–11. https://www.wiwi.uniunibonn.de/bgsepapers/boncrc/CRCTR224_2019_074.pdf

Calvi A, Kotzinos D (2023) Enhancing AI fairness through impact assessment in the European Union: a legal and computer science perspective. https://doi.org/10.1145/3593013.3594076

Desjardins J (2019, March 19) How the Tech Giants Make Their Billions. https://www.visualcapitalist.com/how-tech-giants-make-billions/

Dinwoodie GB (2017) A Comparative Analysis of the Secondary Liability of Online Service Providers. Secondary Liability of Internet Service Providers 1–72. https://doi.org/10.1007/978-3-319-55030-5_1

Erickson K, Kretschmer M (2018) What motivates takedown of usergenerated content by copyright owners? evidence from the removal of music video parodies on youtube. J Intellect Prop Inf Technol E-Commer Law 9(1):75–89

European Commission (2014) Communication from the Commission to the European Parliament, the Council, the European Economic and Social Committee and the Committee of the Regions towards a thriving data-driven economy. https://eur-lex.europa.eu/legal-content/EN/TXT/PDF/?uri=CELEX:52014DC0442&from=EN

European Commission (2017) Working document on the free flow of data and emerging issues of the European data economy COM (2017) 9 final. https://eur-lex.europa.eu/legal-content/EN/TXT/HTML/?uri=CELEX:52017SC0002&from=EN

European Commission (2020) European Commission 2020 work programme: An ambitious roadmap for a Union that strives for more. https://ec.europa.eu/commission/presscorner/detail/en/ip_20_124. Accessed 29 Aug 2025

European Parliament (2022) European Parliament legislative resolution of 5 July 2022 on the proposal for a regulation of the European Parliament and of the council on a single market for digital services (Digital Services Act) and amending Directive 2000/31/EC (COM(2020)0825 – C9- 0418/2020 – 2020/0361(COD)). https://www.europarl.europa.eu/doceo/document/TA-9-2022-0269_EN.html

G'sell, F (2023) The Digital Services Act (DSA): A General Assessment. Content Regulation in the European Union – the Digital Services Act, Trier Studies on Digital Law, Volume 1, Verein für Recht und Digitalisierung e.V., Institute for Digital Law (IRDT), Trier April 2023, Available at SSRN: https://ssrn.com/abstract=4403433 or https://doi.org/10.2139/ssrn.4403433

Genç-Gelgeç B (2022) Regulating Digital Platforms: Will the DSA Correct Its Predecessor's Deficiencies?, 18 CYELP 25, available at https://www.cyelp.com/index.php/cyelp/article/view/485

Geyser W (2022) What Are MCNs for YouTube Creators (+ Top Multi-Channel Networks). https://influencermarketinghub.com/mcn-youtube-creators. Accessed 29 Aug 2025

Gillespie T. (2017) Regulation of and by Platforms, in "The SAGE Handbook of Social Media", available at https://sk.sagepub.com/hnbk/edvol/the-sage-handbook-of-social-media/chpt/14-regulation-and-by-platforms

Gorwa R, Binns R, Katzenbach C (2020) Algorithmic content moderation: Technical and political challenges in the automation of platform governance. Big Data & Society 7(1). https://doi.org/10.1177/2053951719897945

Haimson OL, Delmonaco D, Nie P, Wegner A (2021) Disproportionate Removals and Differing Content Moderation Experiences for Conservative, Transgender, and Black Social Media Users: Marginalization and Moderation Gray Areas. Proc ACM Hum Comput Interact 5(CSCW2):1–35. https://doi.org/10.1145/3479610

Hill RK (2016) What an Algorithm Is. Philos Technol 29(1):35–59. https://doi.org/10.1007/s13347-014-0184-5

Hornik J, llera V (2017) An Economic Analysis of Liability of Hosting Services: Uncertainty and Incentives Online. Bruges European Economic Research Papers 37/2017—Archive of European Integration. Pitt.edu. http://aei.pitt.edu/92487/1/beer37.pdf

Husovec M (2017) Injunctions Against Intermediaries in the European Union: Accountable But Not Liable?. Cambridge University Press. Sartor, Giovanni (2017) Providers Liability: From the eCommerce Directive to the future. Study for the European Parliament

Kaiser K, Ratcliff C (2022) Digital Services Act and Digital Markets act: Opportunities and Challenges for the Digital Single Market and Consumer Protection

Kaye DBV, Gray JE (2021) Copyright Gossip: Exploring Copyright Opinions, Theories, and Strategies on YouTube. Social Media + Society, 7(3), 205630512110369. sagepub. https://doi.org/10.1177/20563051211036940

Kuczerawy A (2022) Remedying Overremoval: The Three-Tiered Approach of the DSA. Verfassungsblog. https://doi.org/10.17176/20221103-215534-0

Morais Carvalho, J, Arga e Lima F, Farinha M (2021, May 24) Introduction to the Digital Services Act, Content Moderation and Consumer Protection. Papers.ssrn.com. https://ssrn.com/abstract=3852280

Mylly UM (2023) Transparent AI? Navigating Between Rules on Trade Secrets and Access to Information. Int Rev Intellect Prop Compet Law. https://doi.org/10.1007/s40319-023-01328-5

Nordemann JB (2018) Liability of Online Service Providers for Copyrighted Content – Regulatory Action Needed? In-Depth Analysis for the IMCO Committee of the European Parliament, European Parliament

Penney JW (2019) Privacy and Legal Automation: The DMCA as a Case Study, pp. 412–486, available at https://law.stanford.edu/publications/privacy-and-legal-automation/

Quintais JP (2020) The New Copyright in the Digital Single Market Directive: A Critical Look. Eur Intellect Prop Rev 42(1):28–41. https://doi.org/10.2139/ssrn.3424770

Quintais JP, Mezei P, Harkai I, Vieira Magalhães J, Katzenbach C, Schwemer SF, Riis T (2022) Copyright Content Moderation in the EU: An Interdisciplinary Mapping Analysis. SSRN Electron J. https://doi.org/10.2139/ssrn.4210278

Quintais JP, Schwemer SF (2022) The Interplay between the Digital Services Act and Sector Regulation: How Special Is Copyright? Eur J Risk Regul 1–31. https://doi.org/10.1017/err.2022.1

Reda F, Selinger J (2021) Digital Services Act: European Parliament discusses website blocking against platforms. Verfassungsblog. https://doi.org/10.17176/20211118-202001-0

Sartor G, Loreggia A (2020) Study: The impact of algorithms for online content filtering or moderation ("upload filters") (pp. 1–69). https://doi.org/10.2861/824506

Savin A (2022) Designing EU Digital Laws. Copenhagen Business School. CBS LAW Research Paper No. 22–13. https://papers.ssrn.com/sol3/papers.cfm?abstract_id=4293314

Savora D et al (2022) The Digital Services Act—What it is and what impact will it have?, available at https://www.cliffordchance.com/content/dam/cliffordchance/briefings/2022/12/the-digital-services-act-what-is-it-and-what-impact-will-it-have-updated-december-2022.pdf

Streel A et al (2020) Online Platforms' Moderation of Illegal Content Online Law, Practices and Options for Reform, available at https://www.europarl.europa.eu/RegData/etudes/STUD/2020/652718/IPOL_STU(2020)652718_EN.pdf

Urban JM, Karaganis J, Schofield B (2017) Notice and takedown in everyday practice. UC Berkeley Public Law Research Paper No. 2755628

Wimmers J (2021) The Out-of-court dispute settlement mechanism in the Digital Services Act: A disservice to its own goals. J Intell Prop Info Tech Elec Com L 12:381

Zeybek B, Van Hoboken J, Buri I (2022) Redressing Infringements of Individuals' Rights Under the Digital Services Act—DSA Observatory. https://dsa-observatory.eu/2022/05/04/redressing-infringements-of-individuals-rights-under-the-digital-services-act

Zingales N (2023) The DSA as a Paradigm Shift for Online Intermediaries' Due Diligence Hail To Meta-Regulation. In Putting the Digital Services Act into Practice Enforcement, Access to Justice, and Global Implications (pp. 216–218). Verfassungsbooks

MIX
Papier aus verantwortungsvollen Quellen
Paper from responsible sources
FSC® C105338

If you have any concerns about our products,
you can contact us on
ProductSafety@springernature.com

In case Publisher is established outside the EU,
the EU authorized representative is:
Springer Nature Customer Service Center GmbH
Europaplatz 3, 69115 Heidelberg, Germany

Printed by Libri Plureos GmbH
in Hamburg, Germany